ATTACK ON TITAN 11

HAJIME ISAYAMA

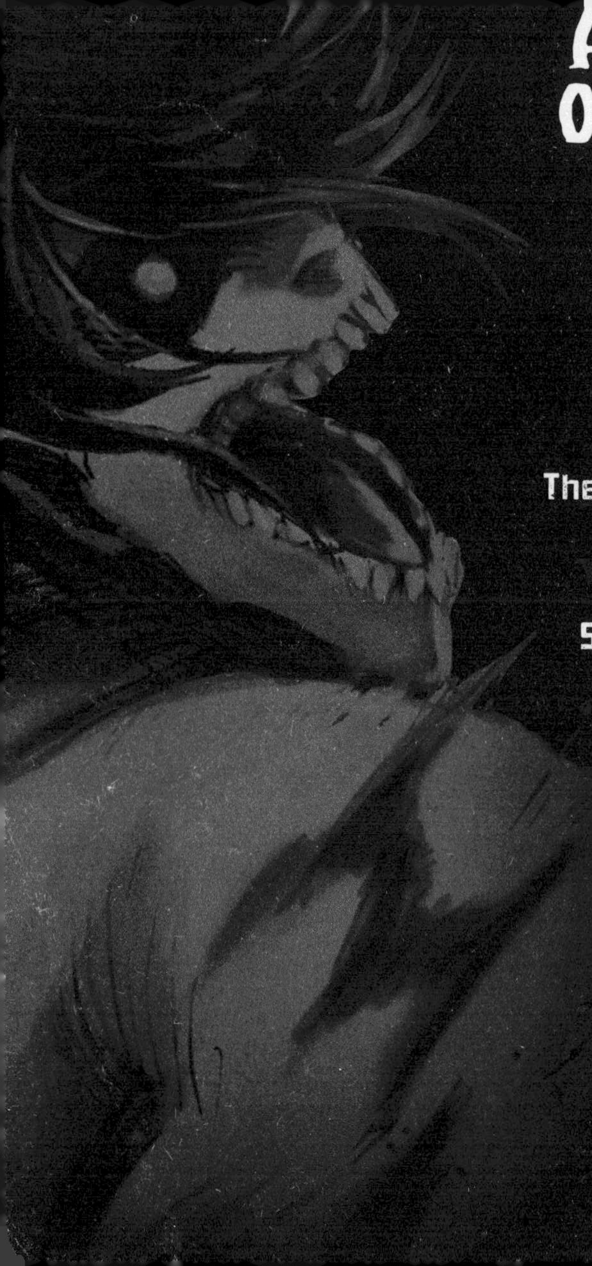

"Attack on Titan" Character Introductions

104th Corps

Graduated at the top of her training corps, Mikasa is a highly talented soldier. Her parents were murdered before her eyes when she was a child, but Eren saved her life. Since then, she has made it her mission to protect him.

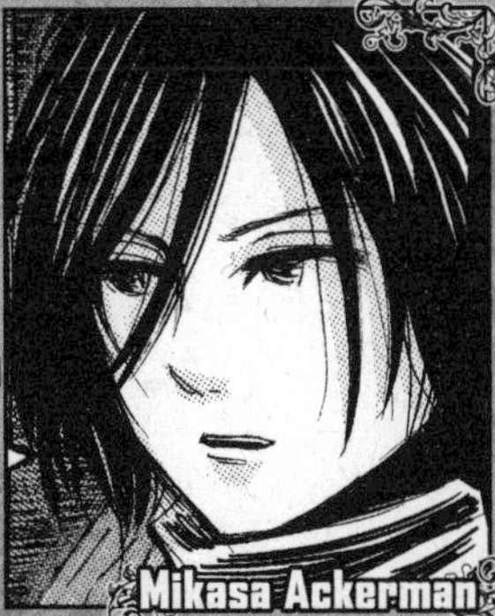

Mikasa Ackerman

Eren joined the Survey Corps out of his longing for the world outside the wall and his hatred of the Titans. He has the power to turn himself into a Titan, but its origins are unknown.

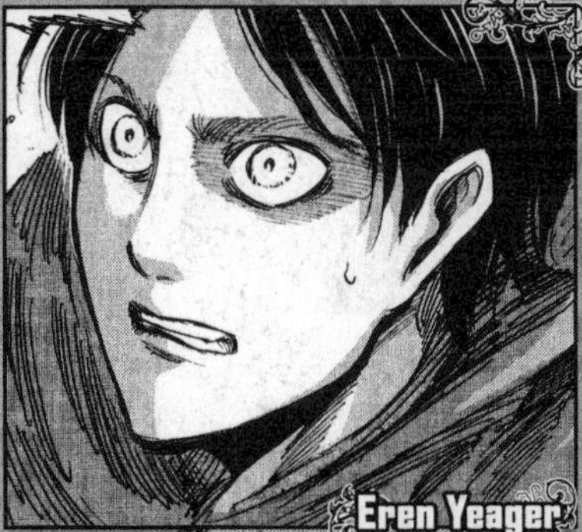

Eren Yeager

Eren and Mikasa's childhood friend. Though Armin isn't athletic in the least, he possesses both sharp observational powers and keen insight, and he exhibits an extraordinary ability to develop strategies.

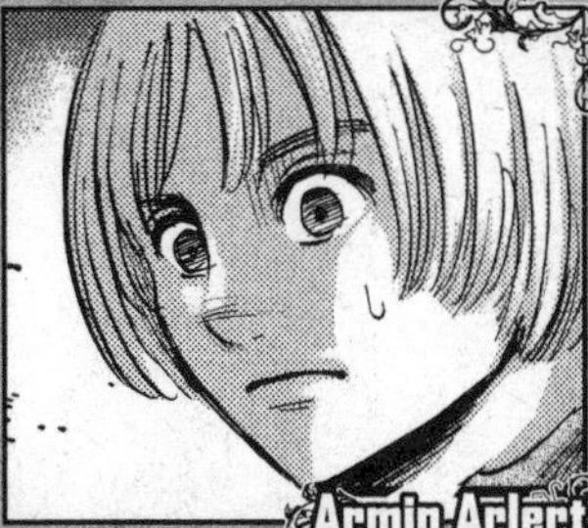

Armin Arlert

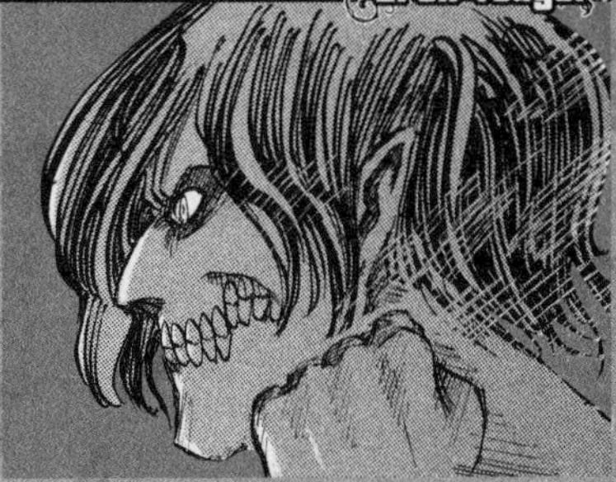

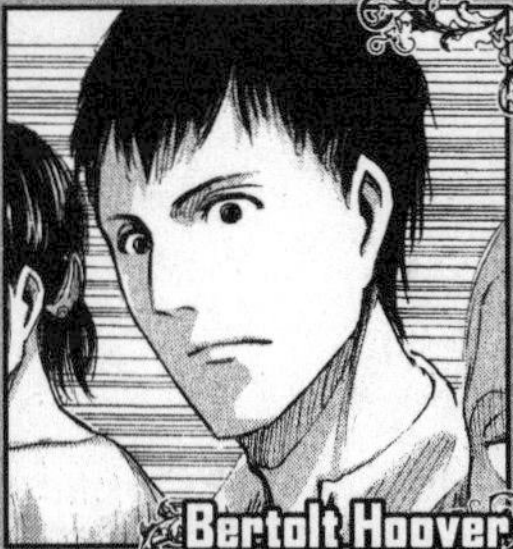

Bertolt Hoover

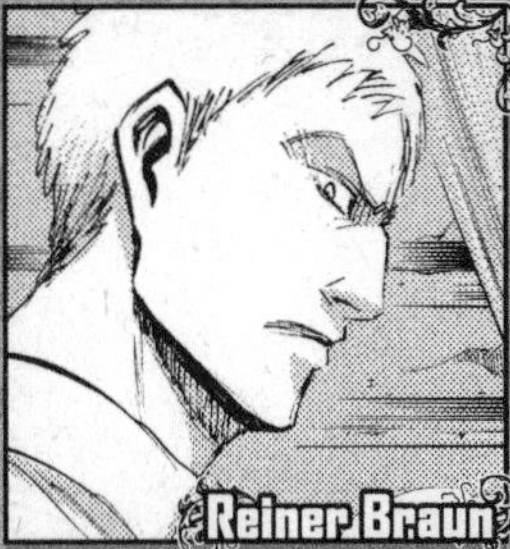

Reiner Braun

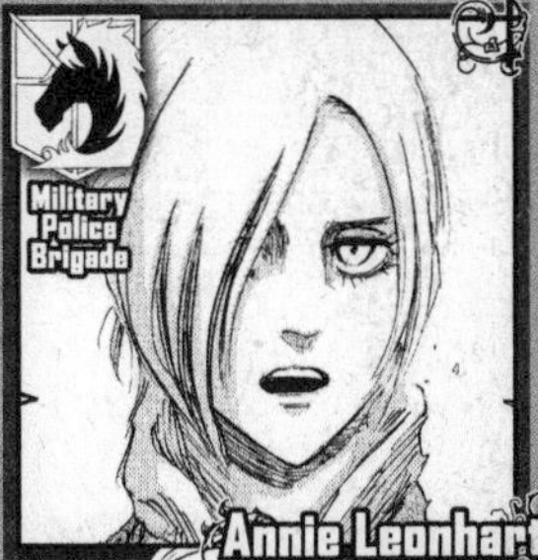
Military Police Brigade

Annie Leonhart

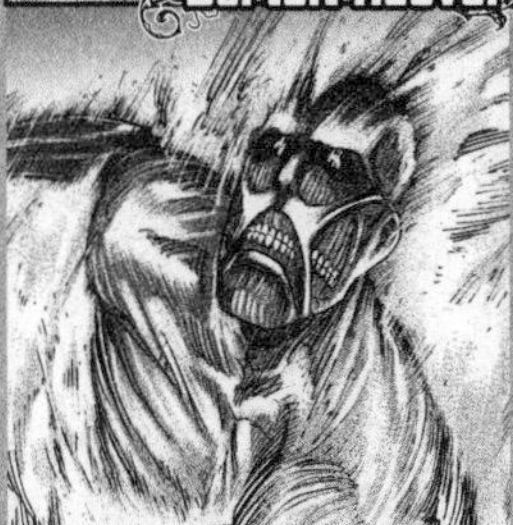

The Colossus Titan

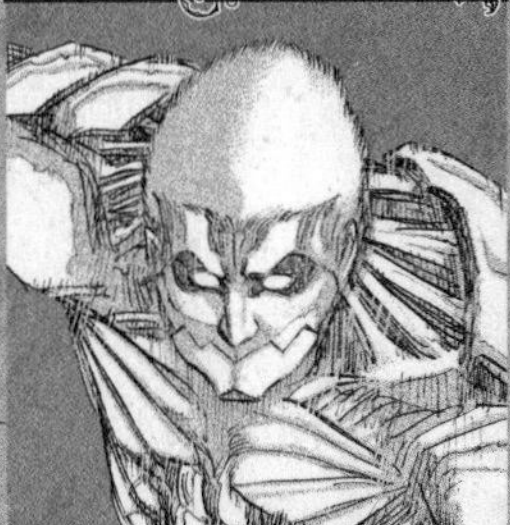

The Armored Titan

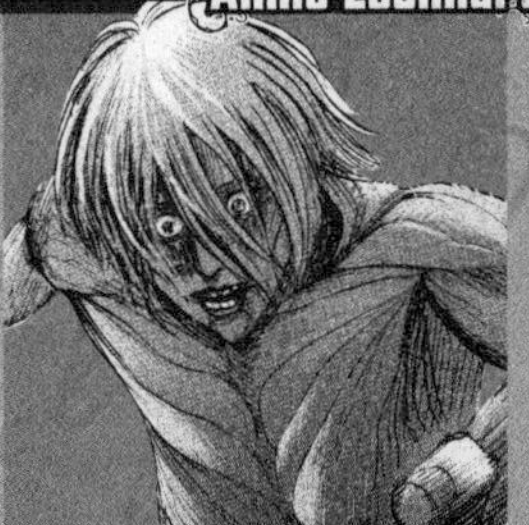

The Female Titan

The Garrison

Defenders of cities who work to reinforce the walls.

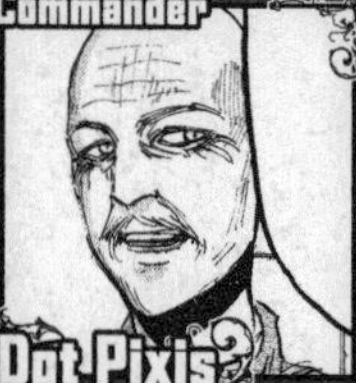
Commander
Dot Pixis

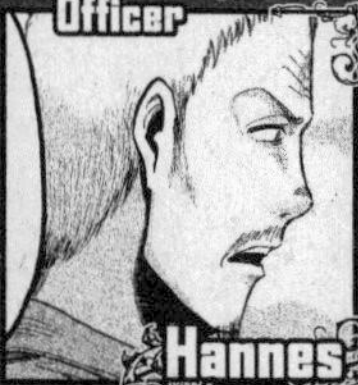
Officer
Hannes

Survey Corps

Soldiers who are prepared to sacrifice themselves as they brave the Titan territory outside the walls.

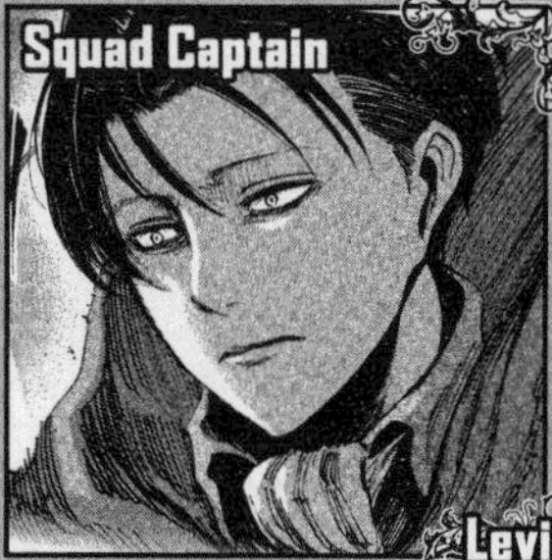
Squad Captain
Levi

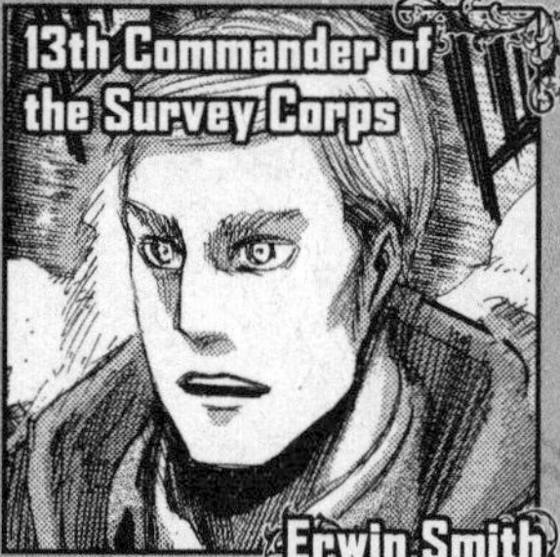
13th Commander of the Survey Corps
Erwin Smith

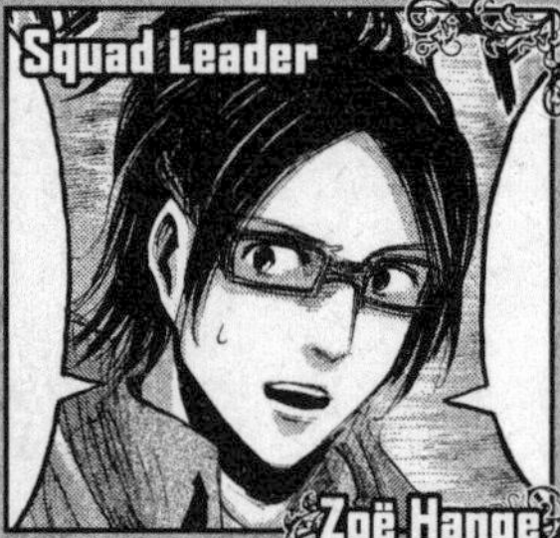
Squad Leader
Zoë Hange

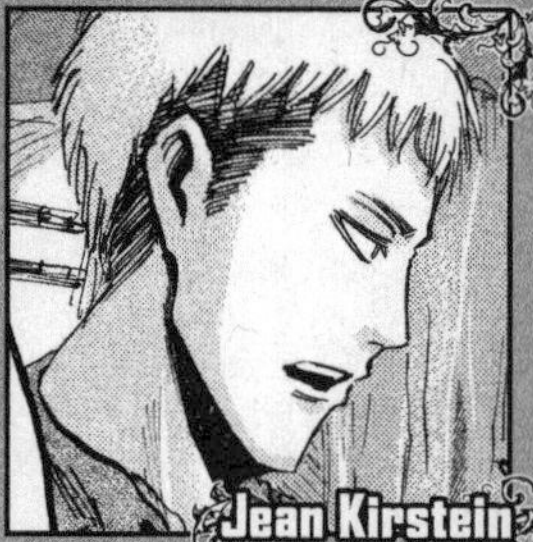
Jean Kirstein

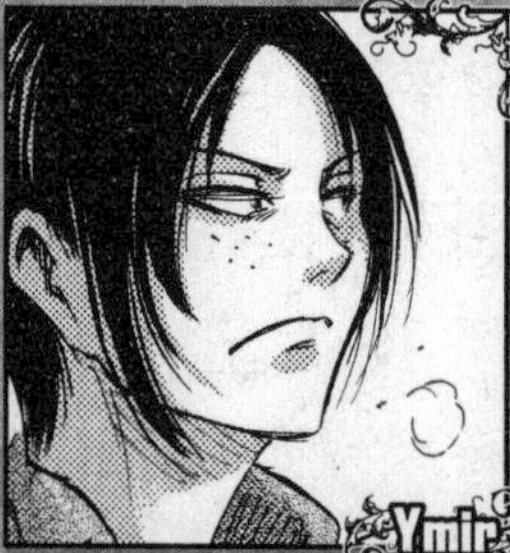
Ymir

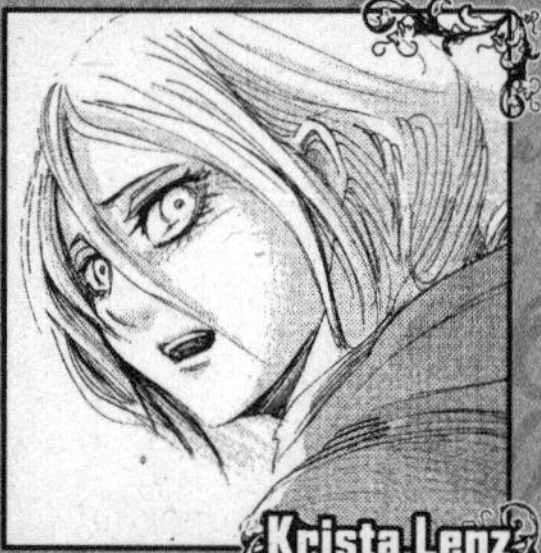
Krista Lenz

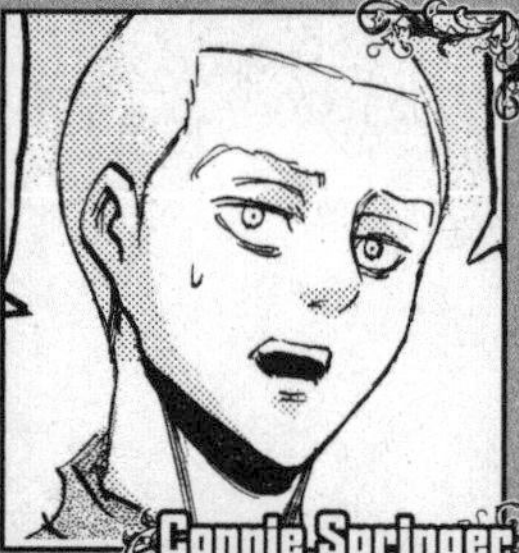
Connie Springer

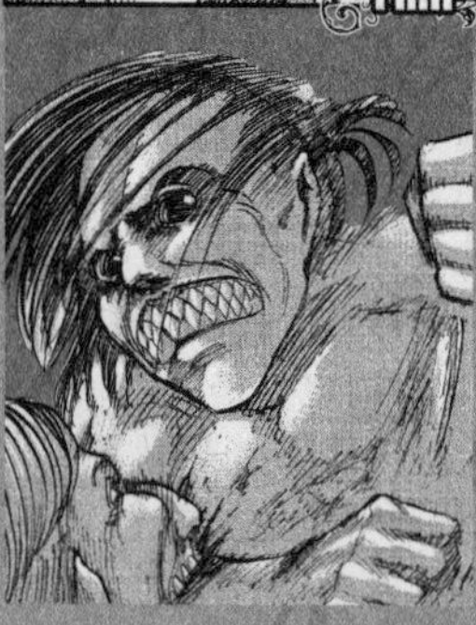

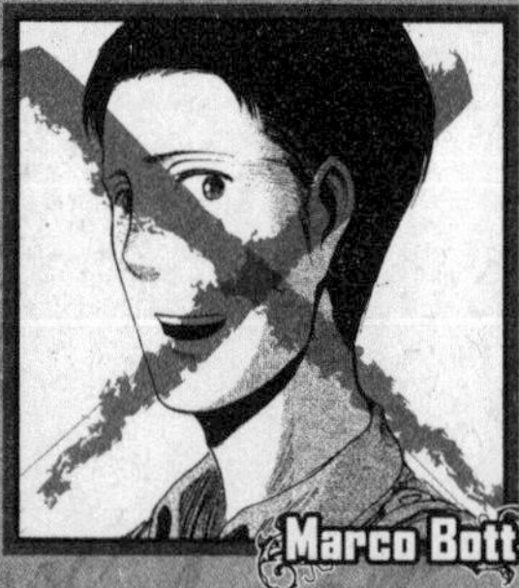
Marco Bott

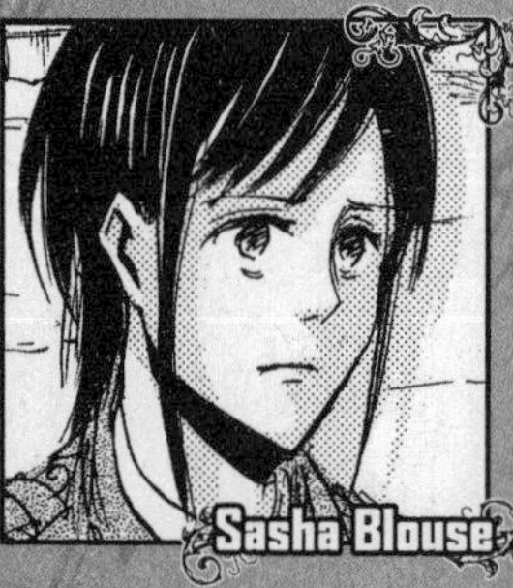
Sasha Blouse

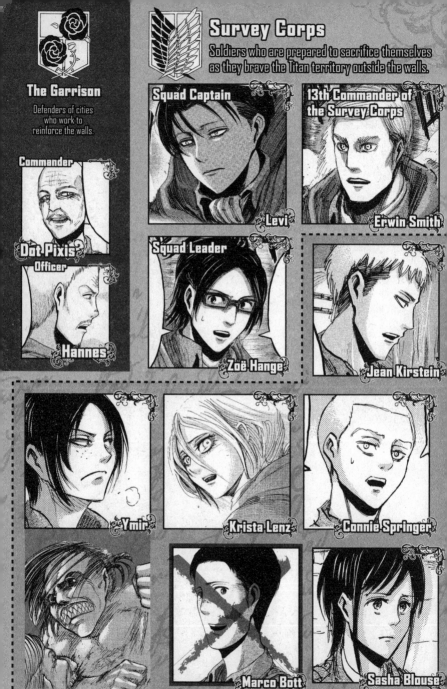

ATTACK on TITAN

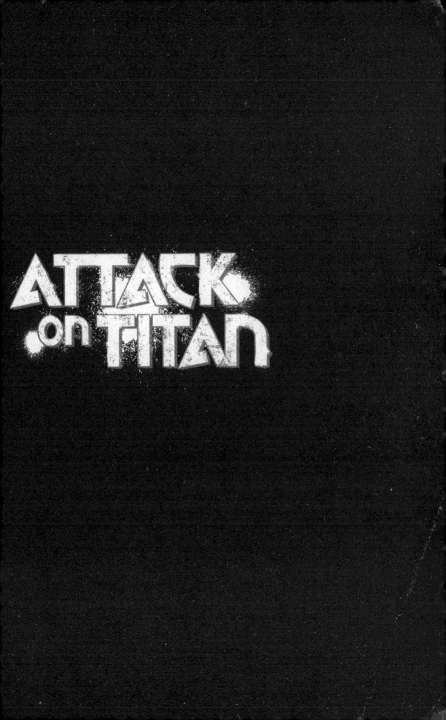

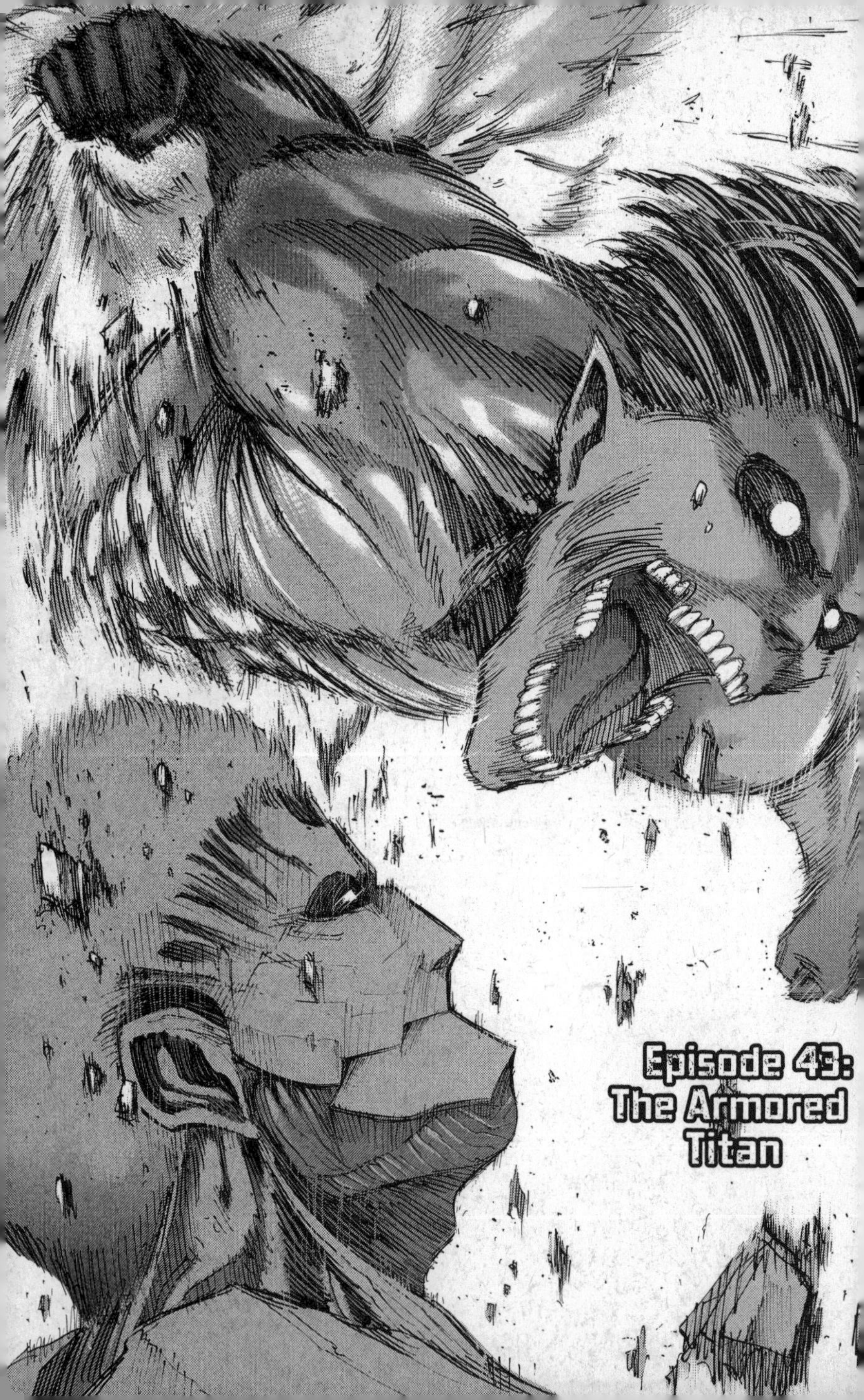
Episode 43: The Armored Titan

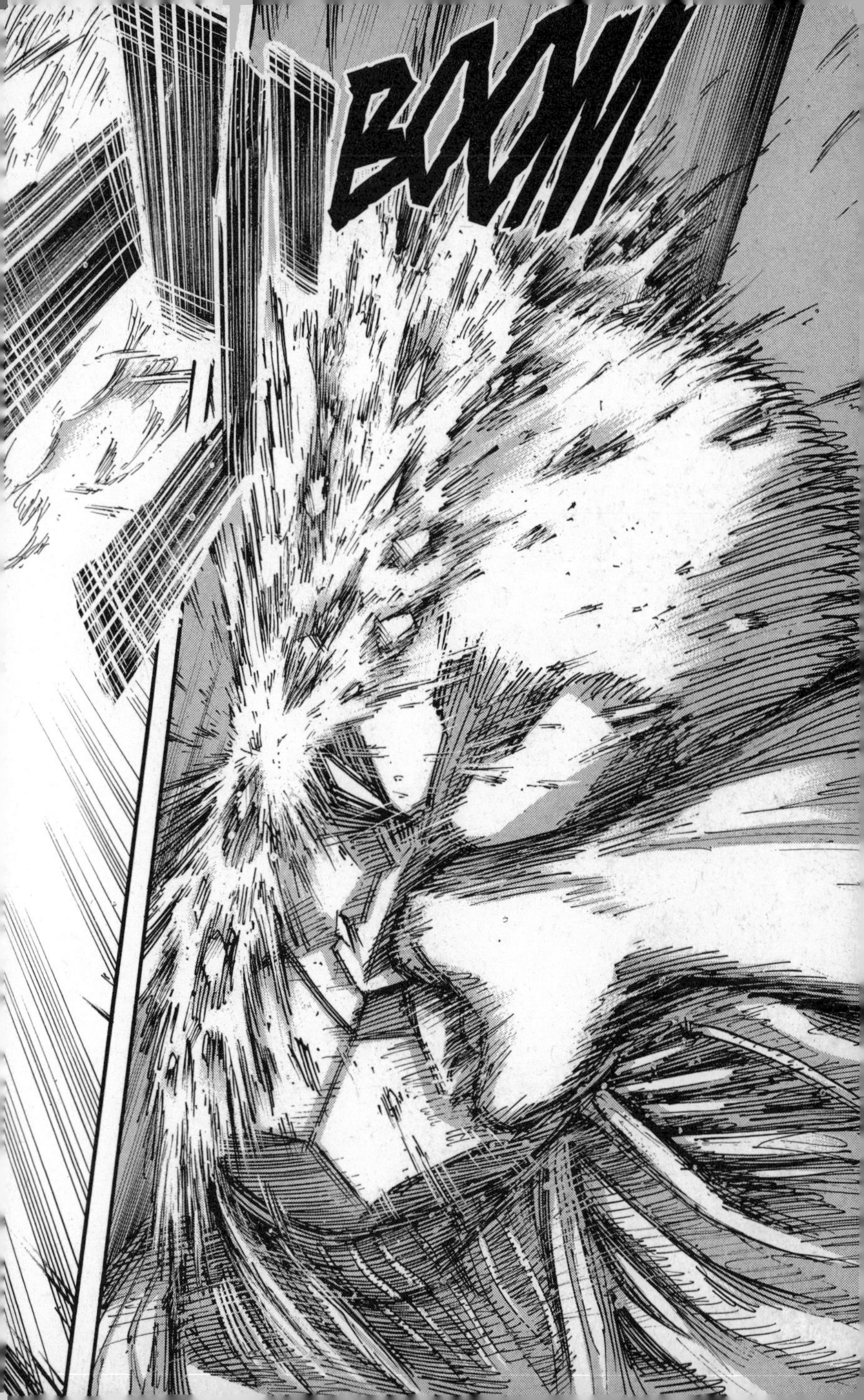
BOOM

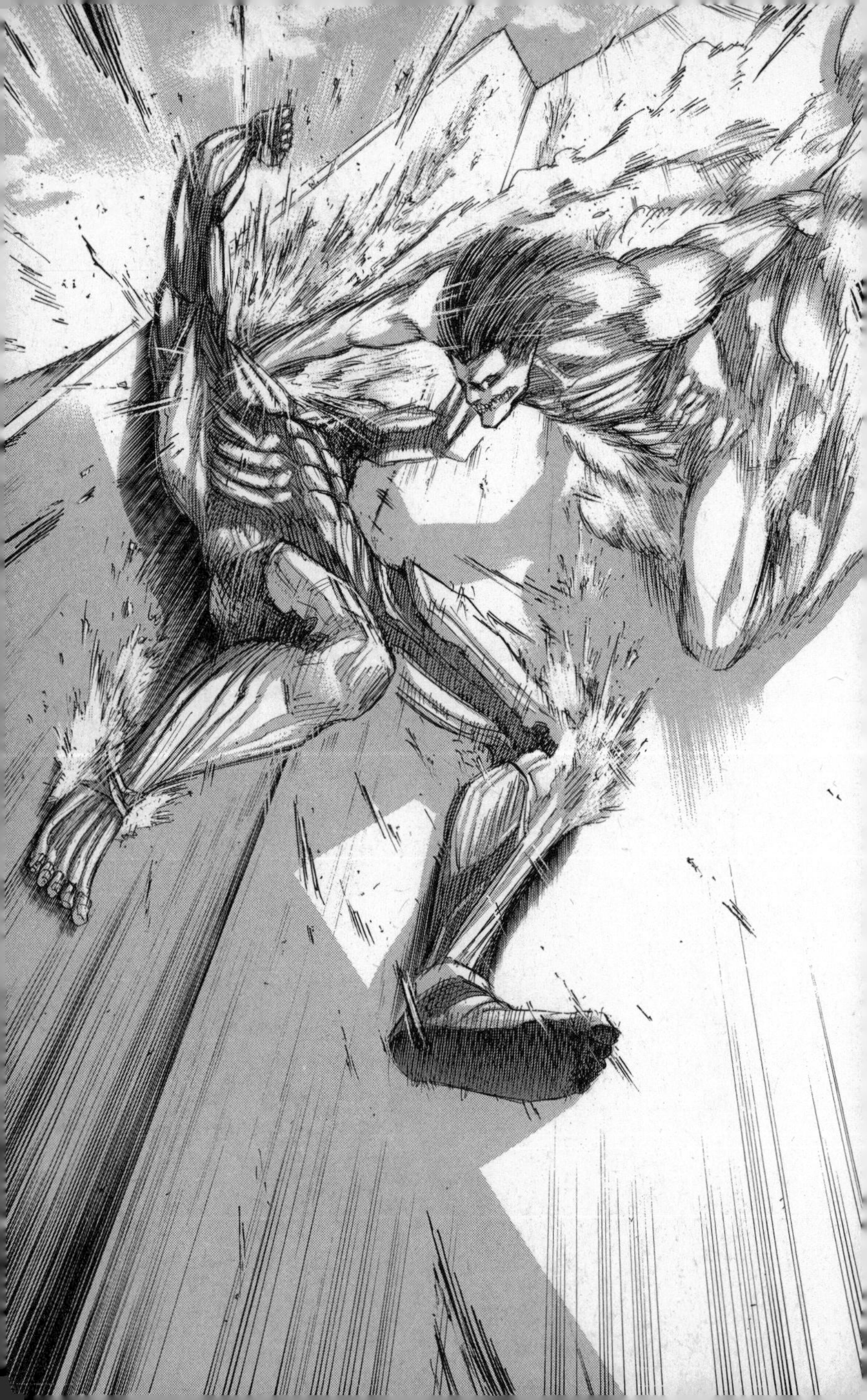

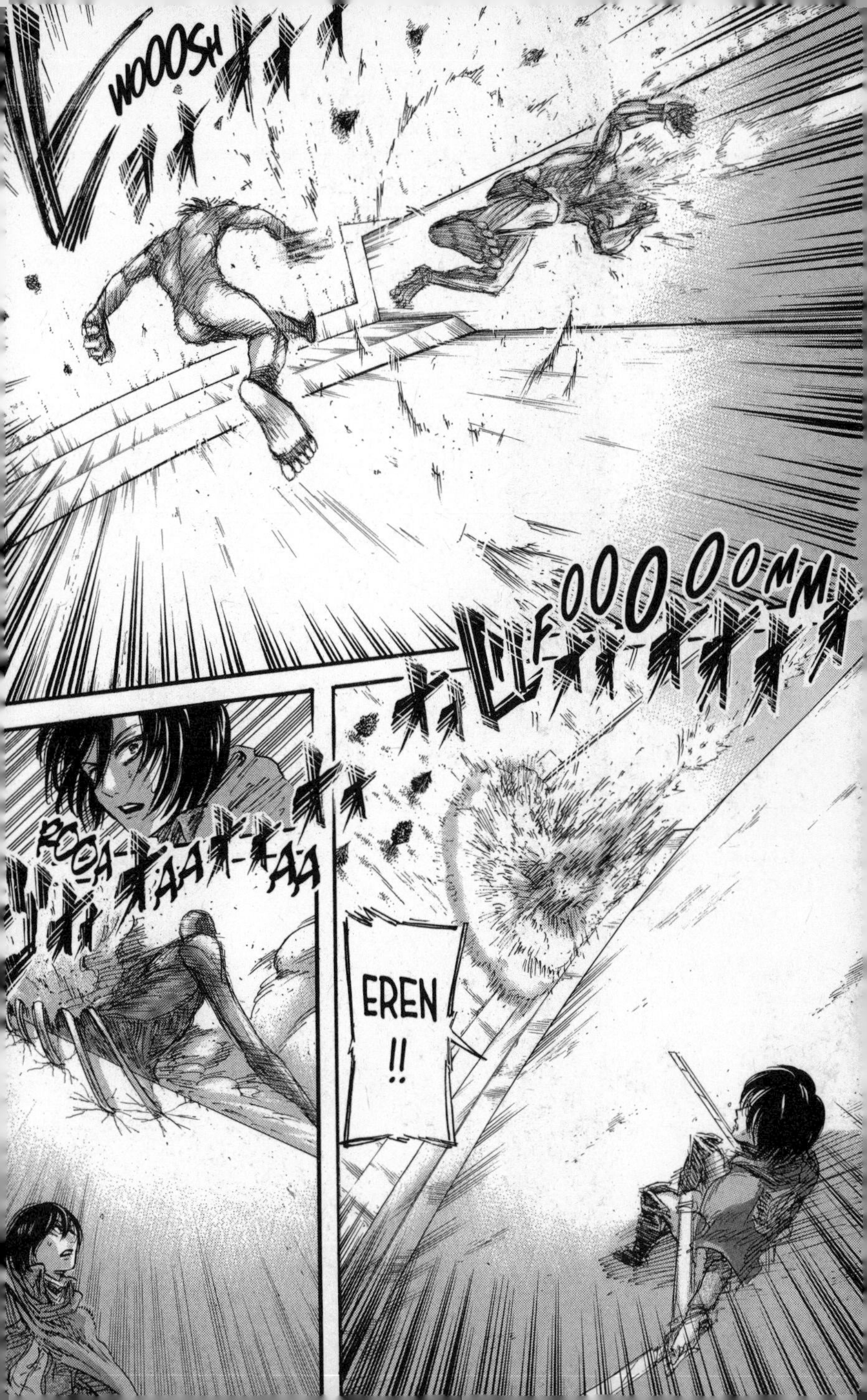
WOOOSH
FOOOOOMM
ROOOAAAAA
EREN !!

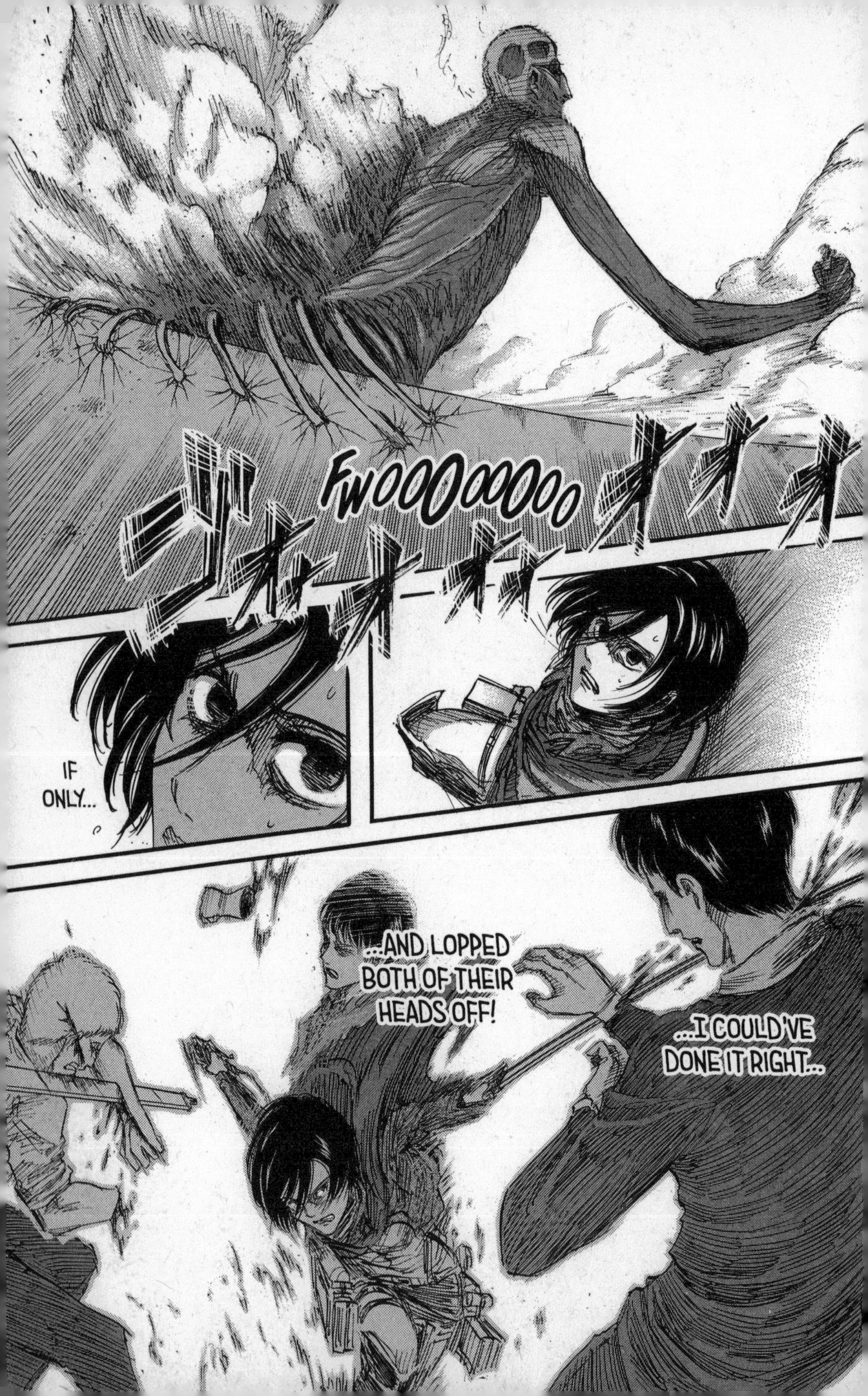
FWOOOOOOOO
IF ONLY...
...I COULD'VE DONE IT RIGHT...
...AND LOPPED BOTH OF THEIR HEADS OFF!

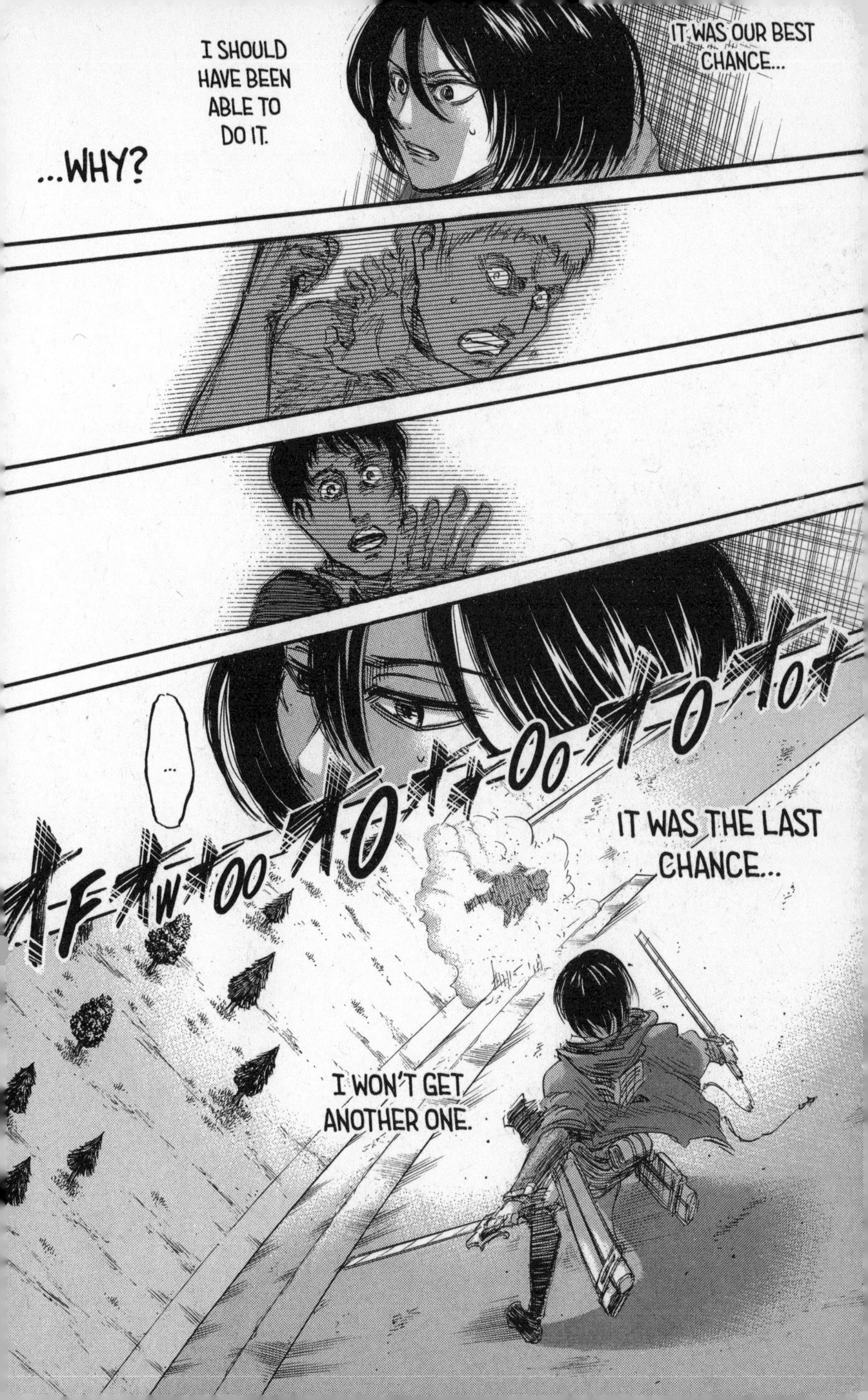
IT WAS OUR BEST CHANCE...
I SHOULD HAVE BEEN ABLE TO DO IT.
...WHY?
...
FWOOOOOOOO
IT WAS THE LAST CHANCE...
I WON'T GET ANOTHER ONE.

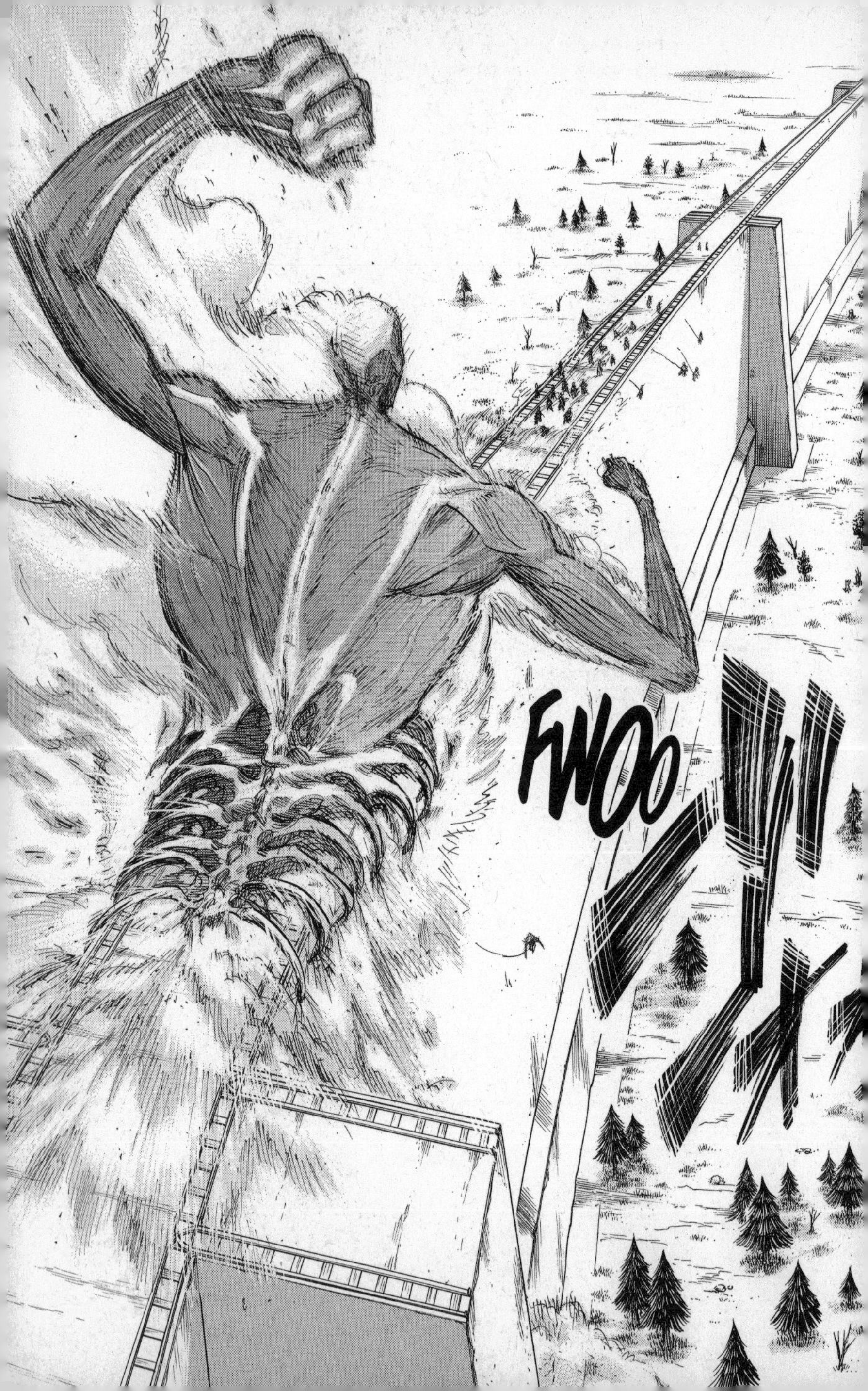
FWOO

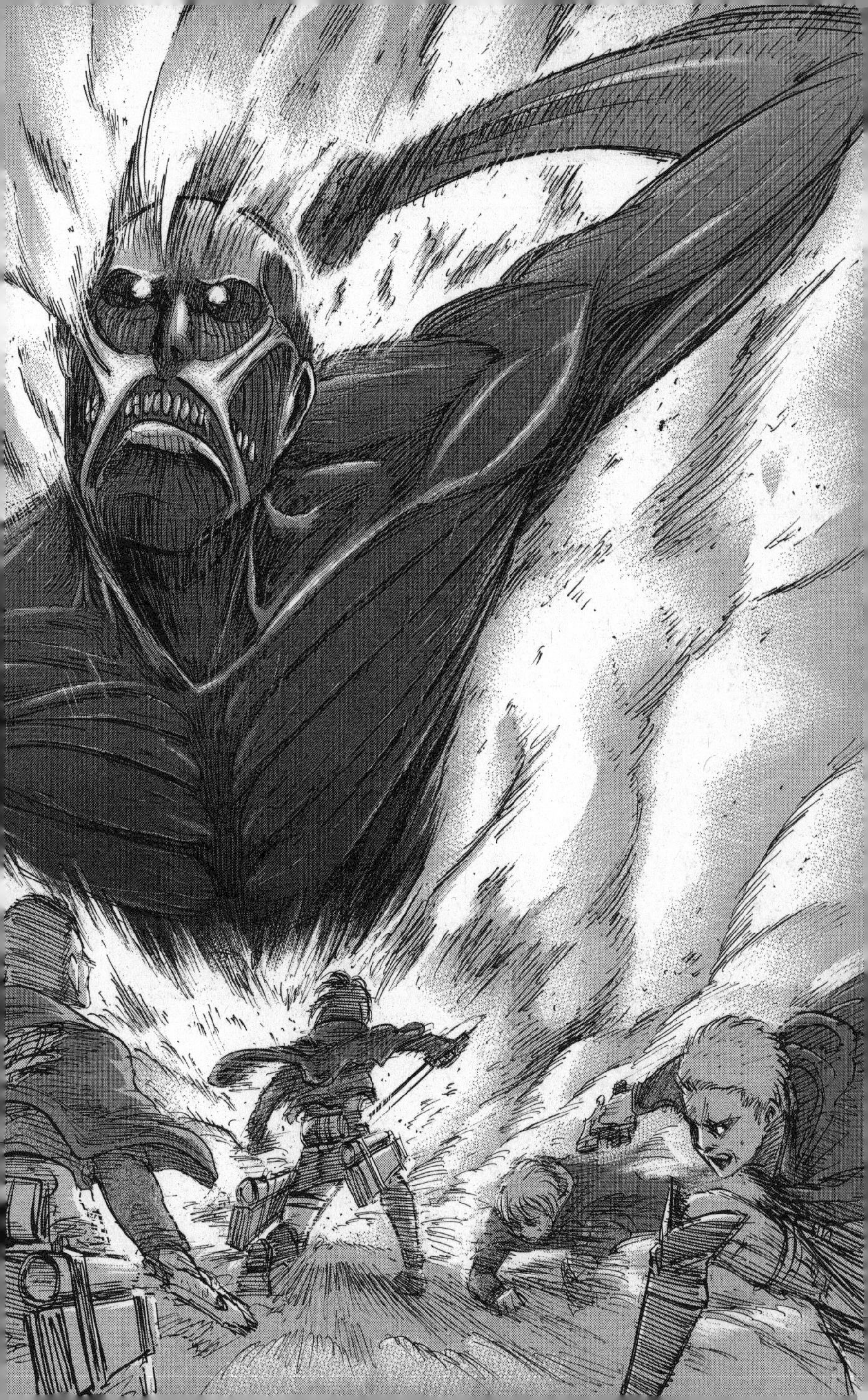

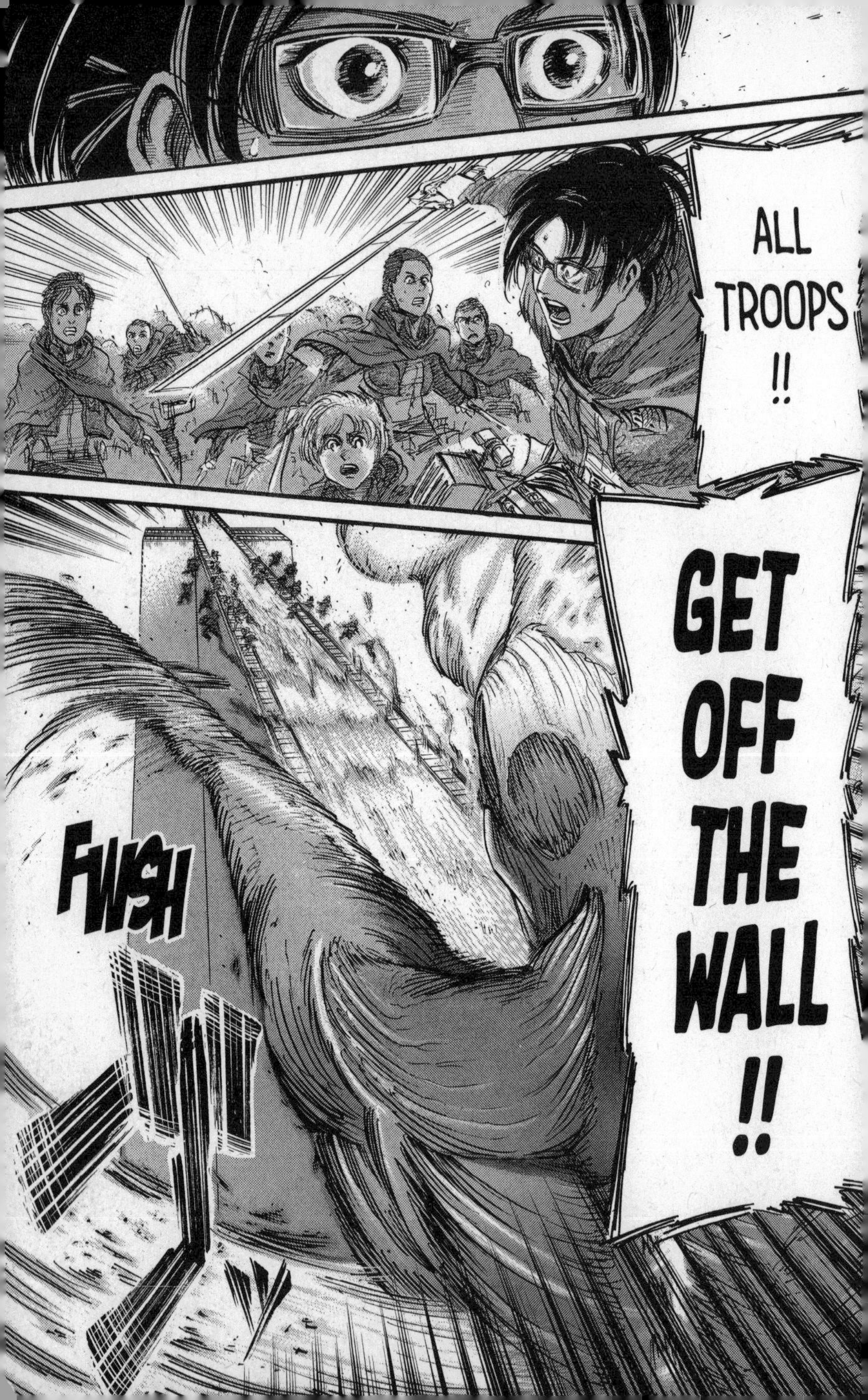
ALL TROOPS !!
GET OFF THE WALL !!
FWSH

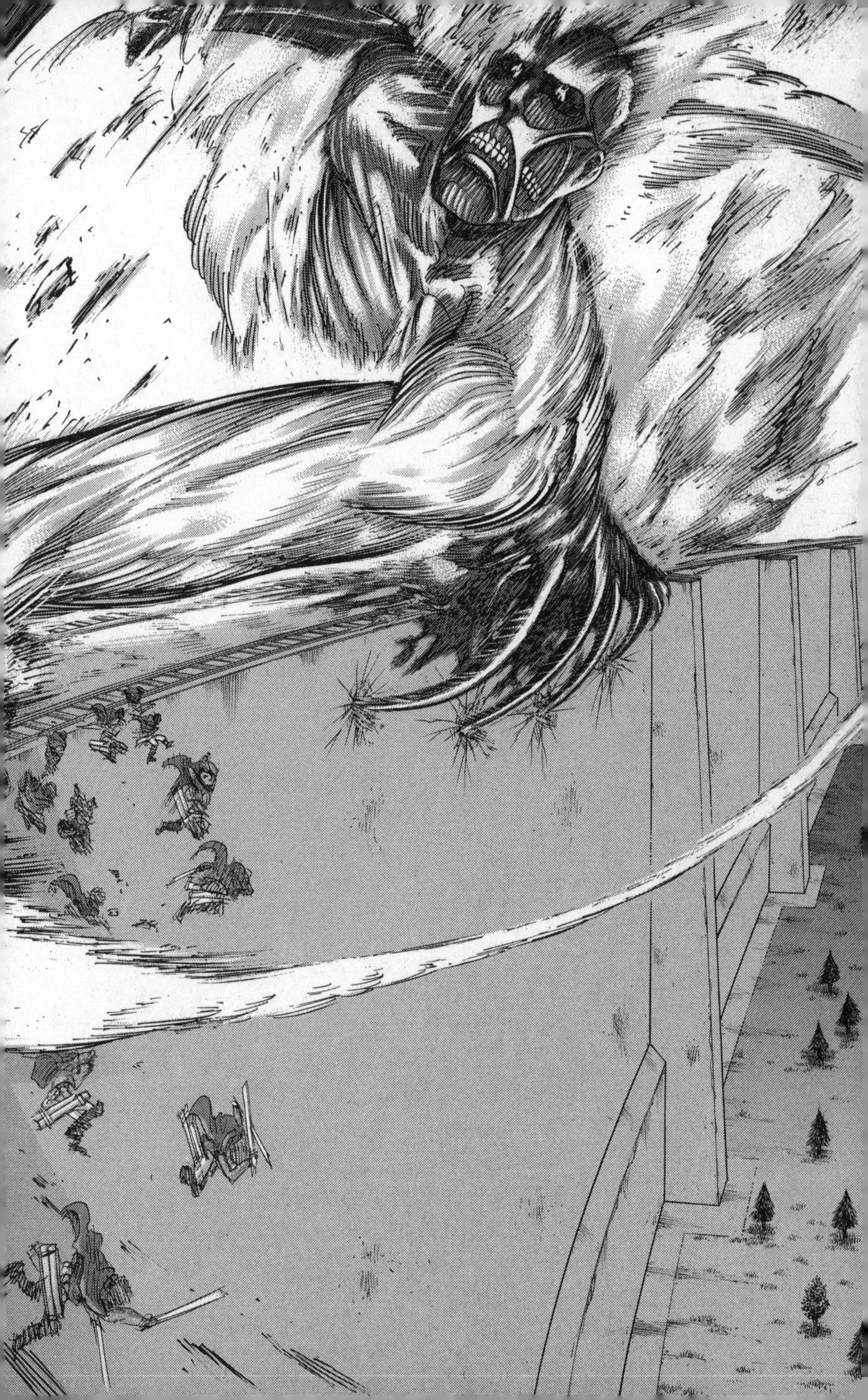

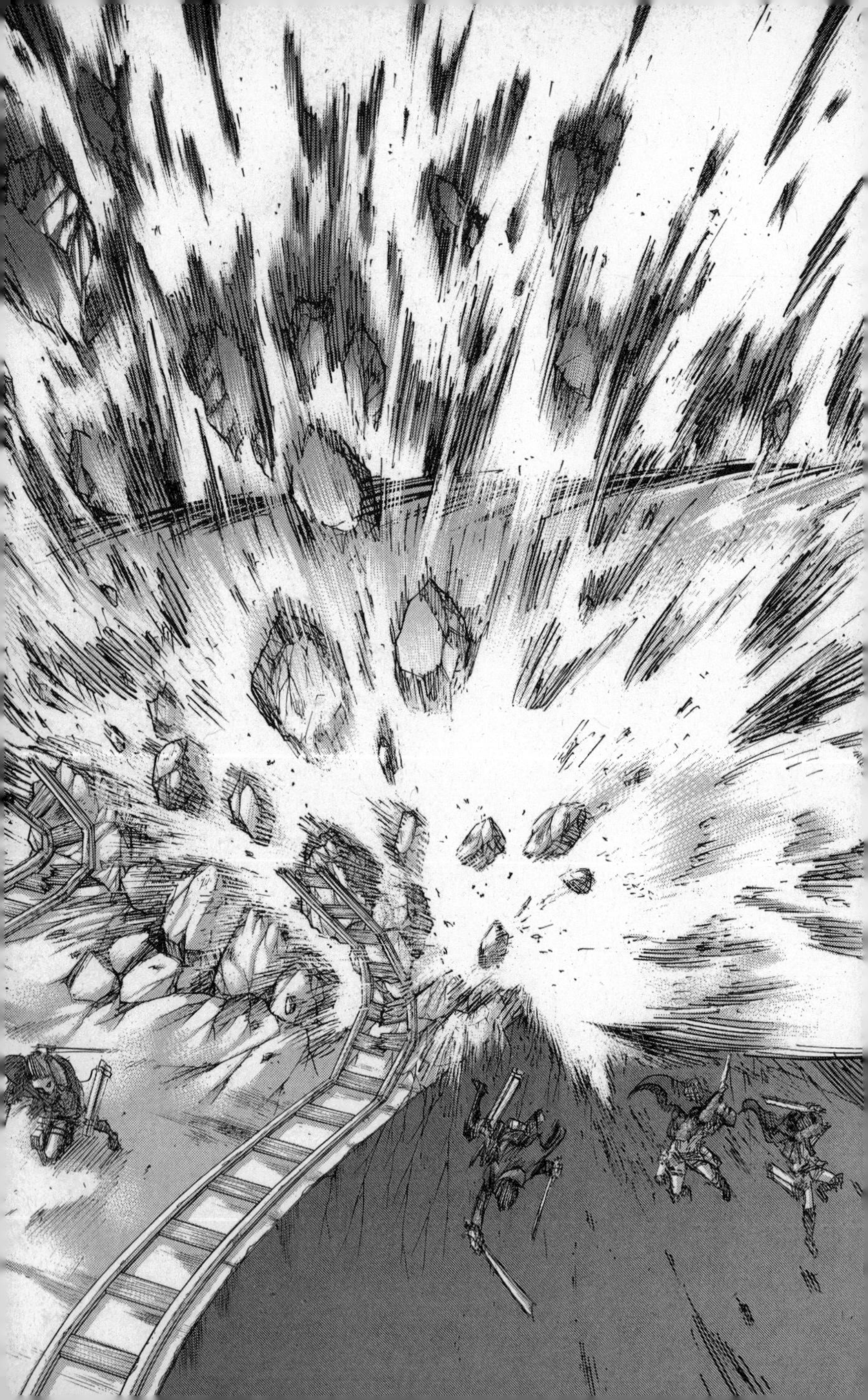

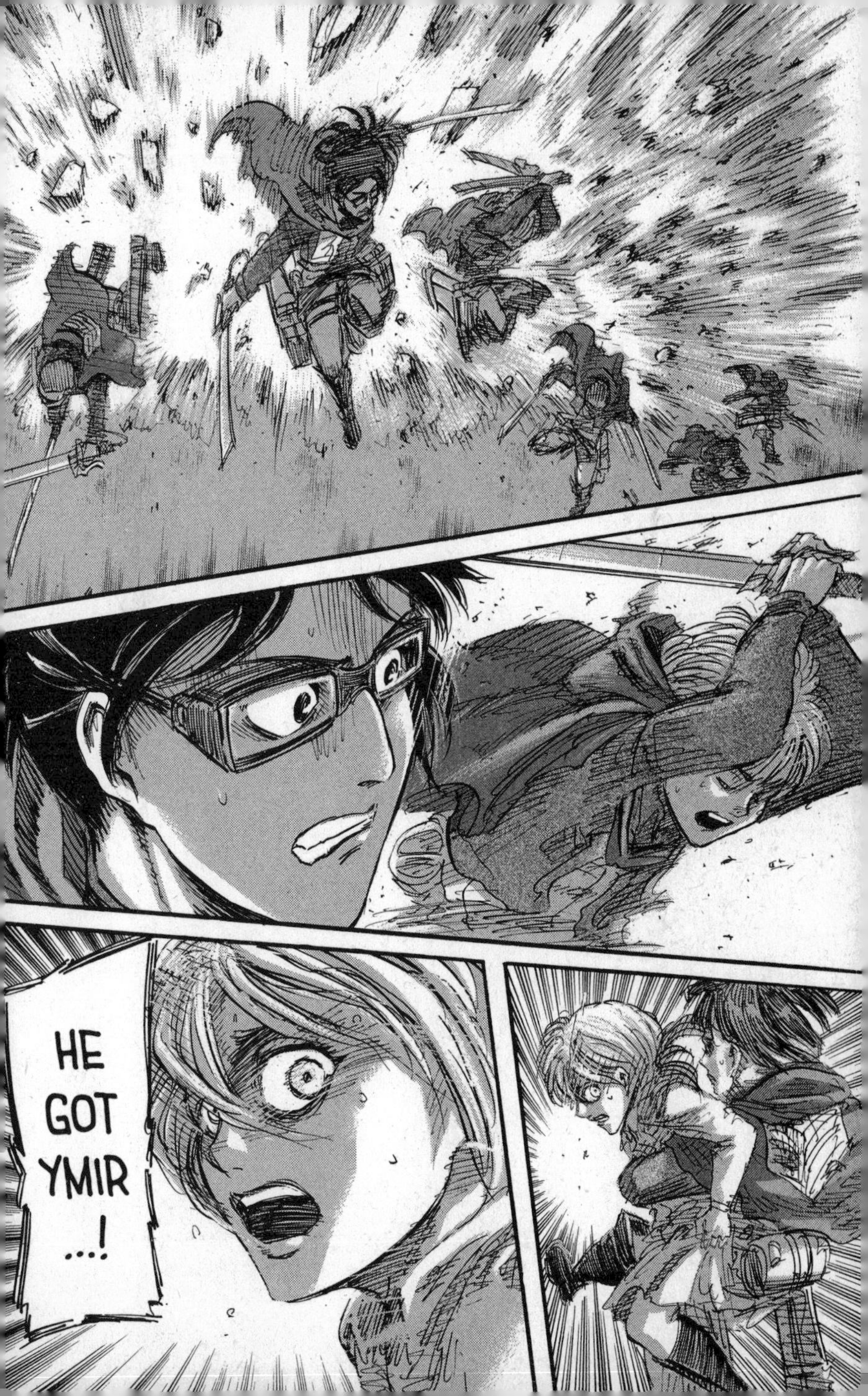
HE GOT YMIR ...!

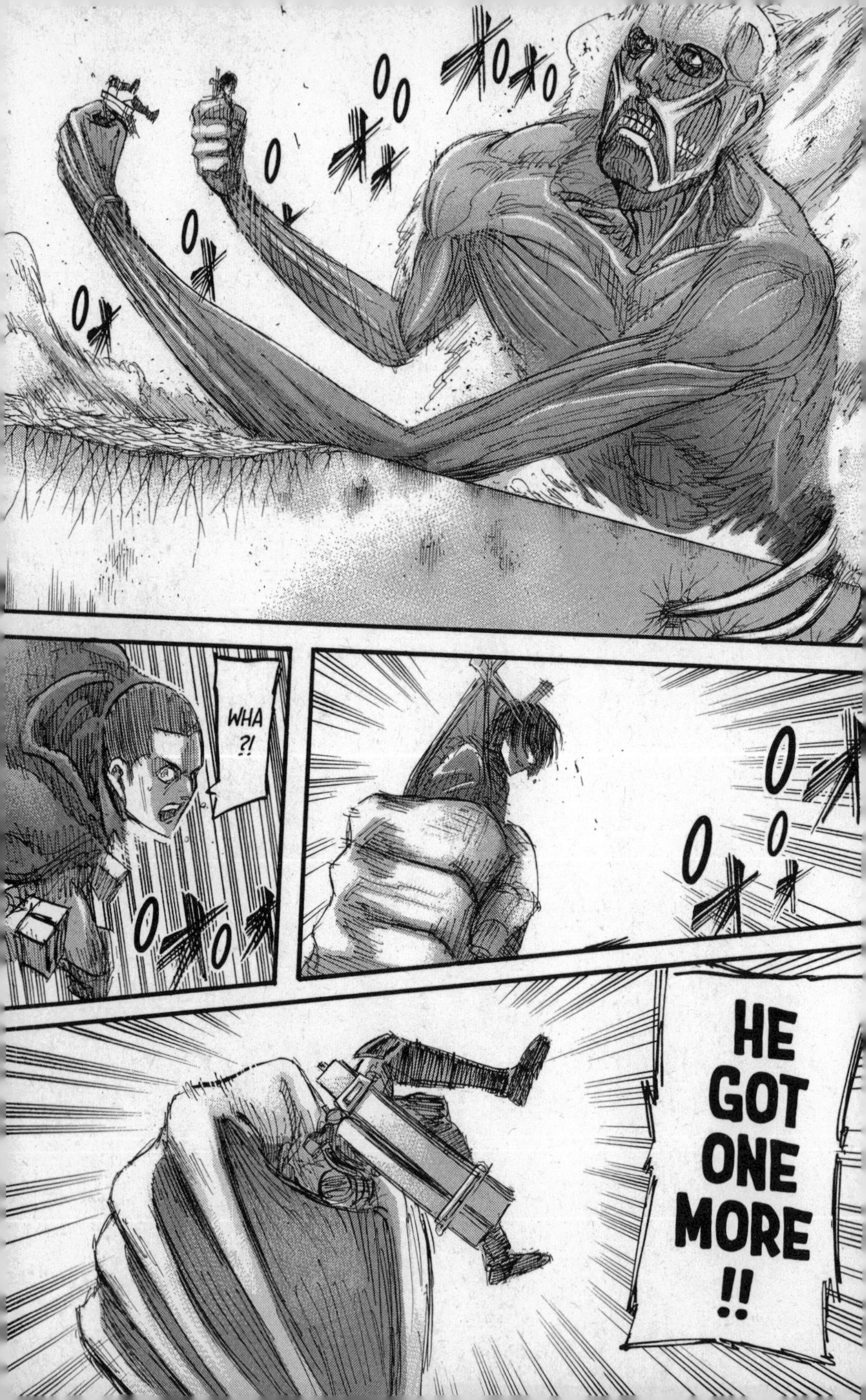
WHA?!
HE GOT ONE MORE!!

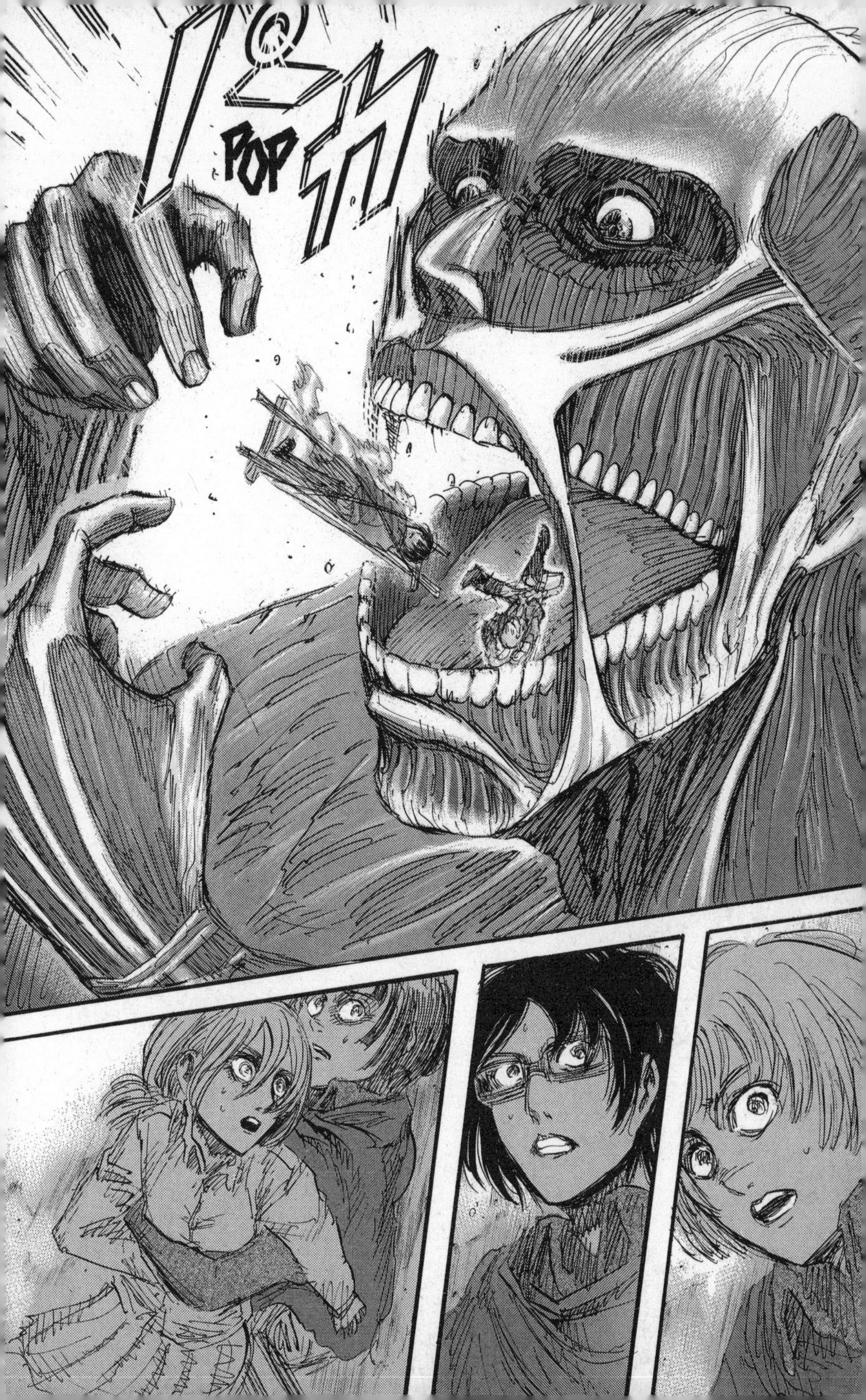
POP

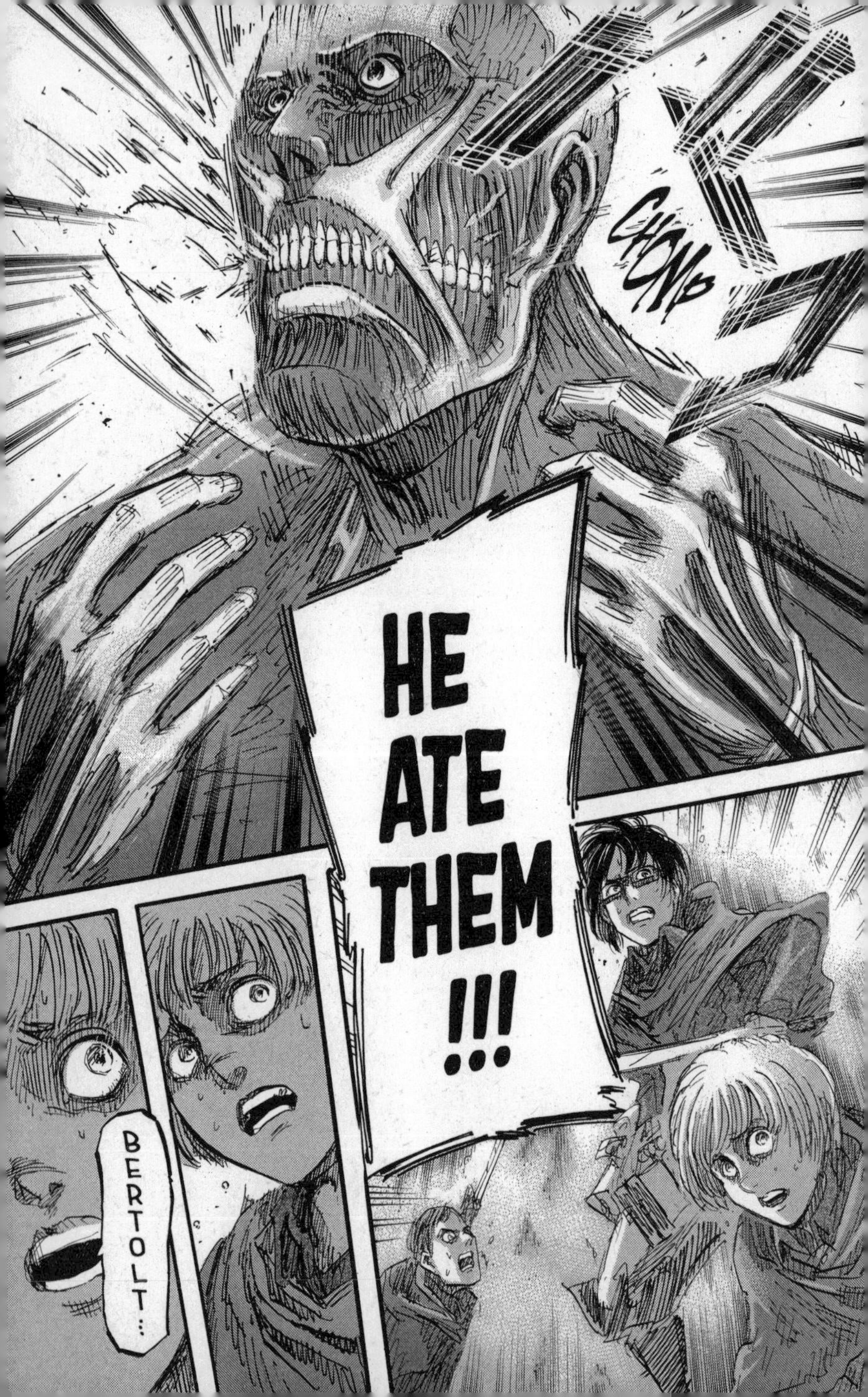
CHOMP
HE ATE THEM!!!
BERTOLT...

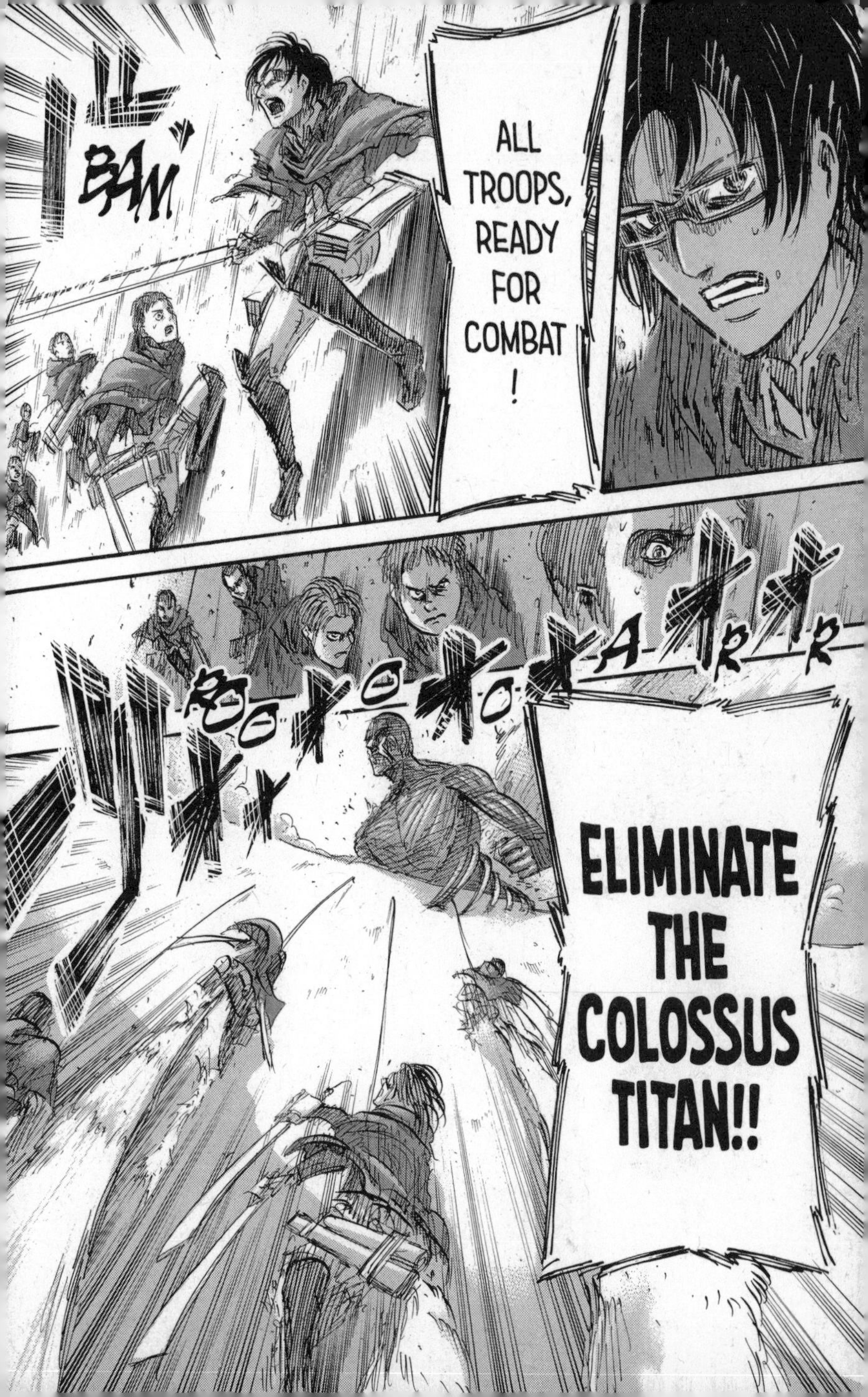

ALL TROOPS, READY FOR COMBAT!
BAM
ROOOOARR
ELIMINATE THE COLOSSUS TITAN!!

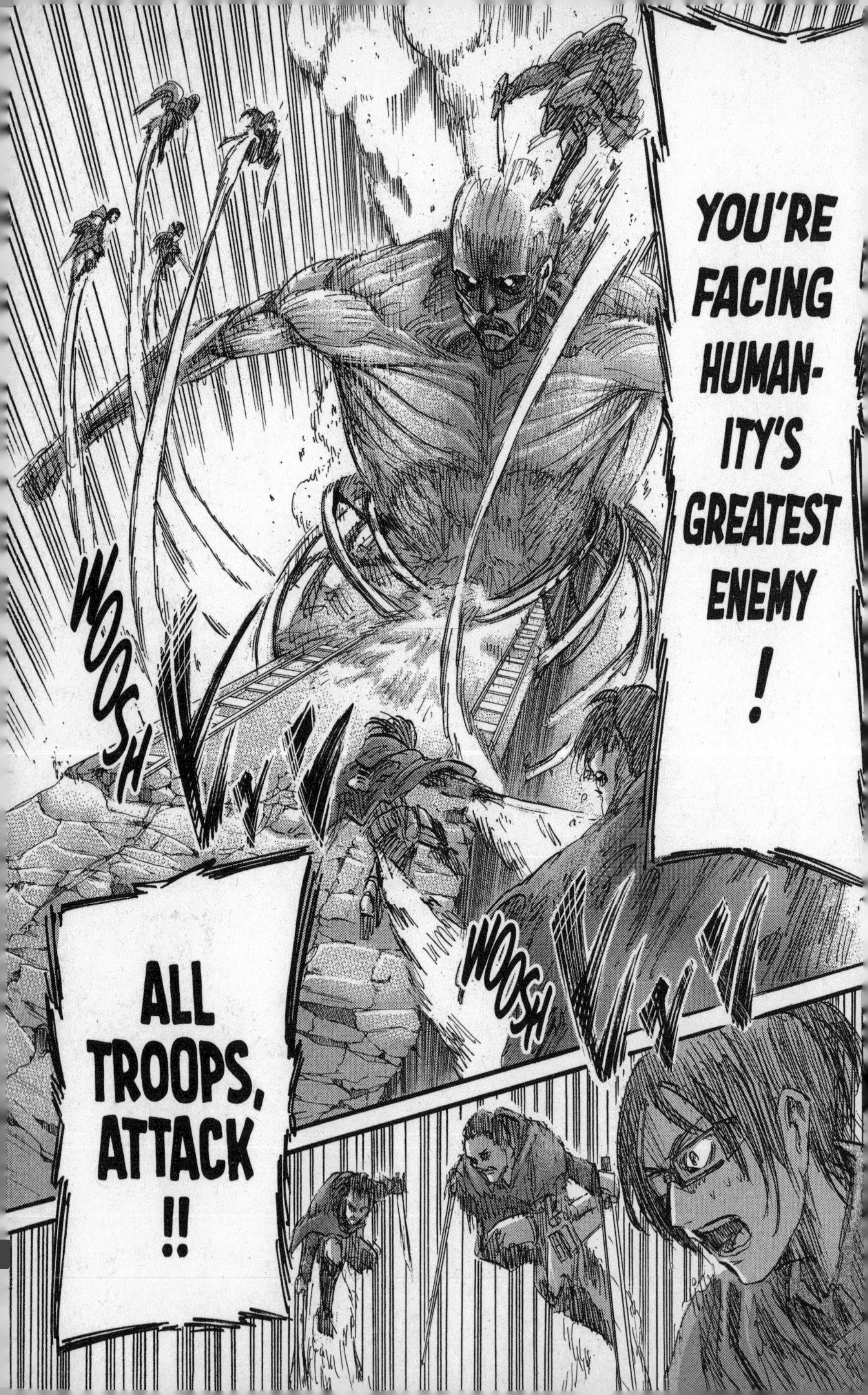
YOU'RE FACING HUMAN-ITY'S GREATEST ENEMY !
WOOSH
ALL TROOPS, ATTACK !!
WOOSH

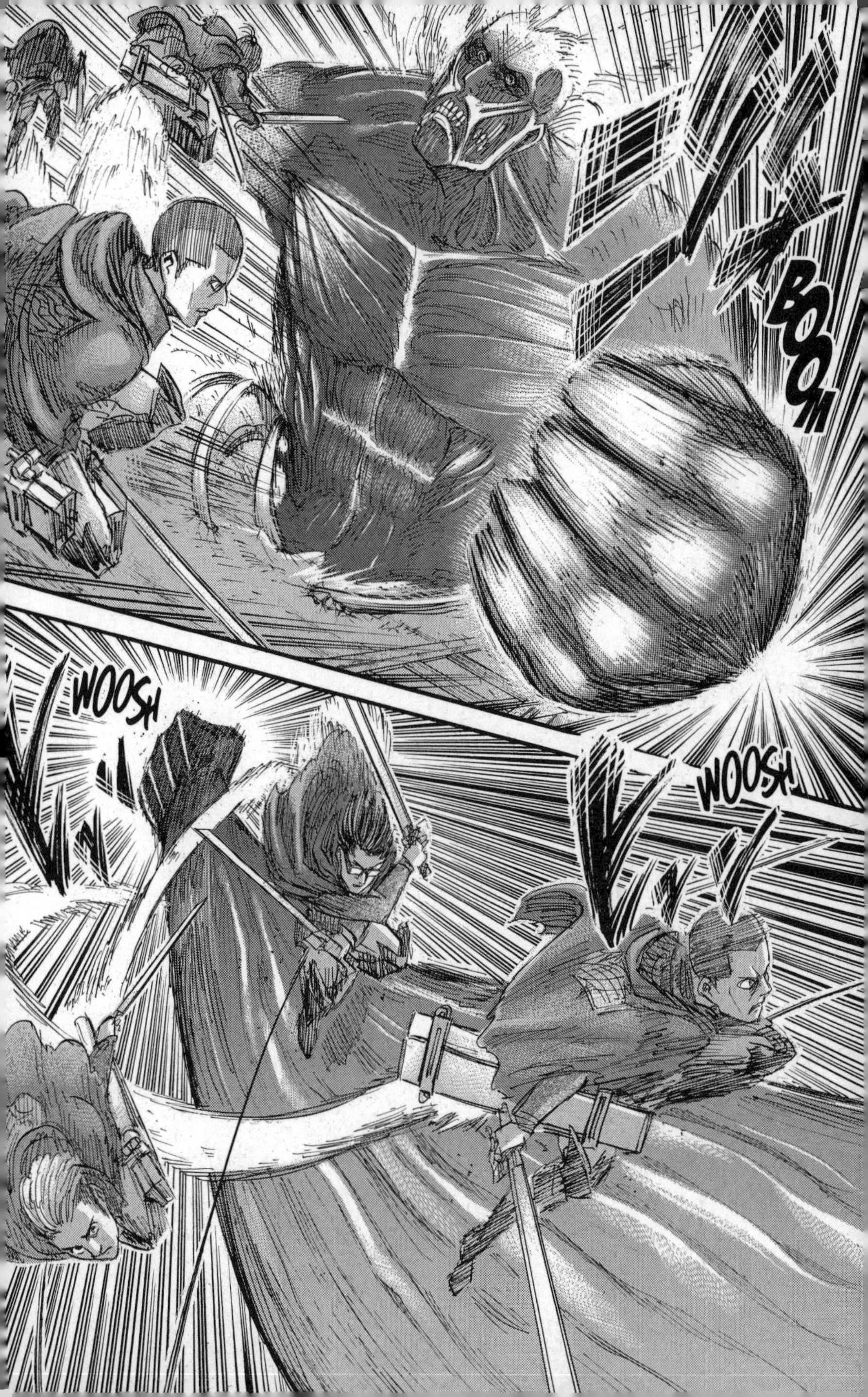
BOOM
WOOSH
WOOSH

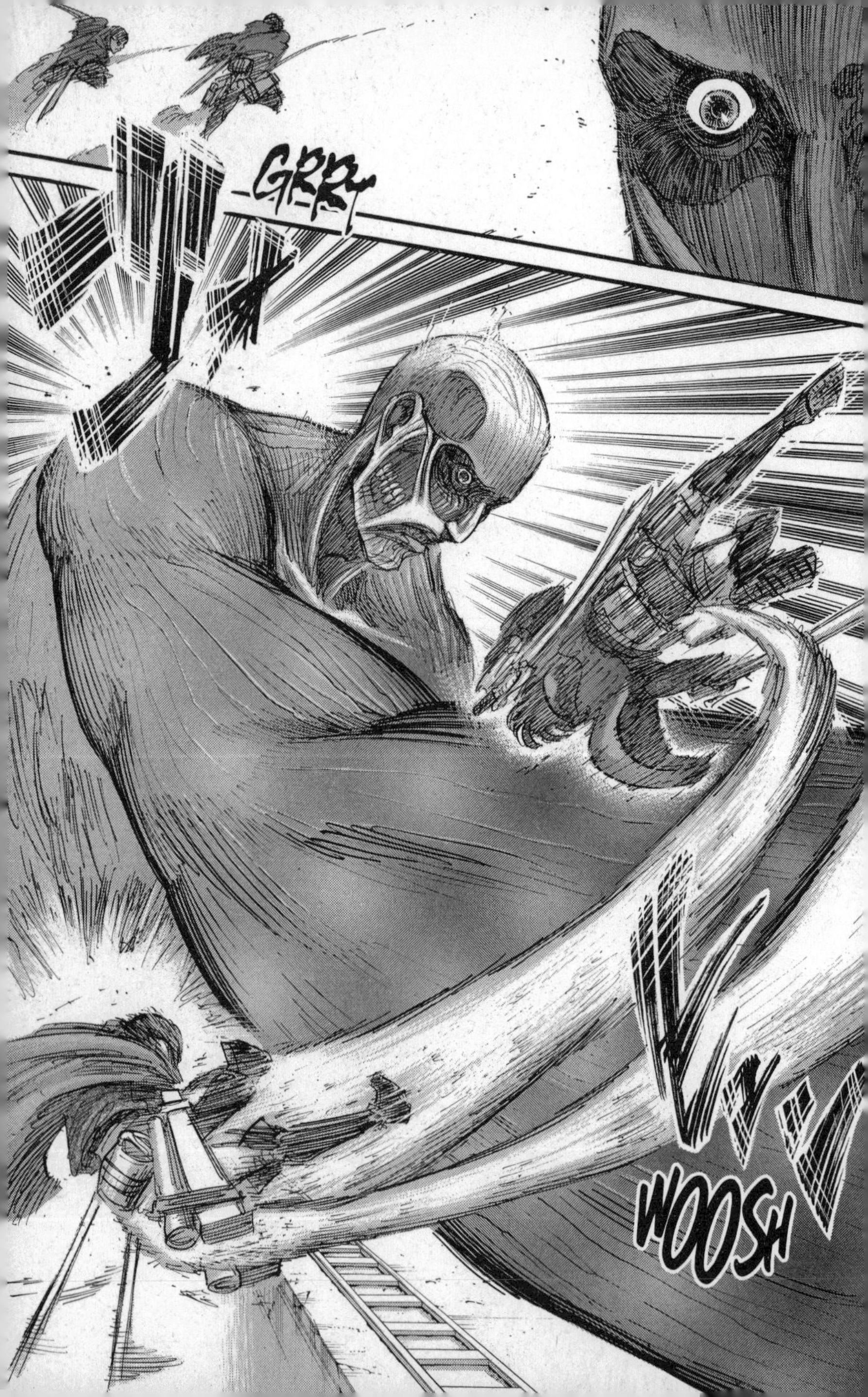
GRRR
WOOSH

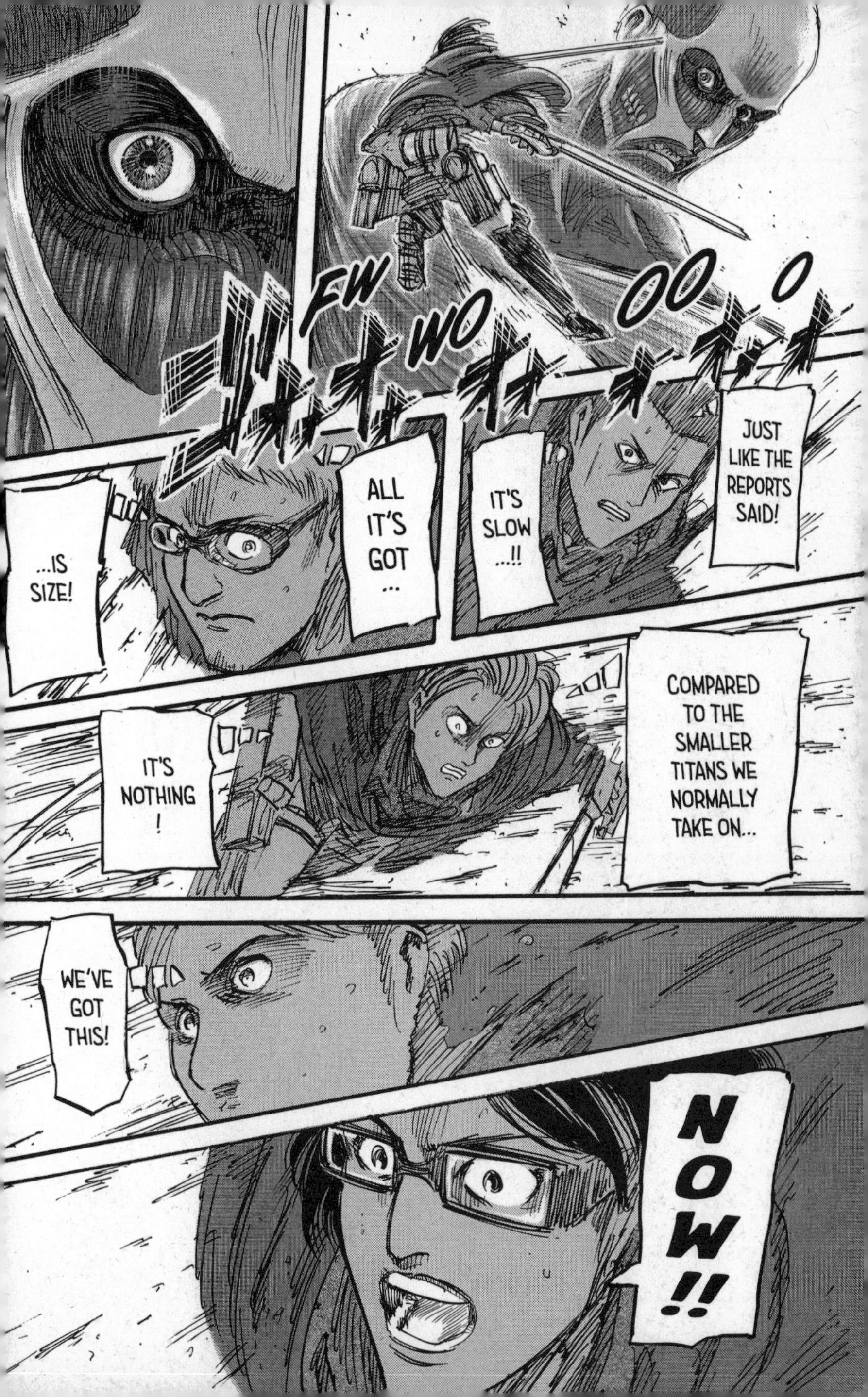
FWWOOOO
JUST LIKE THE REPORTS SAID!
IT'S SLOW ...!!
ALL IT'S GOT ...
...IS SIZE!
COMPARED TO THE SMALLER TITANS WE NORMALLY TAKE ON...
IT'S NOTHING !
WE'VE GOT THIS!
NOW!!

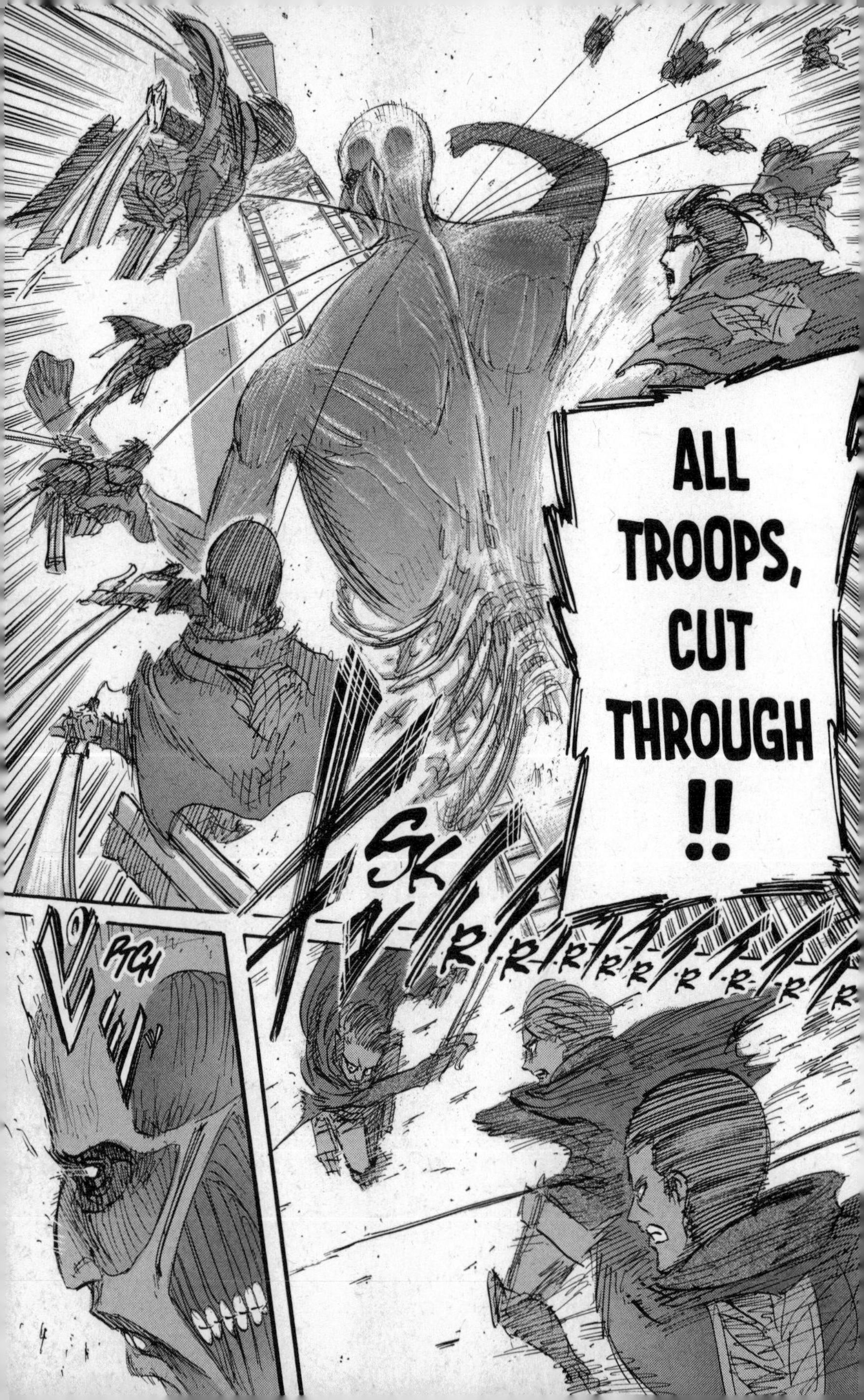
ALL TROOPS, CUT THROUGH!!
SKNRRRRRRRRRRRRRRR
PTCH

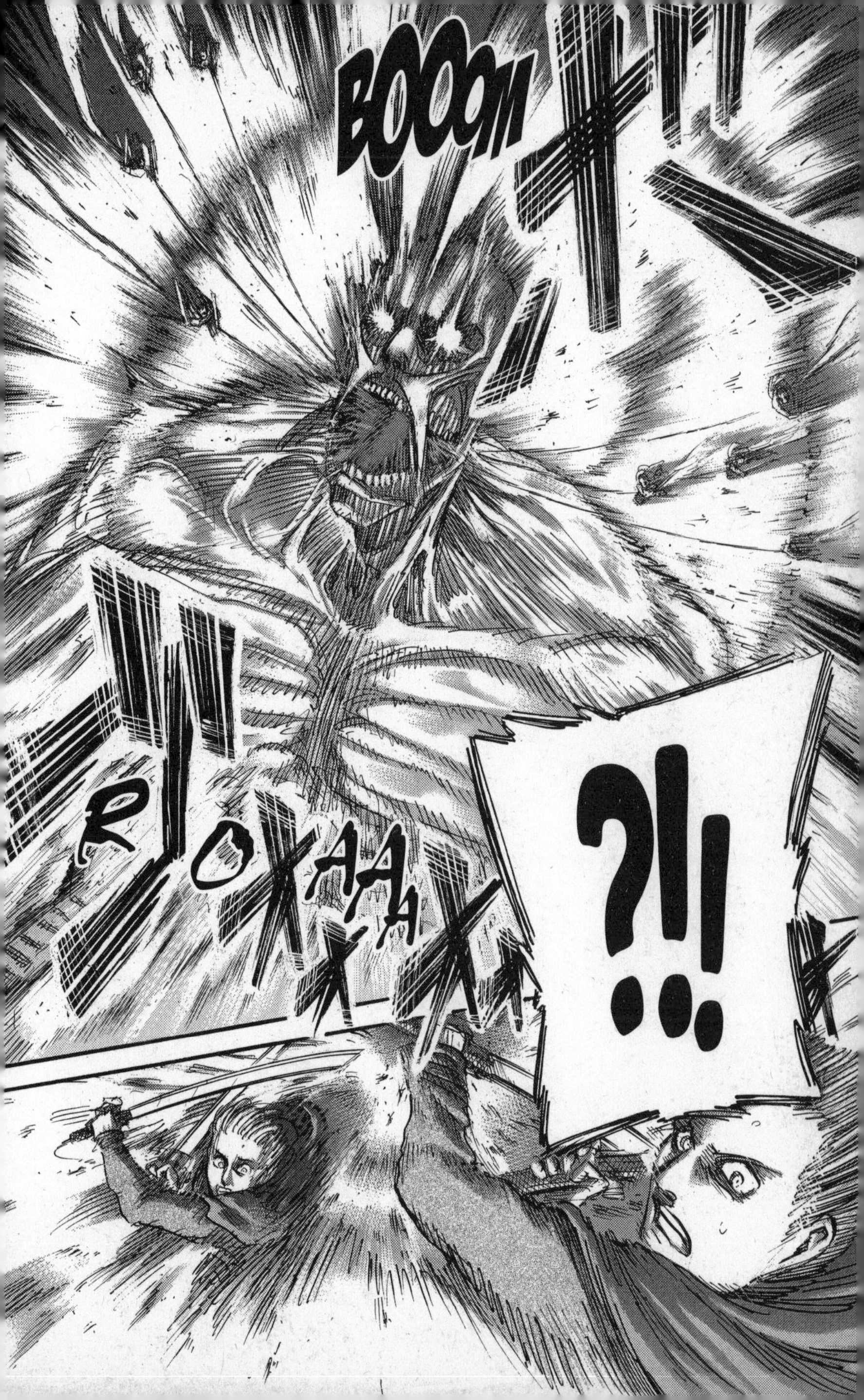
BOOOM
ROAAA
?!!

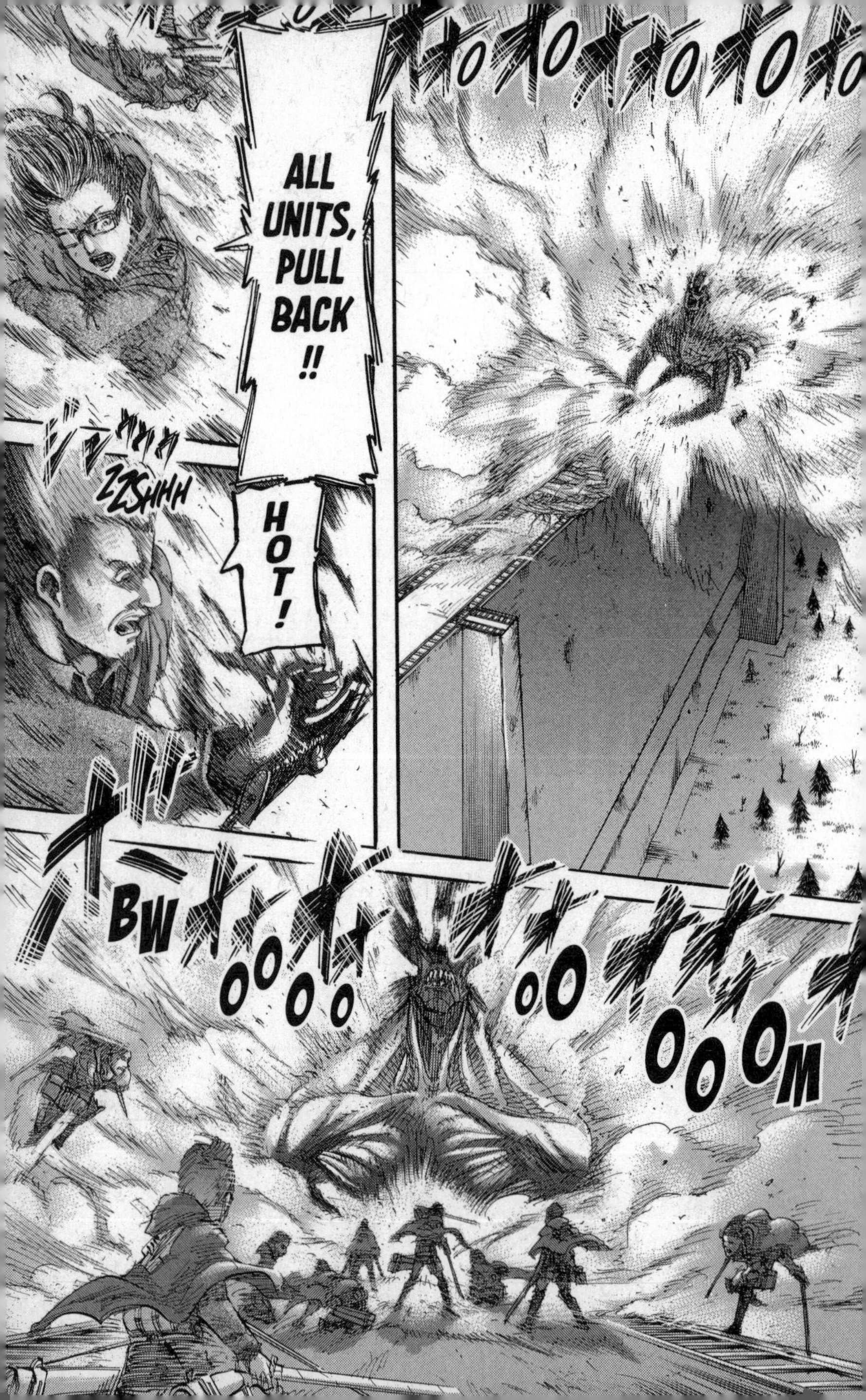
ALL UNITS, PULL BACK!!
ZZSHHH
HOT!
BWOOOOOOOOOOM

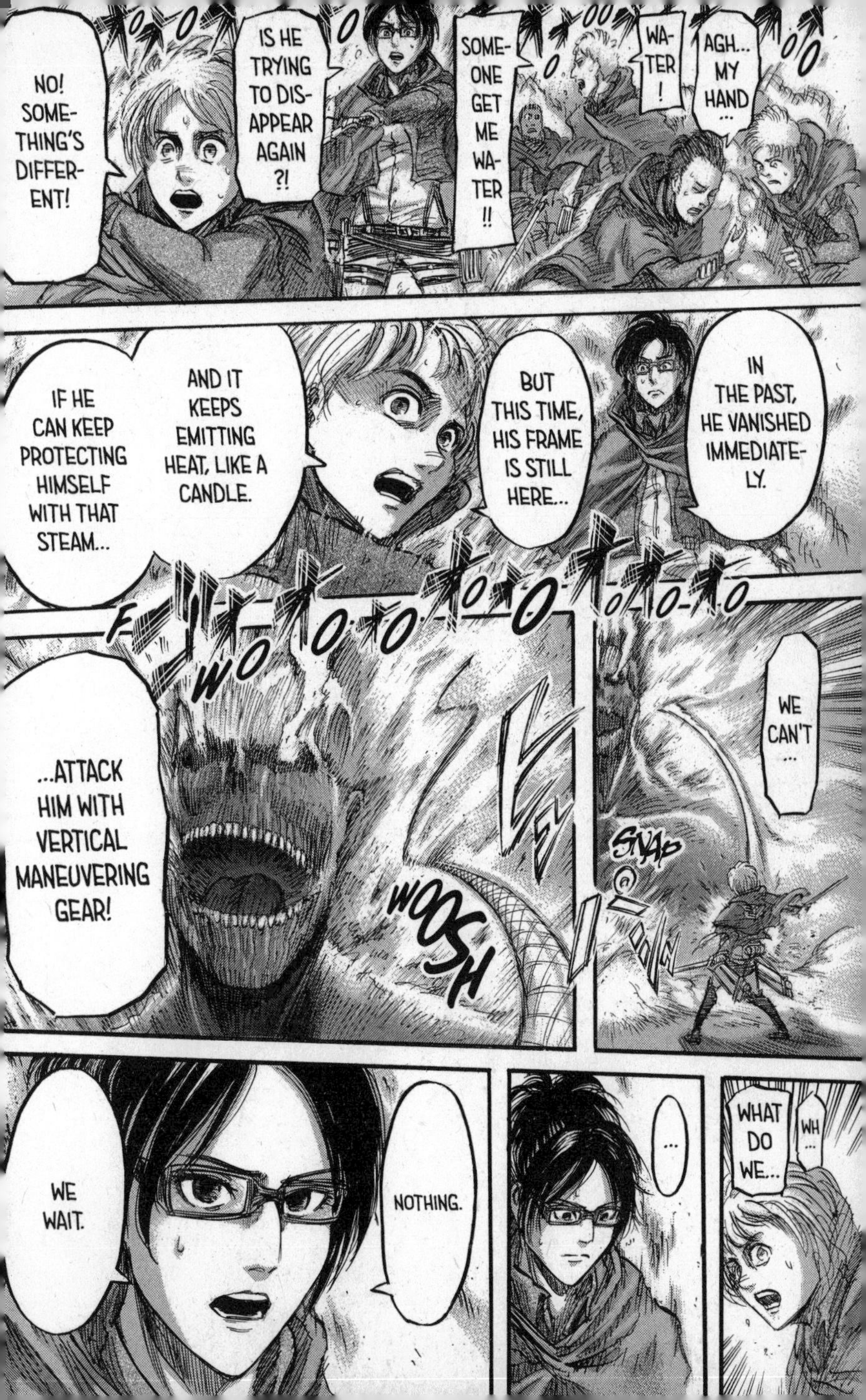
AGH... MY HAND ...
WA-TER!
SOME-ONE GET ME WA-TER!!
IS HE TRYING TO DIS-APPEAR AGAIN?!
NO! SOME-THING'S DIFFER-ENT!
IN THE PAST, HE VANISHED IMMEDIATE-LY.
BUT THIS TIME, HIS FRAME IS STILL HERE...
AND IT KEEPS EMITTING HEAT, LIKE A CANDLE.
IF HE CAN KEEP PROTECTING HIMSELF WITH THAT STEAM...
WE CAN'T ...
SNAP
...ATTACK HIM WITH VERTICAL MANEUVERING GEAR!
WOOSH
WH ...
WHAT DO WE...
...
NOTHING.
WE WAIT.

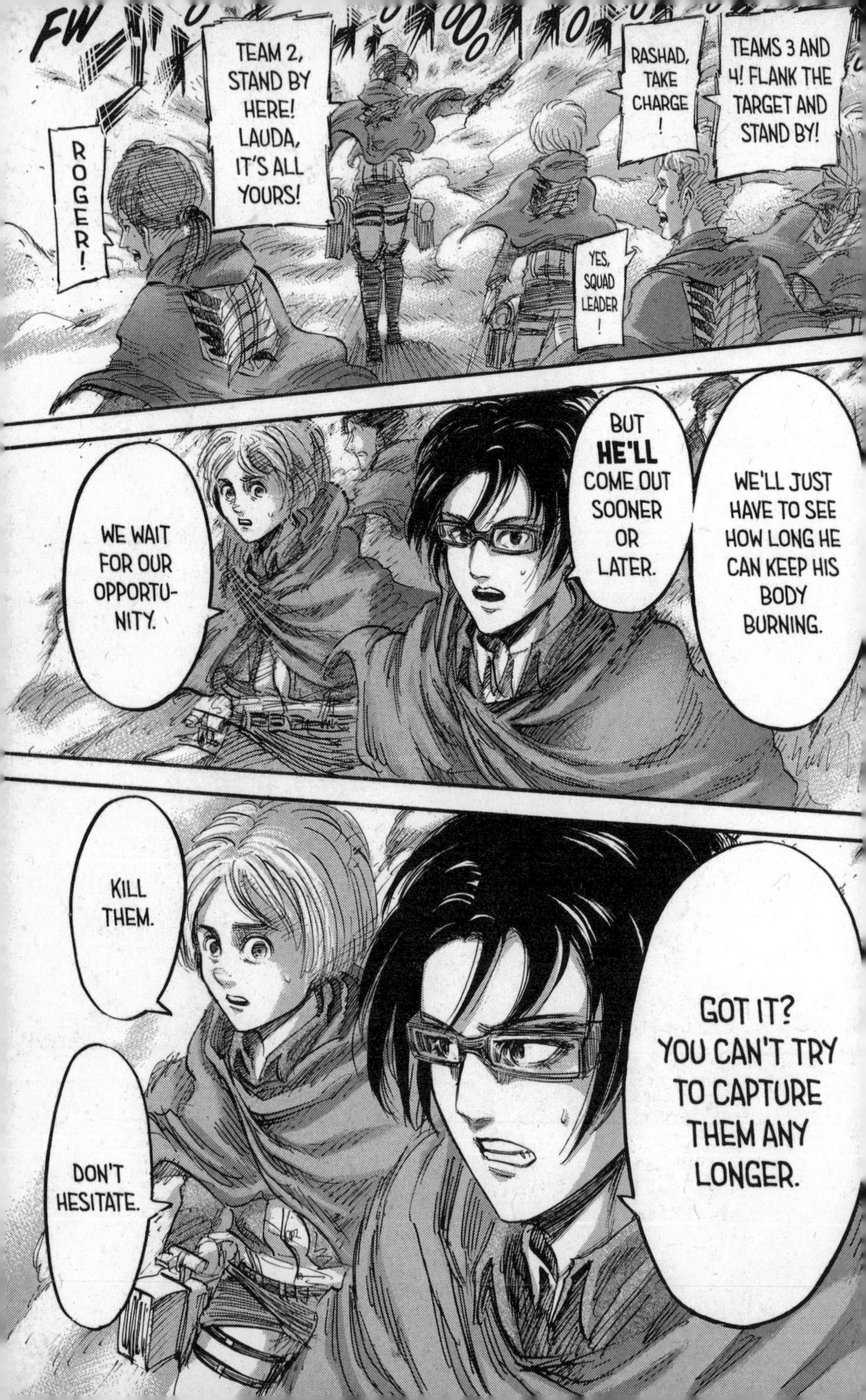
FW
TEAMS 3 AND 4! FLANK THE TARGET AND STAND BY!
RASHAD, TAKE CHARGE!
YES, SQUAD LEADER!
TEAM 2, STAND BY HERE! LAUDA, IT'S ALL YOURS!
ROGER!
WE'LL JUST HAVE TO SEE HOW LONG HE CAN KEEP HIS BODY BURNING.
BUT **HE'LL** COME OUT SOONER OR LATER.
WE WAIT FOR OUR OPPORTUNITY.
GOT IT? YOU CAN'T TRY TO CAPTURE THEM ANY LONGER.
KILL THEM.
DON'T HESITATE.

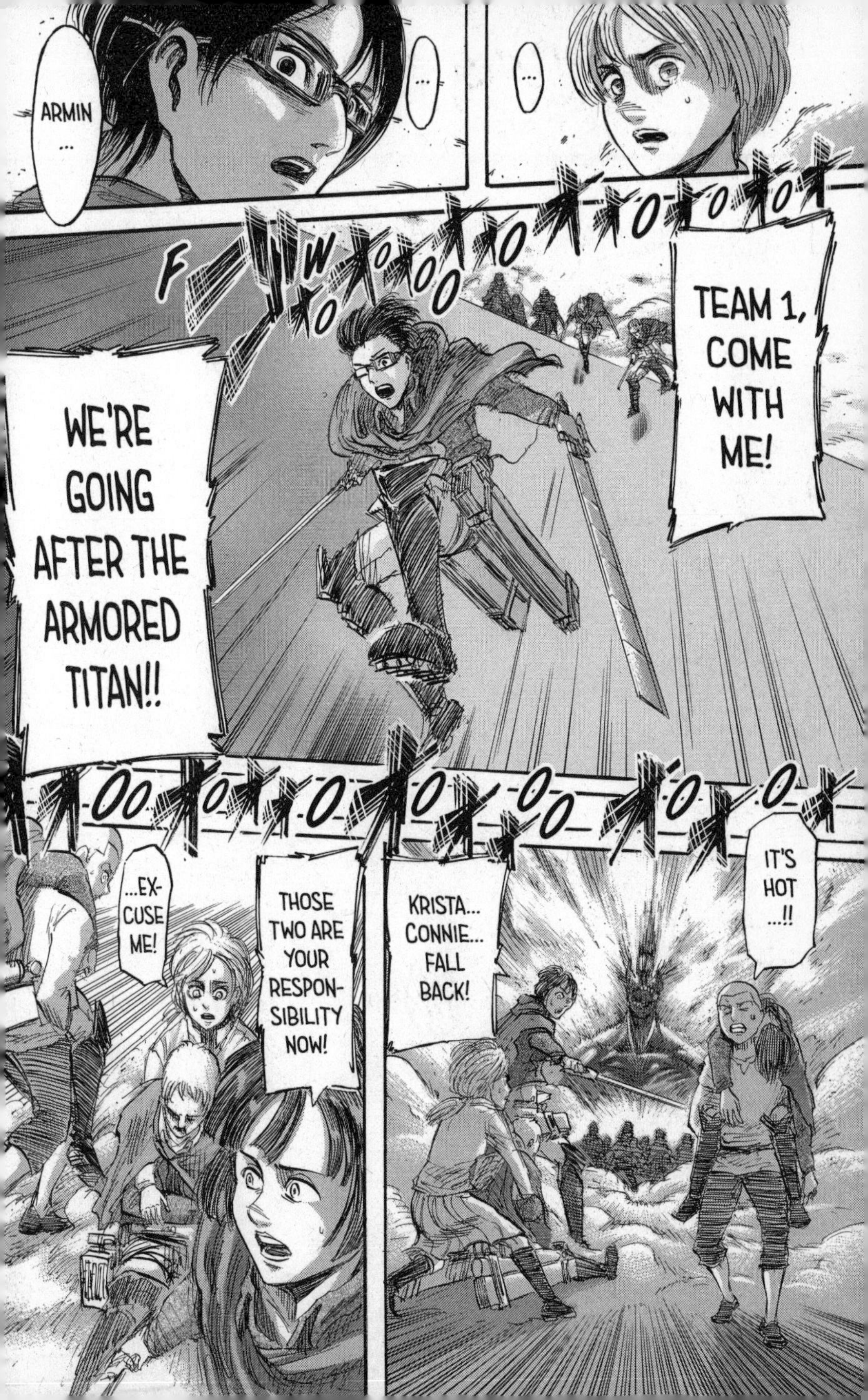
...
...
ARMIN ...
FWOOOO
TEAM 1, COME WITH ME!
WE'RE GOING AFTER THE ARMORED TITAN!!
IT'S HOT ...!!
KRISTA... CONNIE... FALL BACK!
THOSE TWO ARE YOUR RESPONSIBILITY NOW!
...EXCUSE ME!

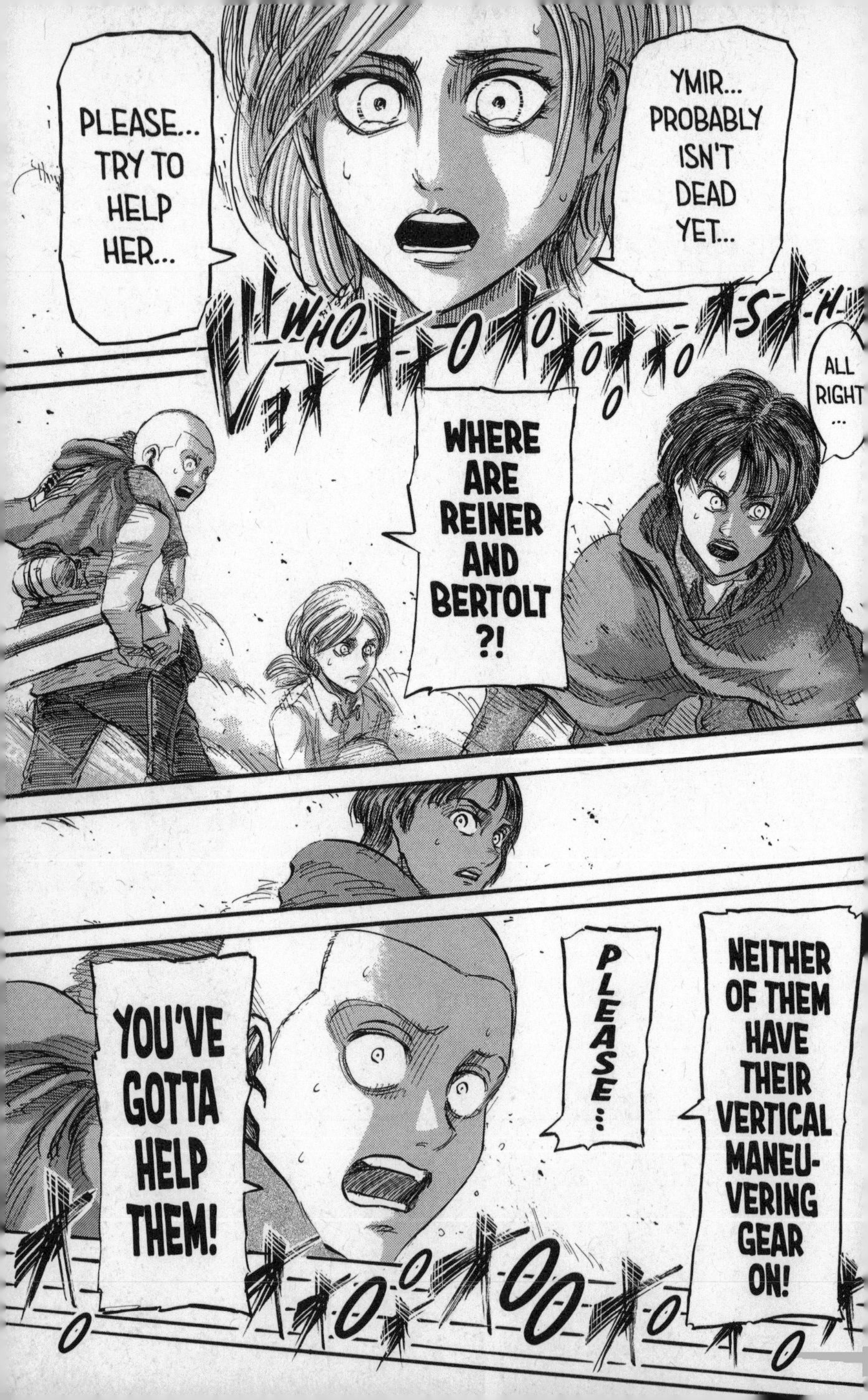
YMIR... PROBABLY ISN'T DEAD YET...
PLEASE... TRY TO HELP HER...
WHO-O-O-O-O-S-H
ALL RIGHT...
WHERE ARE REINER AND BERTOLT?!
NEITHER OF THEM HAVE THEIR VERTICAL MANEU-VERING GEAR ON!
PLEASE...
YOU'VE GOTTA HELP THEM!

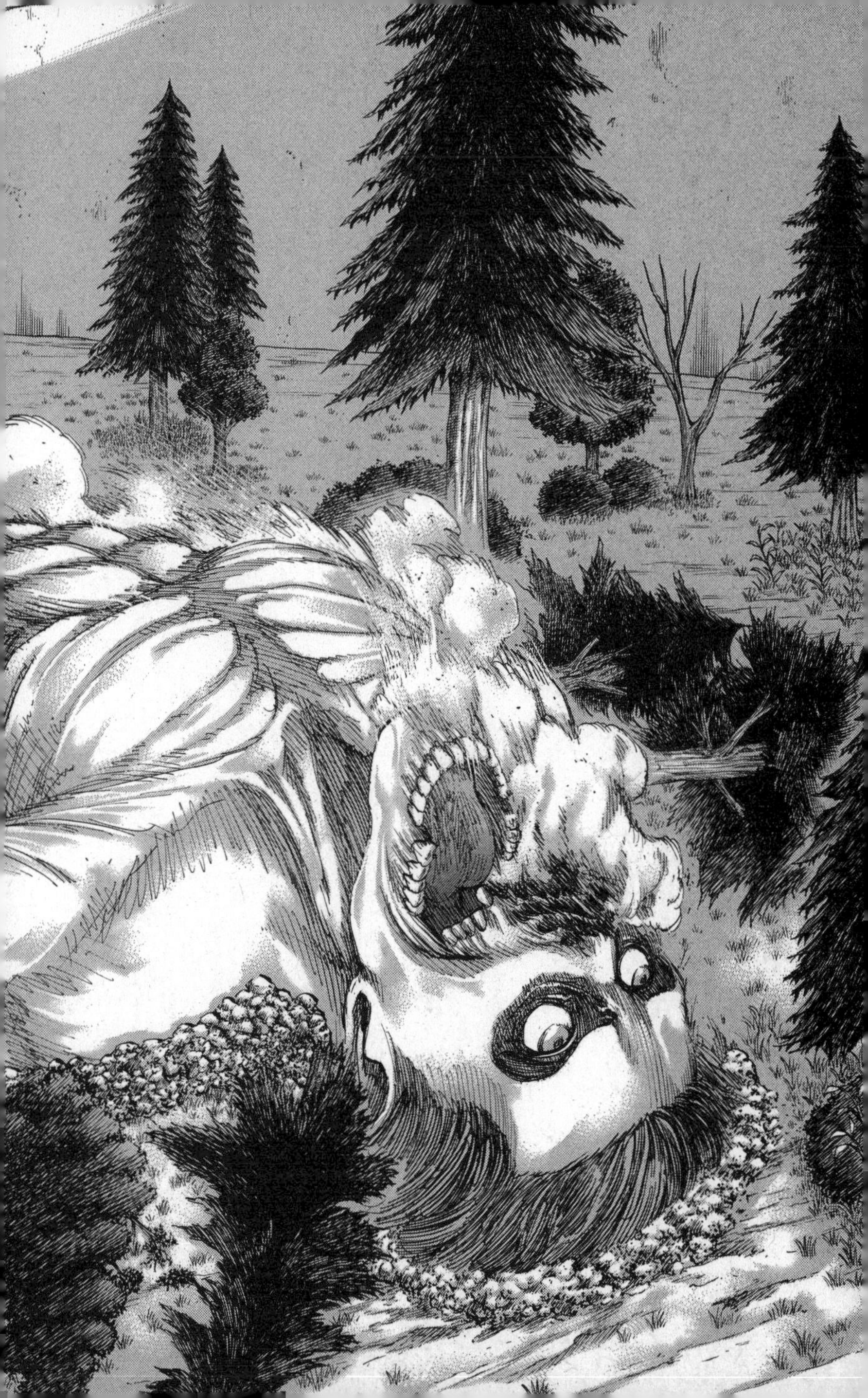

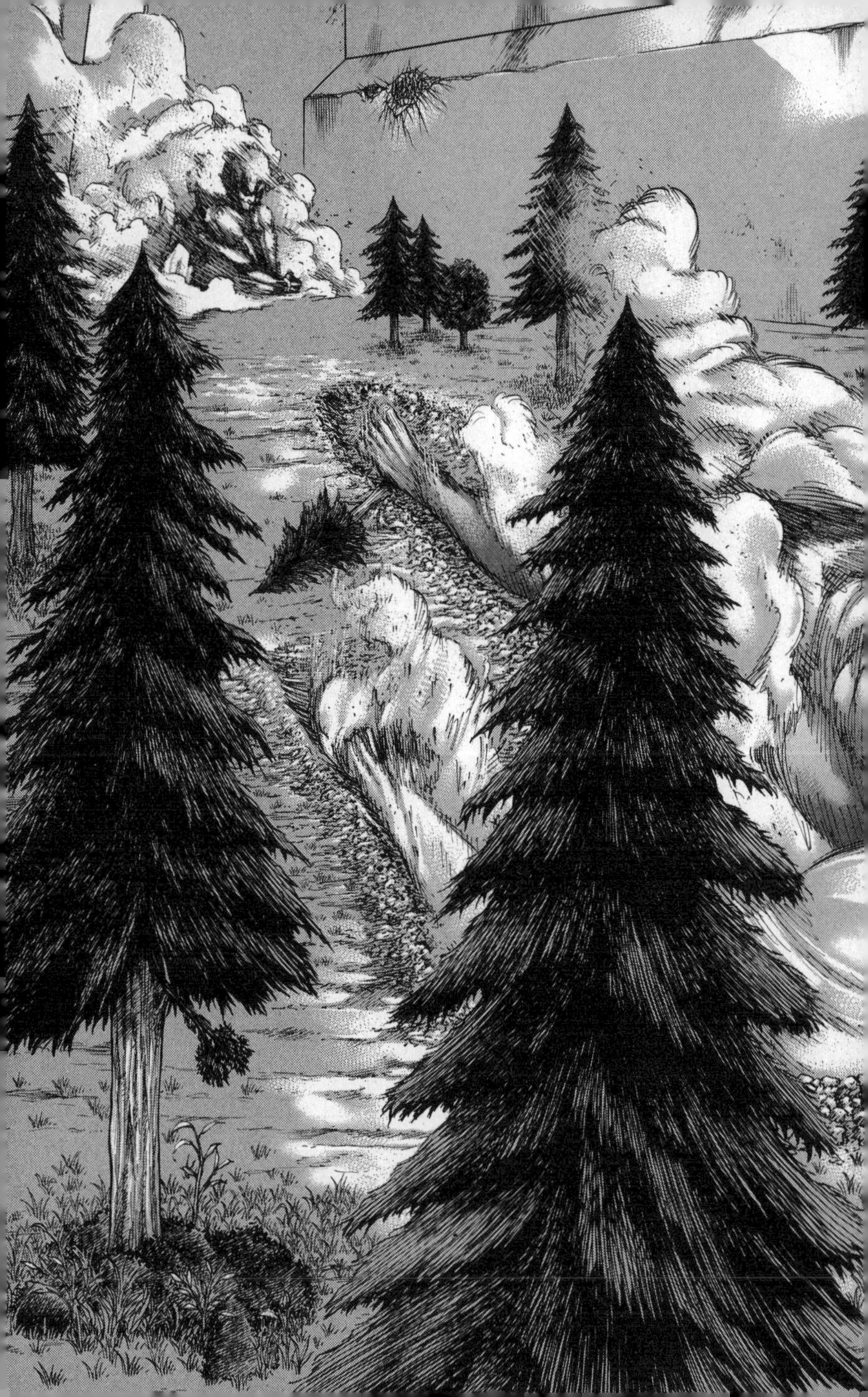

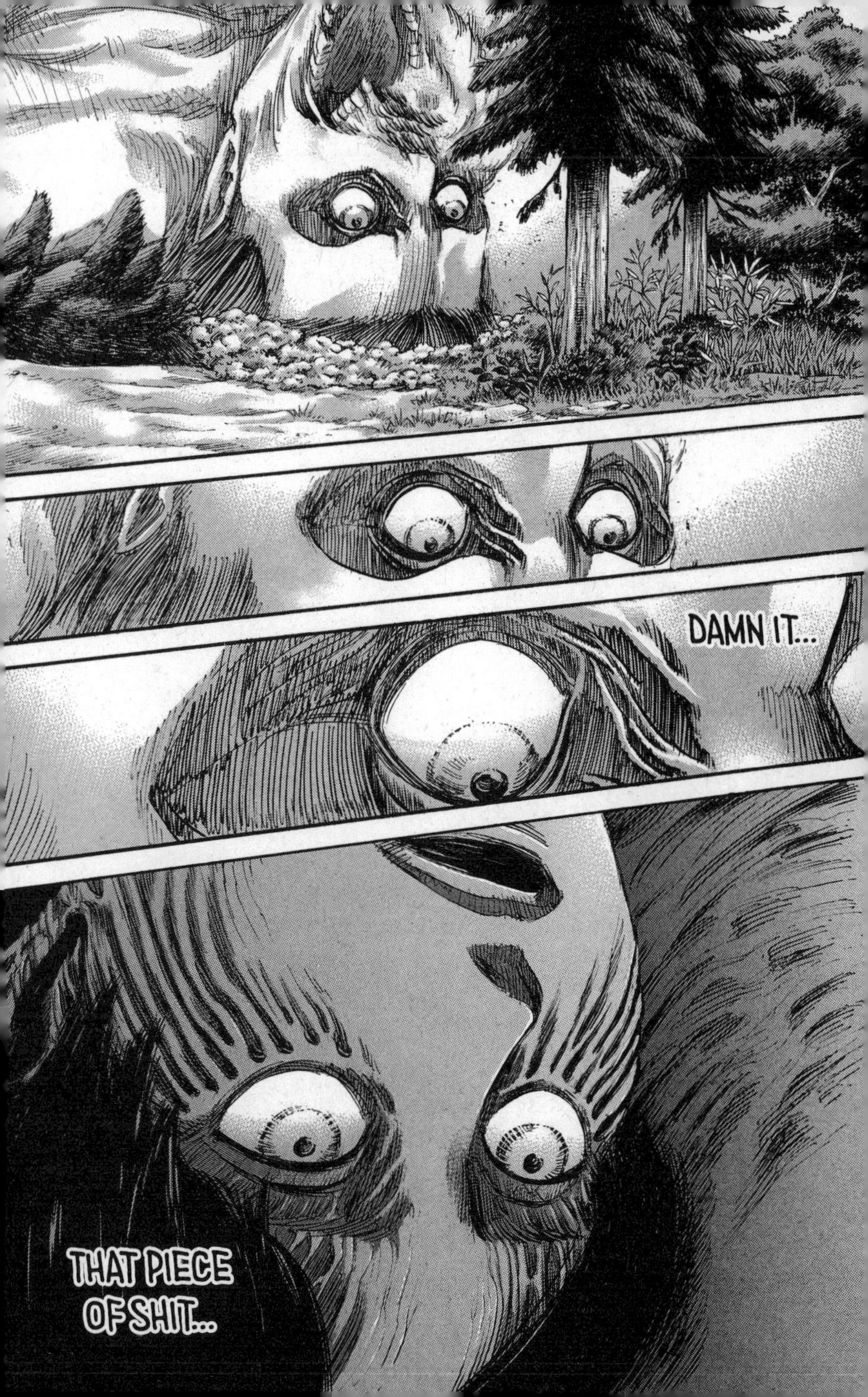

DAMN IT...
THAT PIECE OF SHIT...

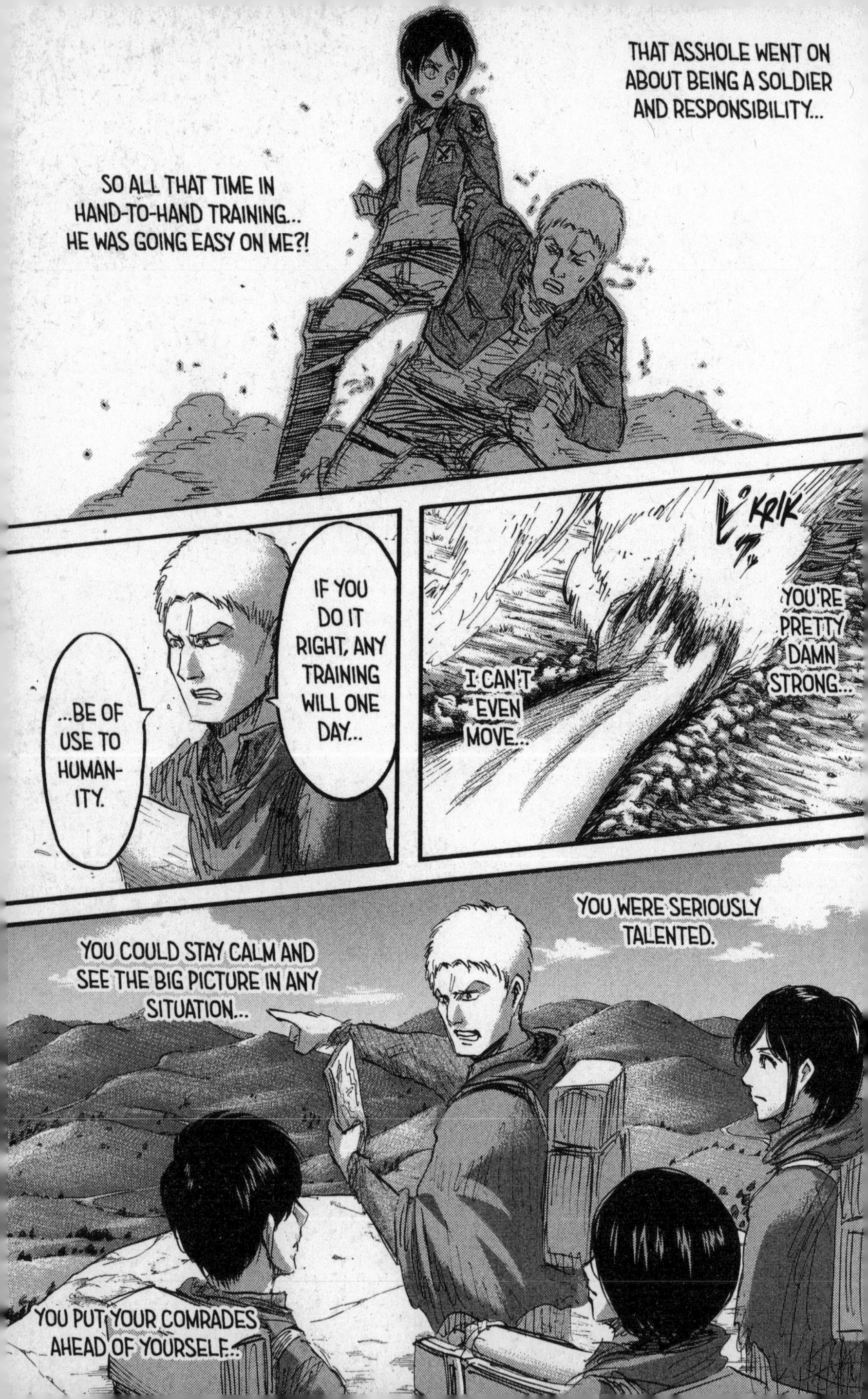
THAT ASSHOLE WENT ON ABOUT BEING A SOLDIER AND RESPONSIBILITY...
SO ALL THAT TIME IN HAND-TO-HAND TRAINING... HE WAS GOING EASY ON ME?!
KRIK
YOU'RE PRETTY DAMN STRONG...
I CAN'T EVEN MOVE...
IF YOU DO IT RIGHT, ANY TRAINING WILL ONE DAY...
...BE OF USE TO HUMAN-ITY.
YOU WERE SERIOUSLY TALENTED.
YOU COULD STAY CALM AND SEE THE BIG PICTURE IN ANY SITUATION...
YOU PUT YOUR COMRADES AHEAD OF YOURSELF...

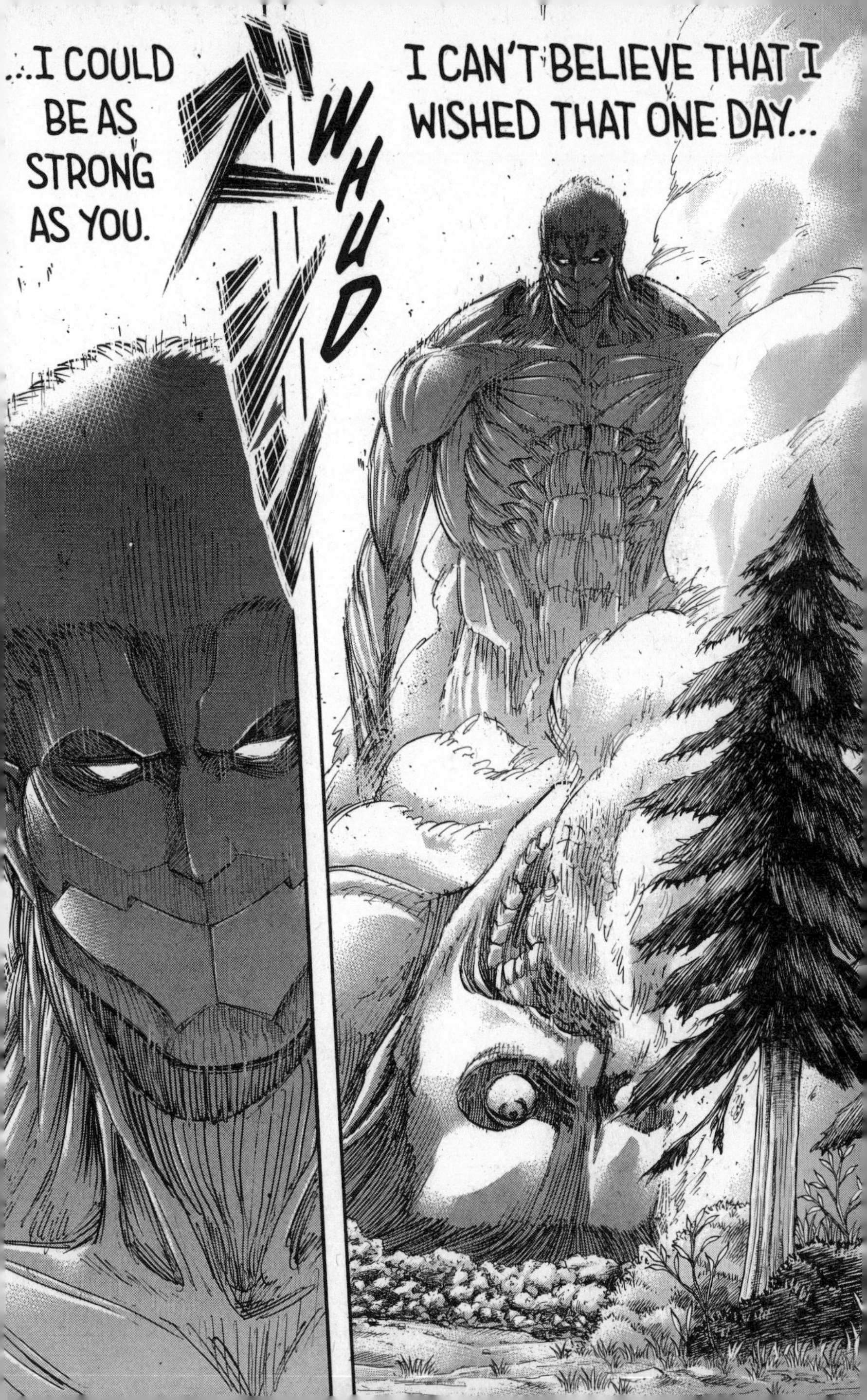
I CAN'T BELIEVE THAT I WISHED THAT ONE DAY...
...I COULD BE AS STRONG AS YOU.
WHUD

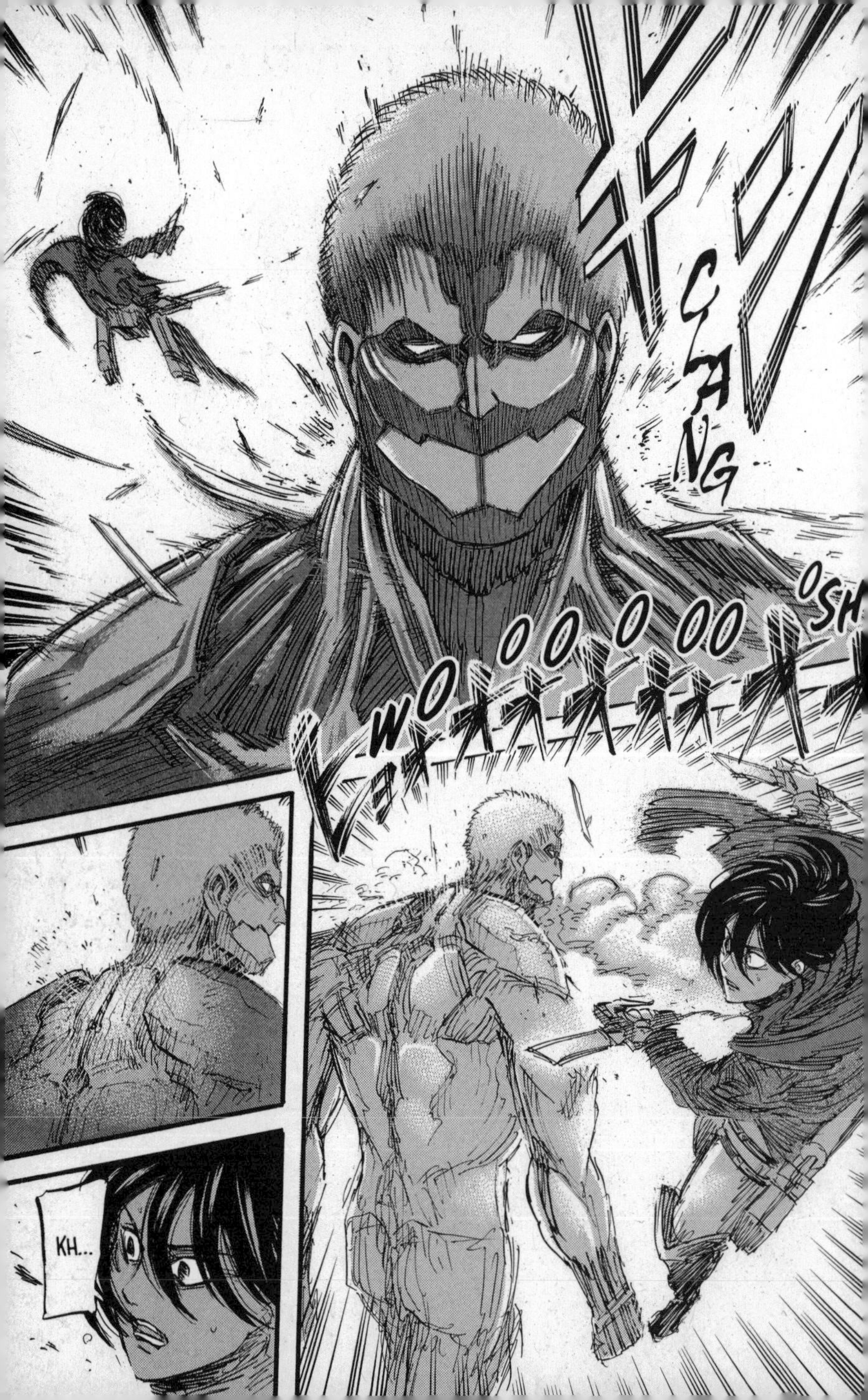
CLANG
WOOOOOOOOSH
KH...

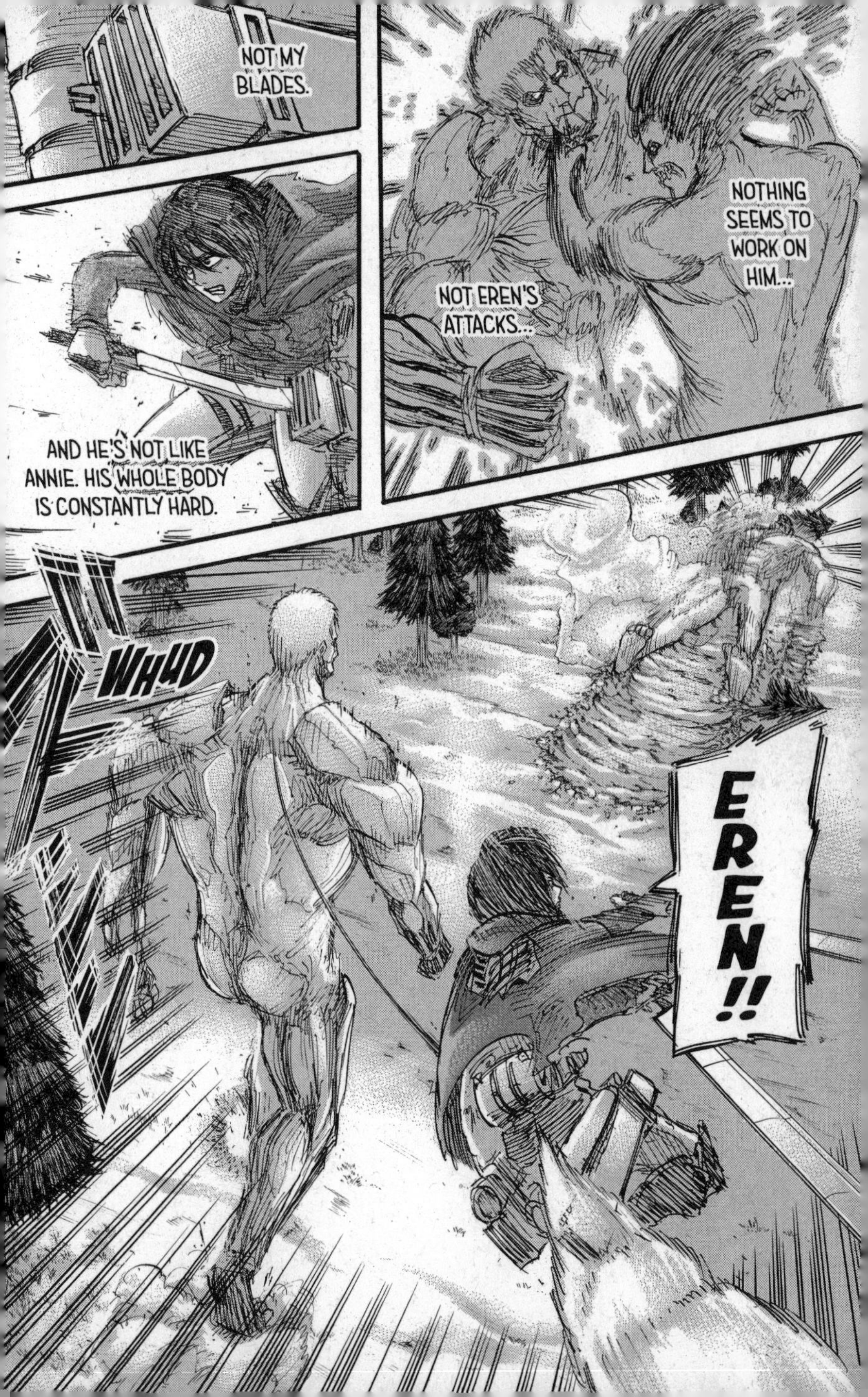
NOTHING SEEMS TO WORK ON HIM...
NOT EREN'S ATTACKS...
NOT MY BLADES.
AND HE'S NOT LIKE ANNIE. HIS WHOLE BODY IS CONSTANTLY HARD.
EREN!!
WHUD

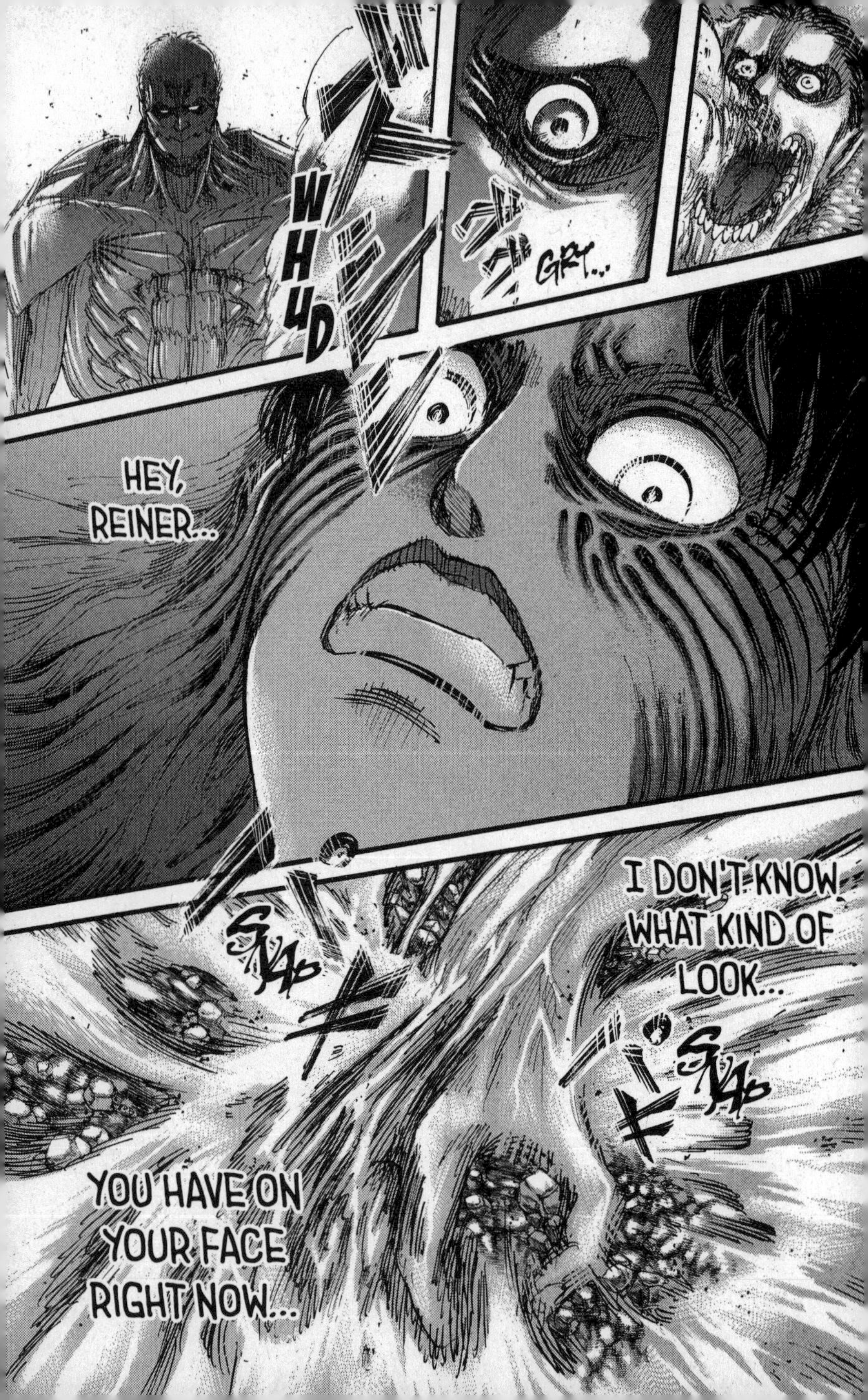
GRT...
WHUD
HEY, REINER...
I DON'T KNOW WHAT KIND OF LOOK...
YOU HAVE ON YOUR FACE RIGHT NOW...

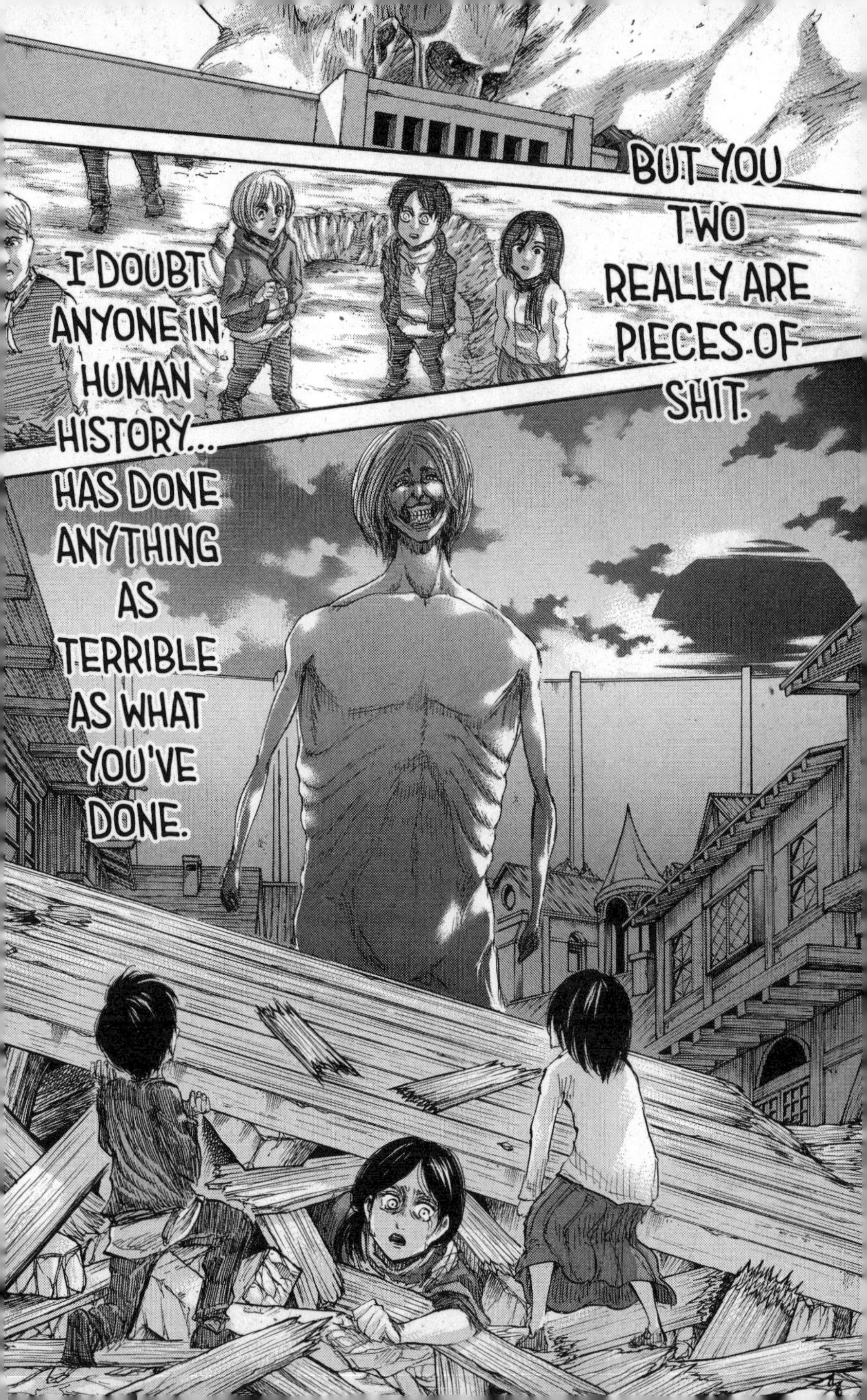
BUT YOU TWO REALLY ARE PIECES OF SHIT.
I DOUBT ANYONE IN HUMAN HISTORY... HAS DONE ANYTHING AS TERRIBLE AS WHAT YOU'VE DONE.

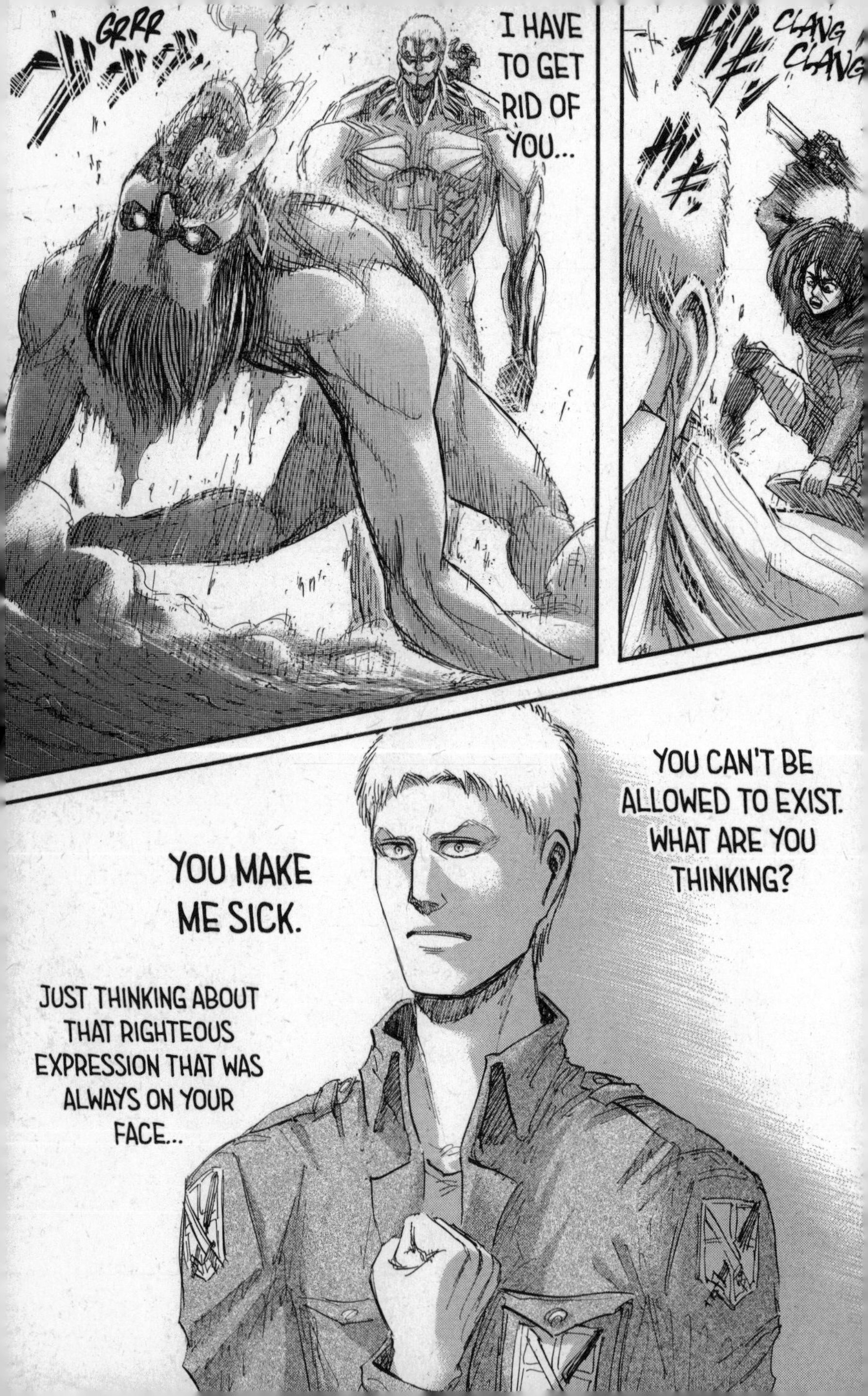
CLANG
CLANG
GRRR
I HAVE TO GET RID OF YOU...
YOU CAN'T BE ALLOWED TO EXIST. WHAT ARE YOU THINKING?
YOU MAKE ME SICK.
JUST THINKING ABOUT THAT RIGHTEOUS EXPRESSION THAT WAS ALWAYS ON YOUR FACE...

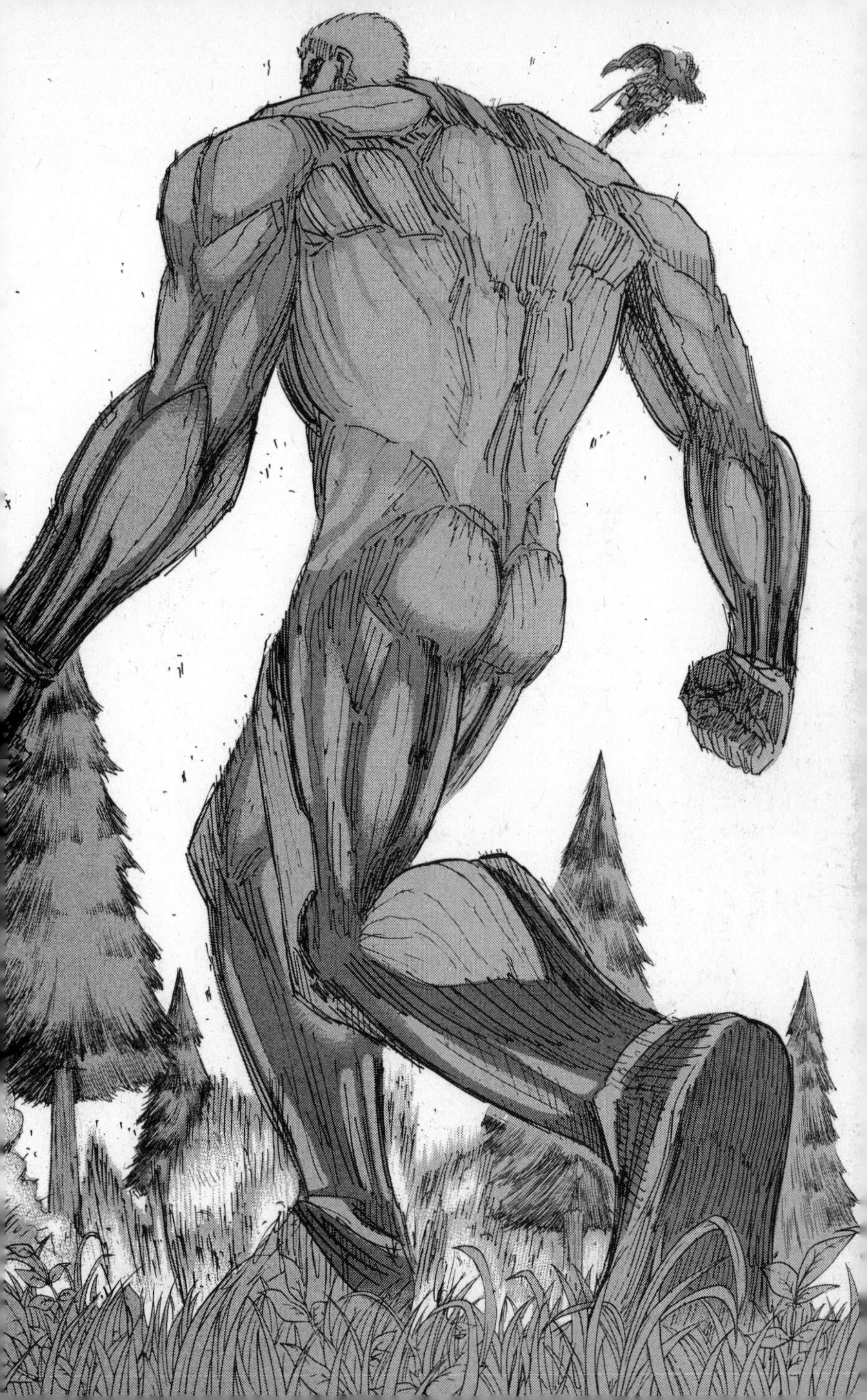

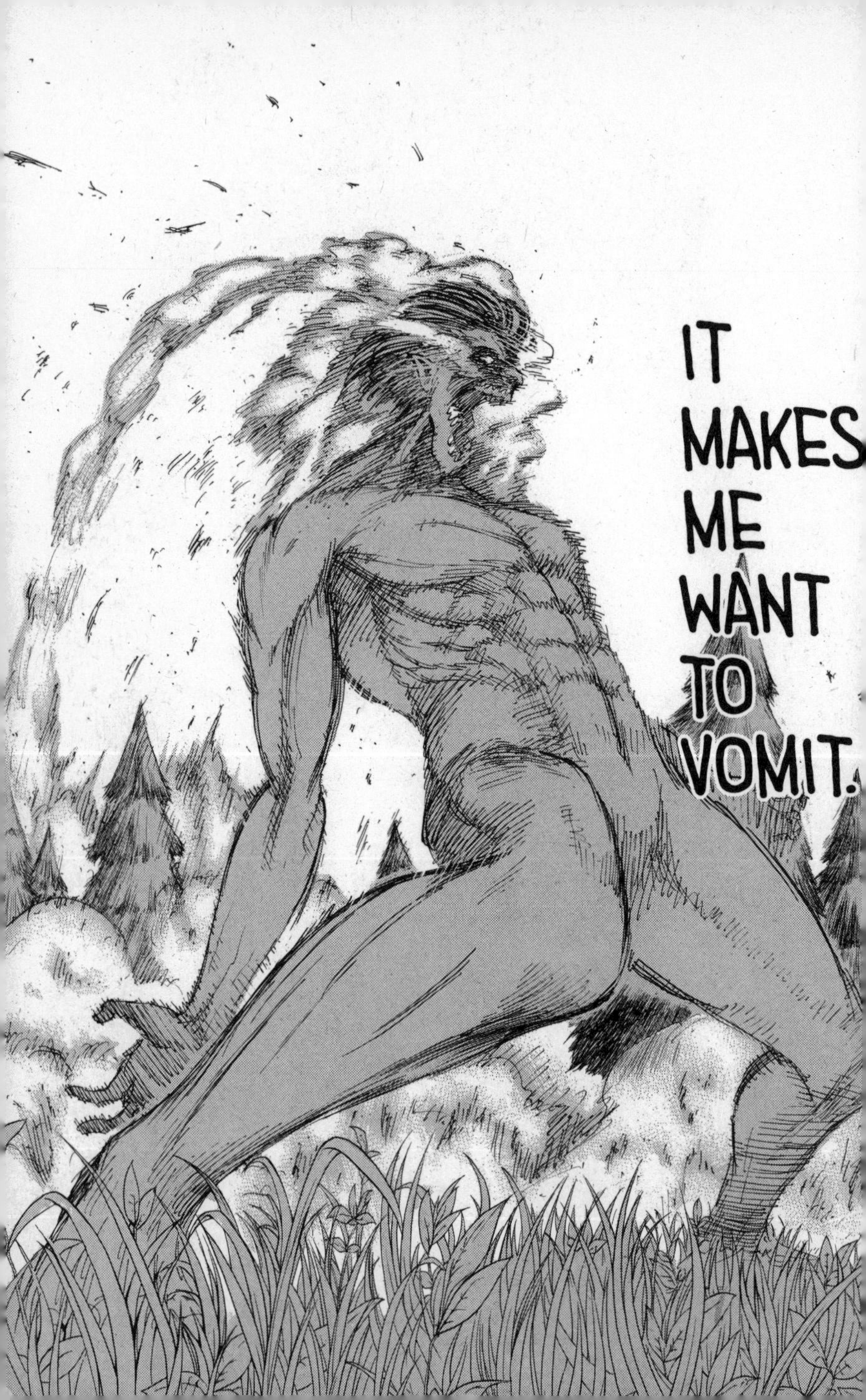
IT MAKES ME WANT TO VOMIT.

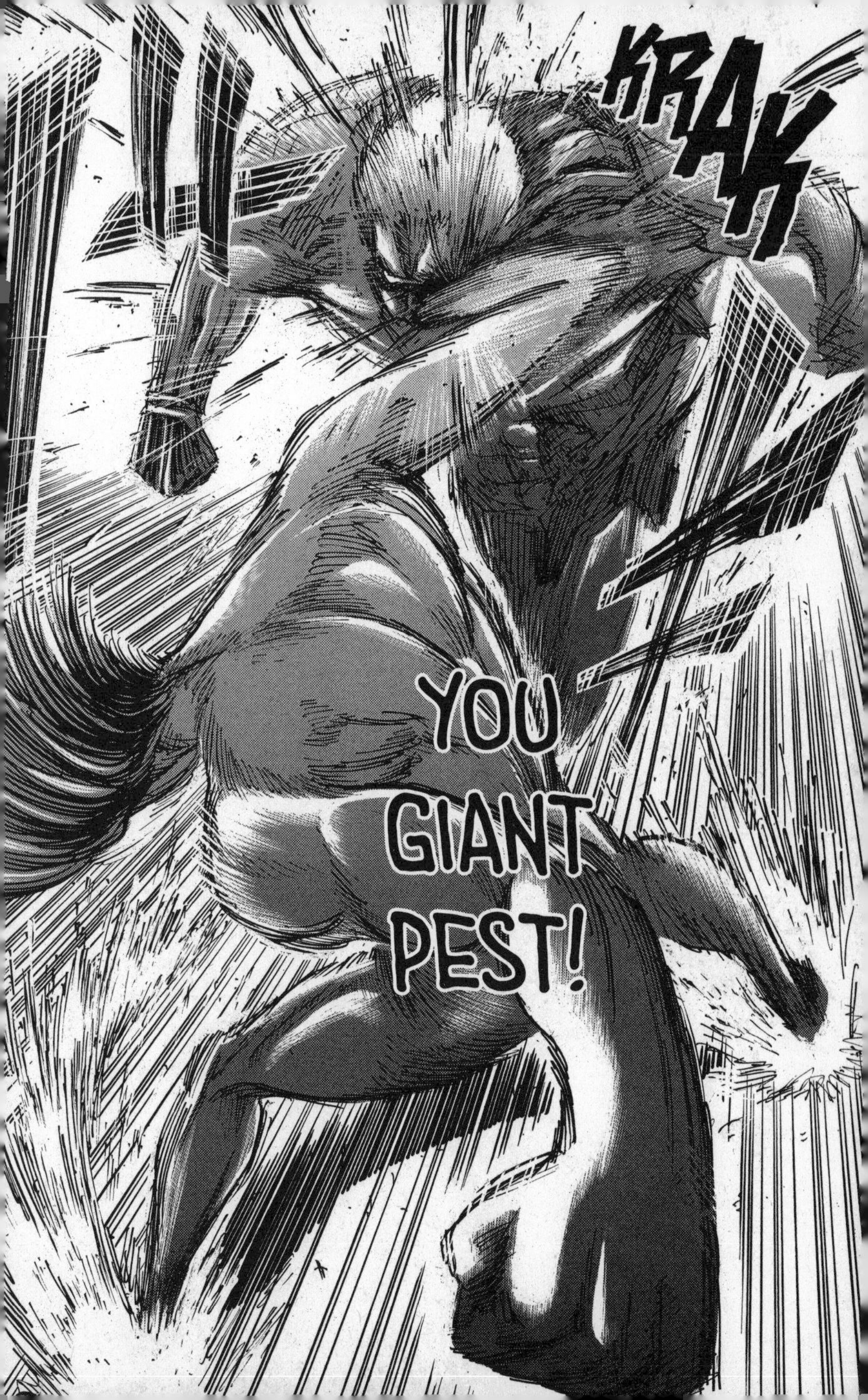
KRAK
YOU GIANT PEST!

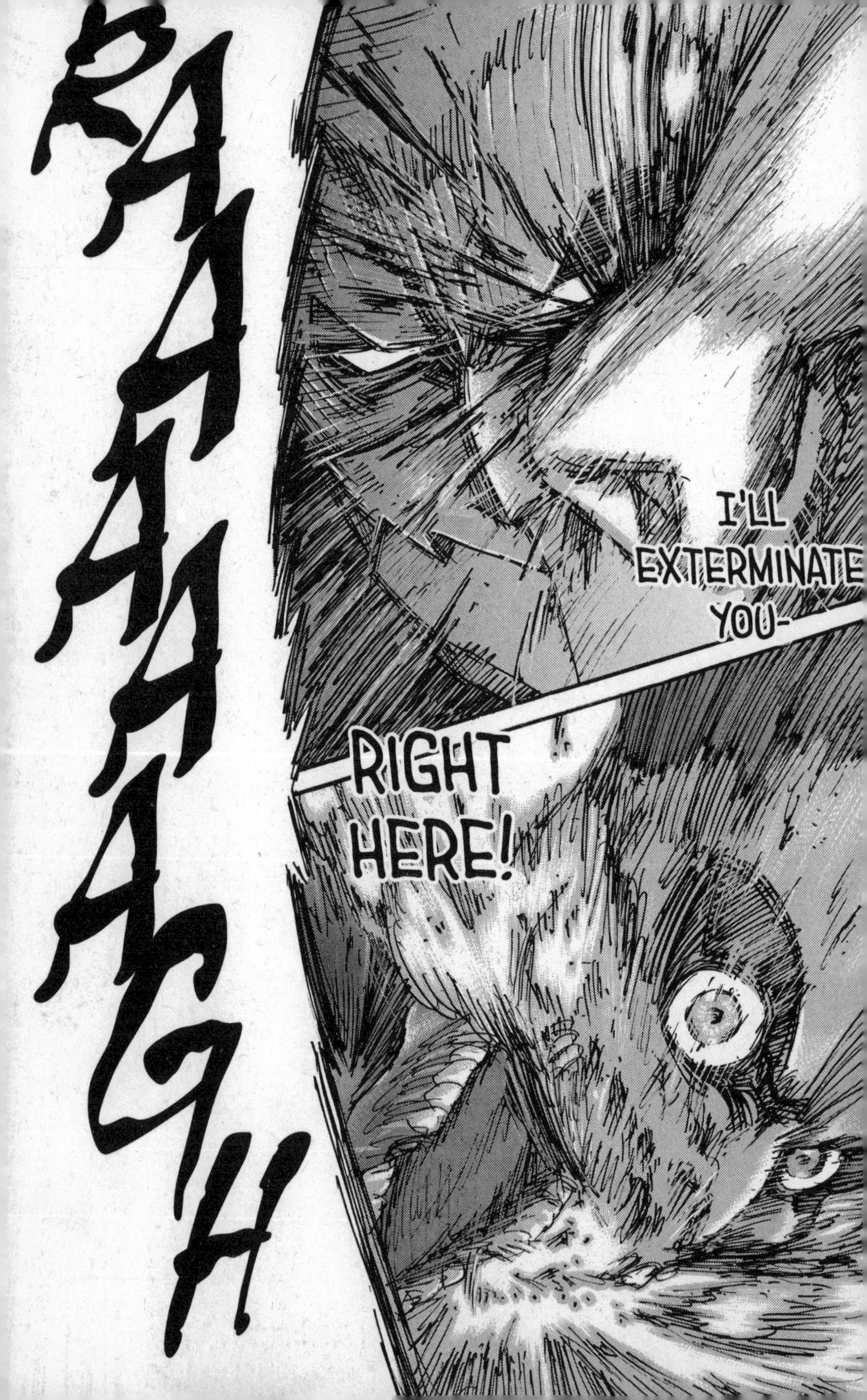
I'LL EXTERMINATE YOU-
RIGHT HERE!
RAAAAAGH!

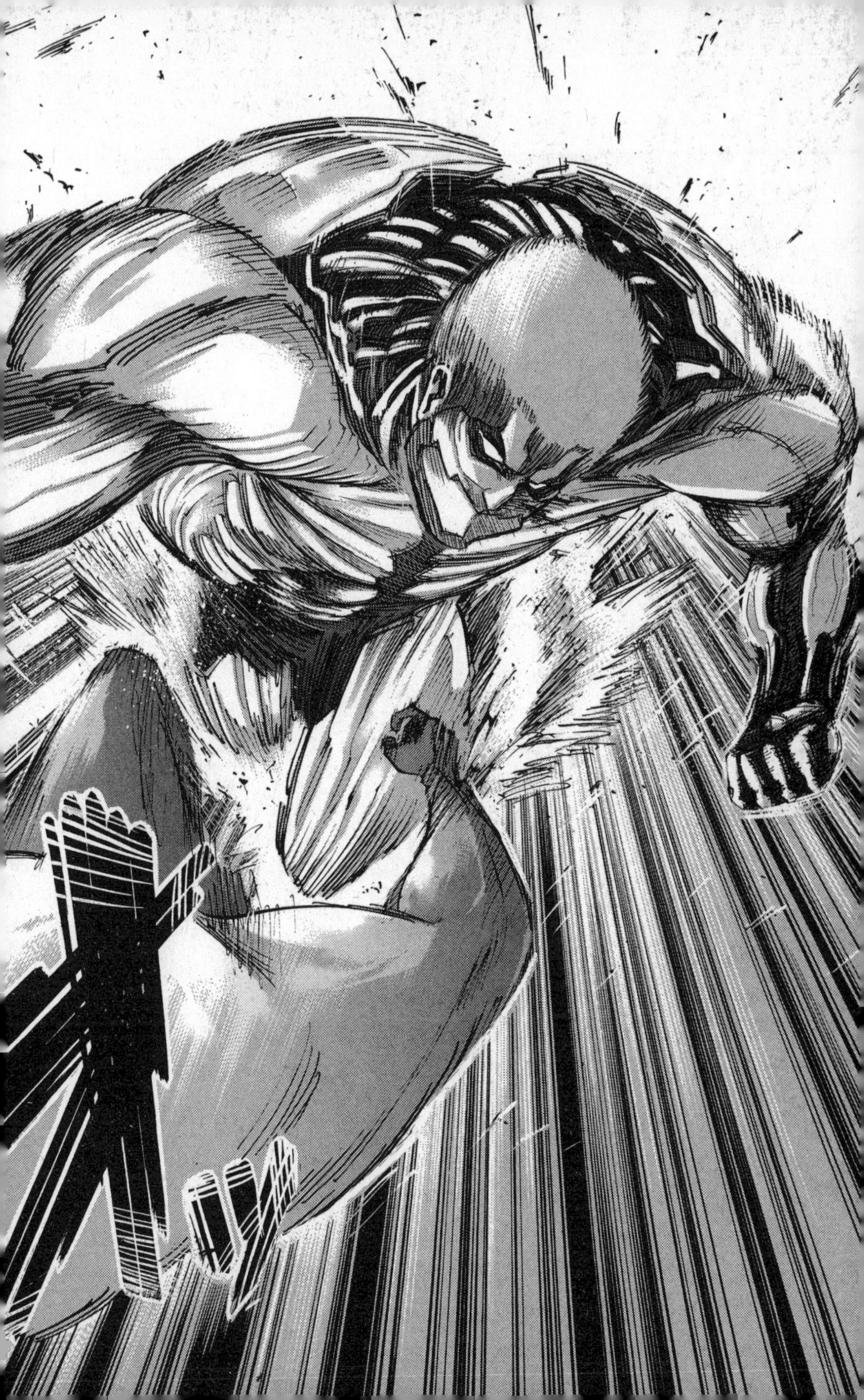

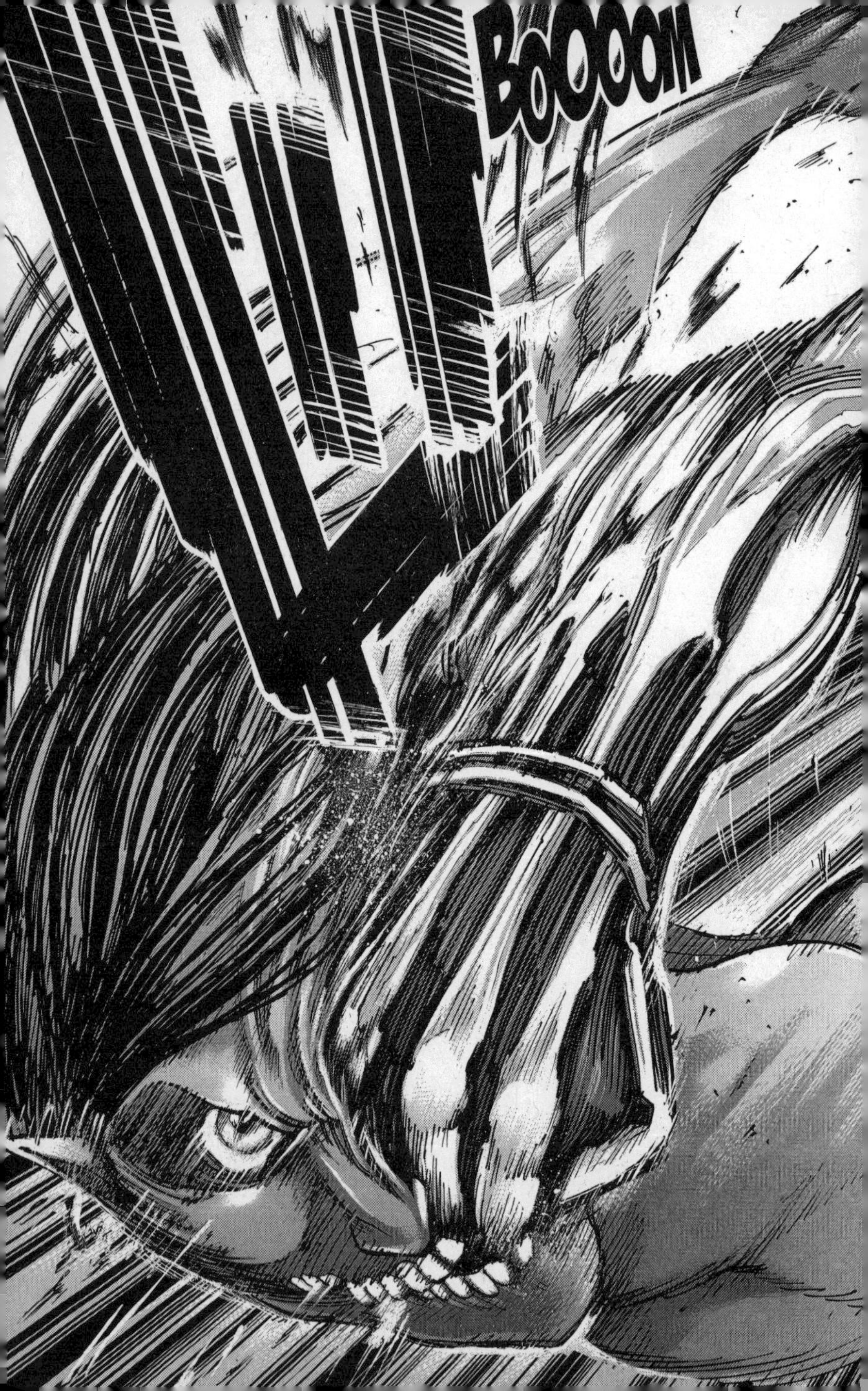
BOOOOM

ATTACK on TITAN

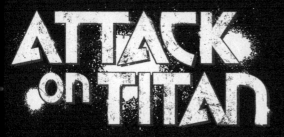

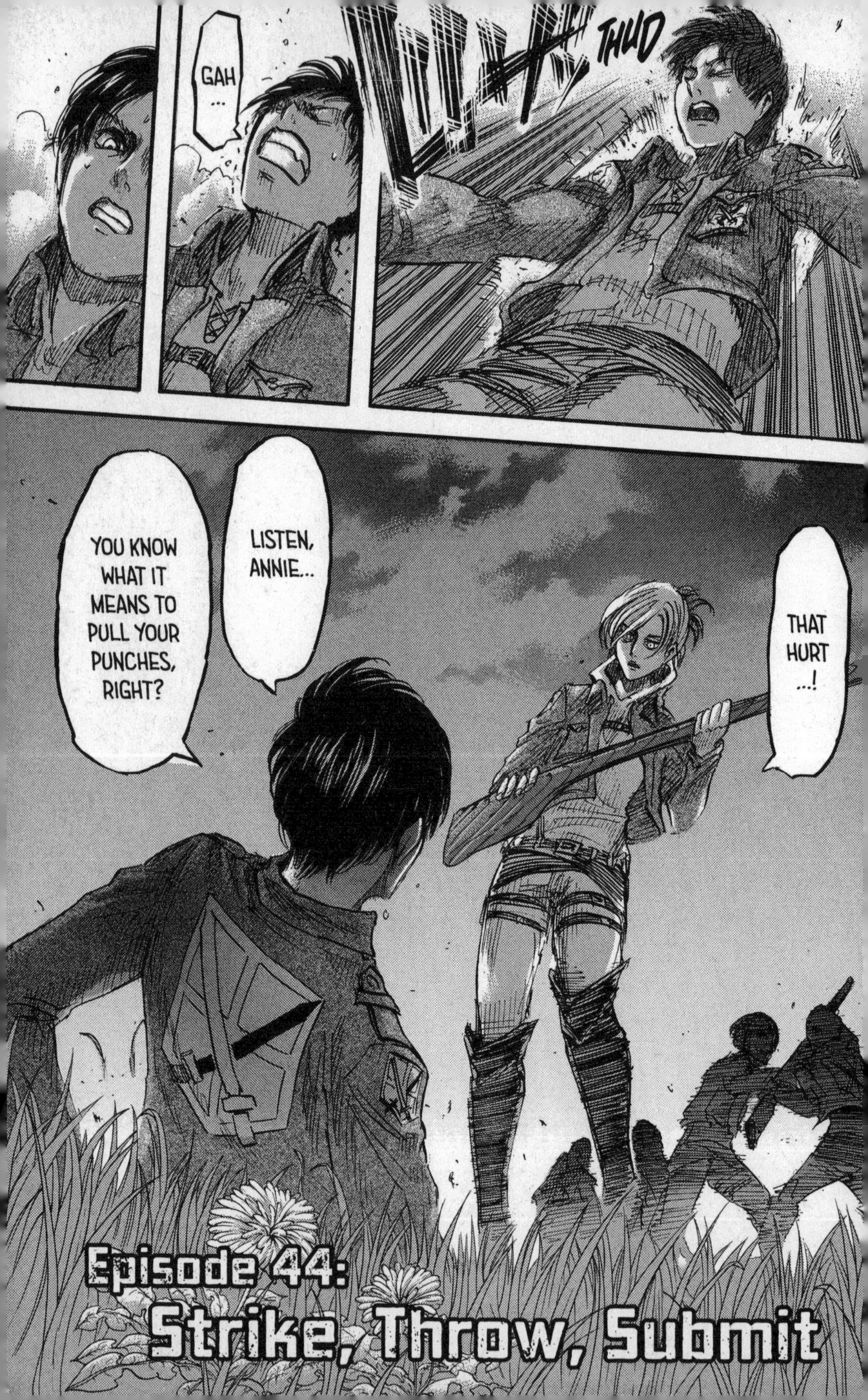
THUD
GAH ...
THAT HURT ...!
LISTEN, ANNIE...
YOU KNOW WHAT IT MEANS TO PULL YOUR PUNCHES, RIGHT?
Episode 44:
Strike, Throw, Submit

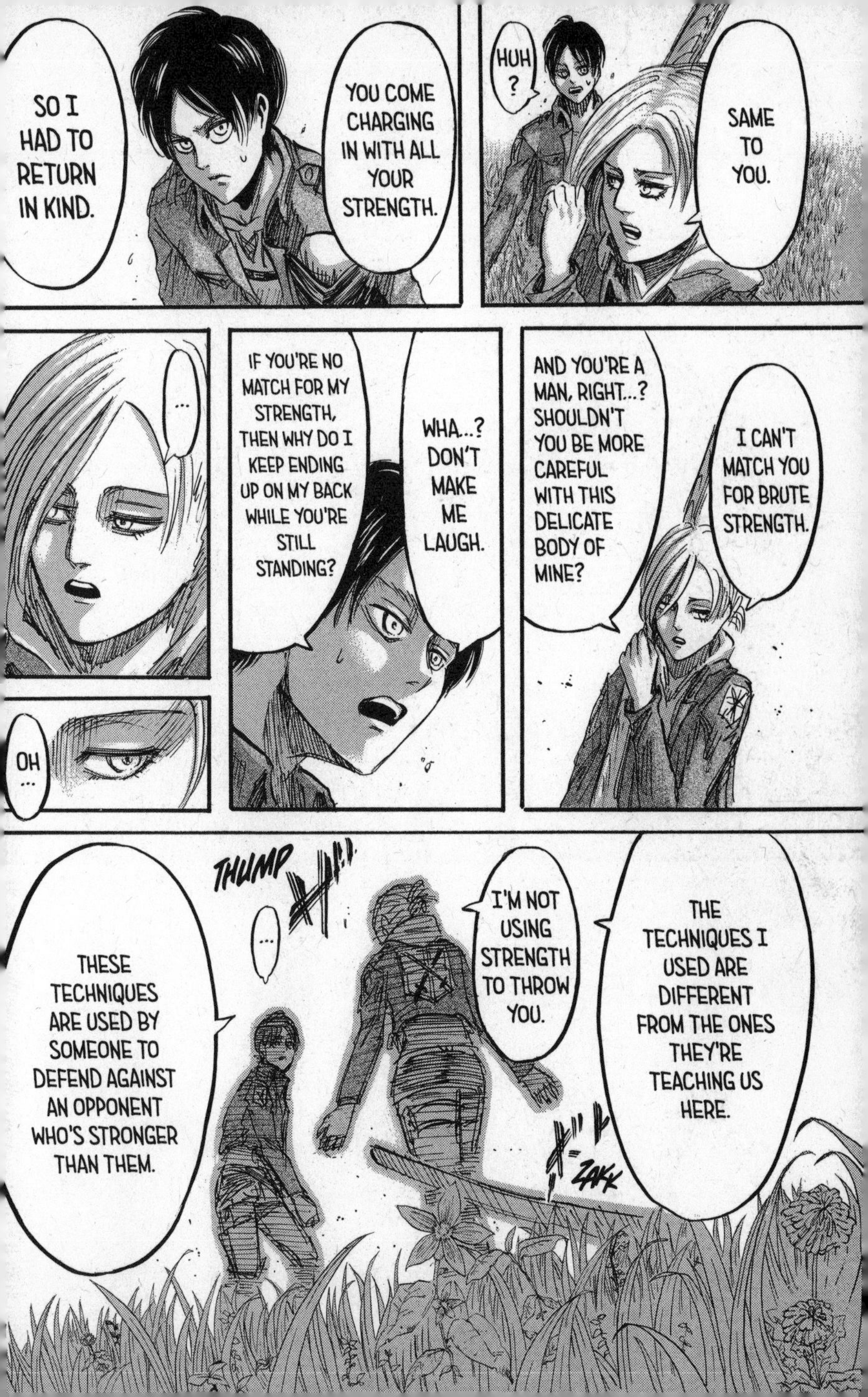
SAME TO YOU.
HUH?
YOU COME CHARGING IN WITH ALL YOUR STRENGTH.
SO I HAD TO RETURN IN KIND.
I CAN'T MATCH YOU FOR BRUTE STRENGTH.
AND YOU'RE A MAN, RIGHT...? SHOULDN'T YOU BE MORE CAREFUL WITH THIS DELICATE BODY OF MINE?
WHA...? DON'T MAKE ME LAUGH.
IF YOU'RE NO MATCH FOR MY STRENGTH, THEN WHY DO I KEEP ENDING UP ON MY BACK WHILE YOU'RE STILL STANDING?
...
OH ...
THE TECHNIQUES I USED ARE DIFFERENT FROM THE ONES THEY'RE TEACHING US HERE.
I'M NOT USING STRENGTH TO THROW YOU.
THUMP
...
THESE TECHNIQUES ARE USED BY SOMEONE TO DEFEND AGAINST AN OPPONENT WHO'S STRONGER THAN THEM.
ZAKK

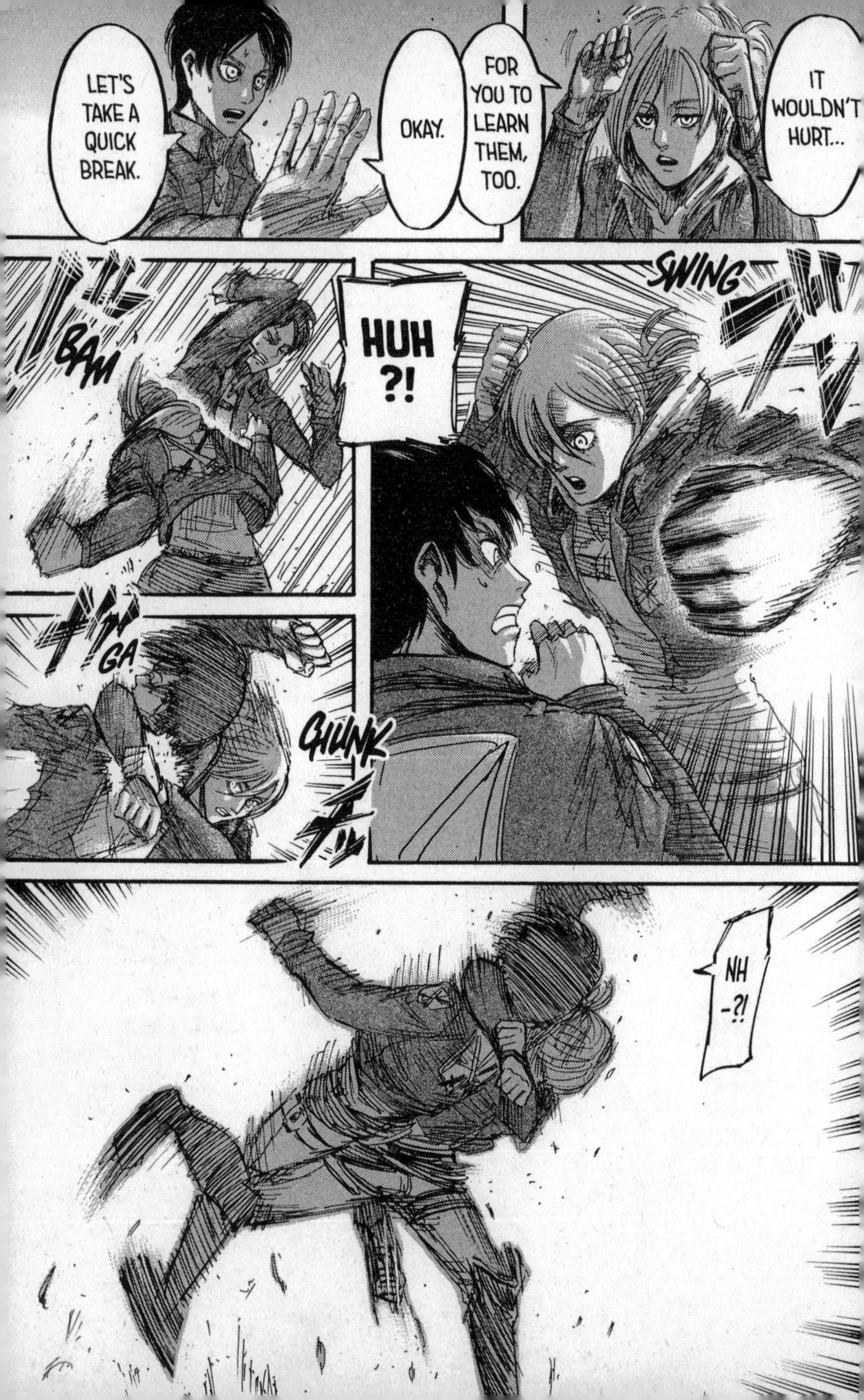
IT WOULDN'T HURT...
FOR YOU TO LEARN THEM, TOO.
OKAY.
LET'S TAKE A QUICK BREAK.
SWING
HUH ?!
BAM
GA
CHUNK
NH -?!

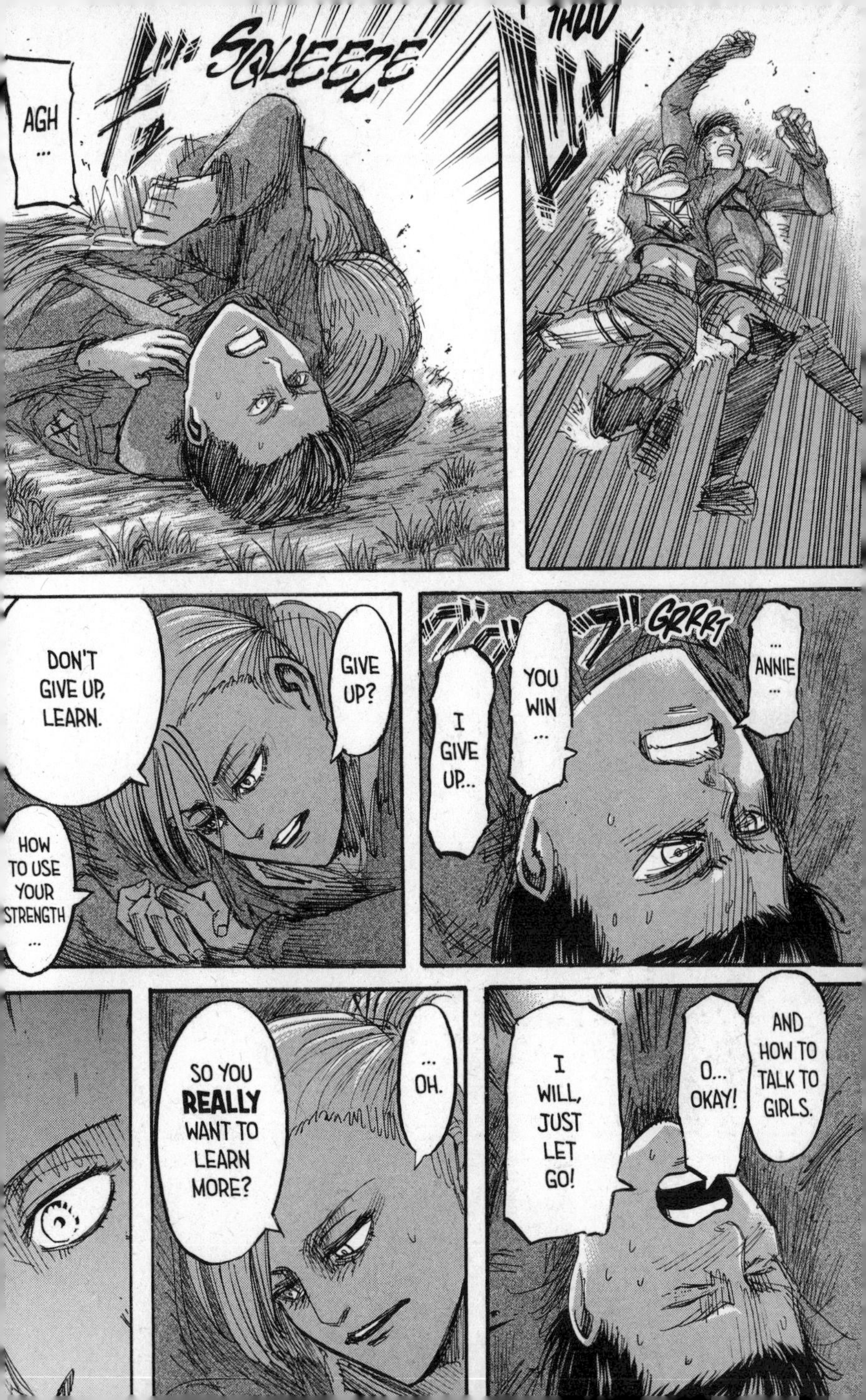
THUD
SQUEEZE
AGH ...
GRRR
... ANNIE ...
YOU WIN ...
I GIVE UP...
GIVE UP?
DON'T GIVE UP, LEARN.
HOW TO USE YOUR STRENGTH ...
AND HOW TO TALK TO GIRLS.
O... OKAY!
I WILL, JUST LET GO!
... OH.
SO YOU **REALLY** WANT TO LEARN MORE?

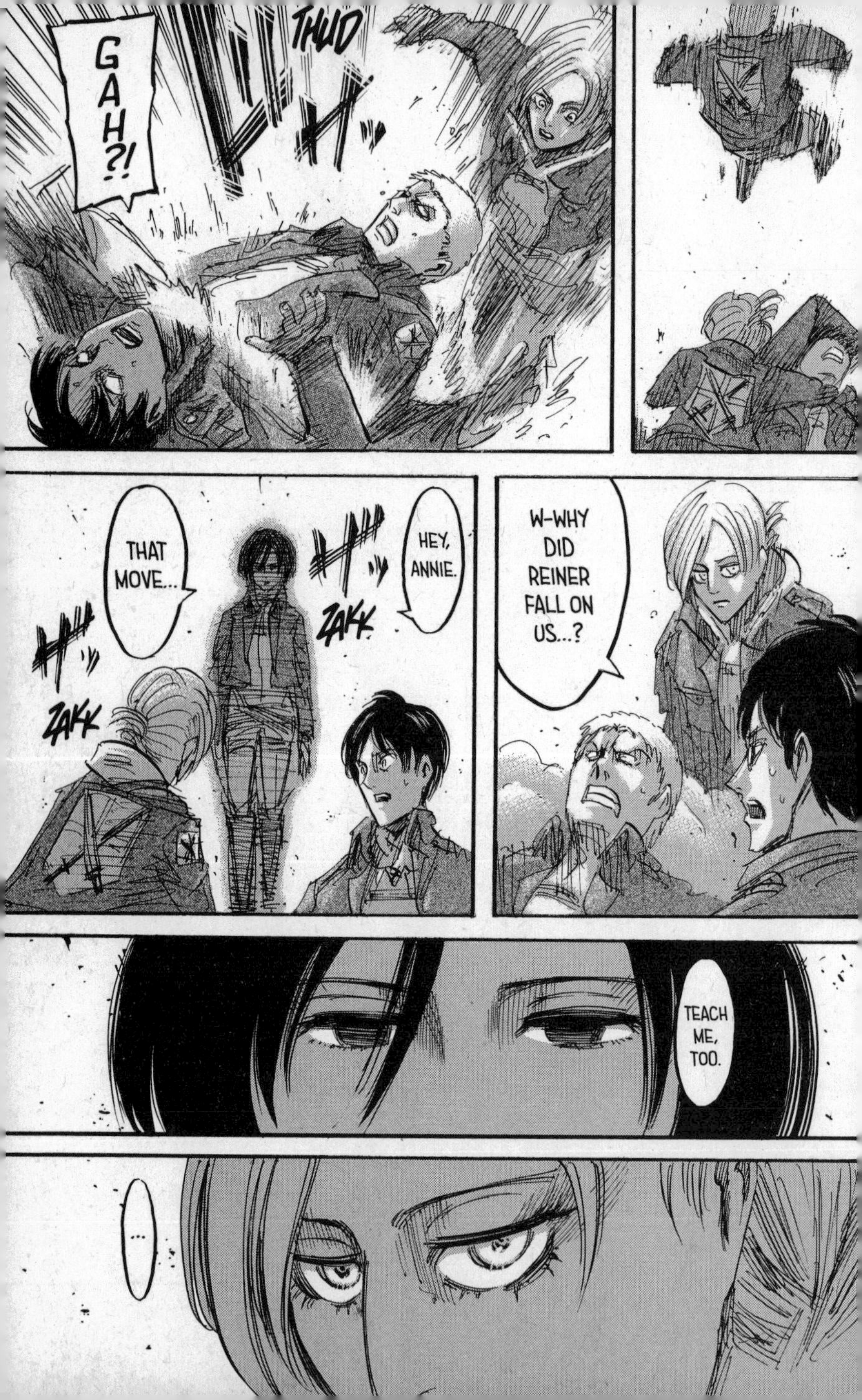
THUD
GAH?!
W-WHY DID REINER FALL ON US...?
HEY, ANNIE.
ZAKK
THAT MOVE...
ZAKK
TEACH ME, TOO.
...

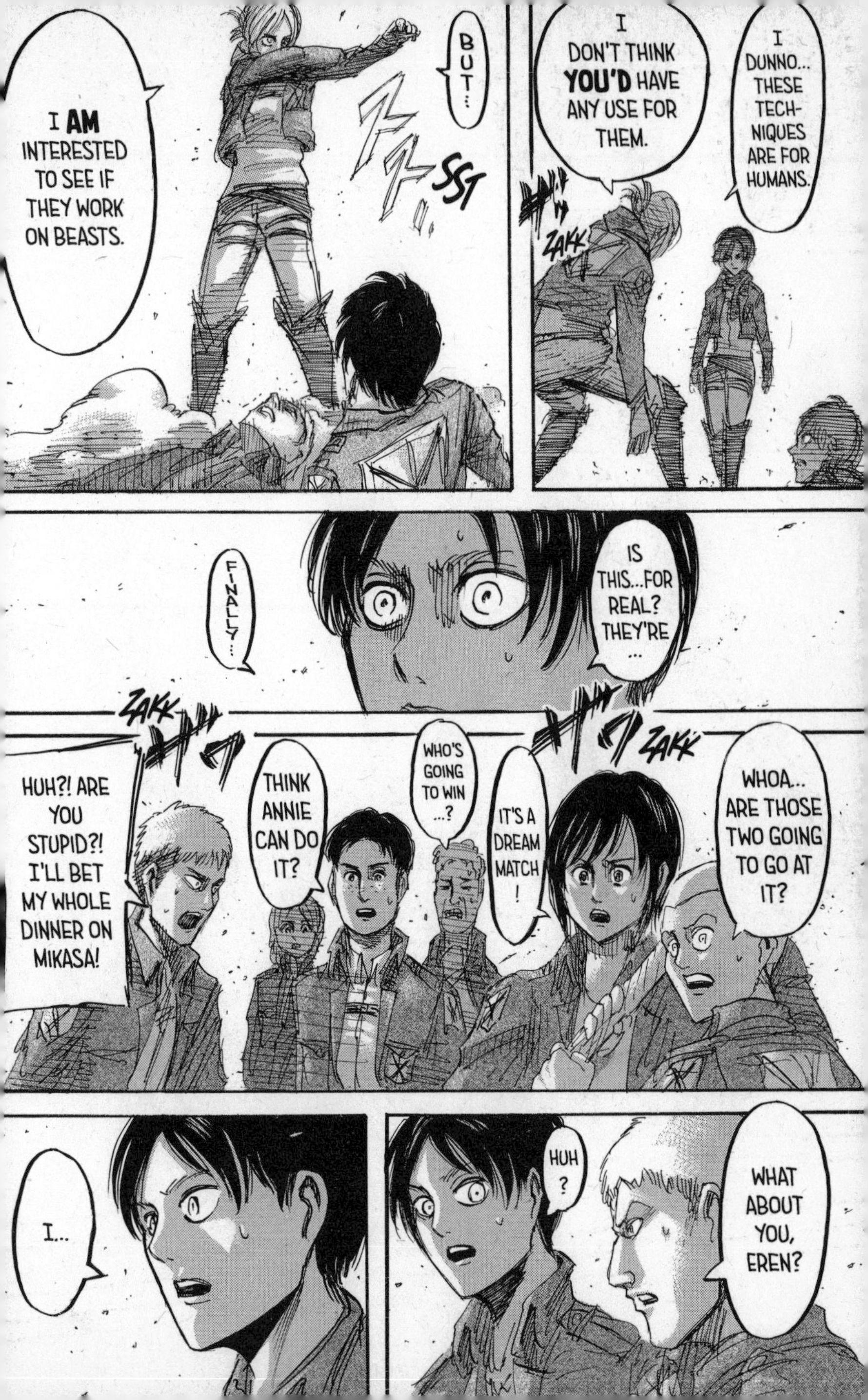
I DUNNO... THESE TECH-NIQUES ARE FOR HUMANS.
I DON'T THINK **YOU'D** HAVE ANY USE FOR THEM.
ZAKK
BUT...
SSST
I **AM** INTERESTED TO SEE IF THEY WORK ON BEASTS.
IS THIS...FOR REAL? THEY'RE ...
FINALLY...
ZAKK
WHOA... ARE THOSE TWO GOING TO GO AT IT?
IT'S A DREAM MATCH!
WHO'S GOING TO WIN ...?
THINK ANNIE CAN DO IT?
HUH?! ARE YOU STUPID?! I'LL BET MY WHOLE DINNER ON MIKASA!
ZAKK
WHAT ABOUT YOU, EREN?
HUH?
I...

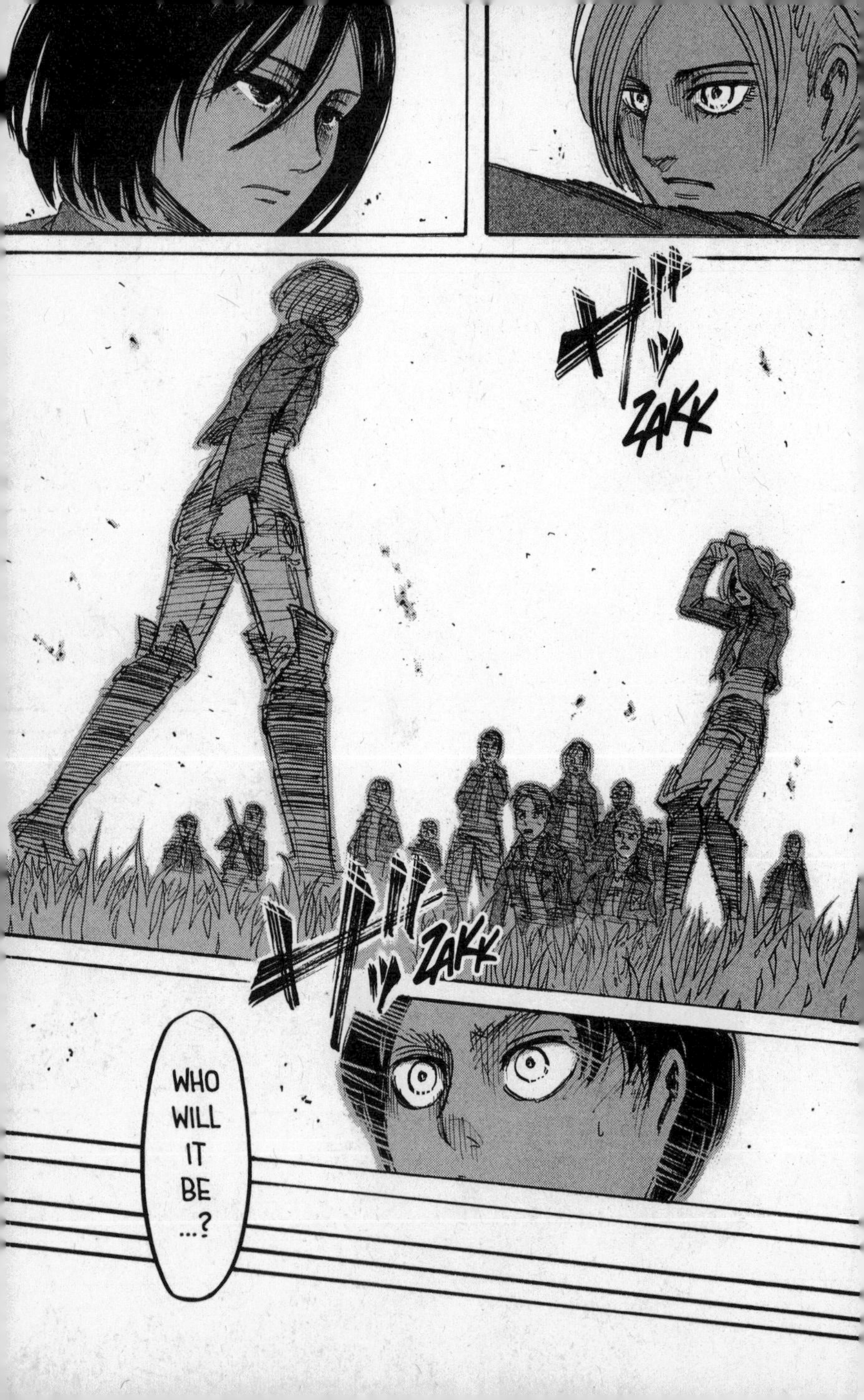
ザッ
ZAKK
ザッ
ZAKK
WHO WILL IT BE ...?

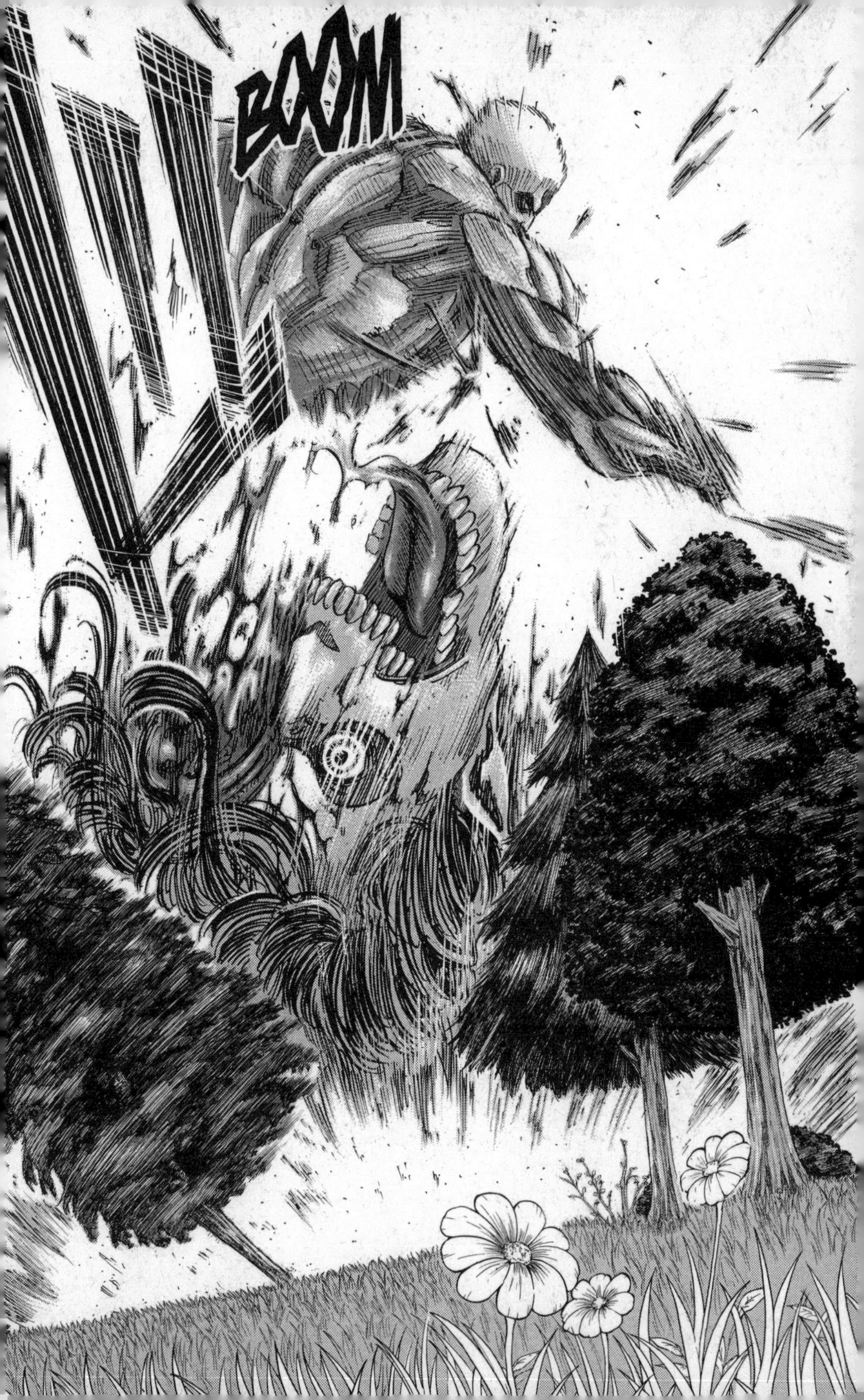
BOOM

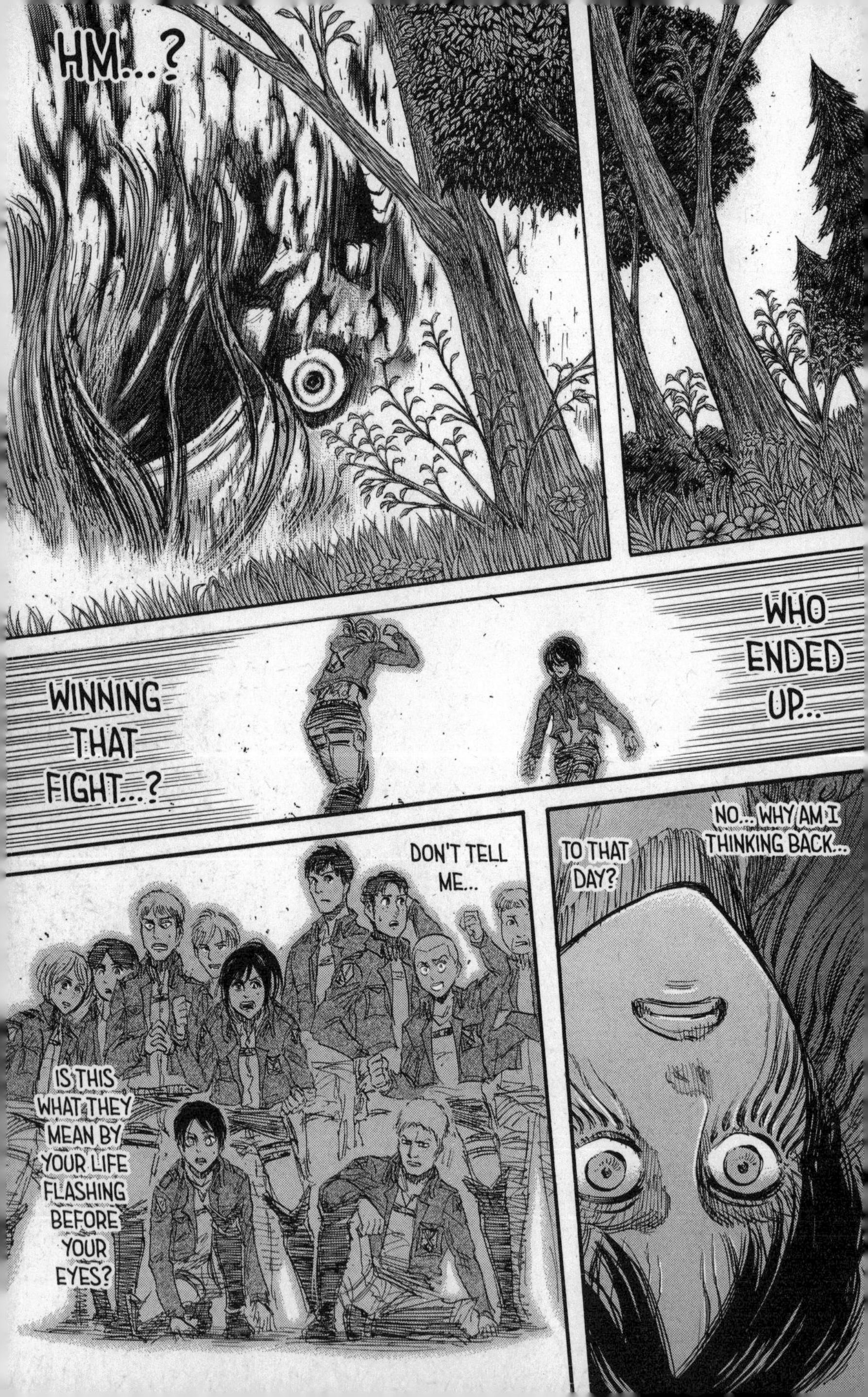
HM...?
WHO ENDED UP...
WINNING THAT FIGHT...?
NO... WHY AM I THINKING BACK...
TO THAT DAY?
DON'T TELL ME...
IS THIS WHAT THEY MEAN BY YOUR LIFE FLASHING BEFORE YOUR EYES?

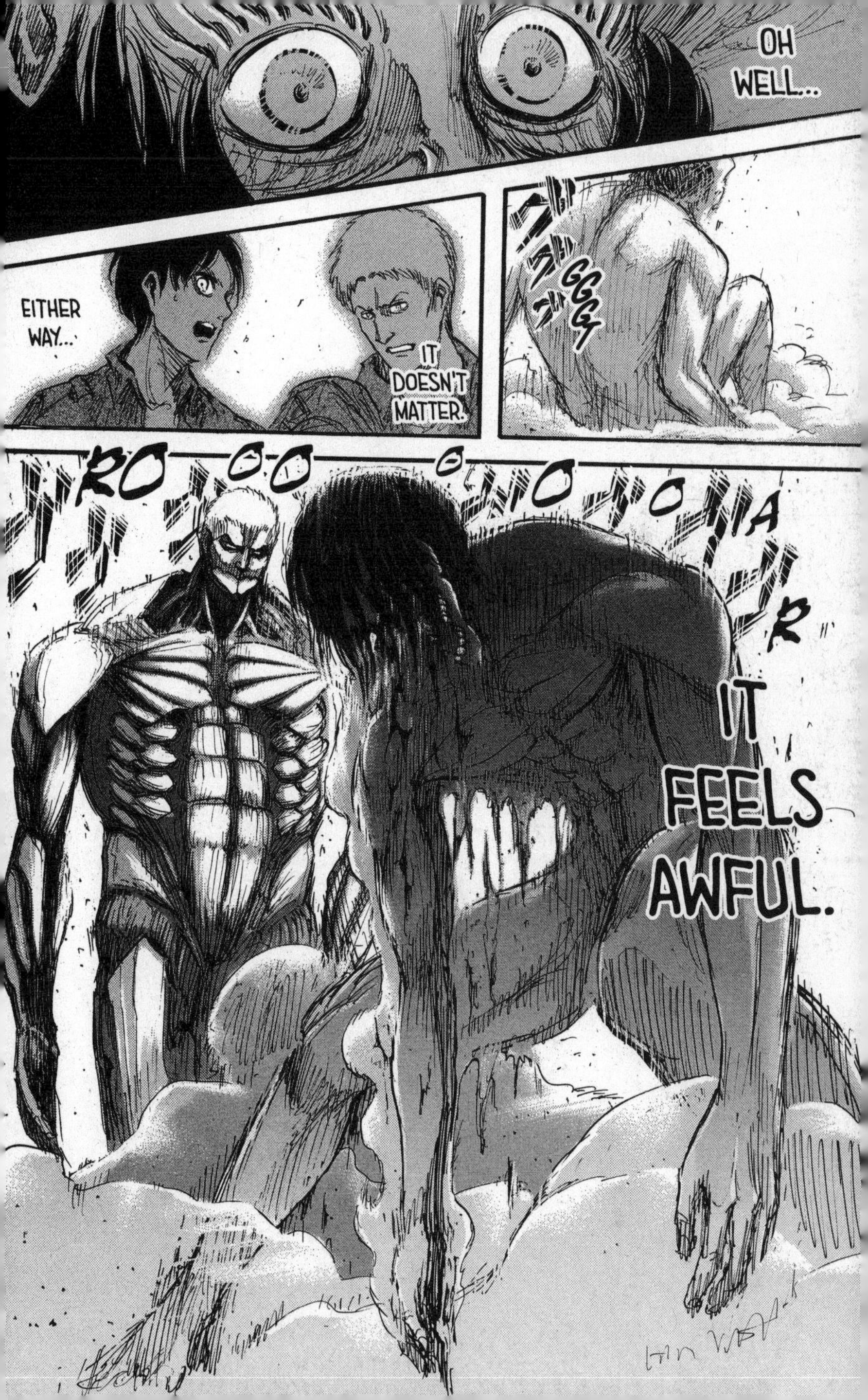
OH WELL...
GGG
EITHER WAY...
IT DOESN'T MATTER.
ROOOOHOOAR
IT FEELS AWFUL.

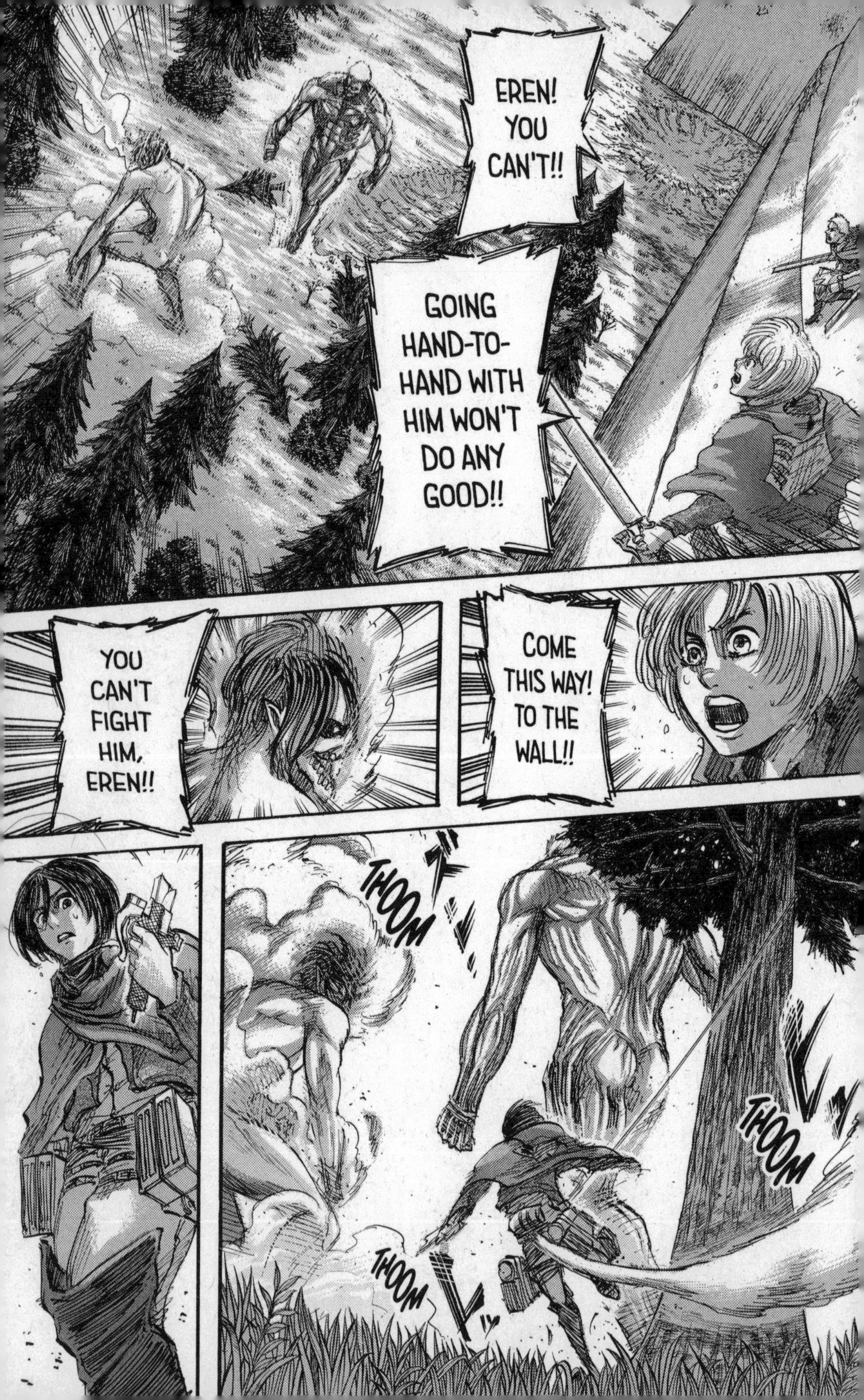
EREN! YOU CAN'T!!
GOING HAND-TO-HAND WITH HIM WON'T DO ANY GOOD!!
COME THIS WAY! TO THE WALL!!
YOU CAN'T FIGHT HIM, EREN!!
THOOM
THOOM
THOOM

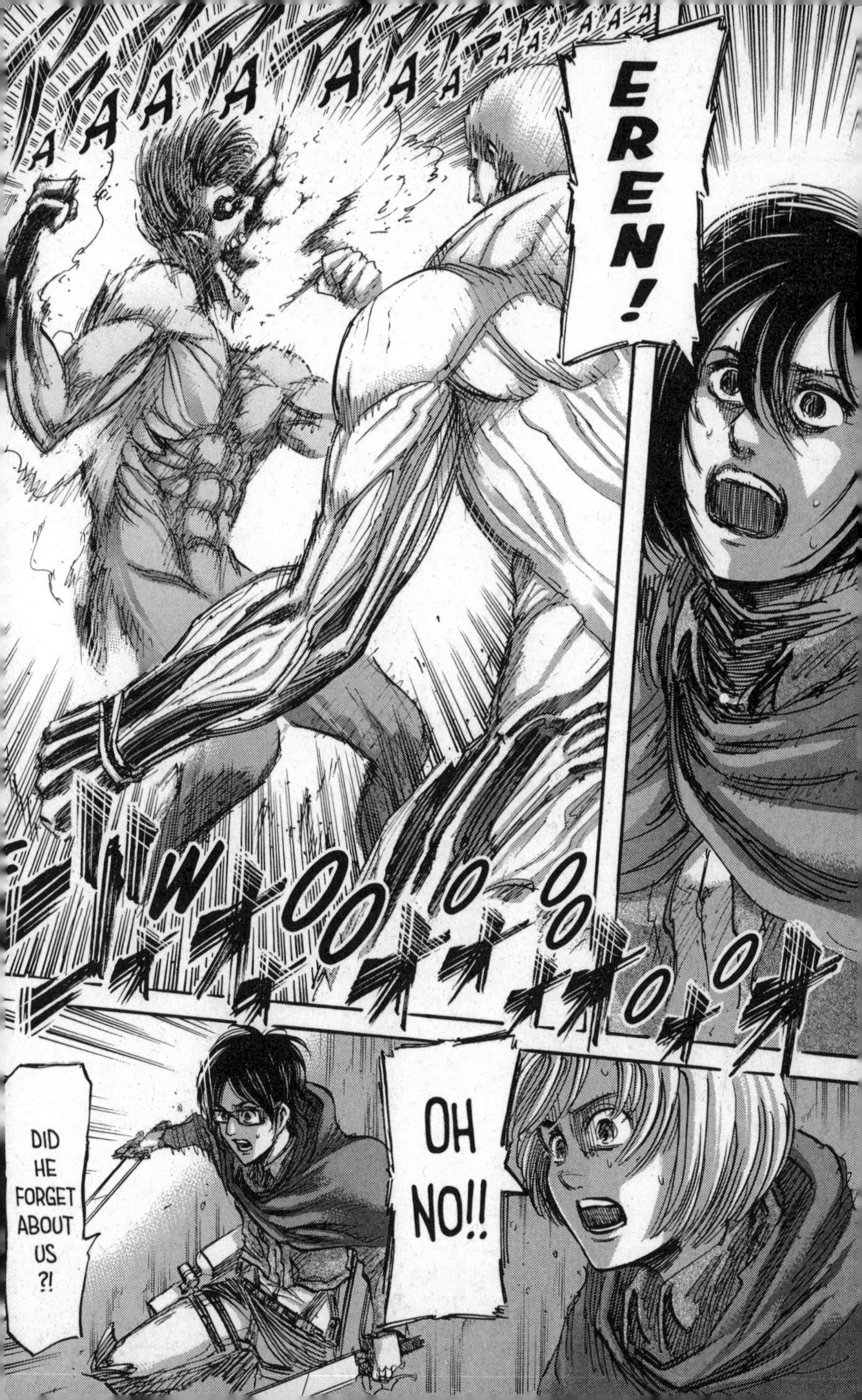

EREN!
AAAAAAAAAAAA
WOOOOOO
OH NO!!
DID HE FORGET ABOUT US ?!

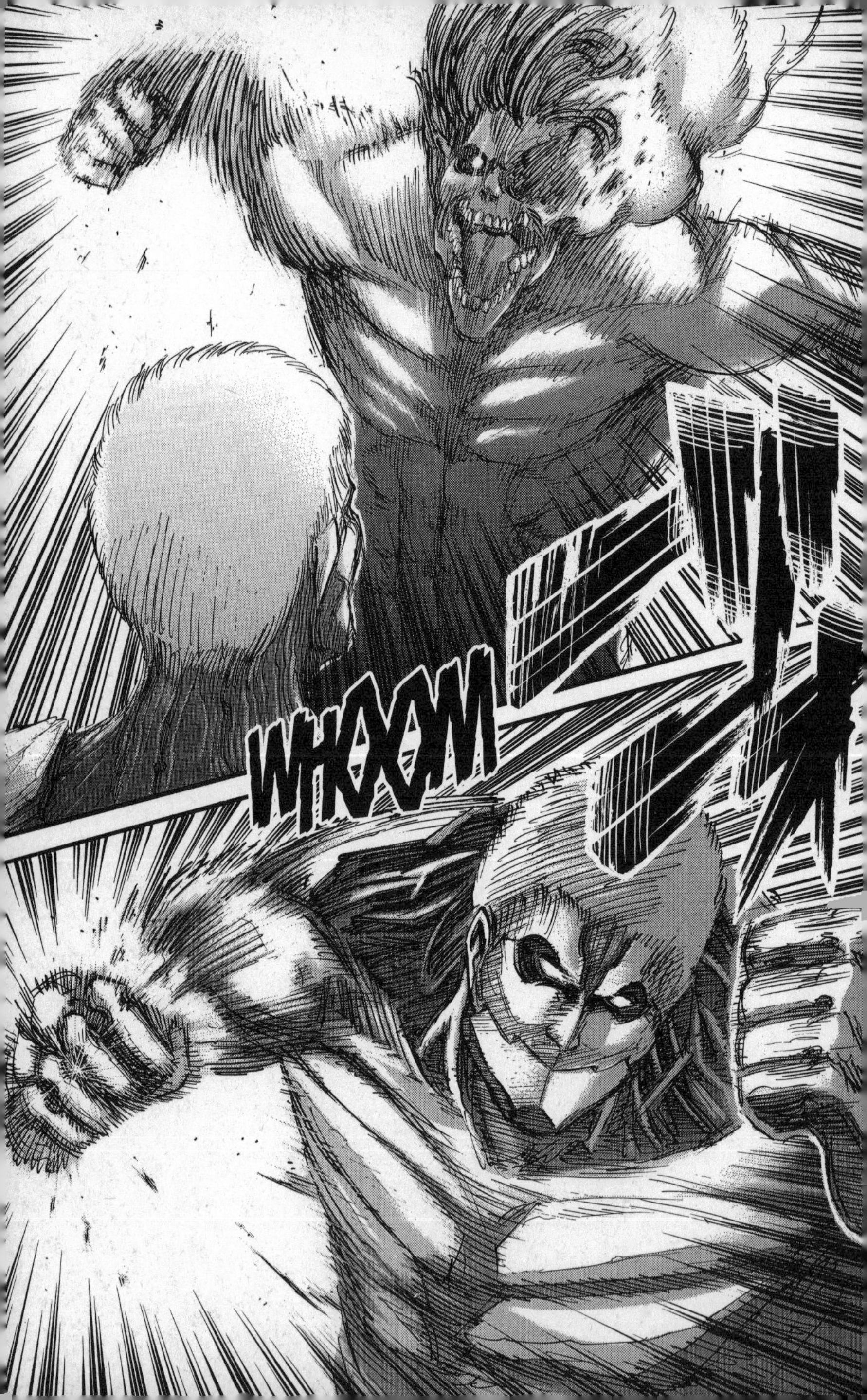
WHOOM

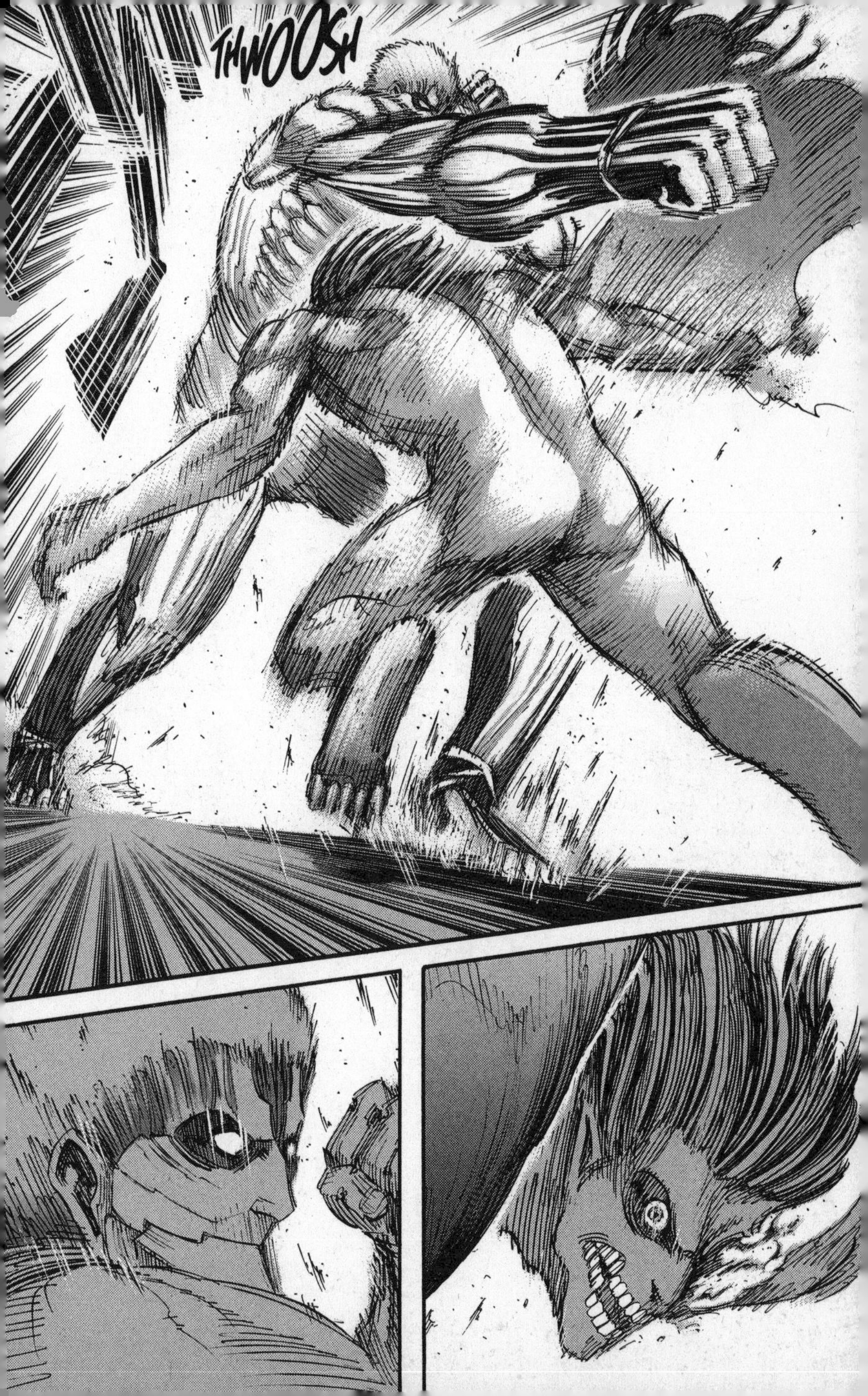
THWOOSH

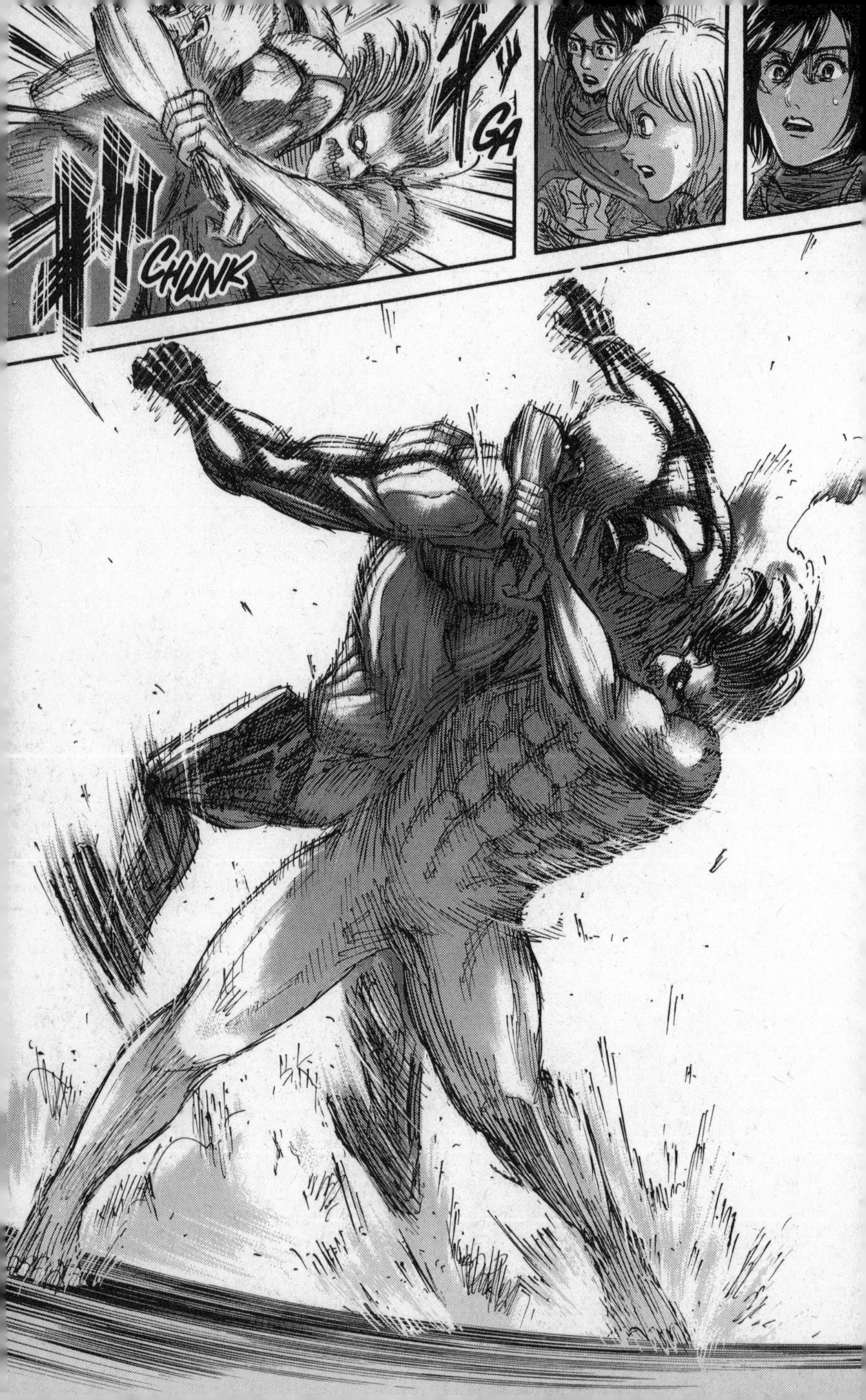
GA
CHUNK

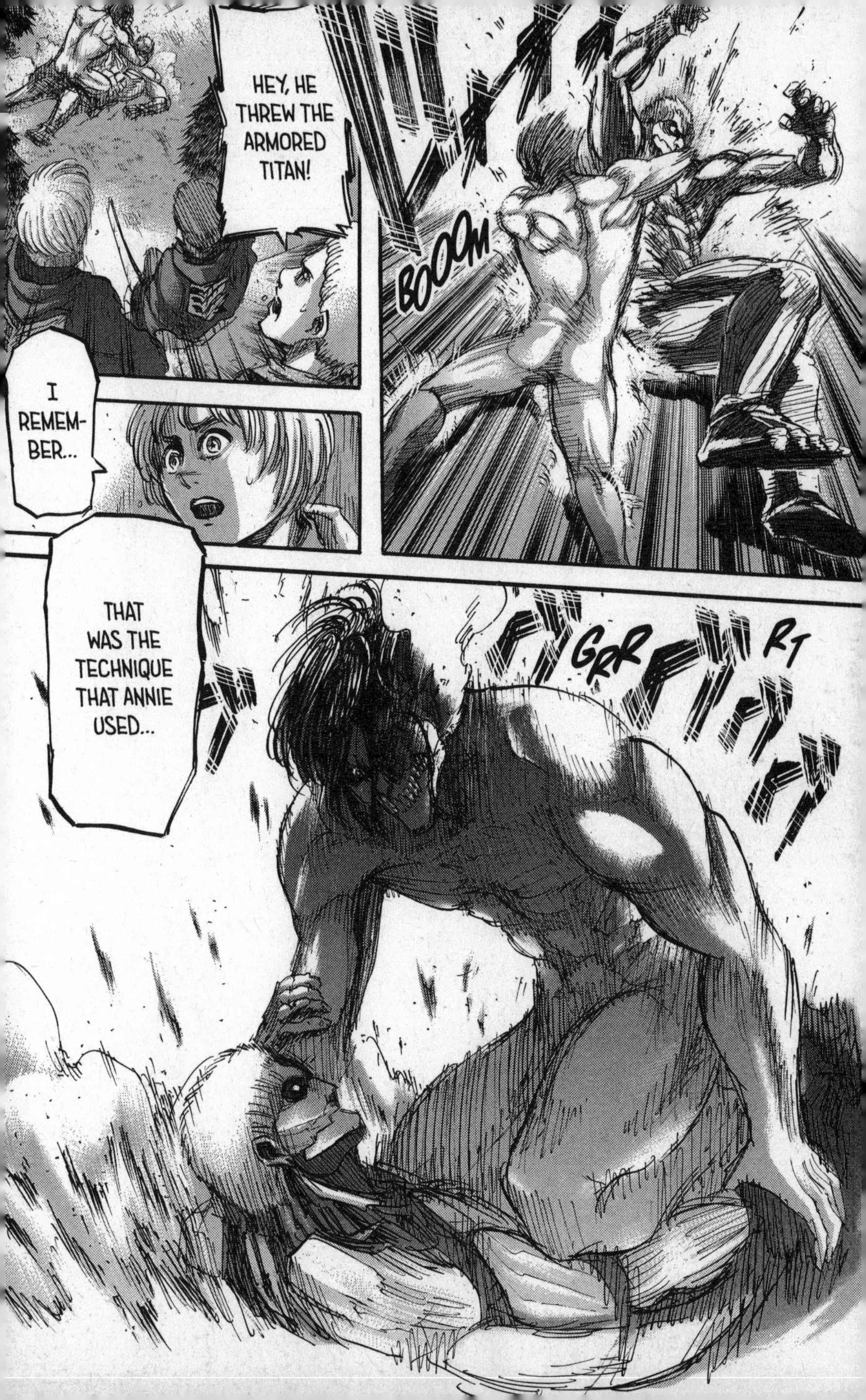
BOOOM
HEY, HE THREW THE ARMORED TITAN!
I REMEMBER...
THAT WAS THE TECHNIQUE THAT ANNIE USED...
GRR
RT

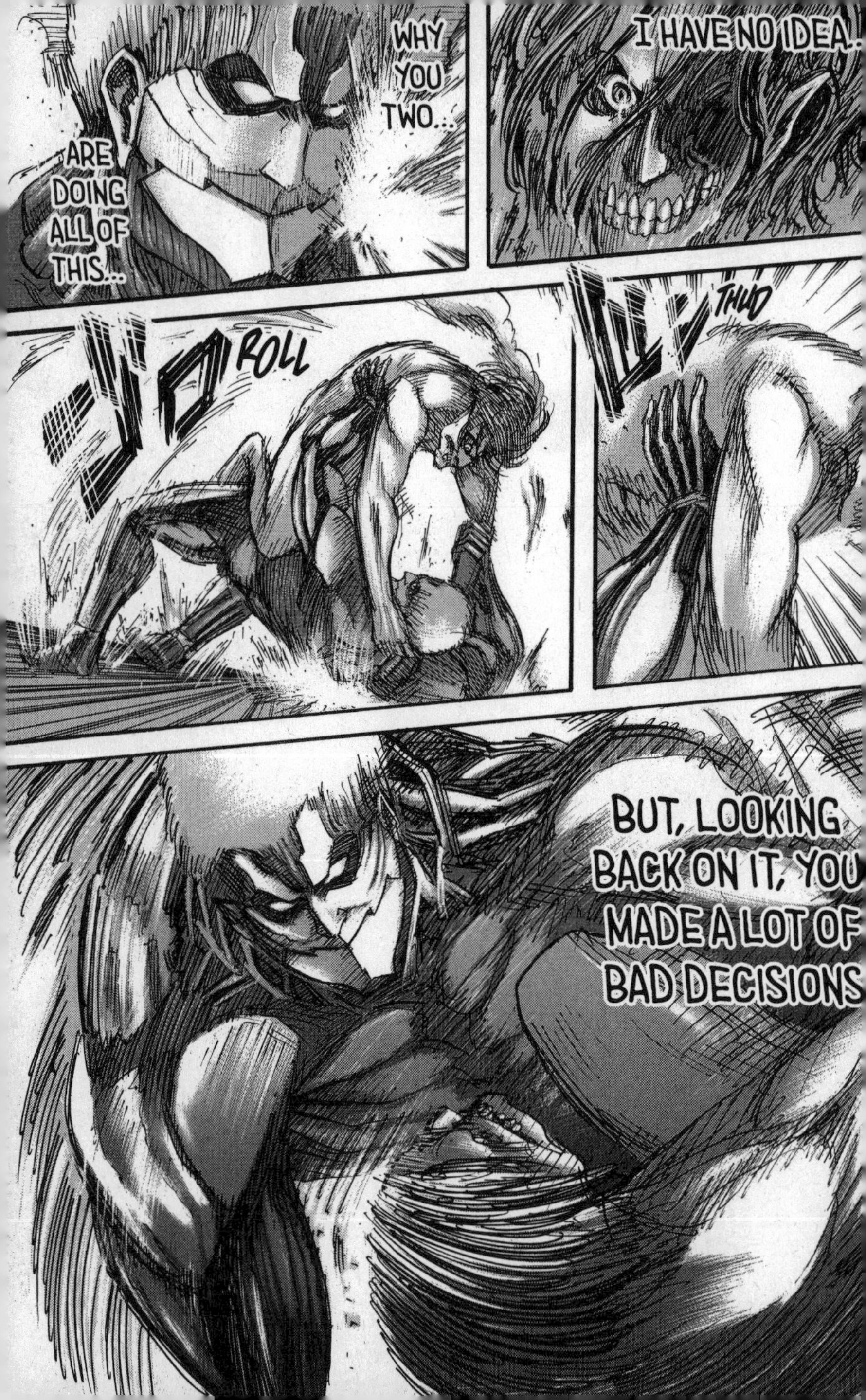

I HAVE NO IDEA...
WHY YOU TWO...
ARE DOING ALL OF THIS...
THUD
ROLL
BUT, LOOKING BACK ON IT, YOU MADE A LOT OF BAD DECISIONS

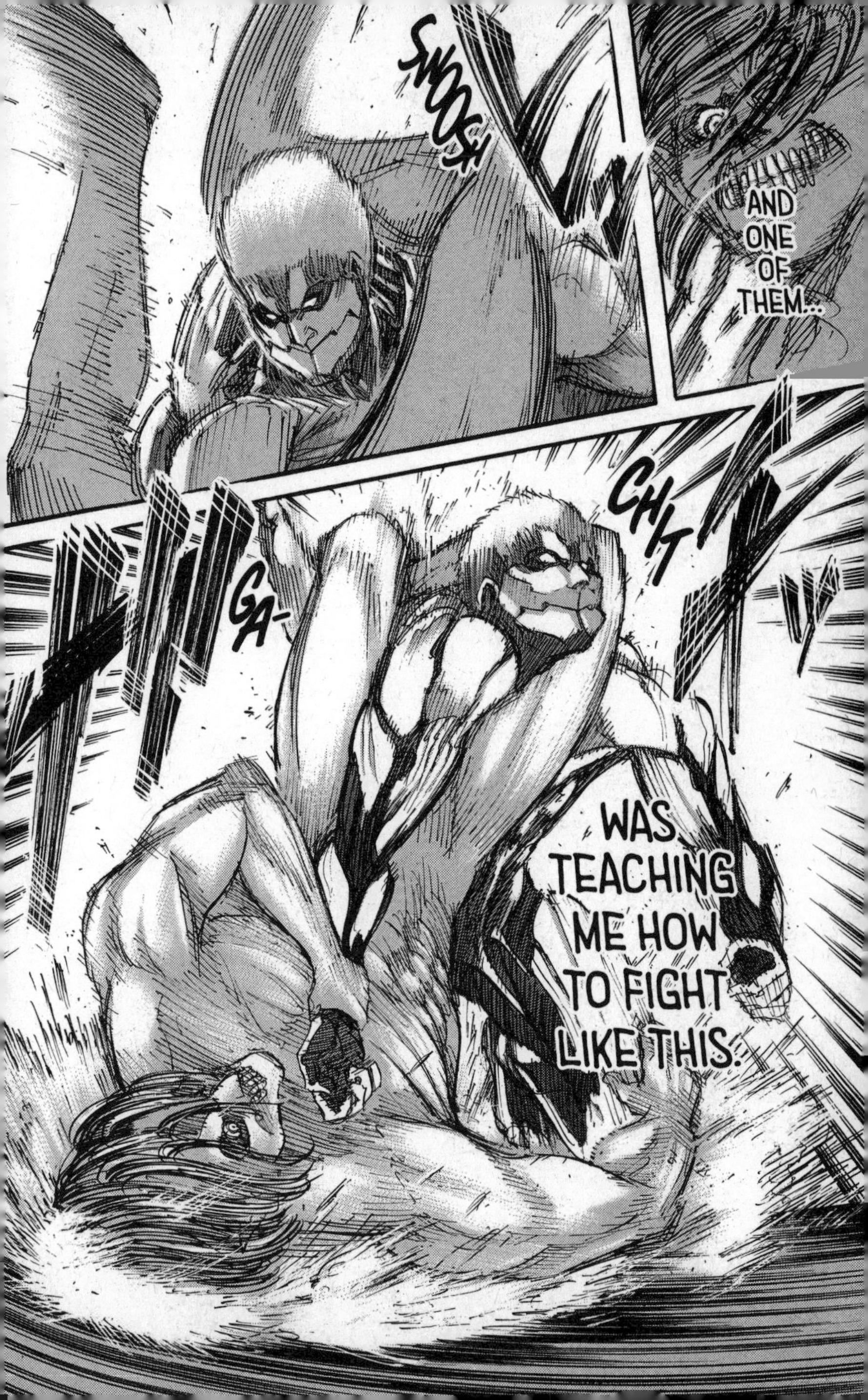
AND ONE OF THEM...
SWOOSH
CHK
GA-
WAS TEACHING ME HOW TO FIGHT LIKE THIS.

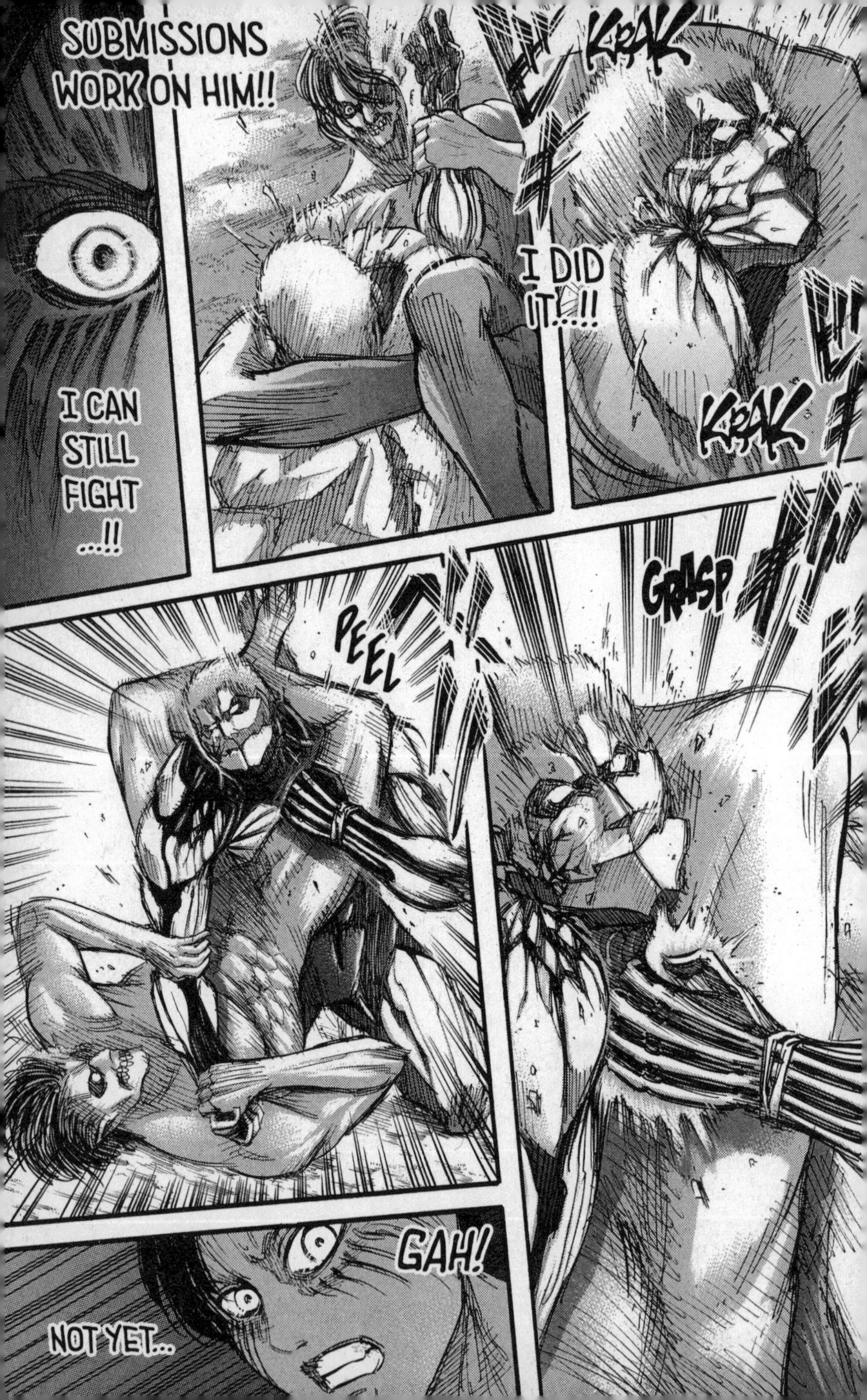

KRAK
I DID IT...!!
KRAK
SUBMISSIONS WORK ON HIM!!
I CAN STILL FIGHT ...!!
GRASP
PEEL
GAH!
NOT YET...

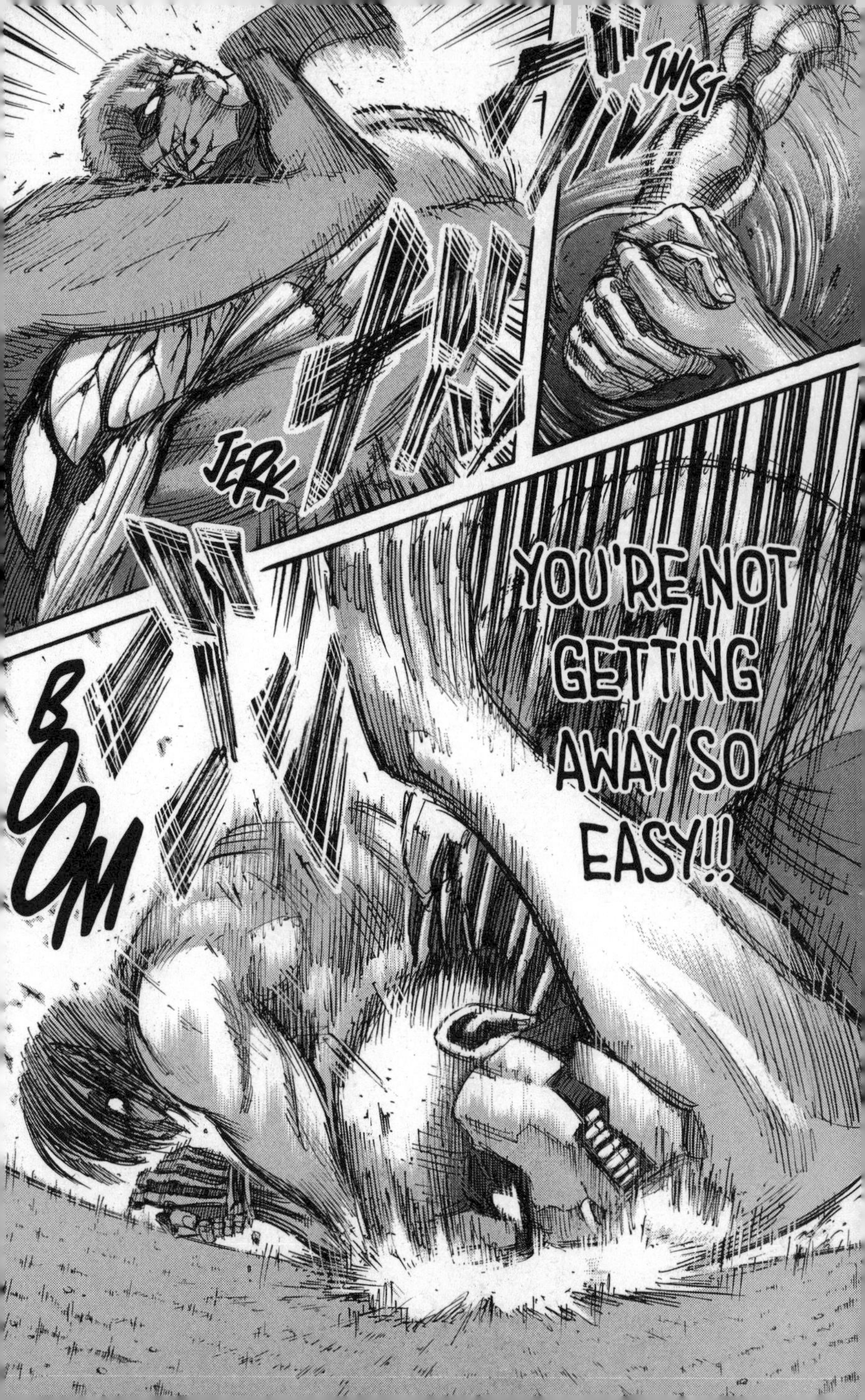
TWIST
JERK
YOU'RE NOT GETTING AWAY SO EASY!!
BOOM

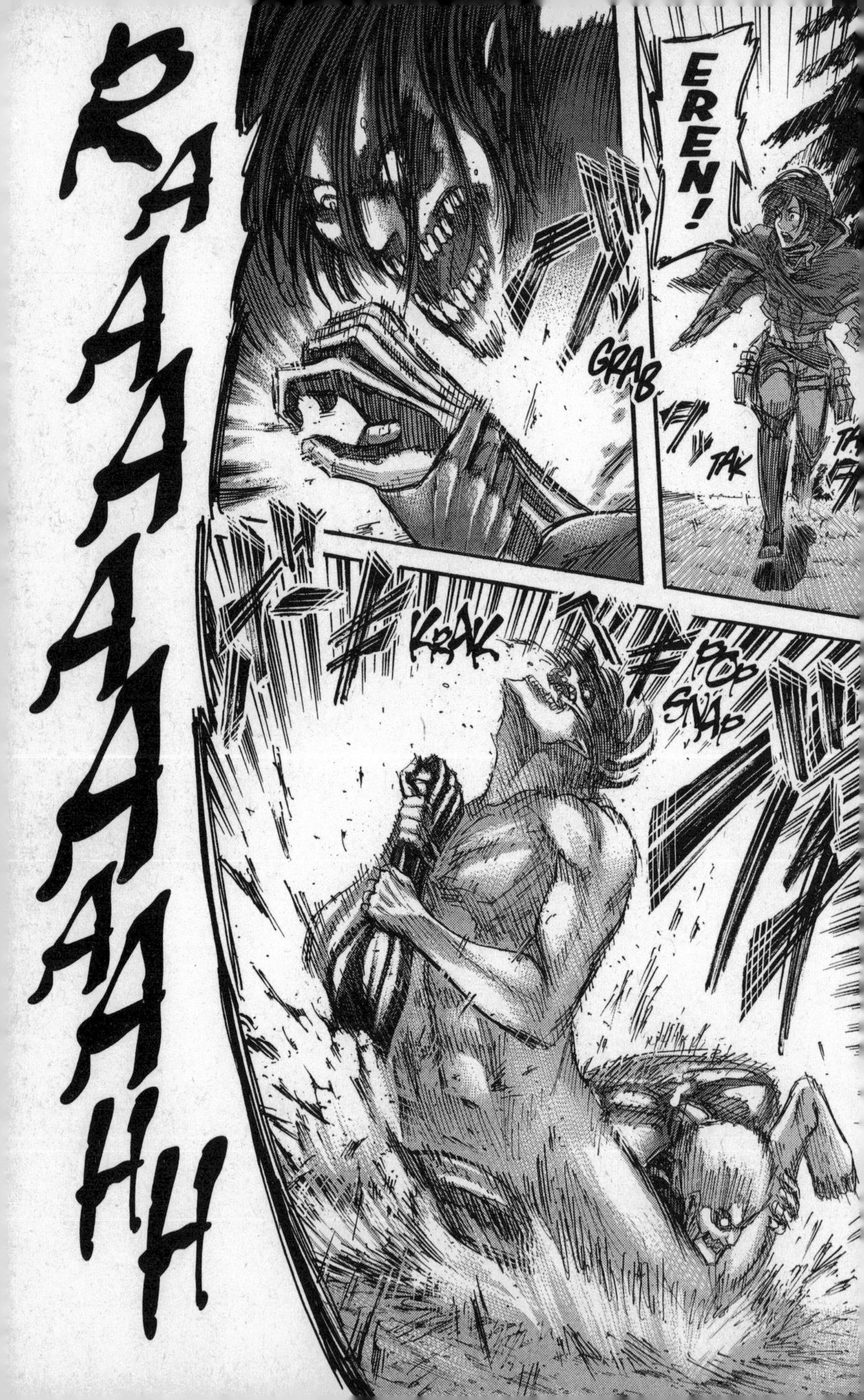
EREN!
TAK
TAK
GRAB
KRAK
POP
SNAP
RAAAAAAAAHH

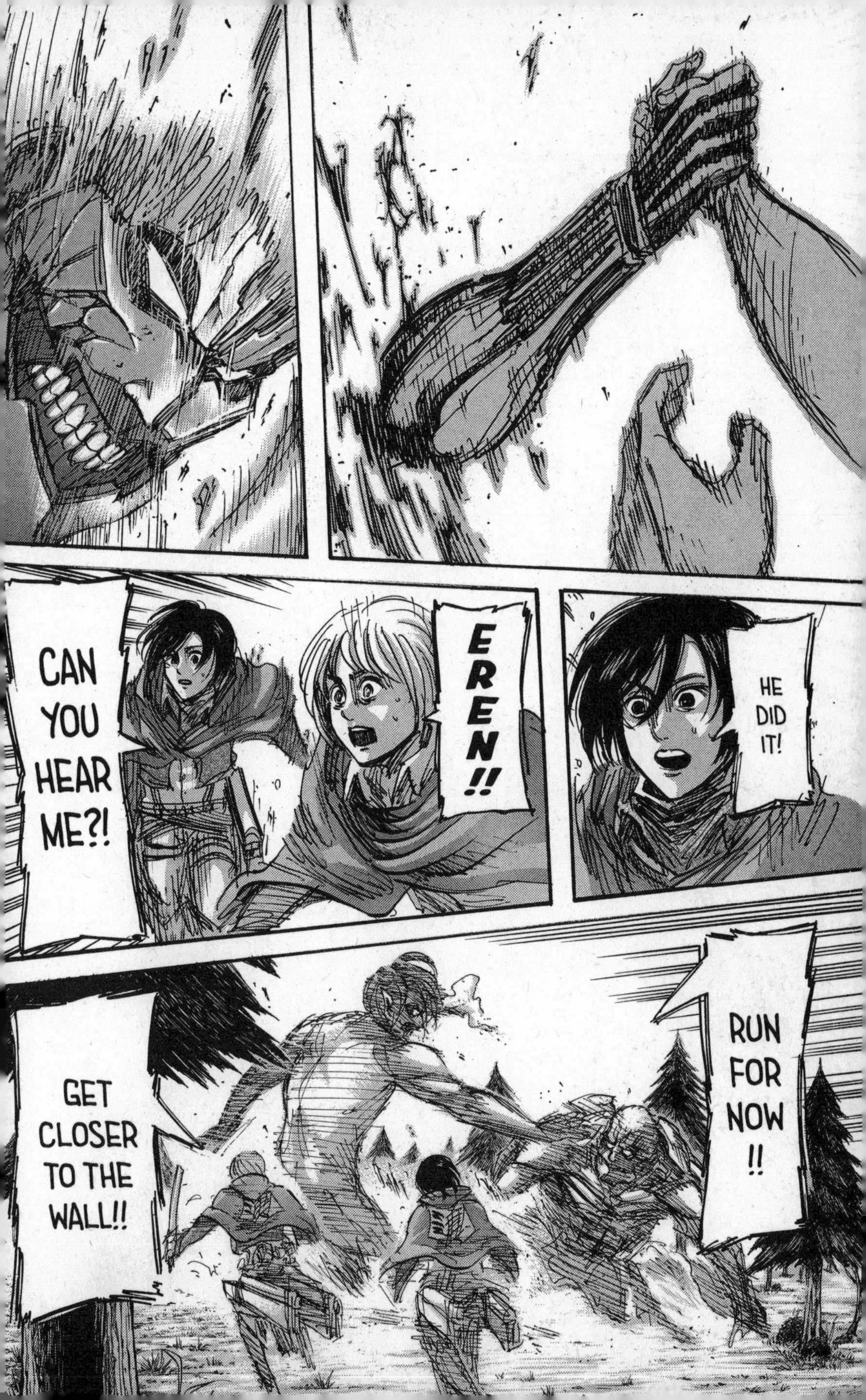
HE DID IT!
EREN!!
CAN YOU HEAR ME?!
RUN FOR NOW!!
GET CLOSER TO THE WALL!!

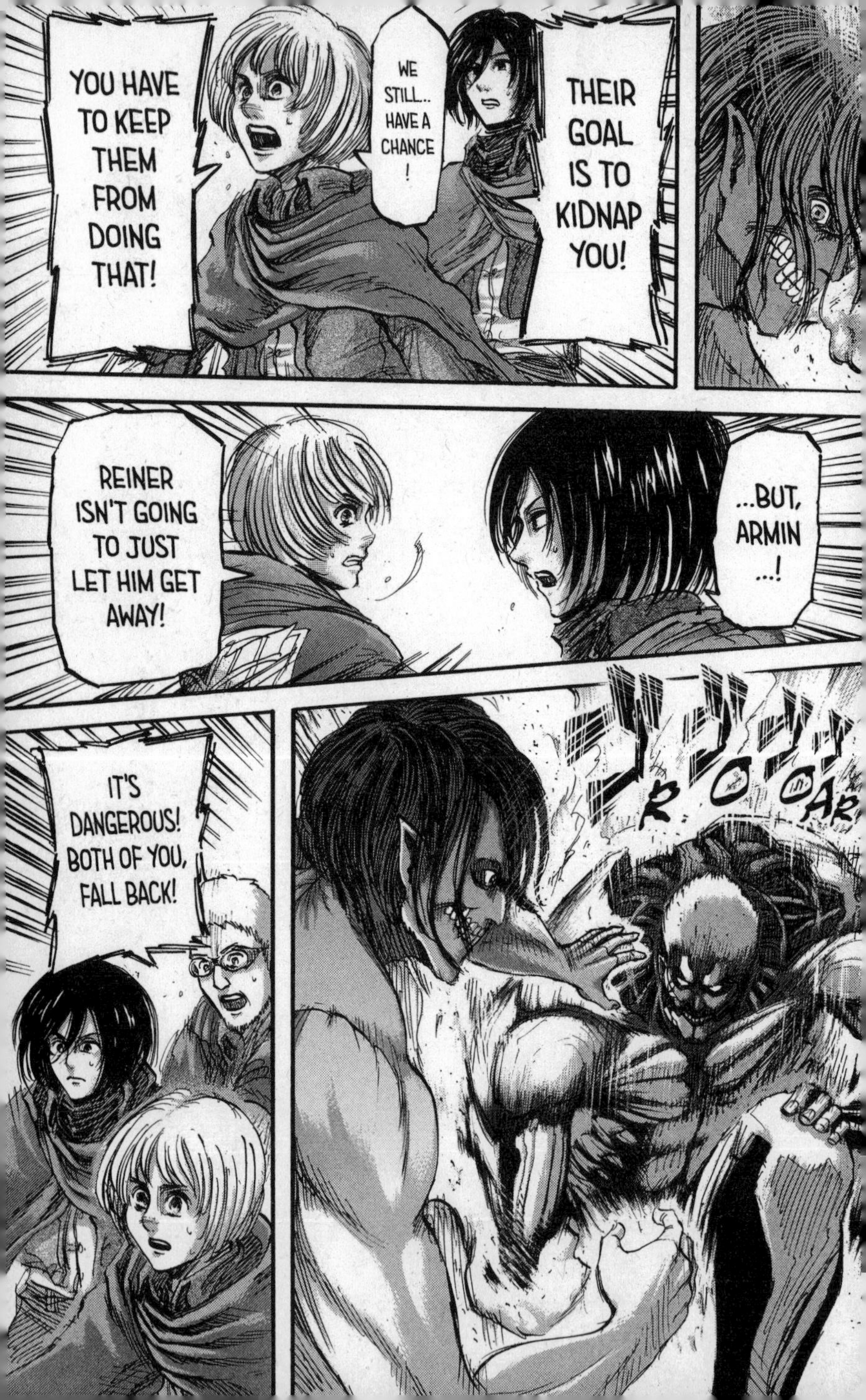
THEIR GOAL IS TO KIDNAP YOU!
WE STILL... HAVE A CHANCE!
YOU HAVE TO KEEP THEM FROM DOING THAT!
...BUT, ARMIN ...!
REINER ISN'T GOING TO JUST LET HIM GET AWAY!
ROOAR
IT'S DANGEROUS! BOTH OF YOU, FALL BACK!

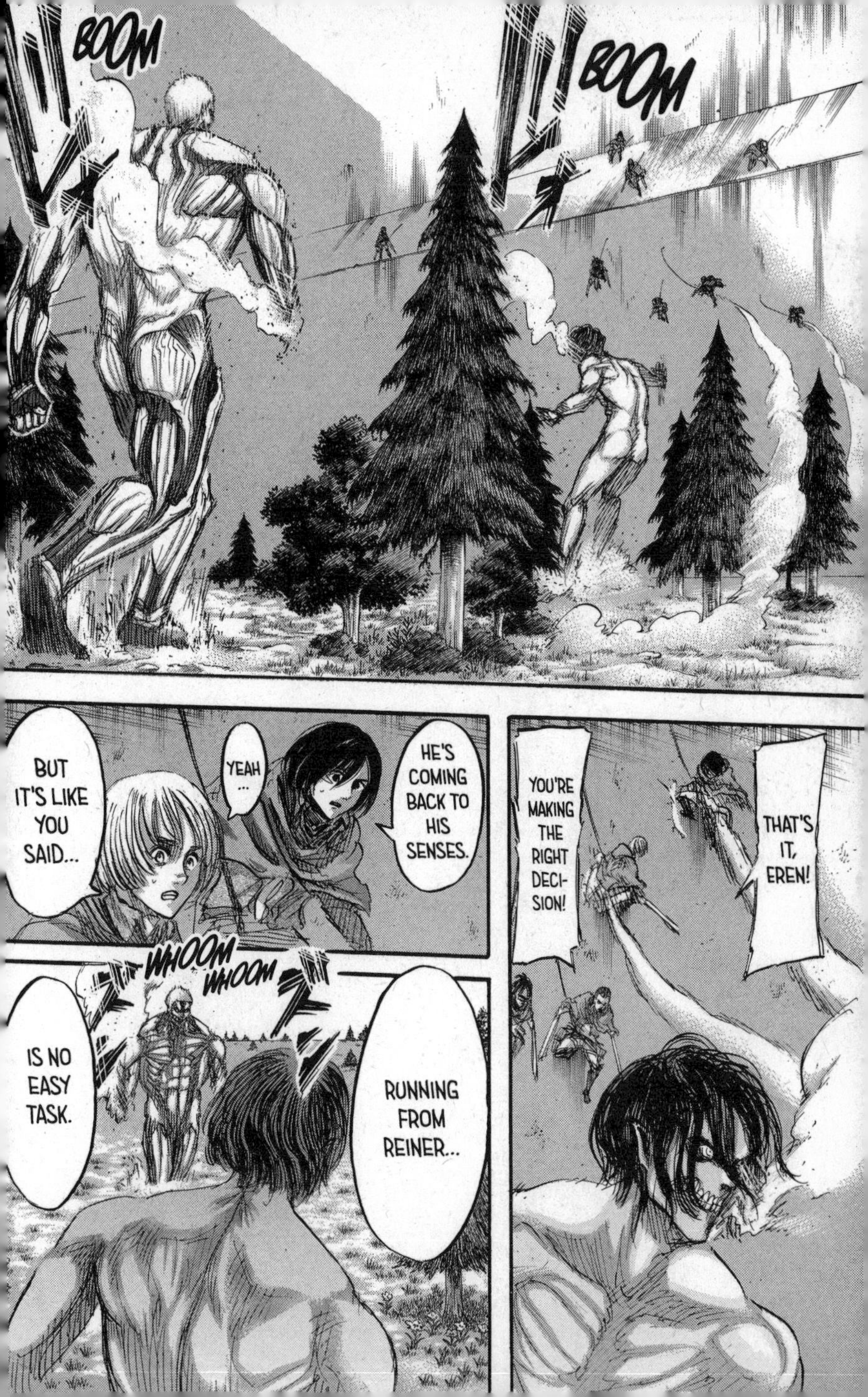
BOOM
BOOM
THAT'S IT, EREN!
YOU'RE MAKING THE RIGHT DECI-SION!
HE'S COMING BACK TO HIS SENSES.
YEAH...
BUT IT'S LIKE YOU SAID...
WHOOM
WHOOM
RUNNING FROM REINER...
IS NO EASY TASK.

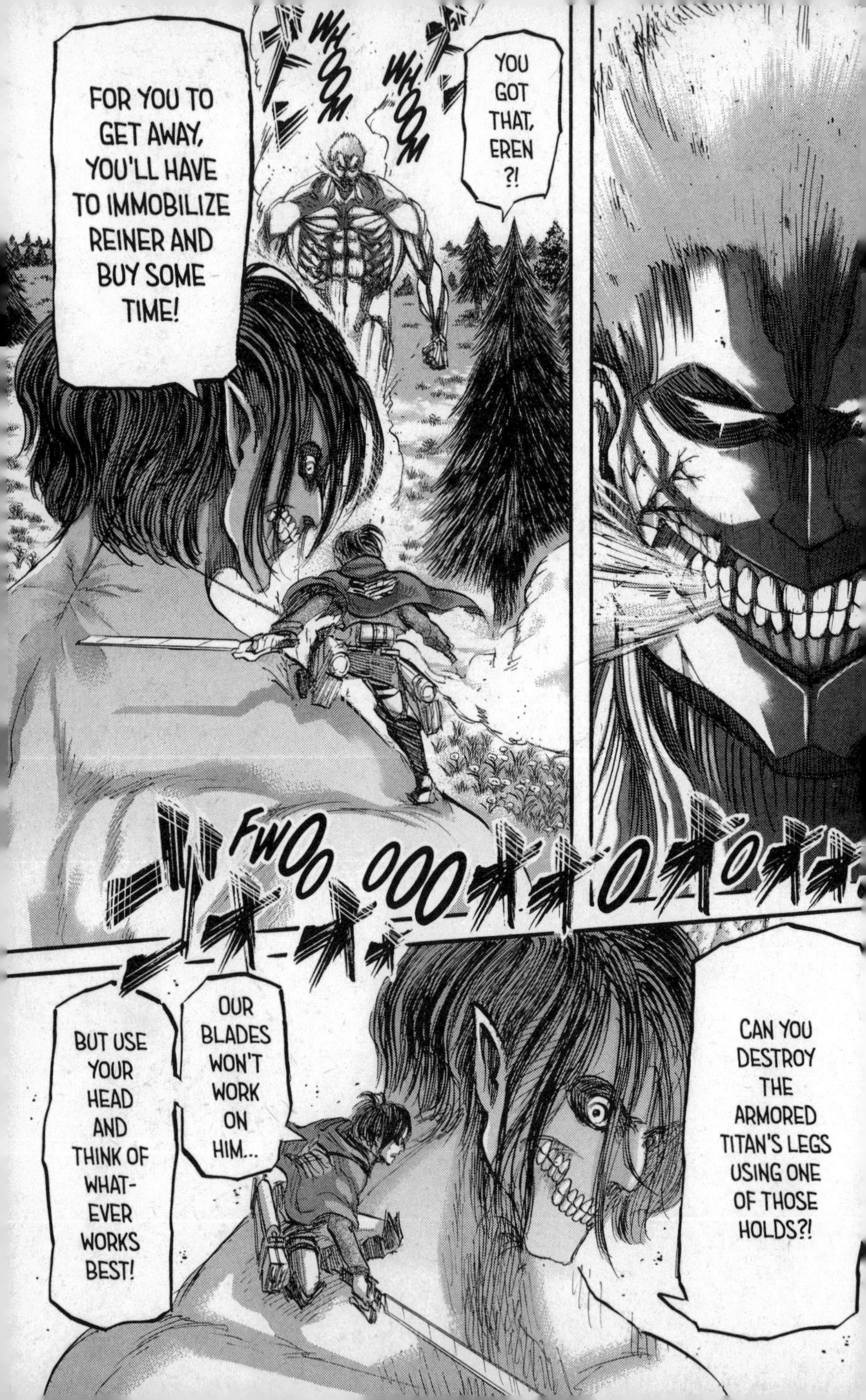
WHOOM
WHOOM
YOU GOT THAT, EREN?!
FOR YOU TO GET AWAY, YOU'LL HAVE TO IMMOBILIZE REINER AND BUY SOME TIME!
FWOOOOOOO
CAN YOU DESTROY THE ARMORED TITAN'S LEGS USING ONE OF THOSE HOLDS?!
OUR BLADES WON'T WORK ON HIM...
BUT USE YOUR HEAD AND THINK OF WHATEVER WORKS BEST!

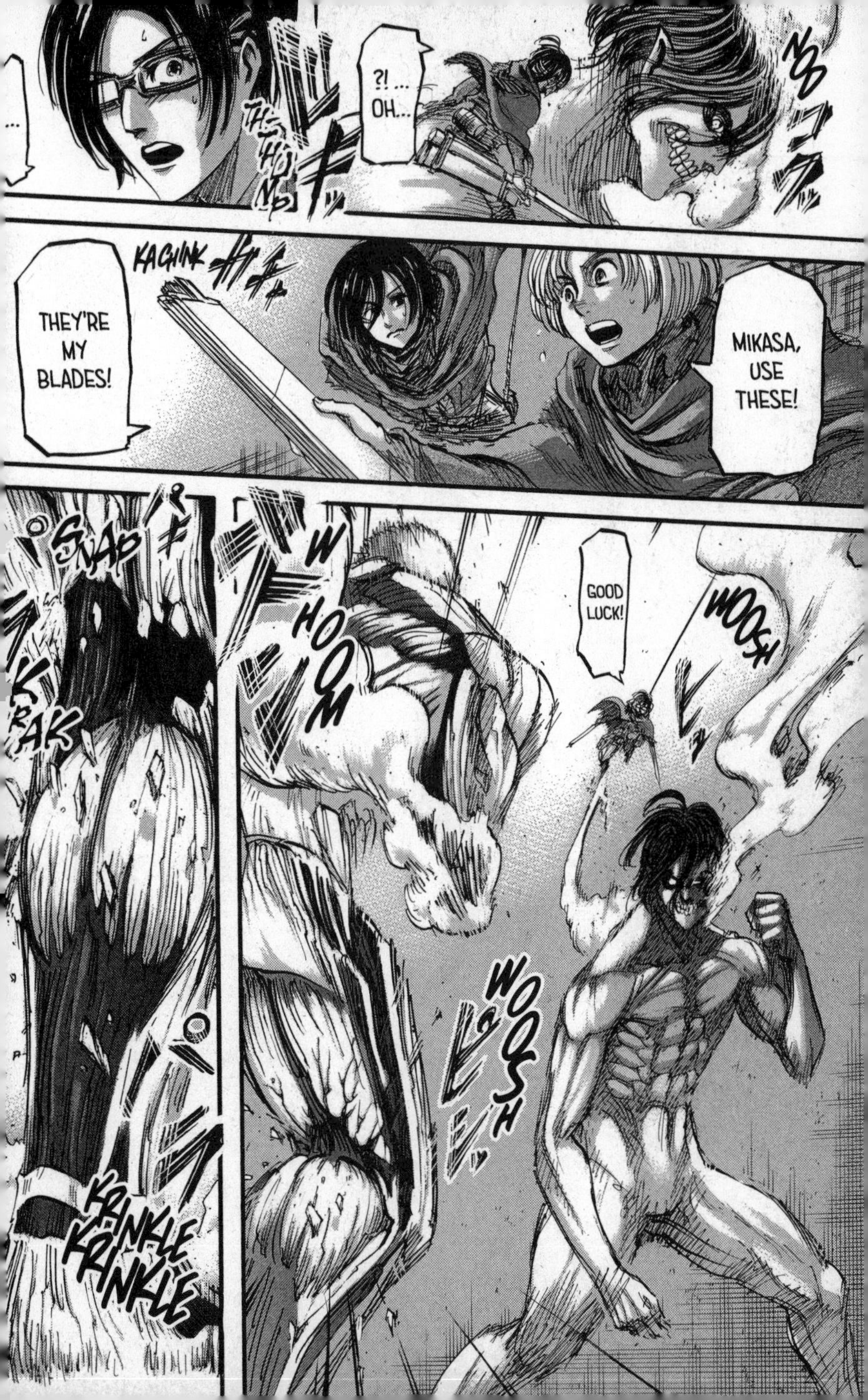
NOO
?! ... OH...
...
MIKASA, USE THESE!
KACHINK
THEY'RE MY BLADES!
GOOD LUCK!
WOOSH
WHOOOM
WOOOSH
SNAP
KRAK
KRINKLE KRINKLE

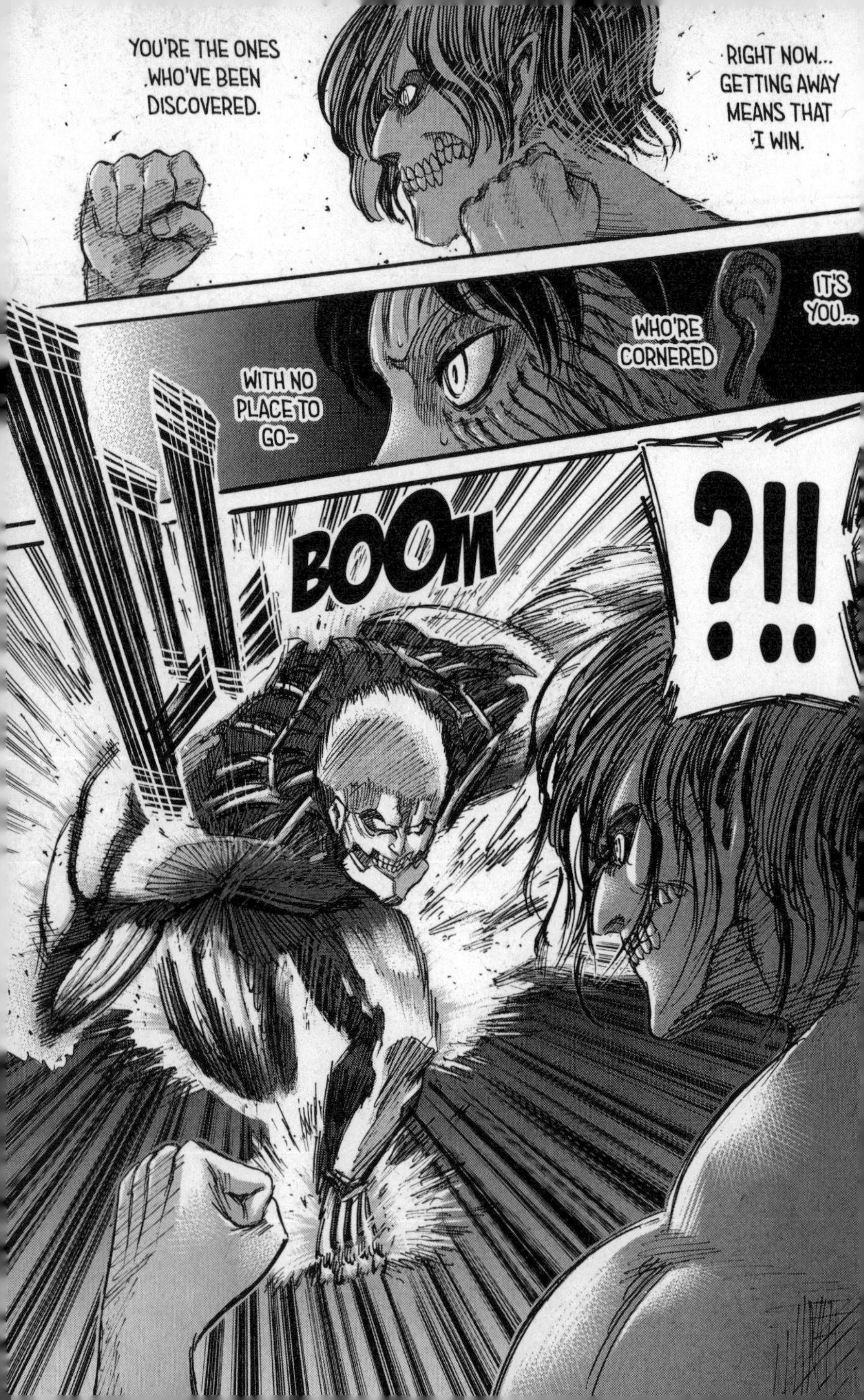
RIGHT NOW... GETTING AWAY MEANS THAT I WIN.
YOU'RE THE ONES WHO'VE BEEN DISCOVERED.
IT'S YOU...
WHO'RE CORNERED
WITH NO PLACE TO GO-
?!!
BOOM

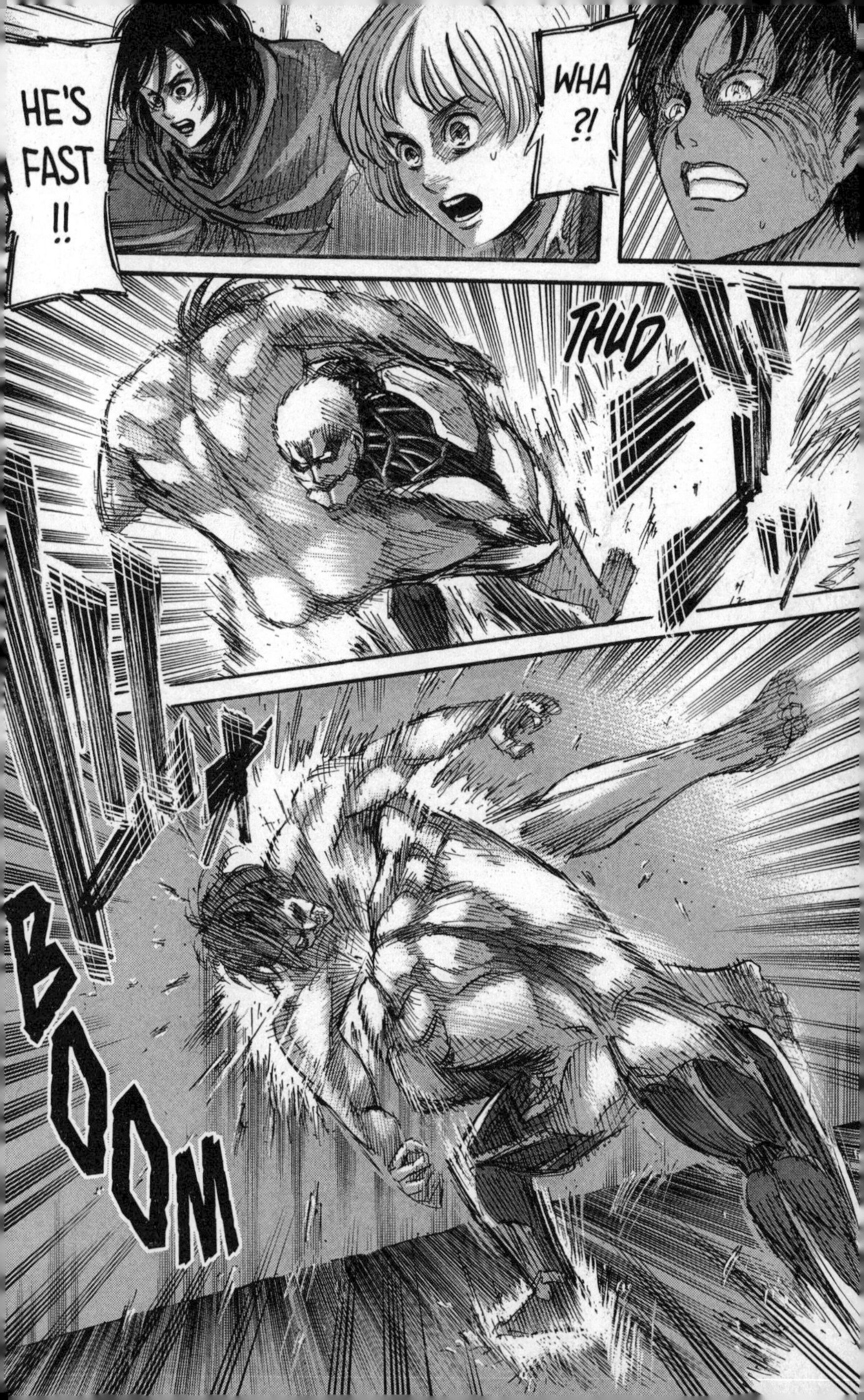
WHA ?!
HE'S FAST !!
THUD
BOOM

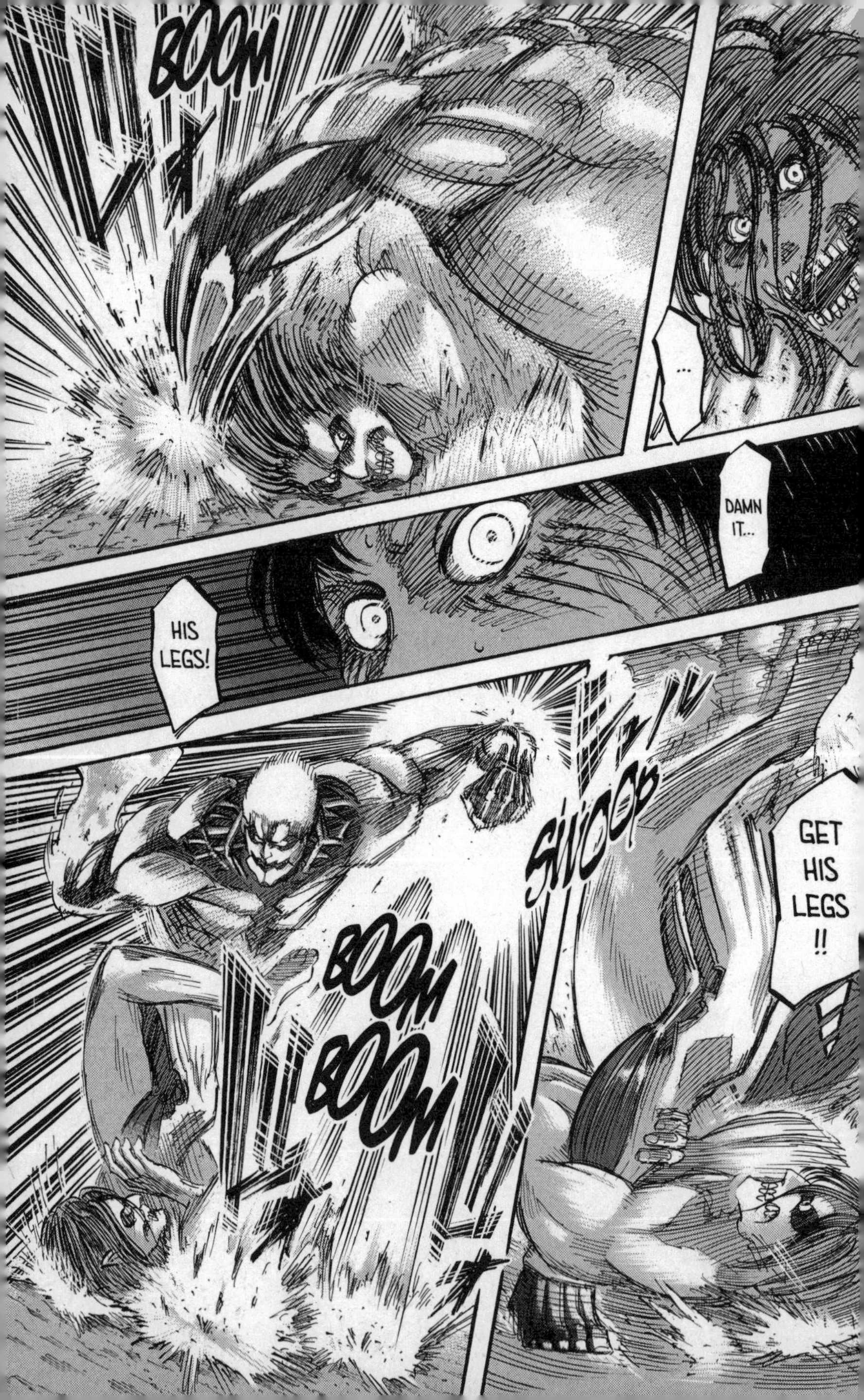
...
BOOM
DAMN IT...
HIS LEGS!
GET HIS LEGS !!
SWOOP
BOOM BOOM BOOM

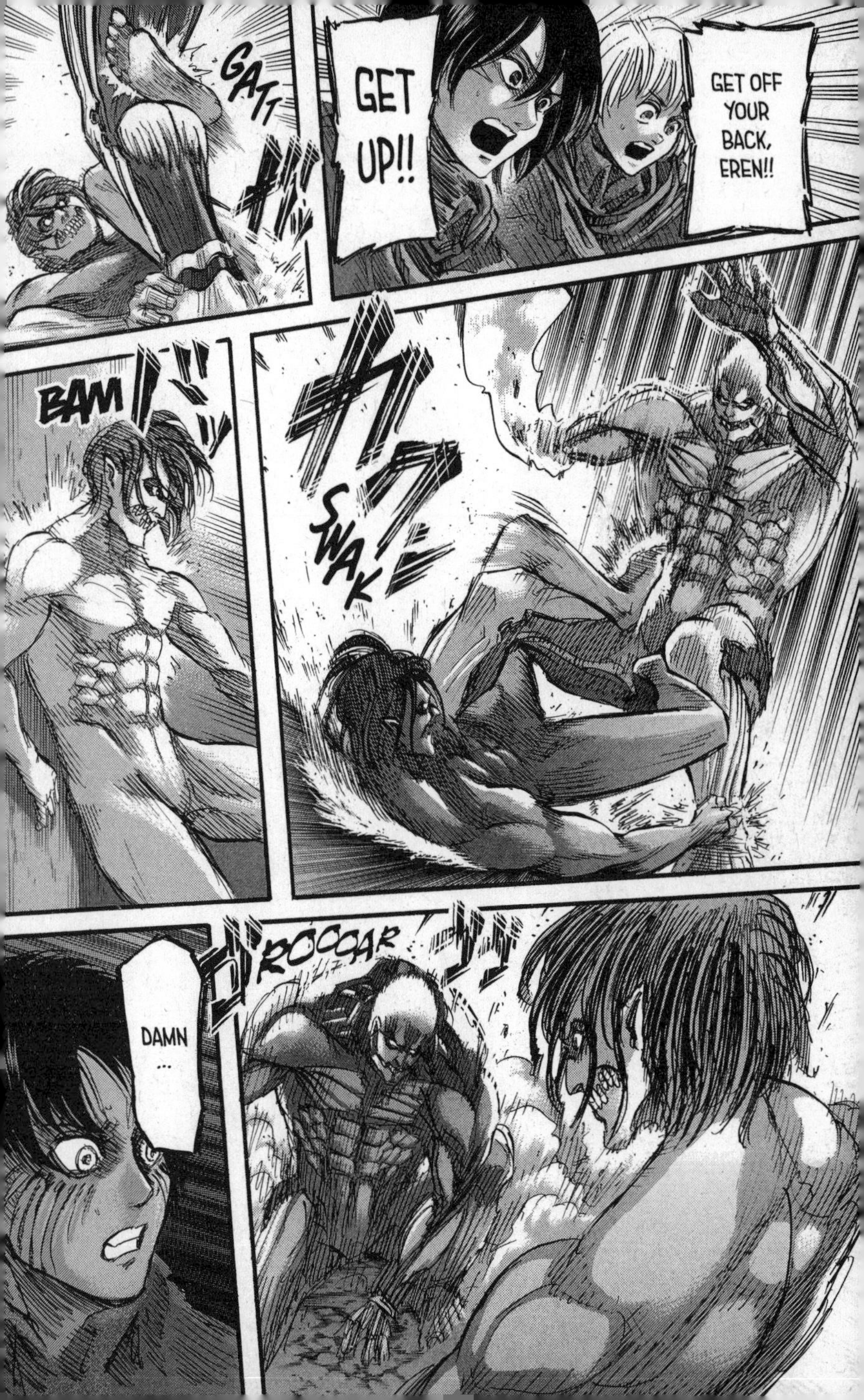
GET OFF YOUR BACK, EREN!!
GET UP!!
GATT
SWAK
BAM
ROOOAR
DAMN ...

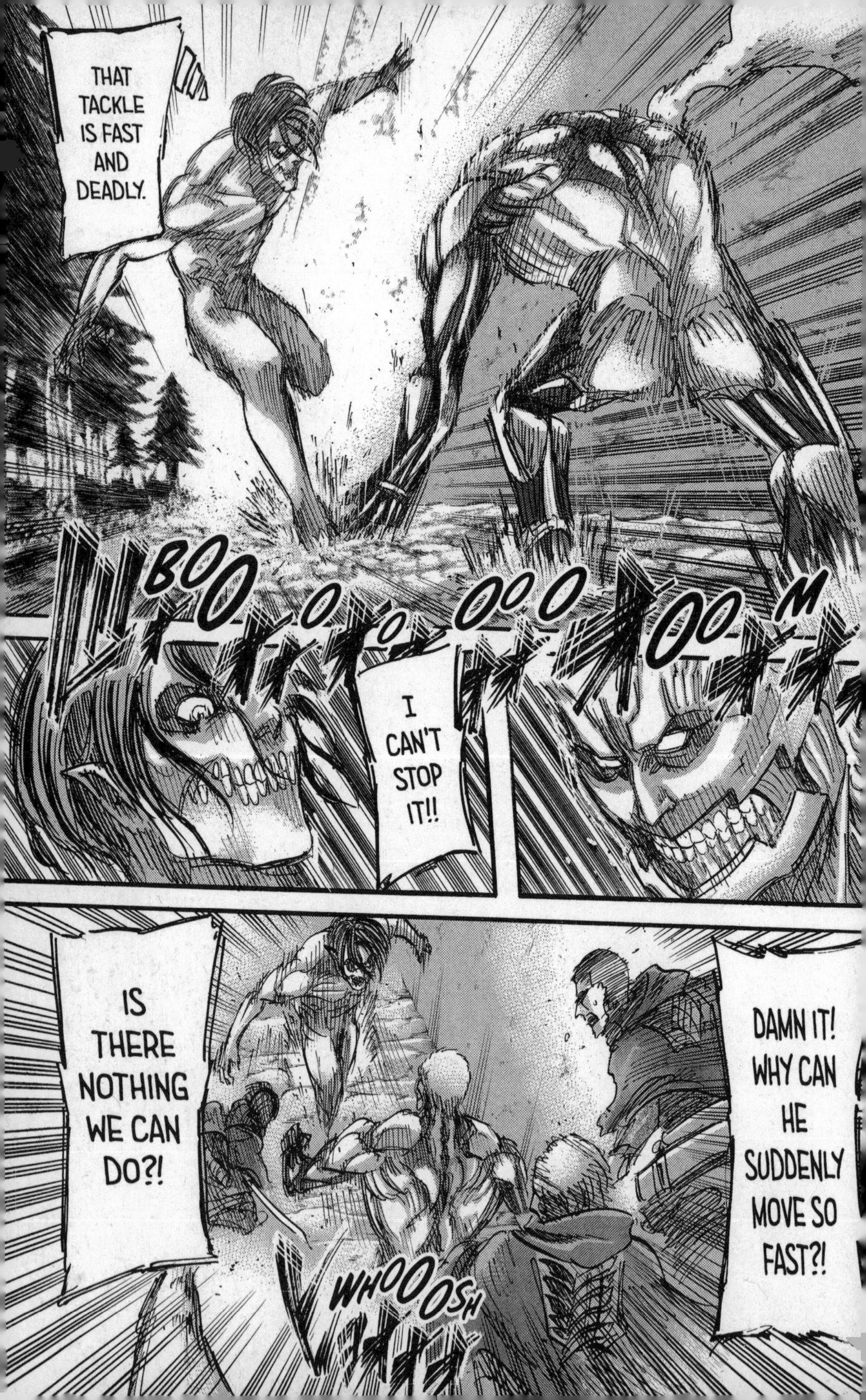
THAT TACKLE IS FAST AND DEADLY.
BOOOOOOOOOM
I CAN'T STOP IT!!
DAMN IT! WHY CAN HE SUDDENLY MOVE SO FAST?!
IS THERE NOTHING WE CAN DO?!
WHOOOOSH

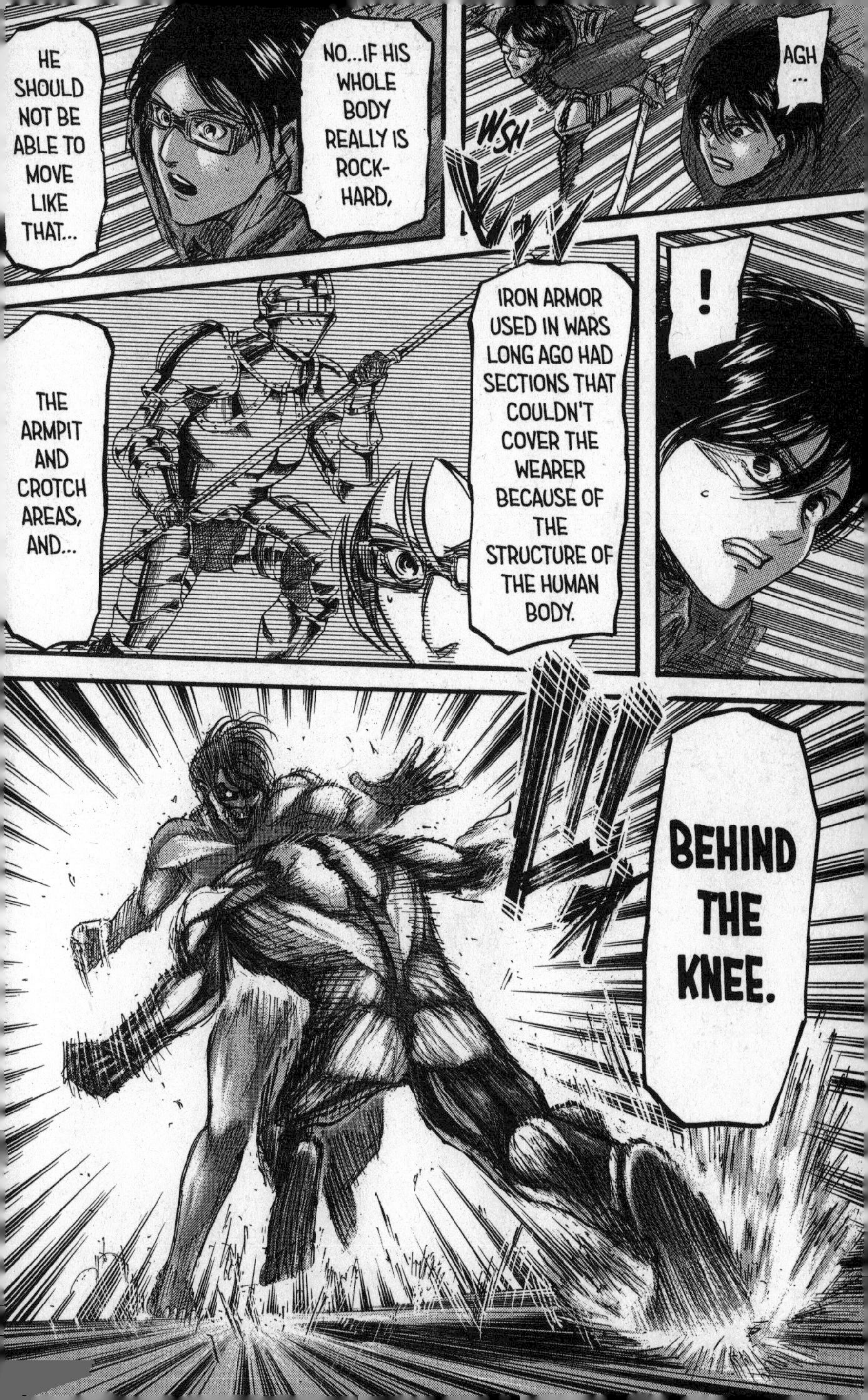
AGH ...
W'SH
NO...IF HIS WHOLE BODY REALLY IS ROCK-HARD,
HE SHOULD NOT BE ABLE TO MOVE LIKE THAT...
!
IRON ARMOR USED IN WARS LONG AGO HAD SECTIONS THAT COULDN'T COVER THE WEARER BECAUSE OF THE STRUCTURE OF THE HUMAN BODY.
THE ARMPIT AND CROTCH AREAS, AND...
BEHIND THE KNEE.

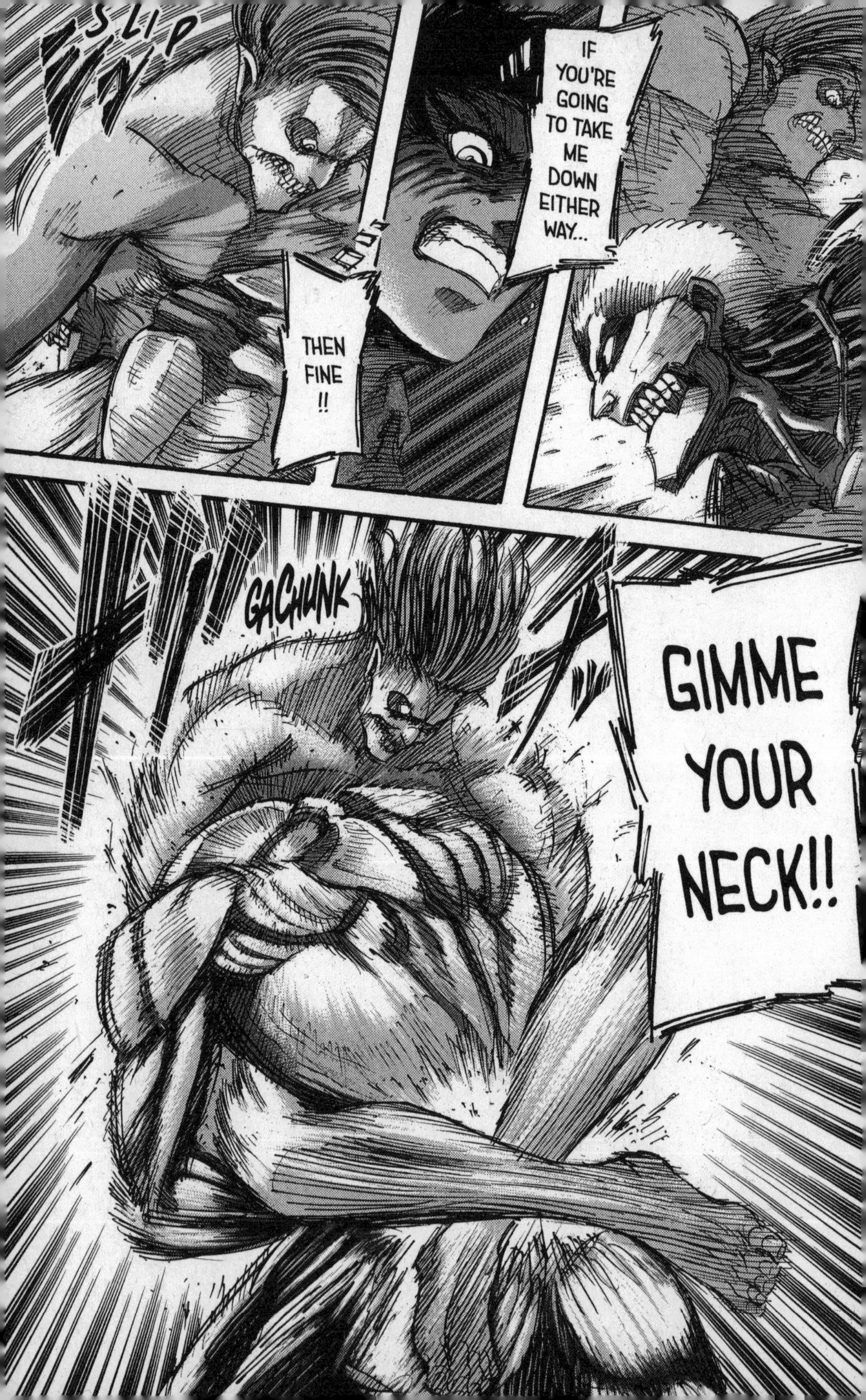
IF YOU'RE GOING TO TAKE ME DOWN EITHER WAY...
THEN FINE!!
SLIP
GIMME YOUR NECK!!
GACHUNK

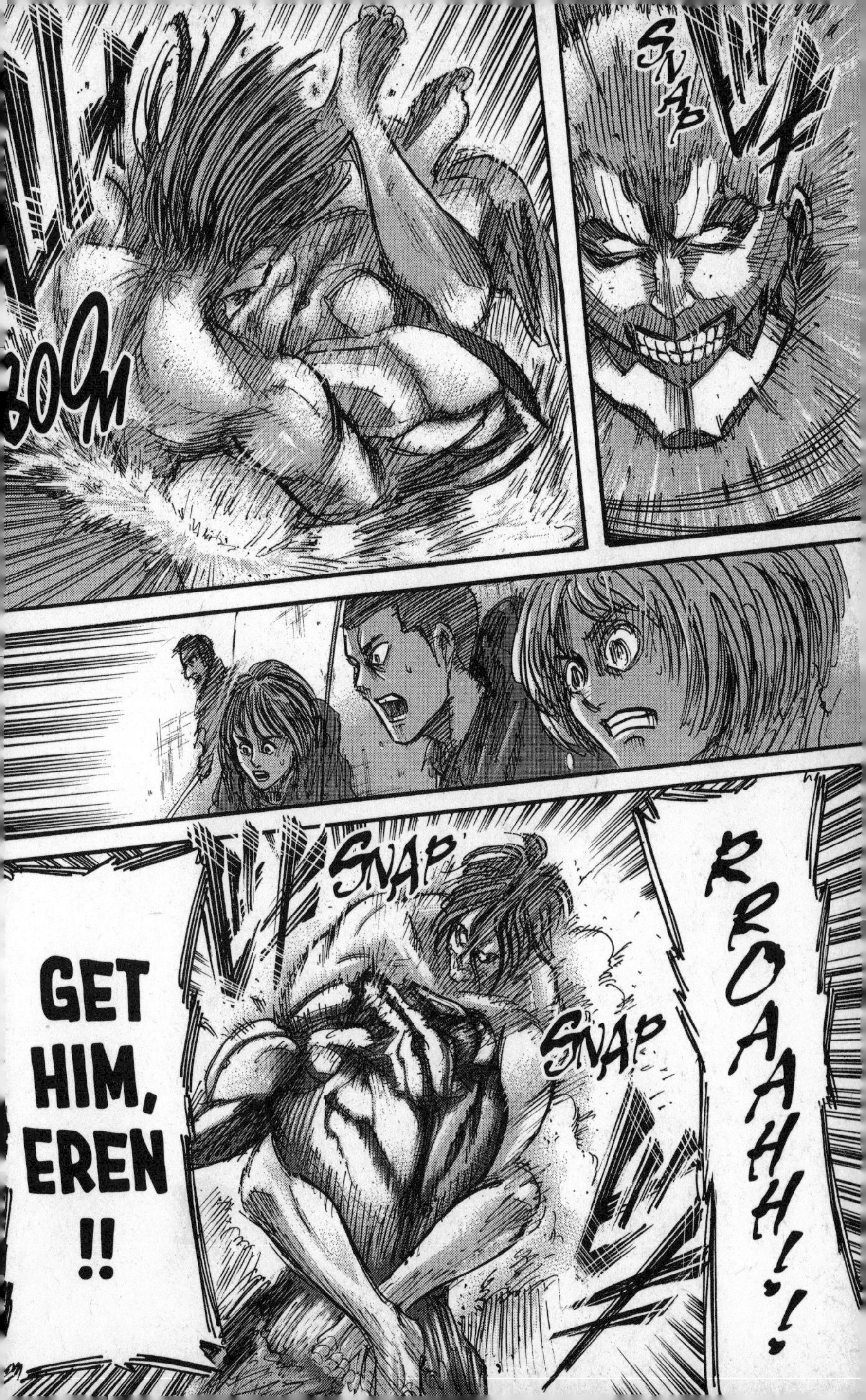
SNAP
BOOM
RROAAHH!!!
SNAP
SNAP
GET HIM, EREN!!

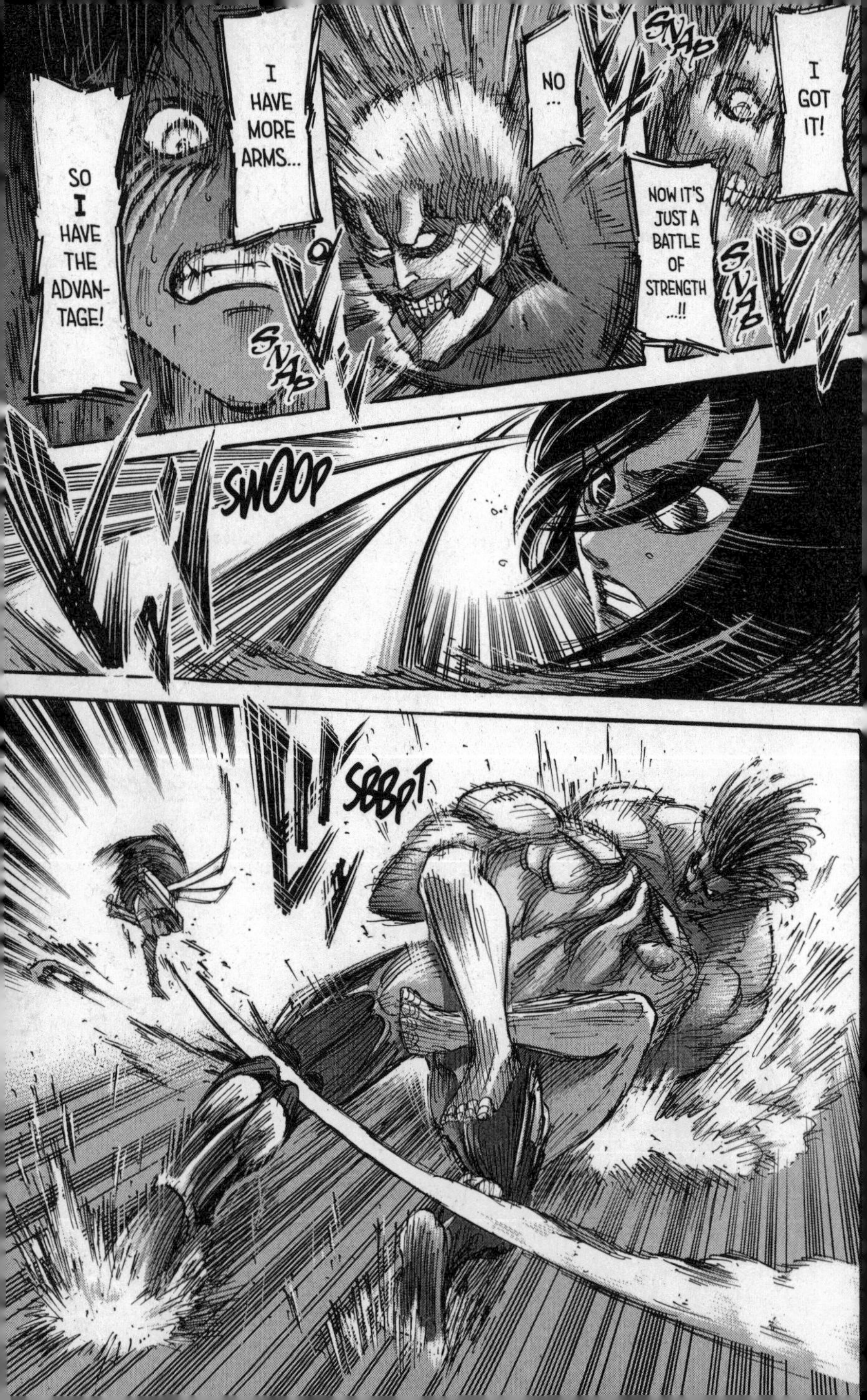
SNAP
I GOT IT!
NOW IT'S JUST A BATTLE OF STRENGTH ...!!
SNAP
NO ...
I HAVE MORE ARMS...
SO I HAVE THE ADVANTAGE!
SNAP
SWOOP
SBBPT

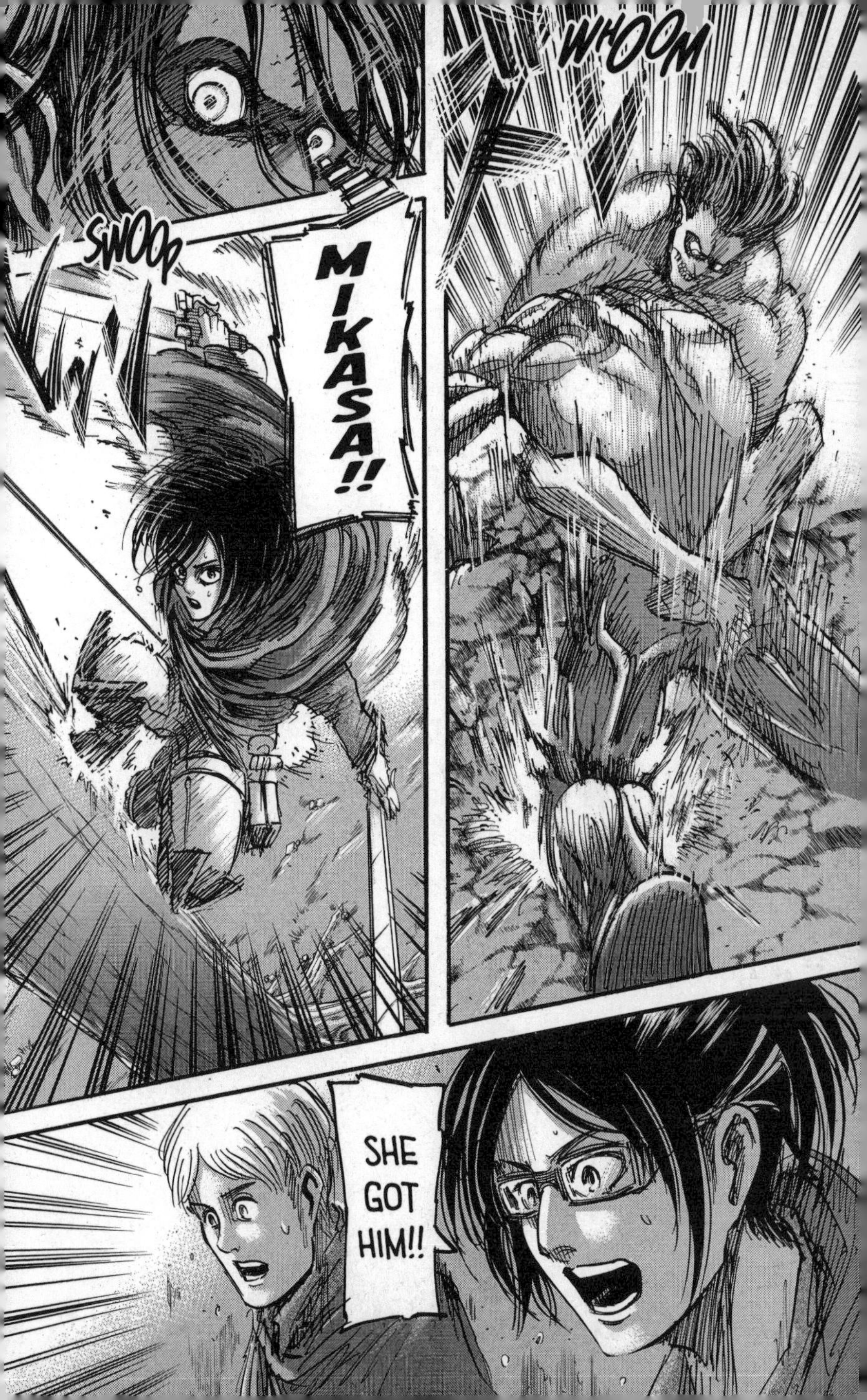
WHOOM
SWOOP
MIKASA!!
SHE GOT HIM!!

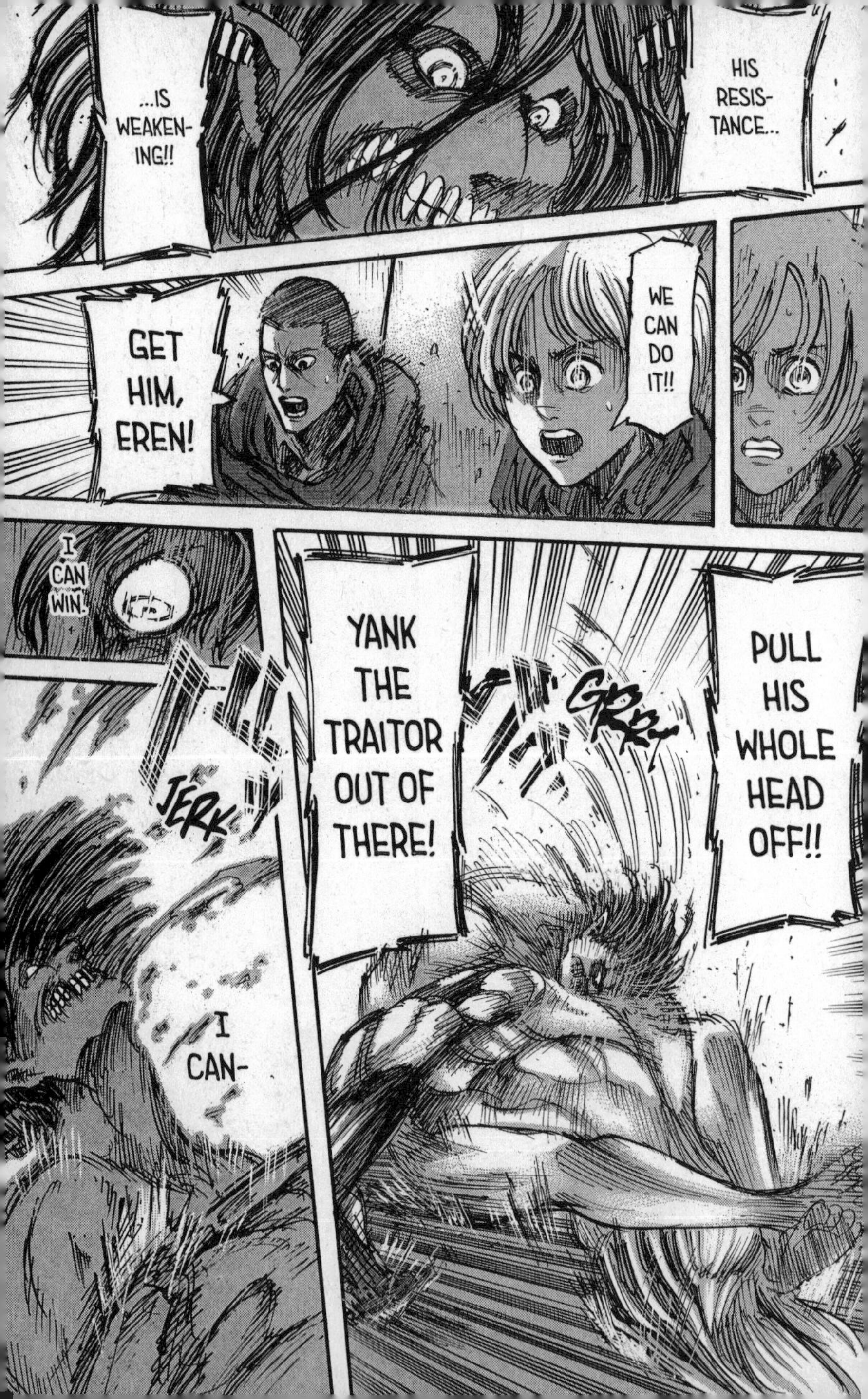

HIS RESISTANCE...
...IS WEAKENING!!
WE CAN DO IT!!
GET HIM, EREN!
PULL HIS WHOLE HEAD OFF!!
GRRR
YANK THE TRAITOR OUT OF THERE!
I CAN WIN.
JERK
I CAN-

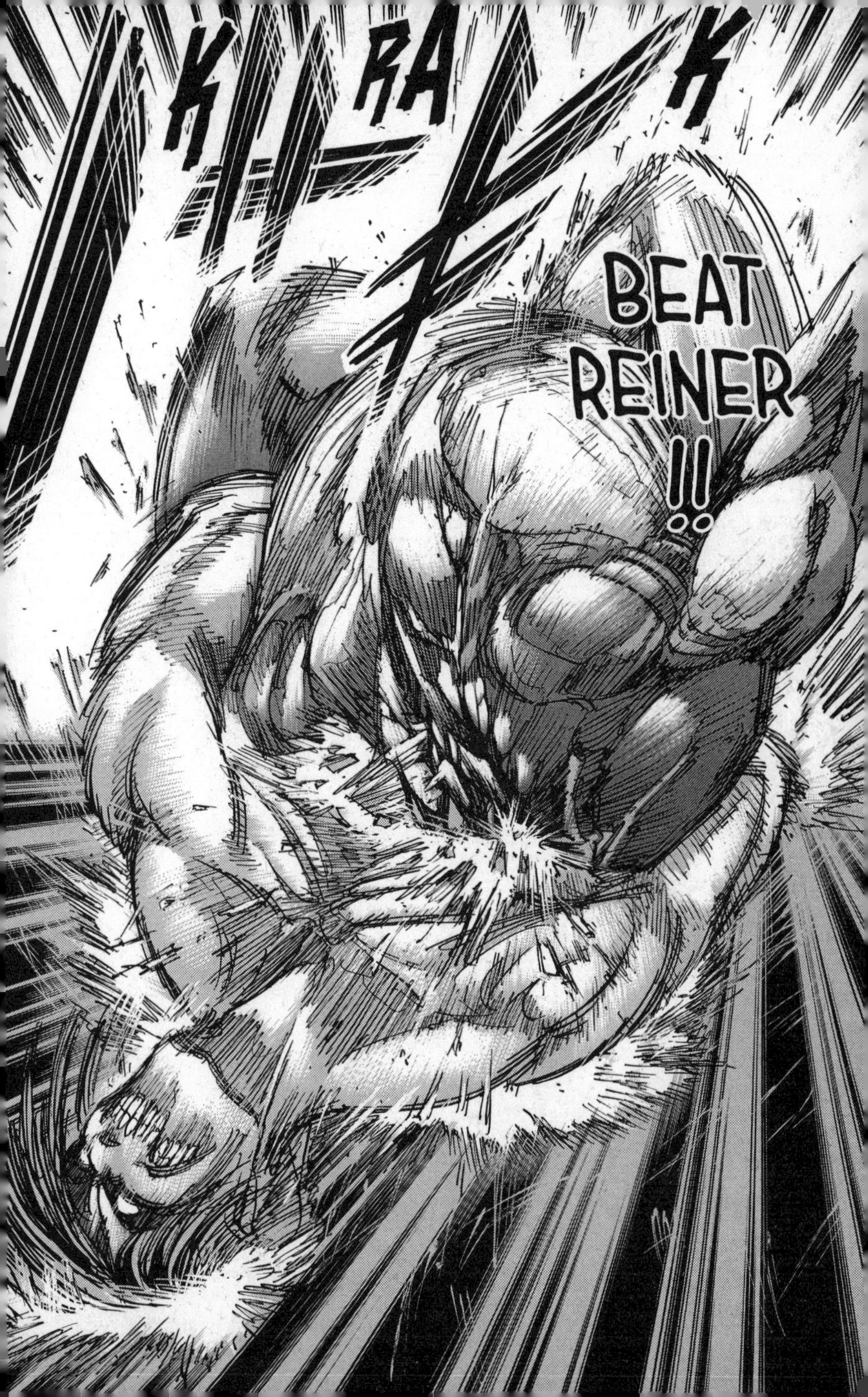
KRAK
BEAT REINER!!

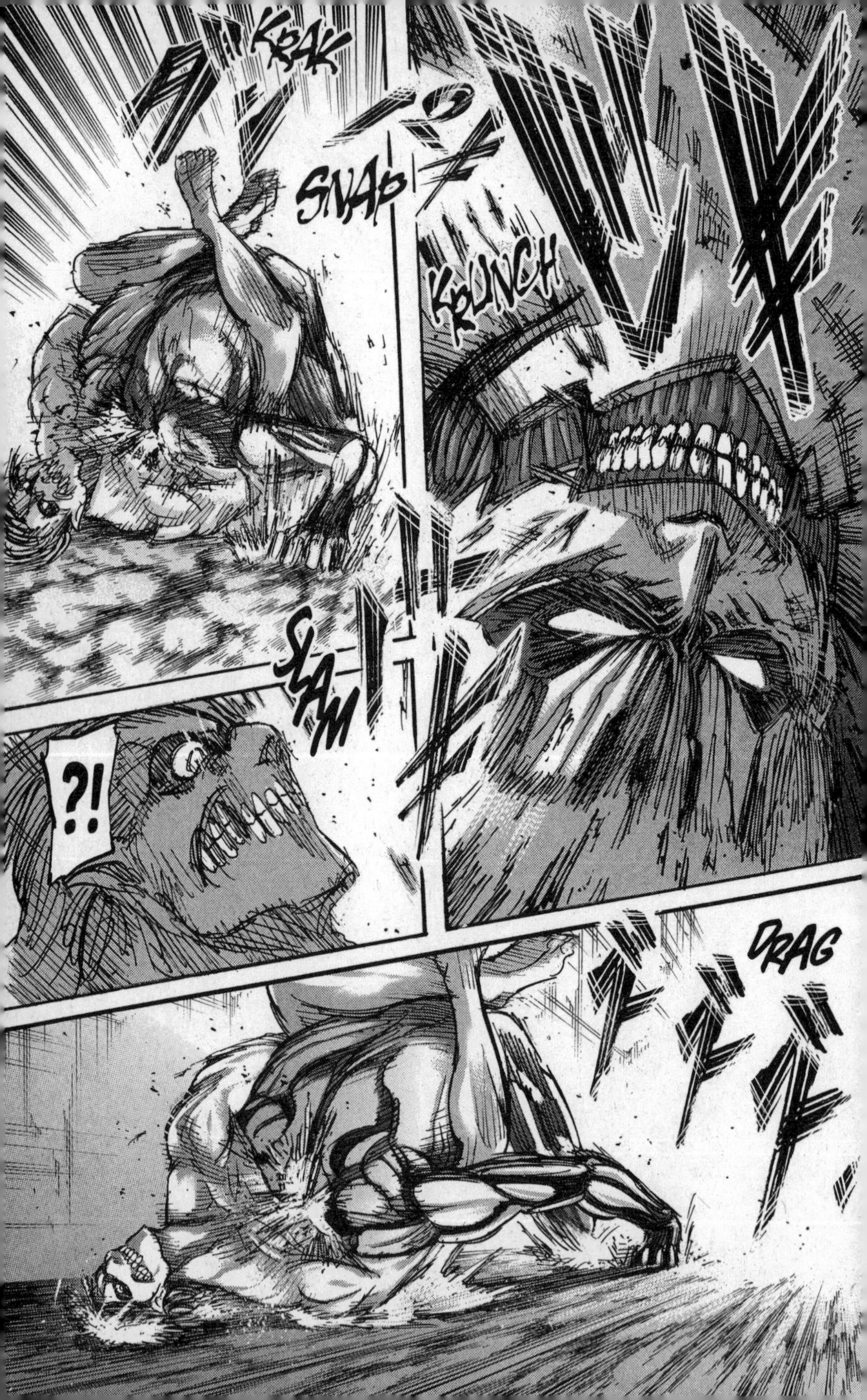
KRUNCH
KRAK
SNAP
SLAM
?!
DRAG

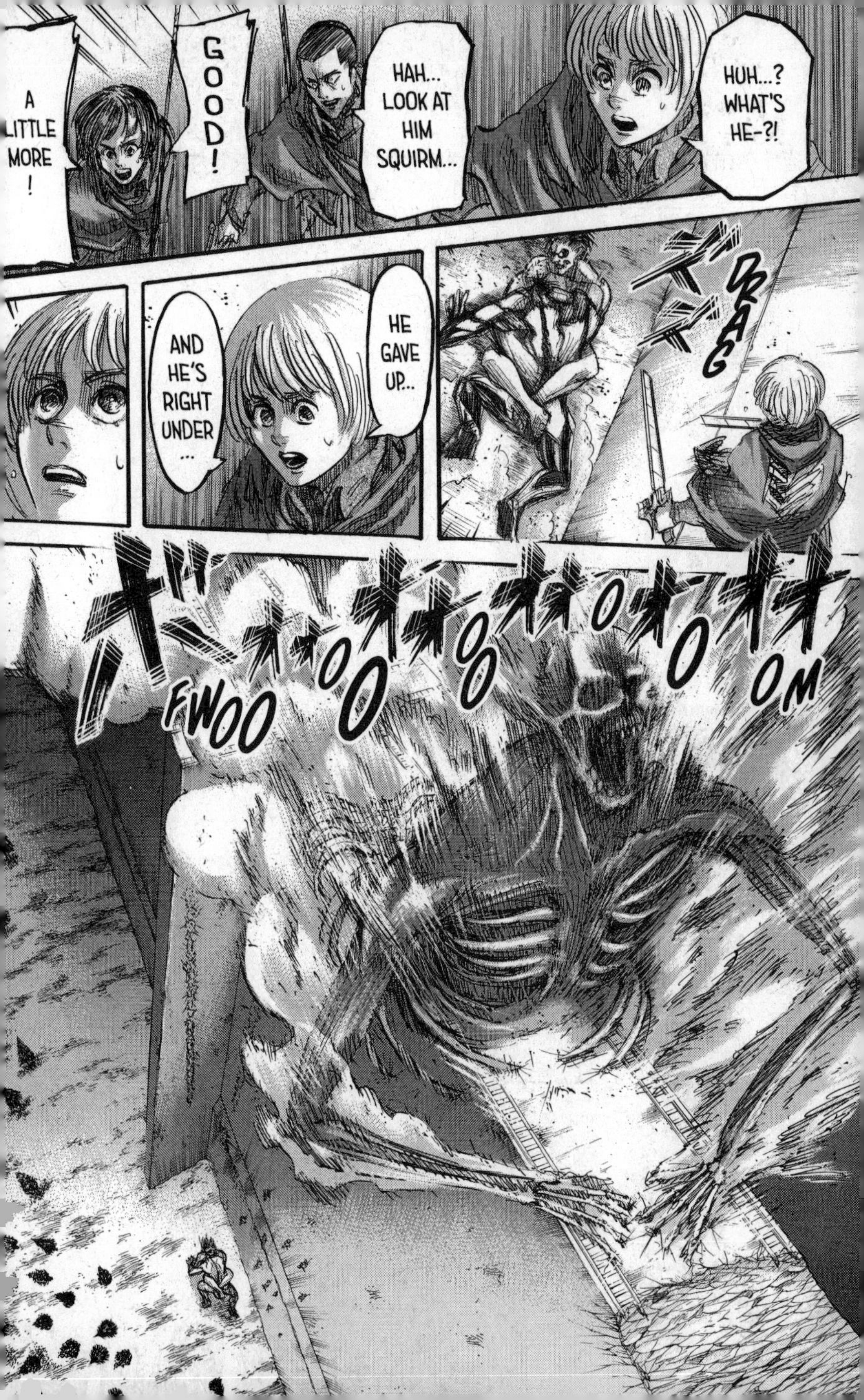
HUH...? WHAT'S HE-?!
HAH... LOOK AT HIM SQUIRM...
GOOD!
A LITTLE MORE!
DRAG
HE GAVE UP...
AND HE'S RIGHT UNDER ...
FWOOOOOOOOOM

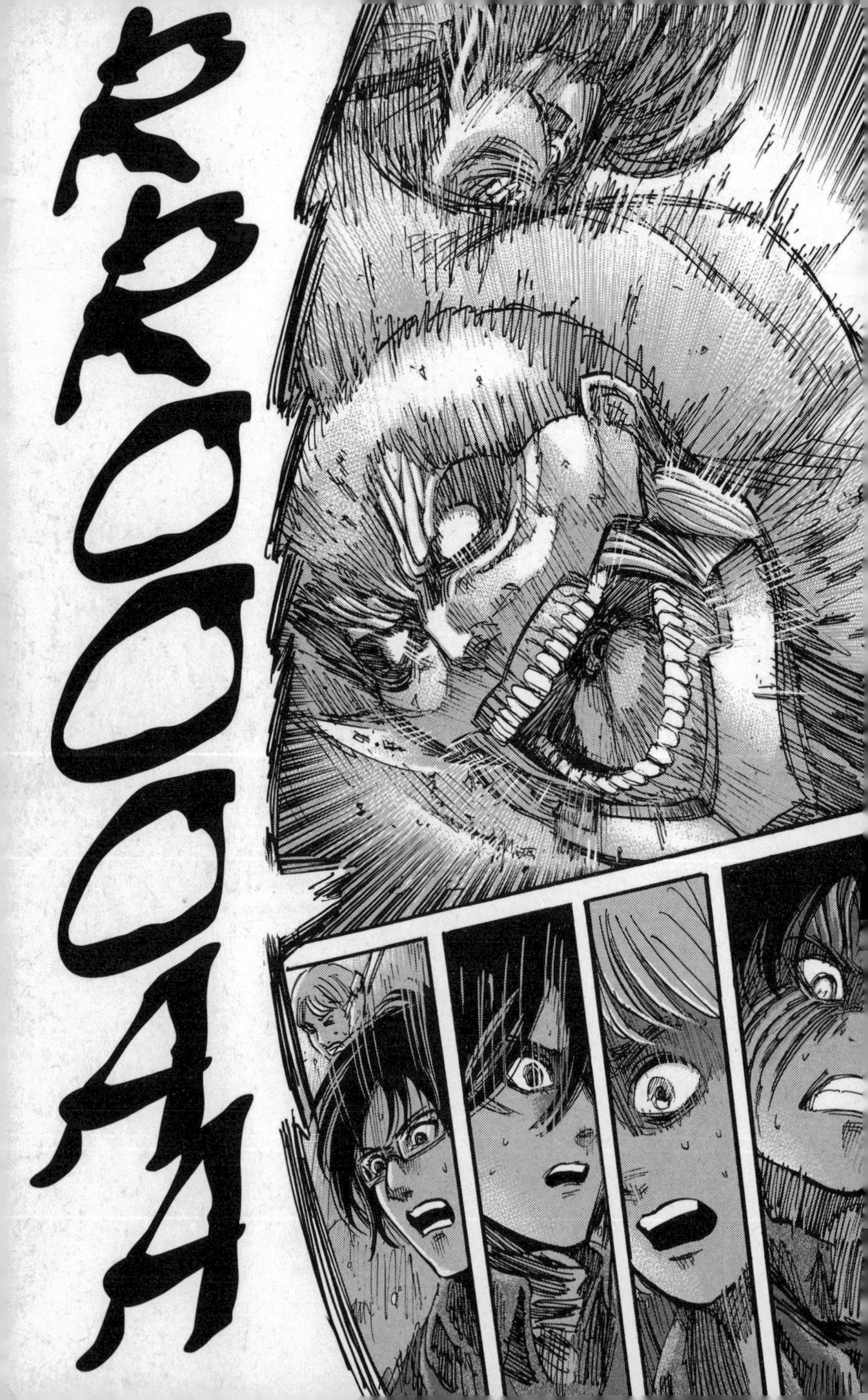
RROOOAA

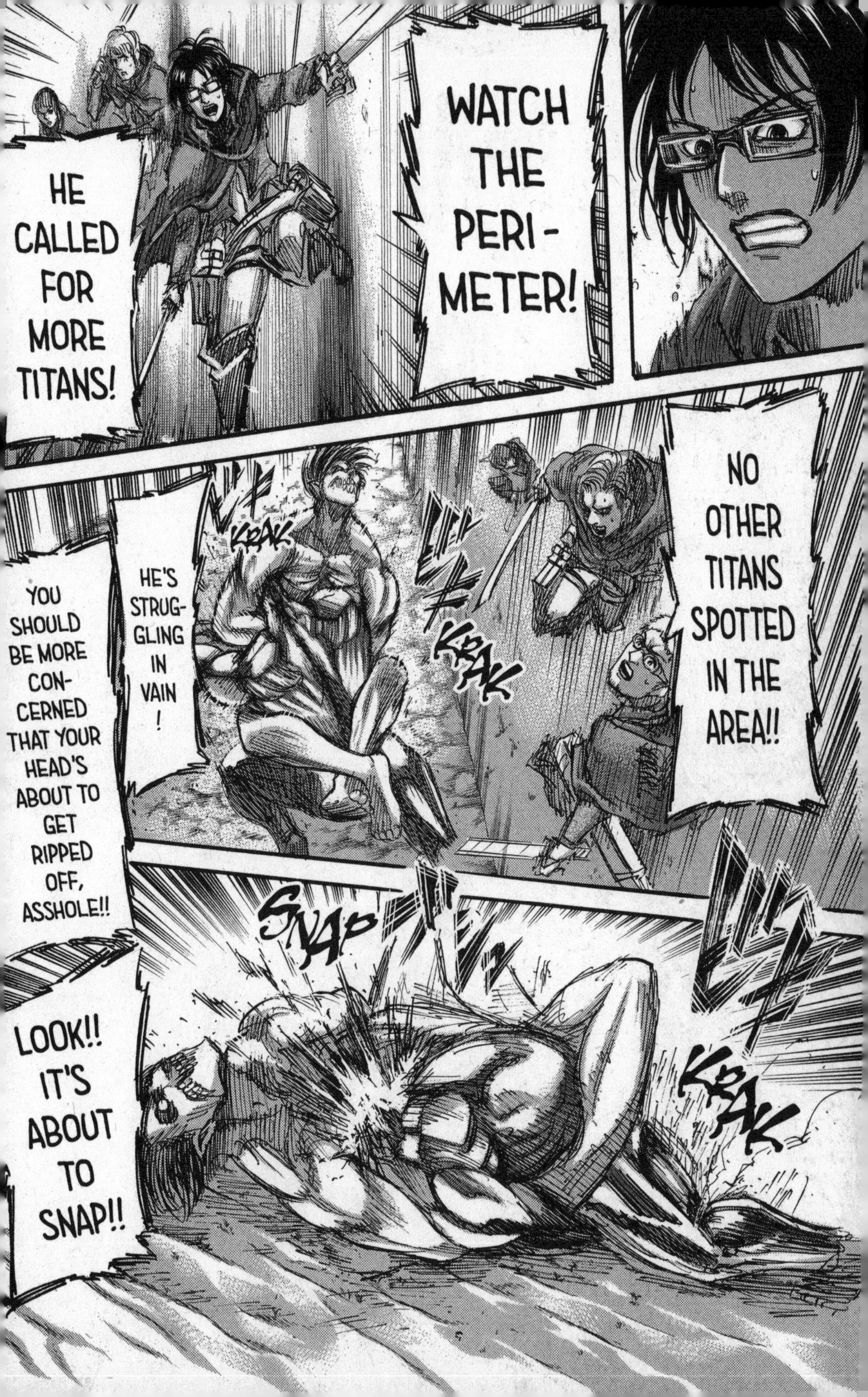
WATCH THE PERI-METER!
HE CALLED FOR MORE TITANS!
NO OTHER TITANS SPOTTED IN THE AREA!!
KRAK
KRAK
HE'S STRUG-GLING IN VAIN!
YOU SHOULD BE MORE CON-CERNED THAT YOUR HEAD'S ABOUT TO GET RIPPED OFF, ASSHOLE!!
KRAK
SNAP
LOOK!! IT'S ABOUT TO SNAP!!

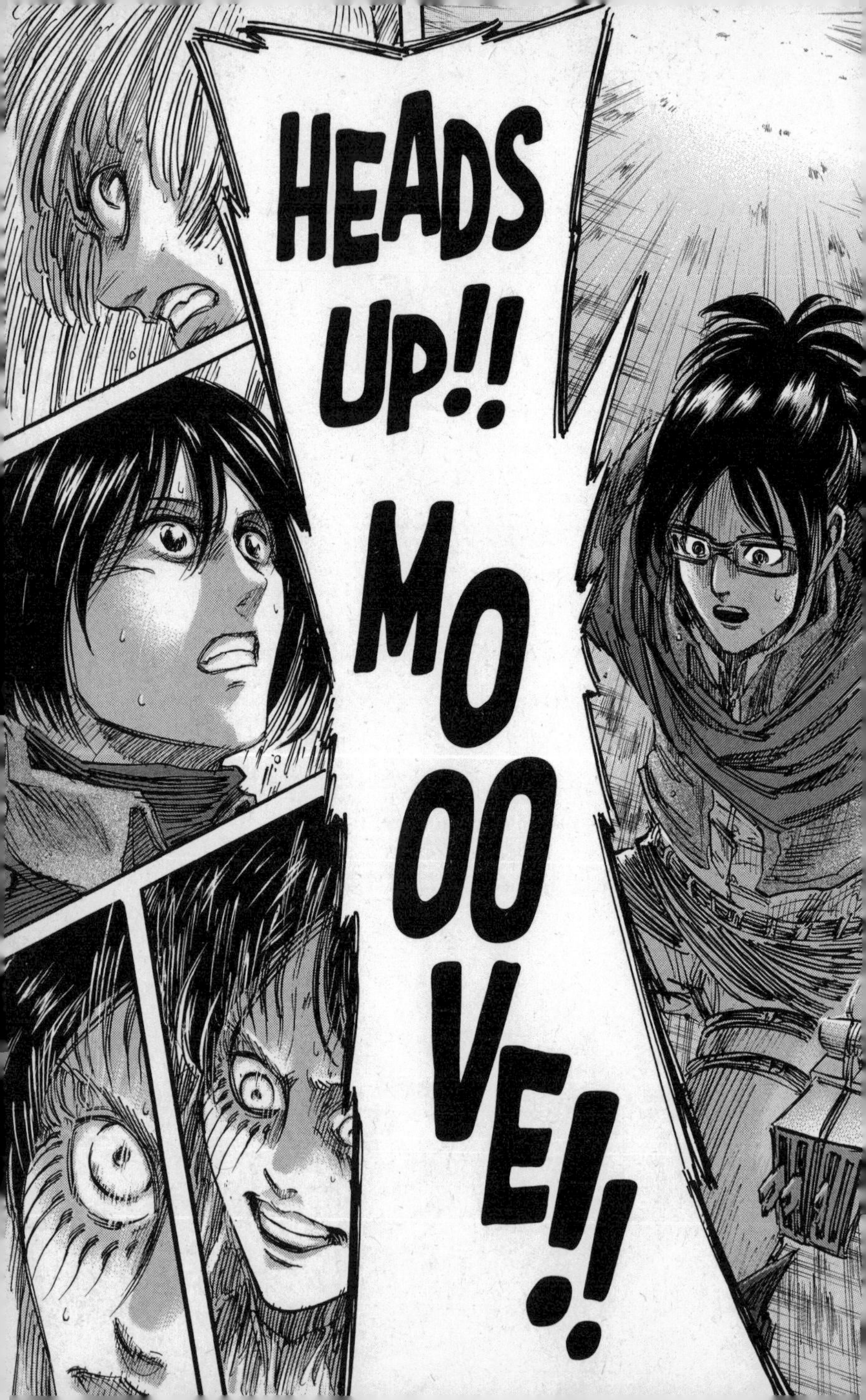
HEADS UP!!
MOOOOVE!!

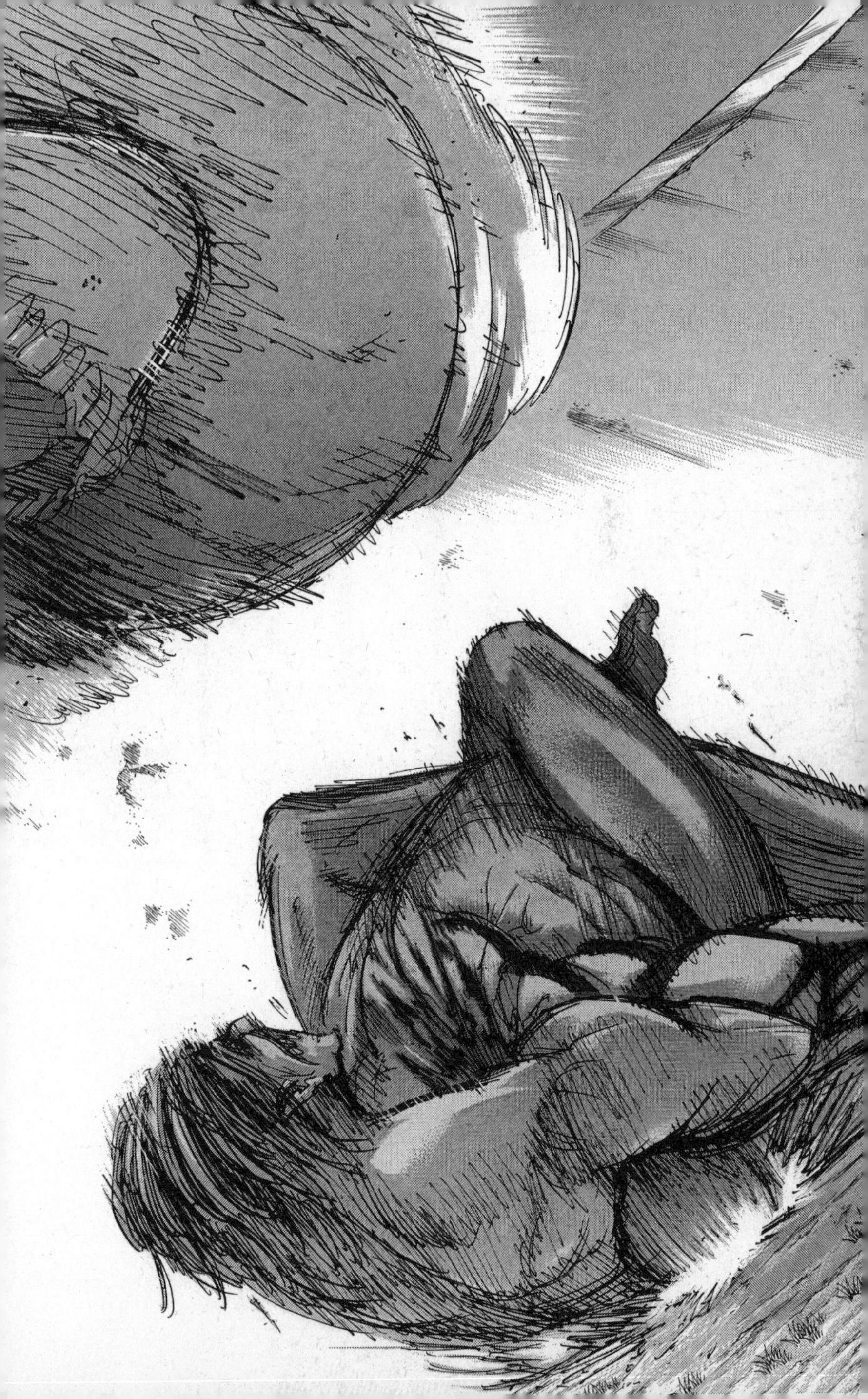

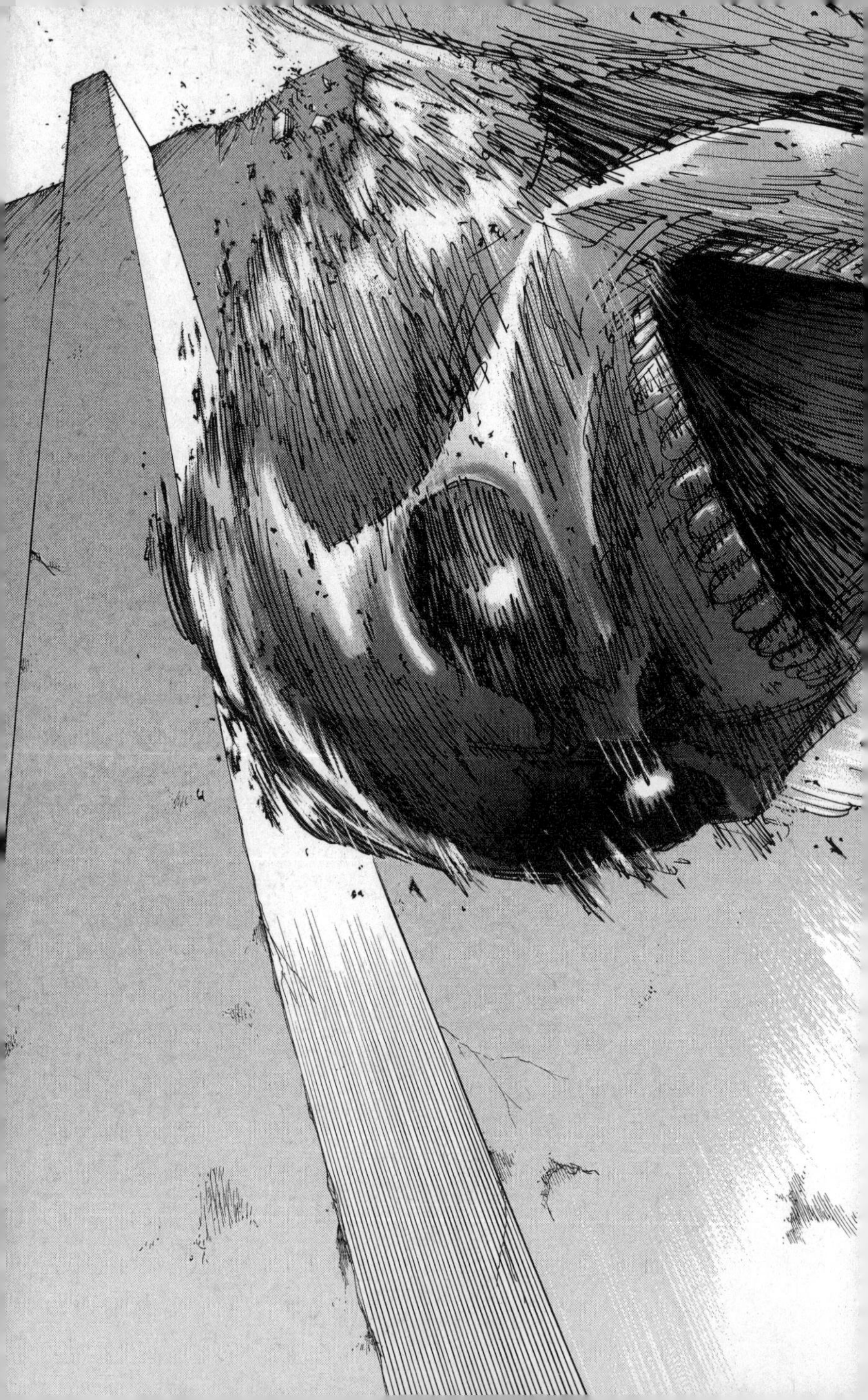

ATTACK on TITAN

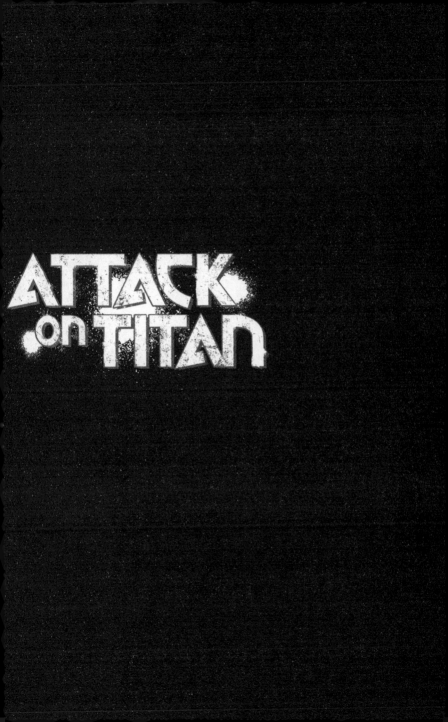

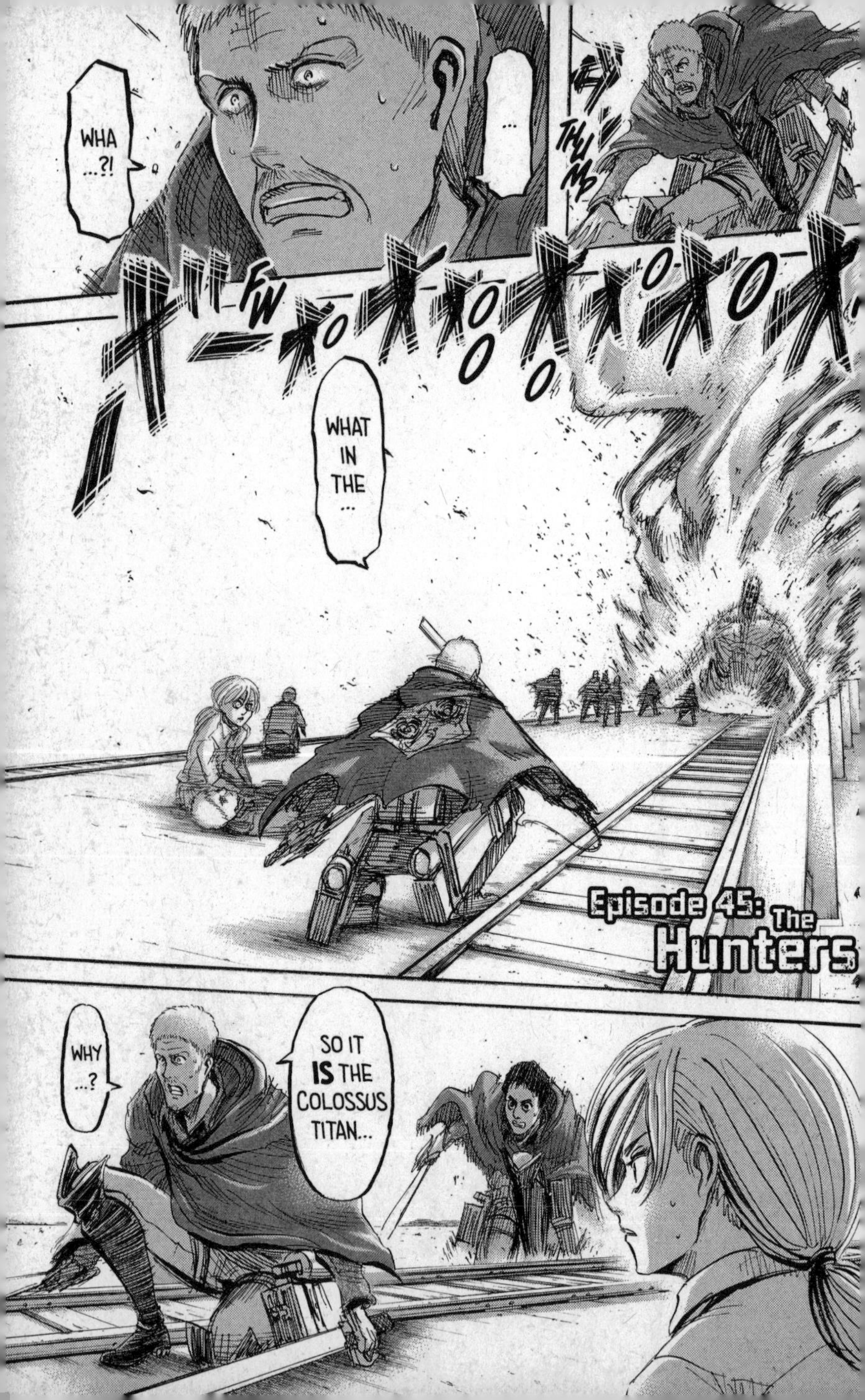
THUMP
...
WHA ...?!
FW
WHAT IN THE ...
Episode 45: The Hunters
SO IT IS THE COLOSSUS TITAN...
WHY ...?

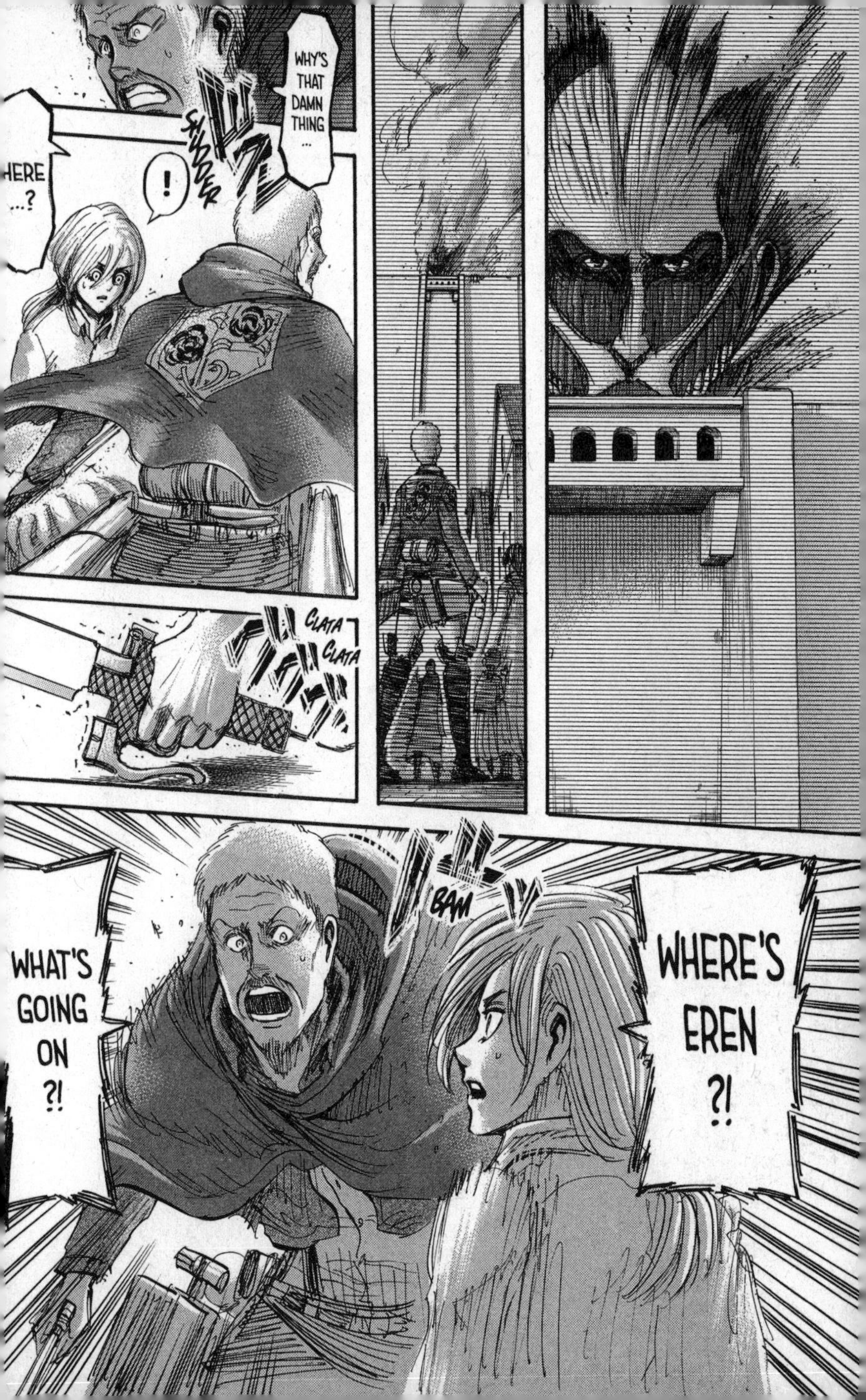

WHY'S THAT DAMN THING ...
SHUDDER
HERE ...?
!
CLATA CLATA
WHERE'S EREN ?!
BAM
WHAT'S GOING ON ?!

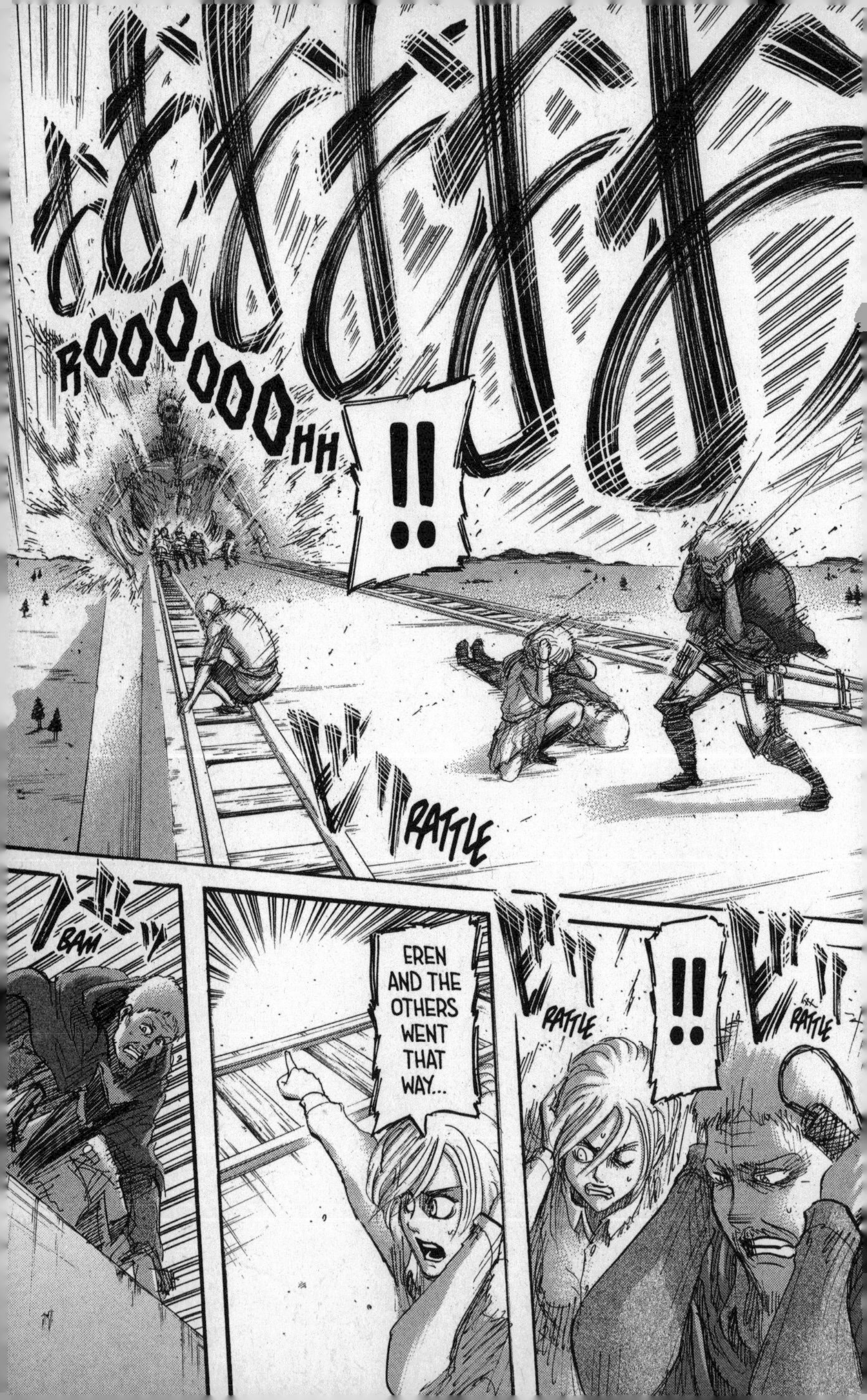
ROOOOOOHH
!!
RATTLE
RATTLE
!!
RATTLE
EREN AND THE OTHERS WENT THAT WAY...
BAM

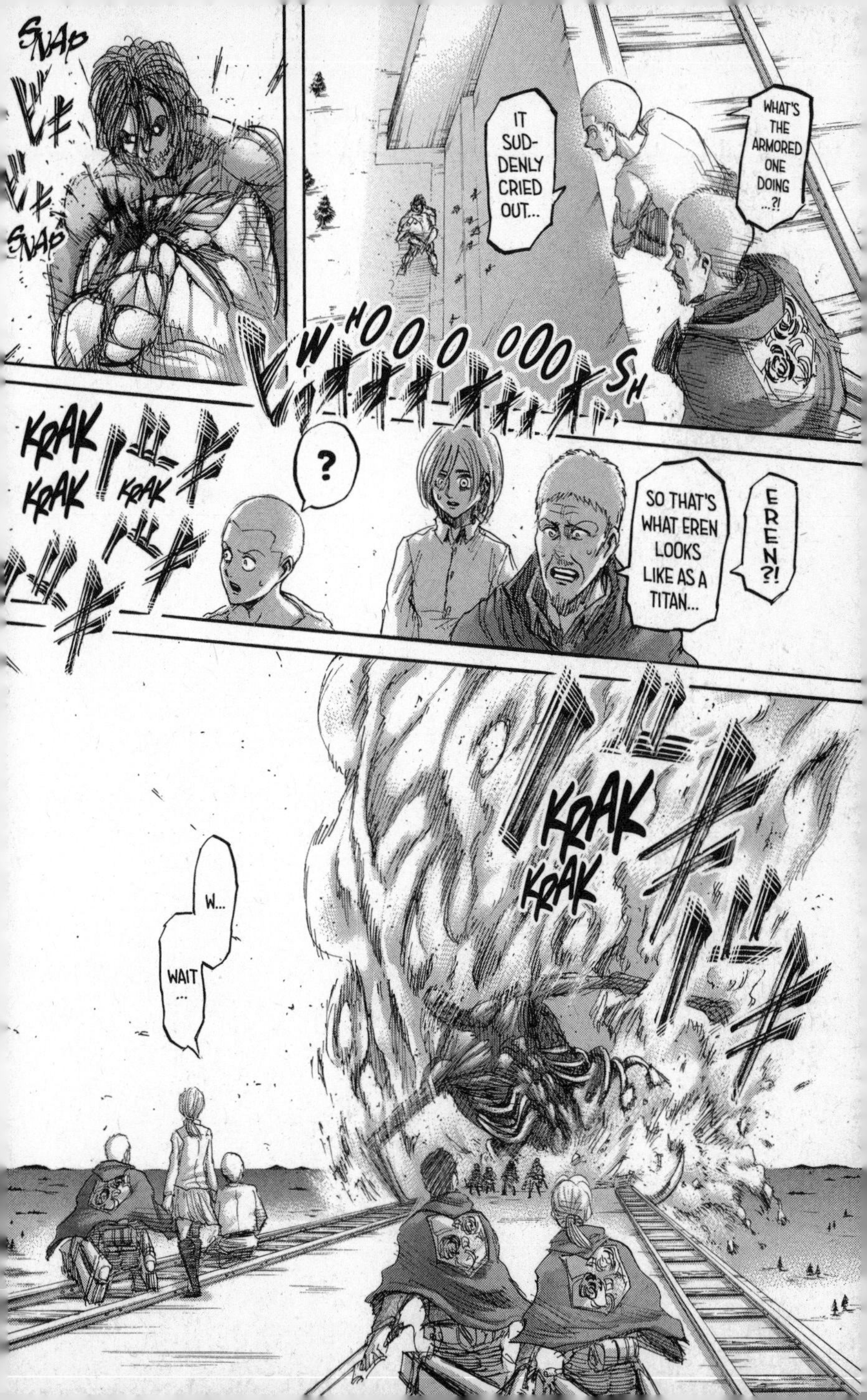
WHAT'S THE ARMORED ONE DOING ...?!
IT SUD-DENLY CRIED OUT...
WHOOOO OOOOSH
SNAP
SNAP
EREN?!
SO THAT'S WHAT EREN LOOKS LIKE AS A TITAN...
?
KRAK KRAK KRAK
KRAK KRAK
W...
WAIT ...

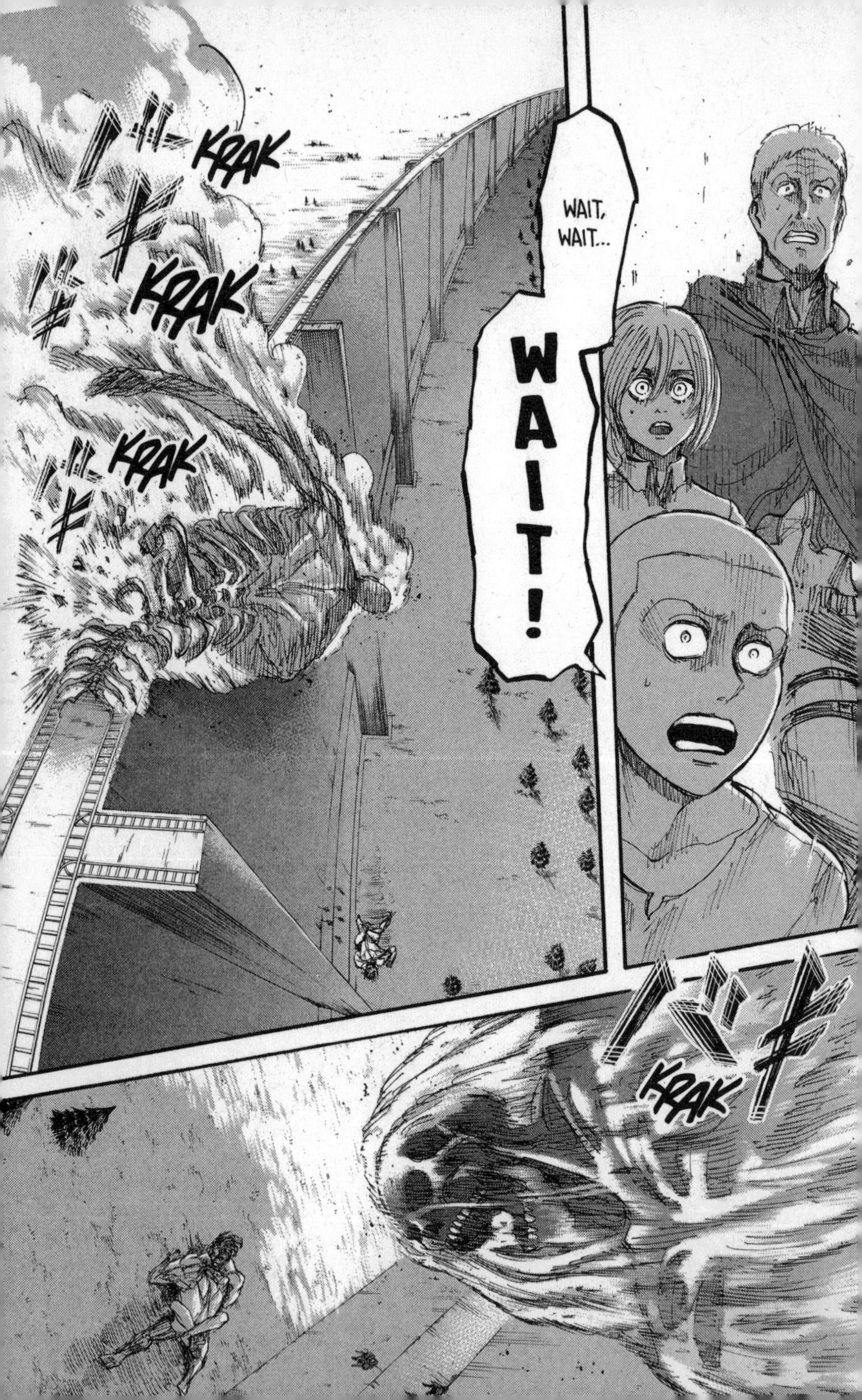
WAIT, WAIT...
WAIT!
KRAK
KRAK
KRAK
KRAK

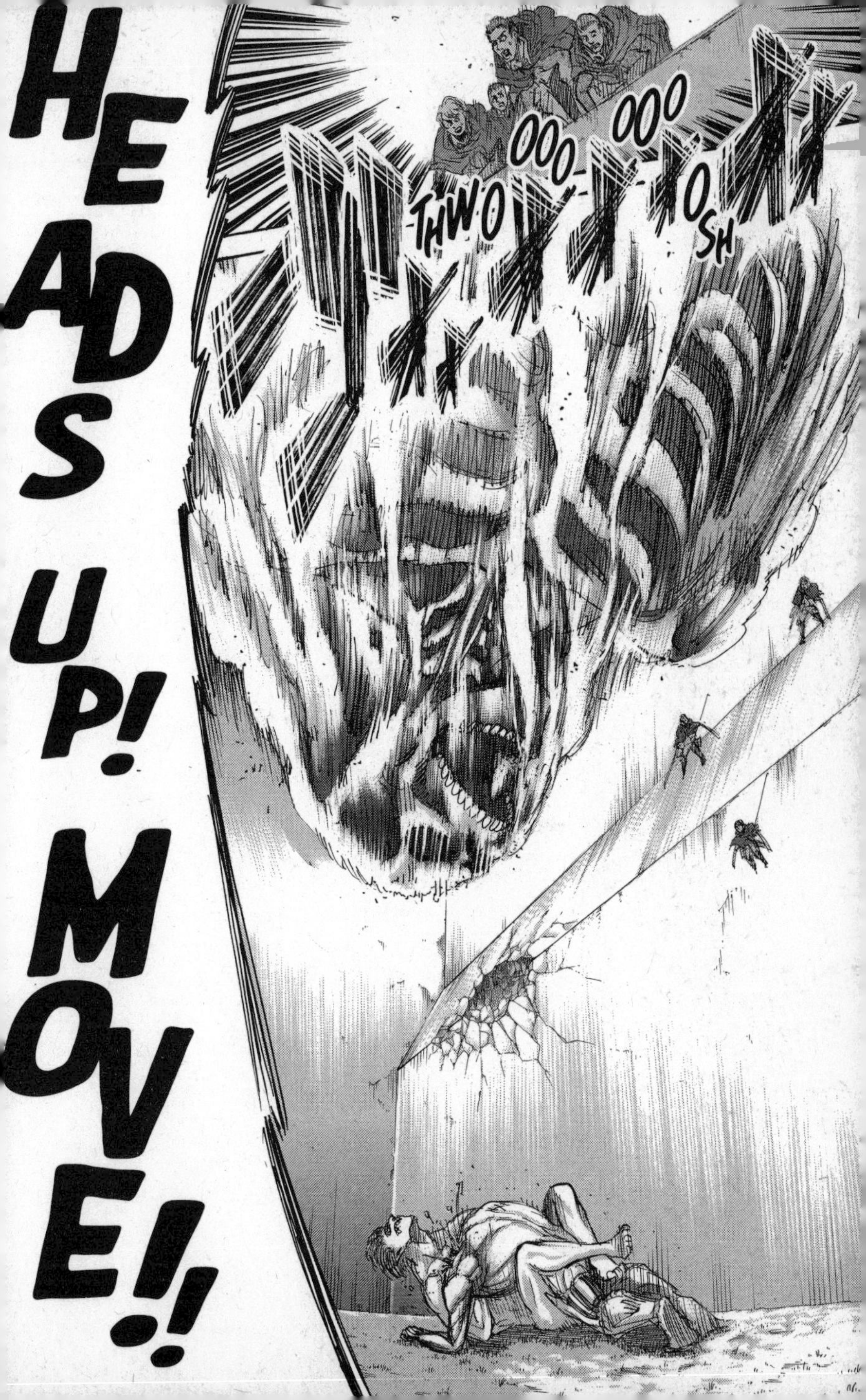
HEADS UP! MOVE!!
THWOOO-OOO-OOSH

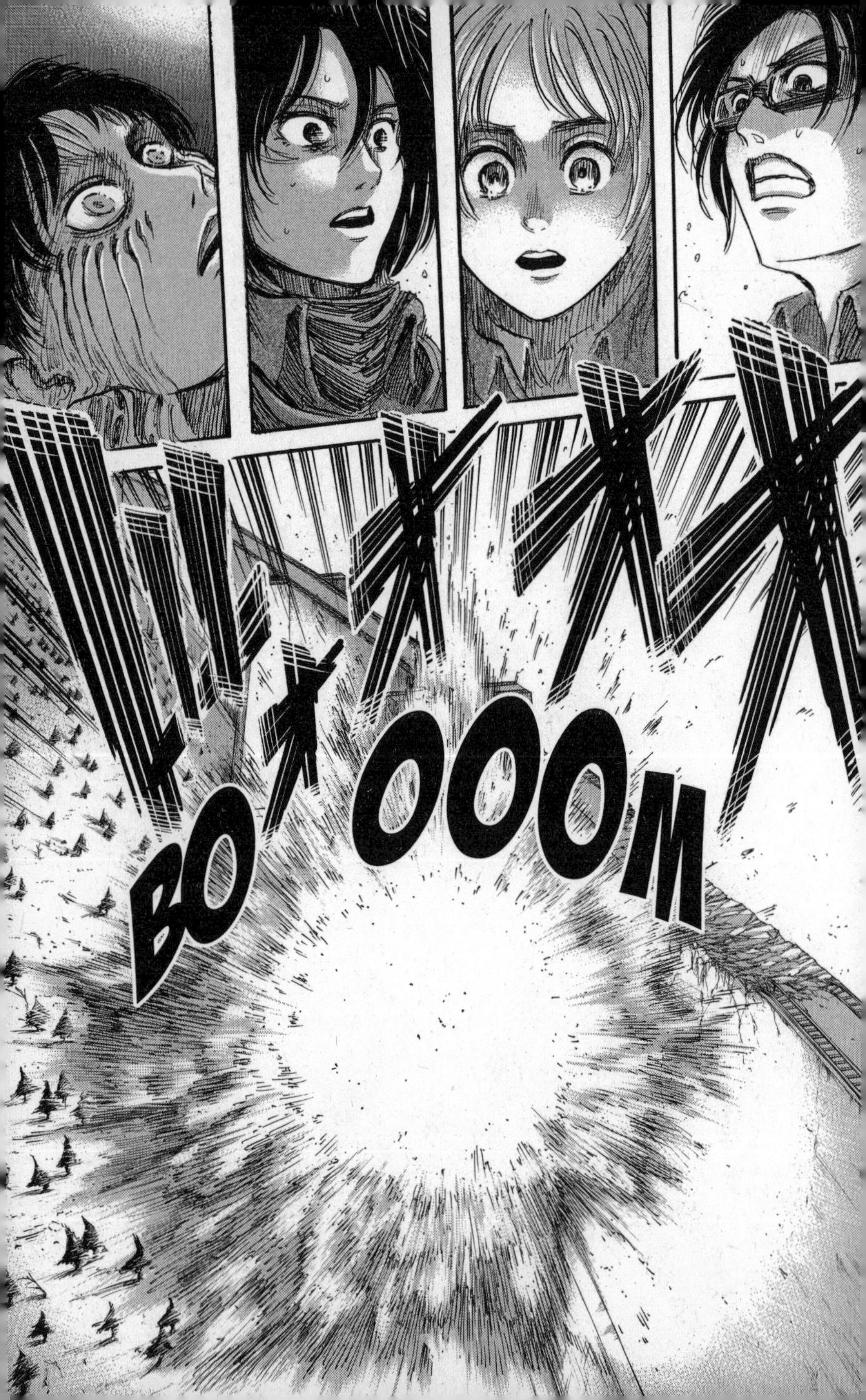
BOOOOM

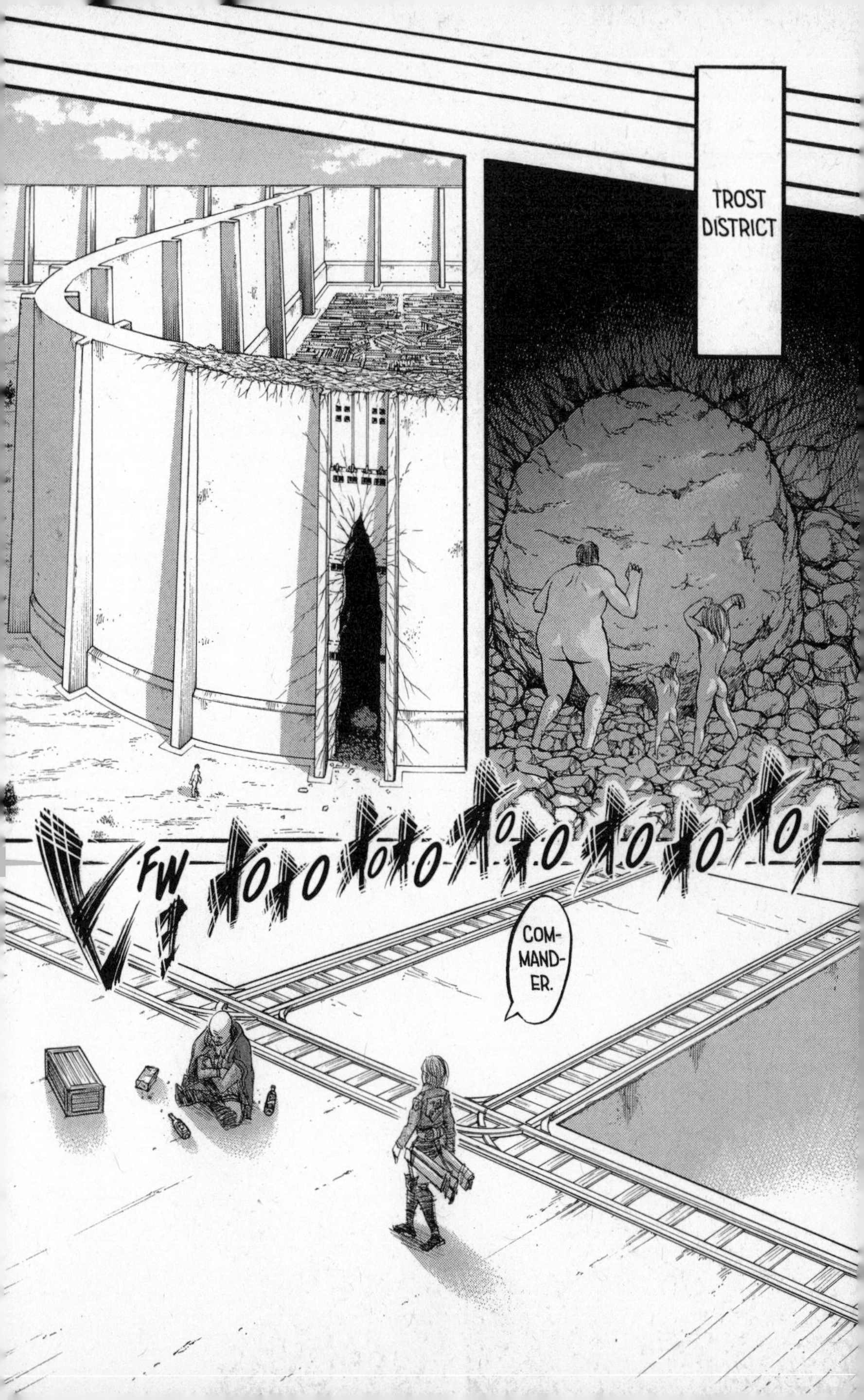
TROST DISTRICT
FWVOOOOOOOOOOOOO
COM-MAND-ER.

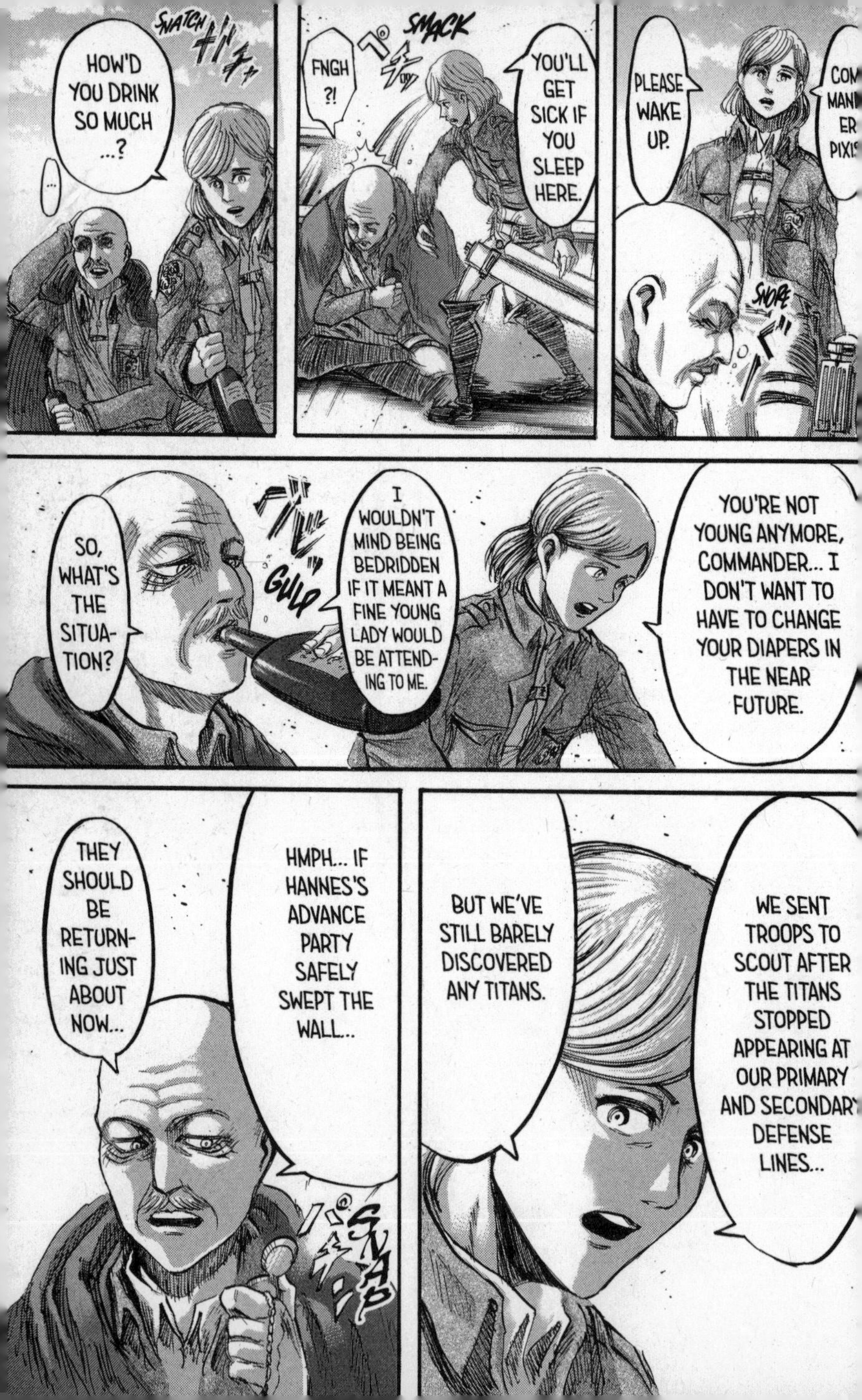
COM MAN ER PIXIS
PLEASE WAKE UP.
SNORE
YOU'LL GET SICK IF YOU SLEEP HERE.
SMACK
FNGH ?!
SNATCH
HOW'D YOU DRINK SO MUCH ...?
...
YOU'RE NOT YOUNG ANYMORE, COMMANDER... I DON'T WANT TO HAVE TO CHANGE YOUR DIAPERS IN THE NEAR FUTURE.
I WOULDN'T MIND BEING BEDRIDDEN IF IT MEANT A FINE YOUNG LADY WOULD BE ATTENDING TO ME.
GULP
SO, WHAT'S THE SITUATION?
WE SENT TROOPS TO SCOUT AFTER THE TITANS STOPPED APPEARING AT OUR PRIMARY AND SECONDARY DEFENSE LINES...
BUT WE'VE STILL BARELY DISCOVERED ANY TITANS.
HMPH... IF HANNES'S ADVANCE PARTY SAFELY SWEPT THE WALL...
THEY SHOULD BE RETURNING JUST ABOUT NOW...
SNAP

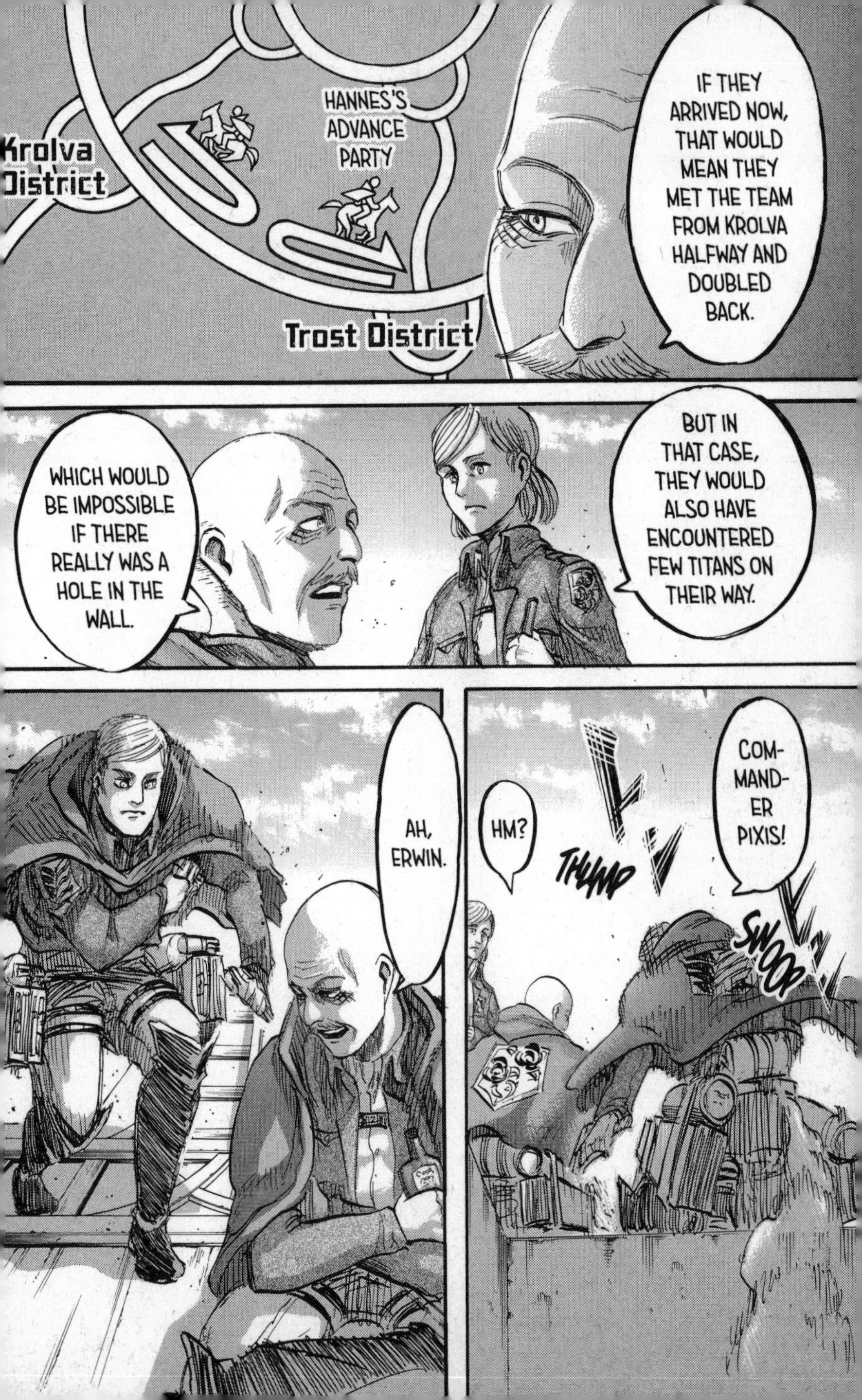
IF THEY ARRIVED NOW, THAT WOULD MEAN THEY MET THE TEAM FROM KROLVA HALFWAY AND DOUBLED BACK.
HANNES'S ADVANCE PARTY
Krolva District
Trost District
BUT IN THAT CASE, THEY WOULD ALSO HAVE ENCOUNTERED FEW TITANS ON THEIR WAY.
WHICH WOULD BE IMPOSSIBLE IF THERE REALLY WAS A HOLE IN THE WALL.
COM-MAND-ER PIXIS!
SWOOP
THUMP
HM?
AH, ERWIN.

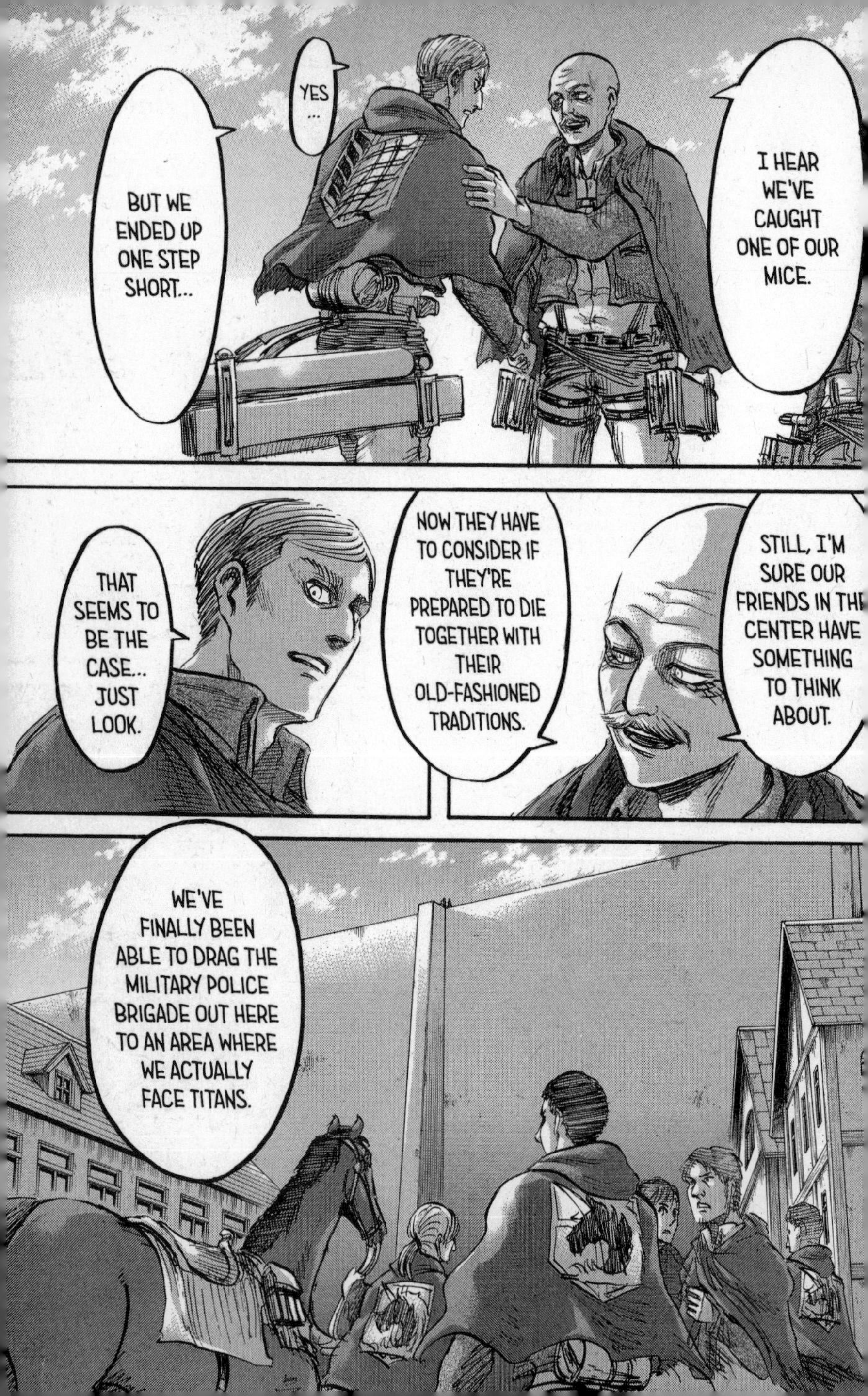
I HEAR WE'VE CAUGHT ONE OF OUR MICE.
YES ...
BUT WE ENDED UP ONE STEP SHORT...
STILL, I'M SURE OUR FRIENDS IN THE CENTER HAVE SOMETHING TO THINK ABOUT.
NOW THEY HAVE TO CONSIDER IF THEY'RE PREPARED TO DIE TOGETHER WITH THEIR OLD-FASHIONED TRADITIONS.
THAT SEEMS TO BE THE CASE... JUST LOOK.
WE'VE FINALLY BEEN ABLE TO DRAG THE MILITARY POLICE BRIGADE OUT HERE TO AN AREA WHERE WE ACTUALLY FACE TITANS.

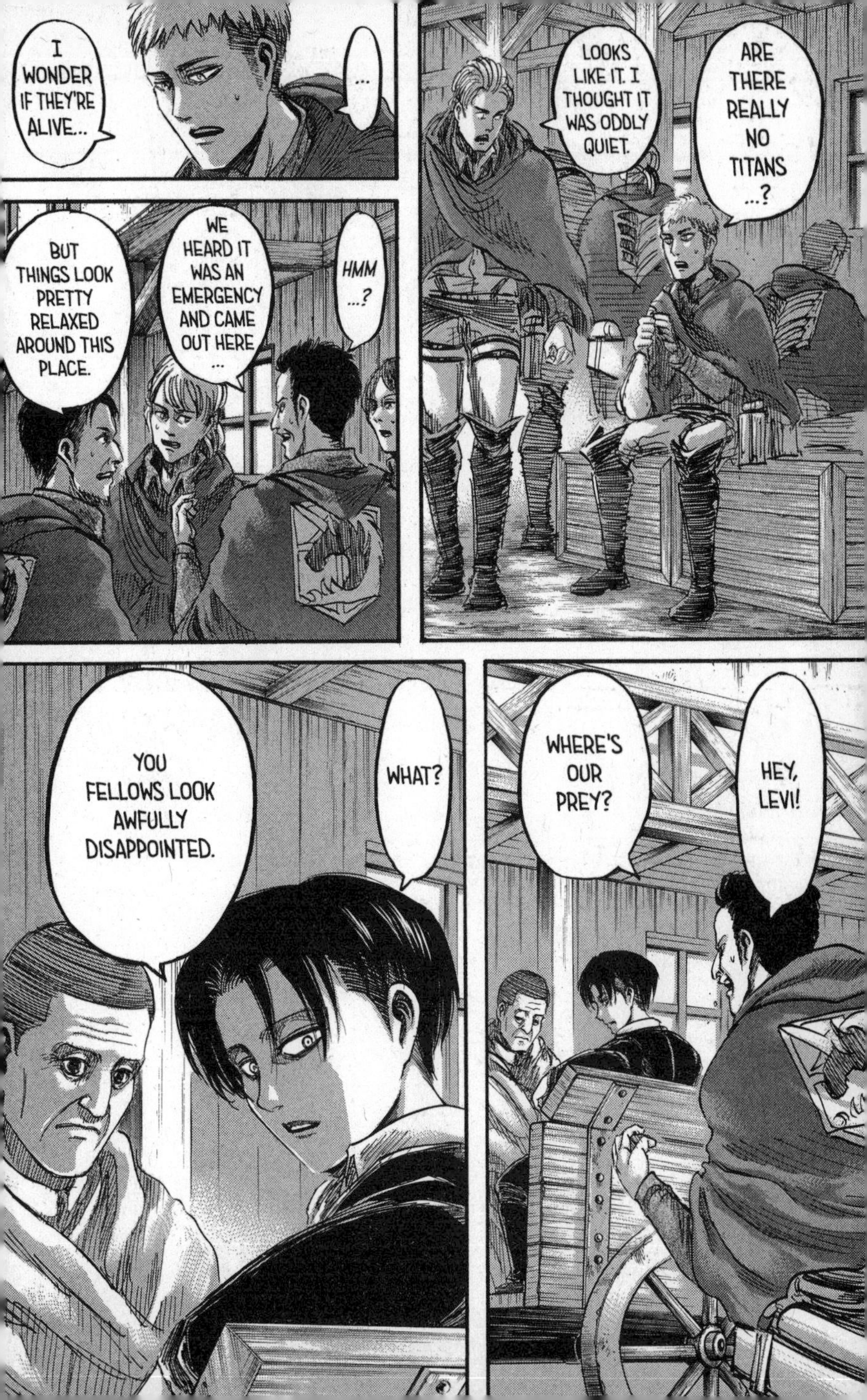
ARE THERE REALLY NO TITANS ...?
LOOKS LIKE IT. I THOUGHT IT WAS ODDLY QUIET.
...
I WONDER IF THEY'RE ALIVE...
HMM ...?
WE HEARD IT WAS AN EMERGENCY AND CAME OUT HERE ...
BUT THINGS LOOK PRETTY RELAXED AROUND THIS PLACE.
HEY, LEVI!
WHERE'S OUR PREY?
WHAT?
YOU FELLOWS LOOK AWFULLY DISAPPOINTED.

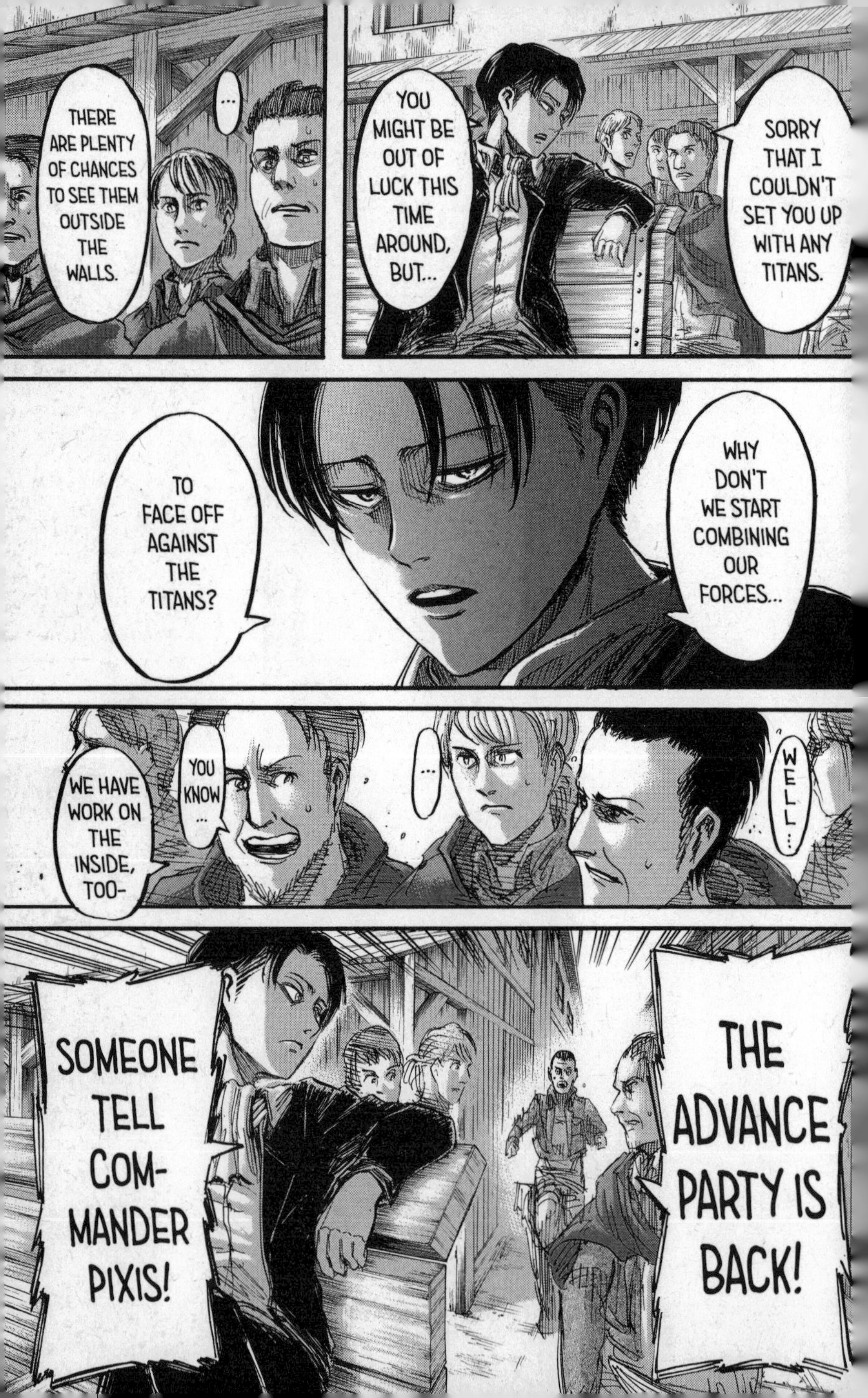
SORRY THAT I COULDN'T SET YOU UP WITH ANY TITANS.
YOU MIGHT BE OUT OF LUCK THIS TIME AROUND, BUT...
...
THERE ARE PLENTY OF CHANCES TO SEE THEM OUTSIDE THE WALLS.
WHY DON'T WE START COMBINING OUR FORCES...
TO FACE OFF AGAINST THE TITANS?
WELL...
...
YOU KNOW...
WE HAVE WORK ON THE INSIDE, TOO-
THE ADVANCE PARTY IS BACK!
SOMEONE TELL COM-MANDER PIXIS!

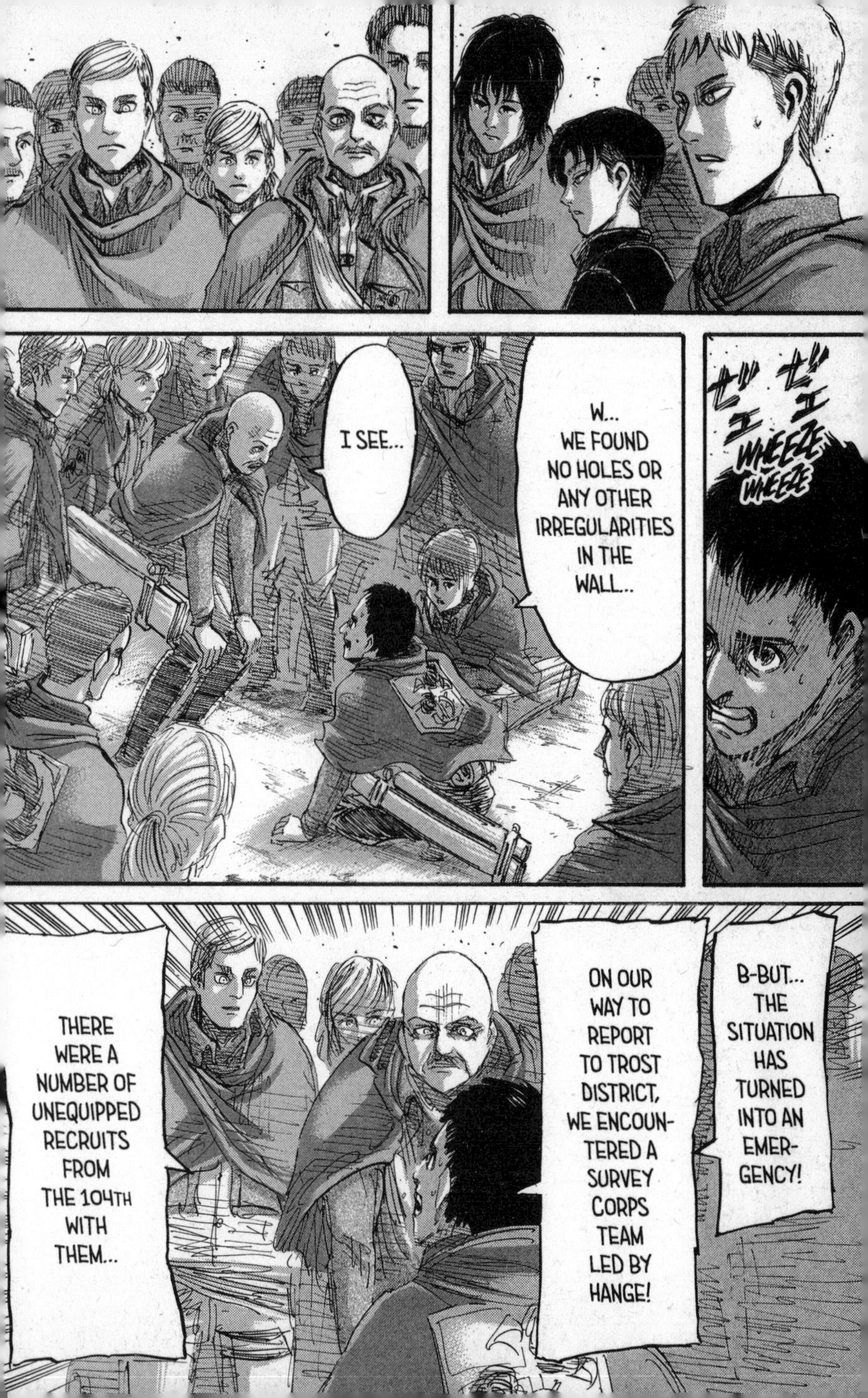
ゼェ ゼェ
WHEEZE WHEEZE
W... WE FOUND NO HOLES OR ANY OTHER IRREGULARITIES IN THE WALL...
I SEE...
B-BUT... THE SITUATION HAS TURNED INTO AN EMER-GENCY!
ON OUR WAY TO REPORT TO TROST DISTRICT, WE ENCOUN-TERED A SURVEY CORPS TEAM LED BY HANGE!
THERE WERE A NUMBER OF UNEQUIPPED RECRUITS FROM THE 104TH WITH THEM...

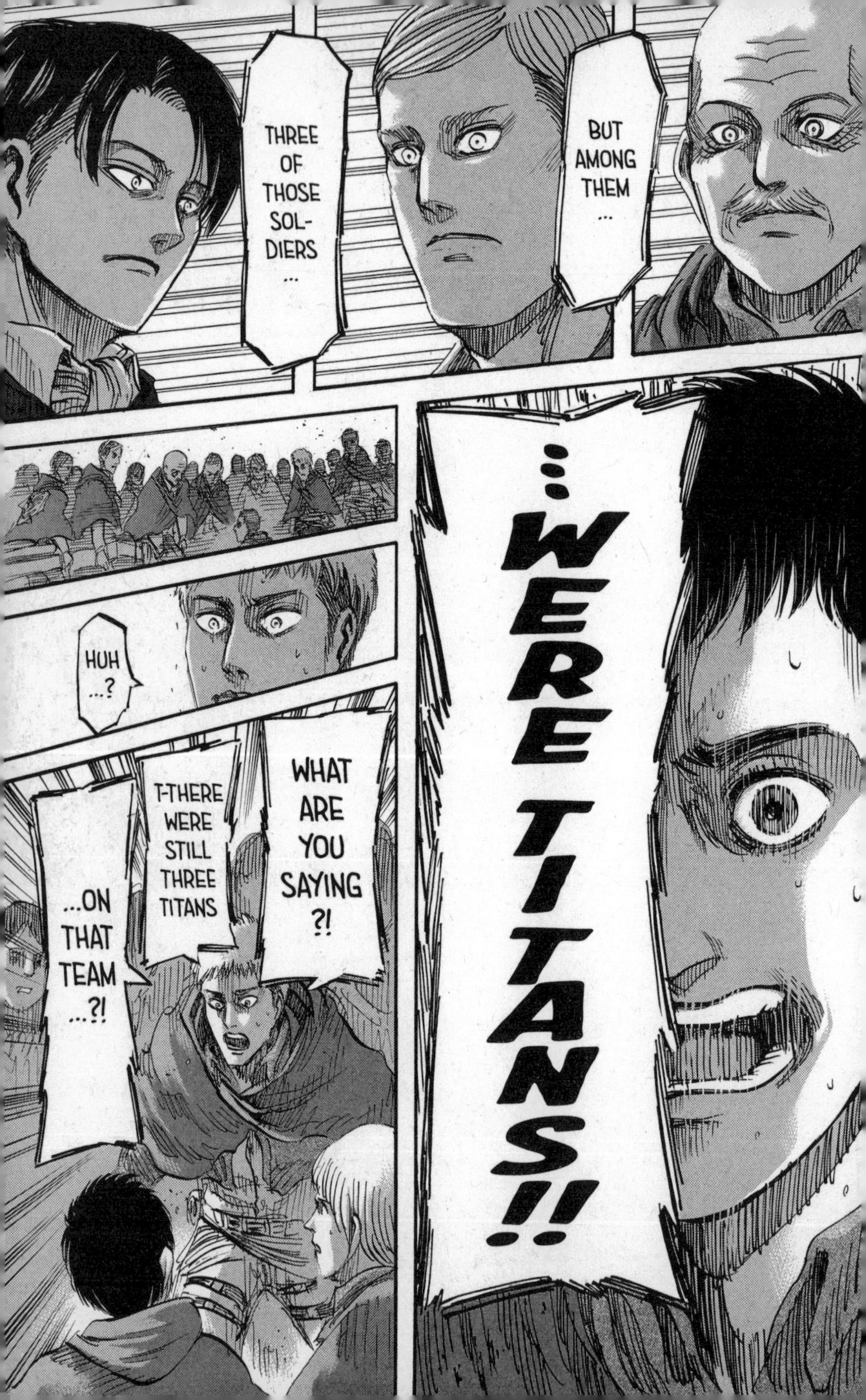

BUT AMONG THEM ...
THREE OF THOSE SOLDIERS ...
...WERE TITANS!!
HUH ...?
WHAT ARE YOU SAYING ?!
T-THERE WERE STILL THREE TITANS
...ON THAT TEAM ...?!

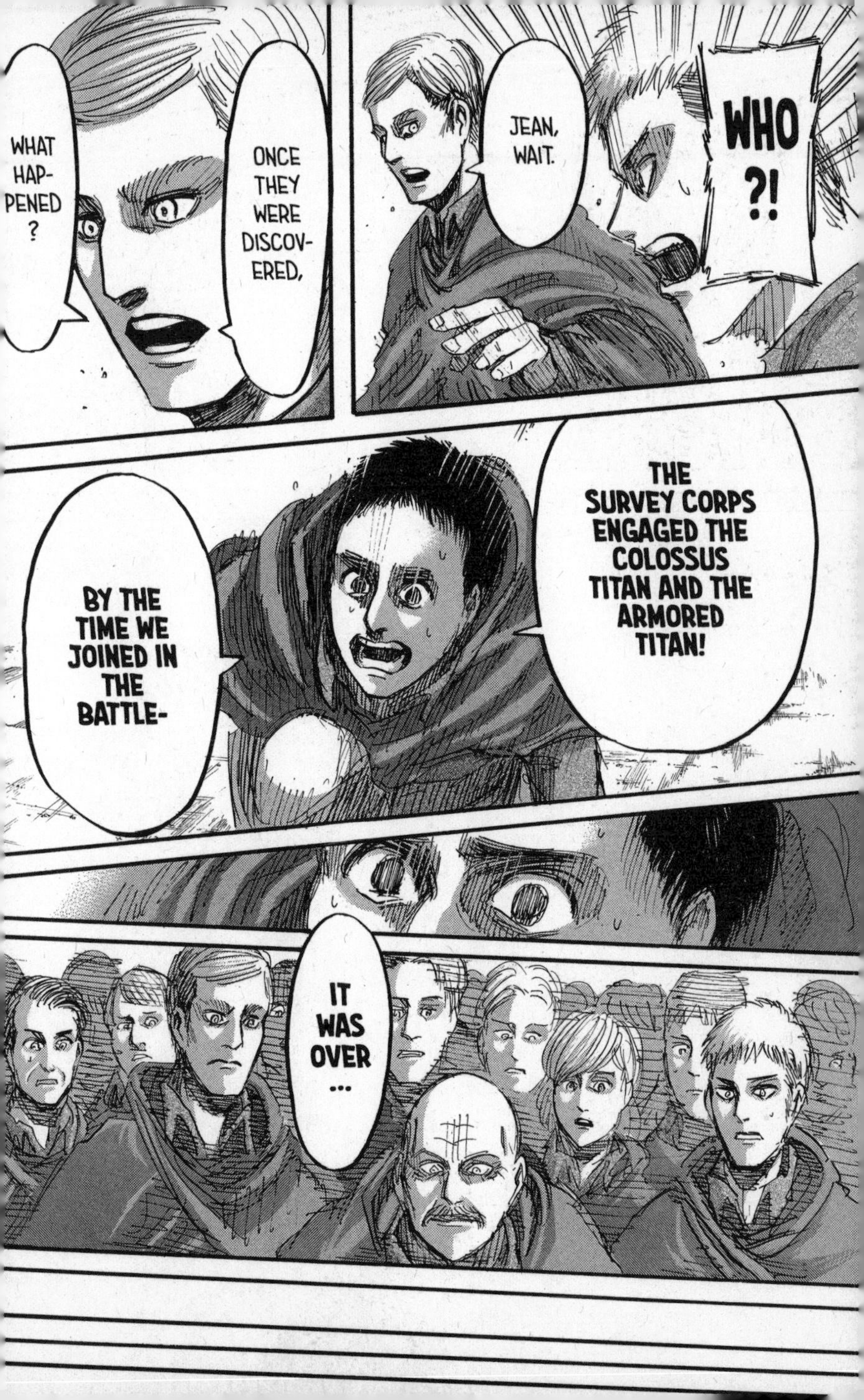
WHO ?!
JEAN, WAIT.
ONCE THEY WERE DISCOVERED,
WHAT HAPPENED ?
THE SURVEY CORPS ENGAGED THE COLOSSUS TITAN AND THE ARMORED TITAN!
BY THE TIME WE JOINED IN THE BATTLE-
IT WAS OVER ...

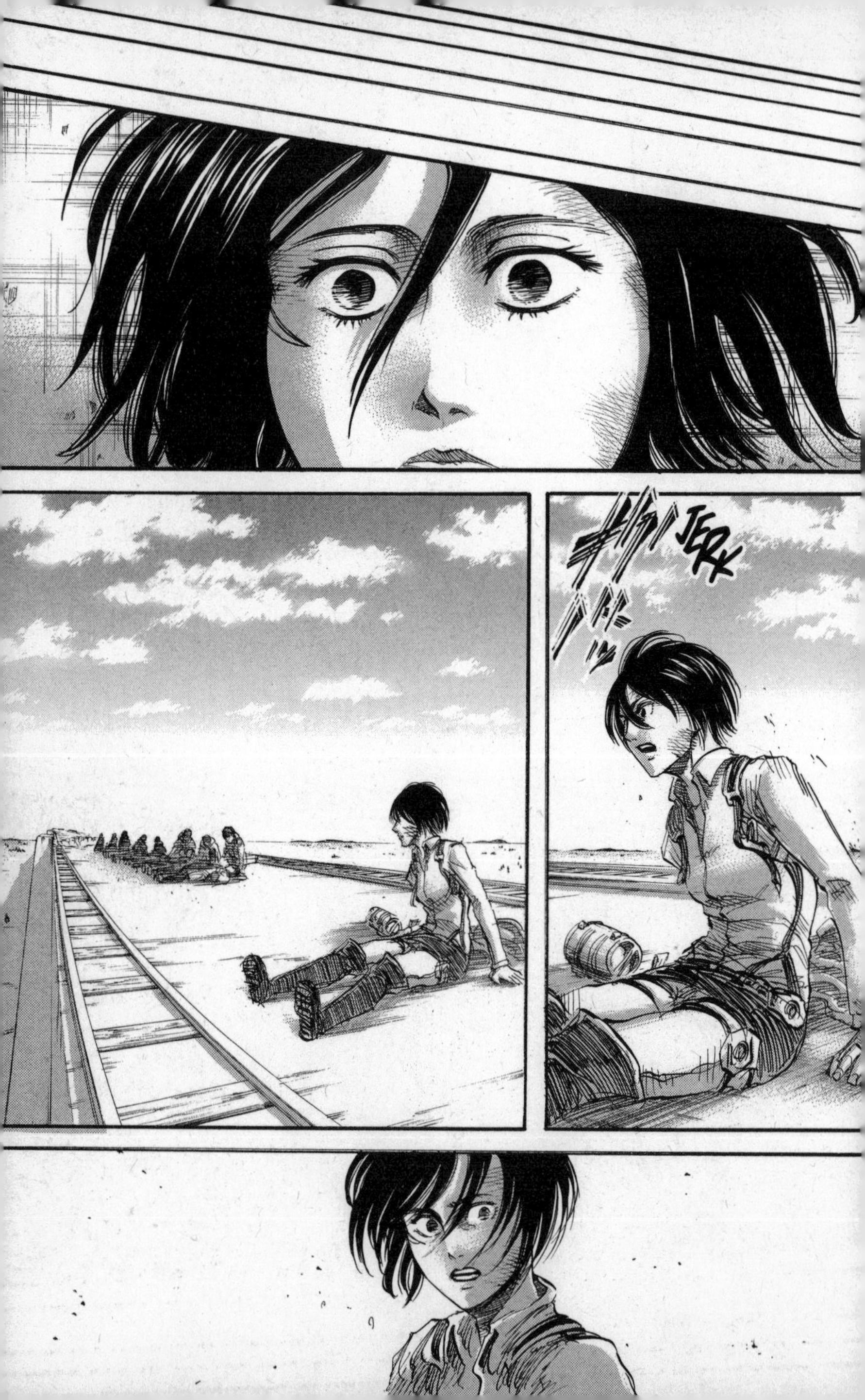
JERK

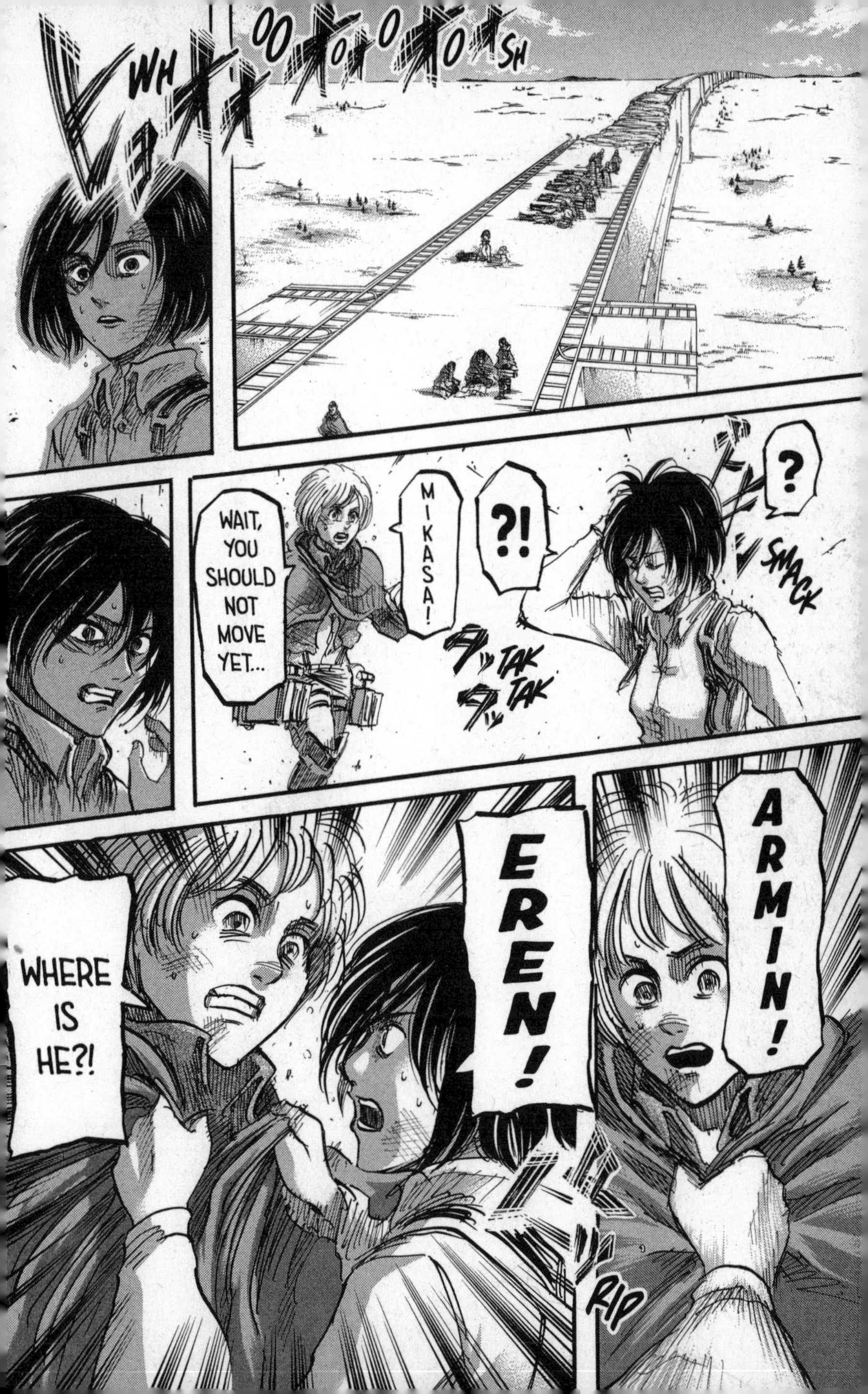
WHOOOOSH
?
SMACK
?!
MIKASA!
TAK TAK
WAIT, YOU SHOULD NOT MOVE YET...
ARMIN!
EREN!
WHERE IS HE?!
RIP

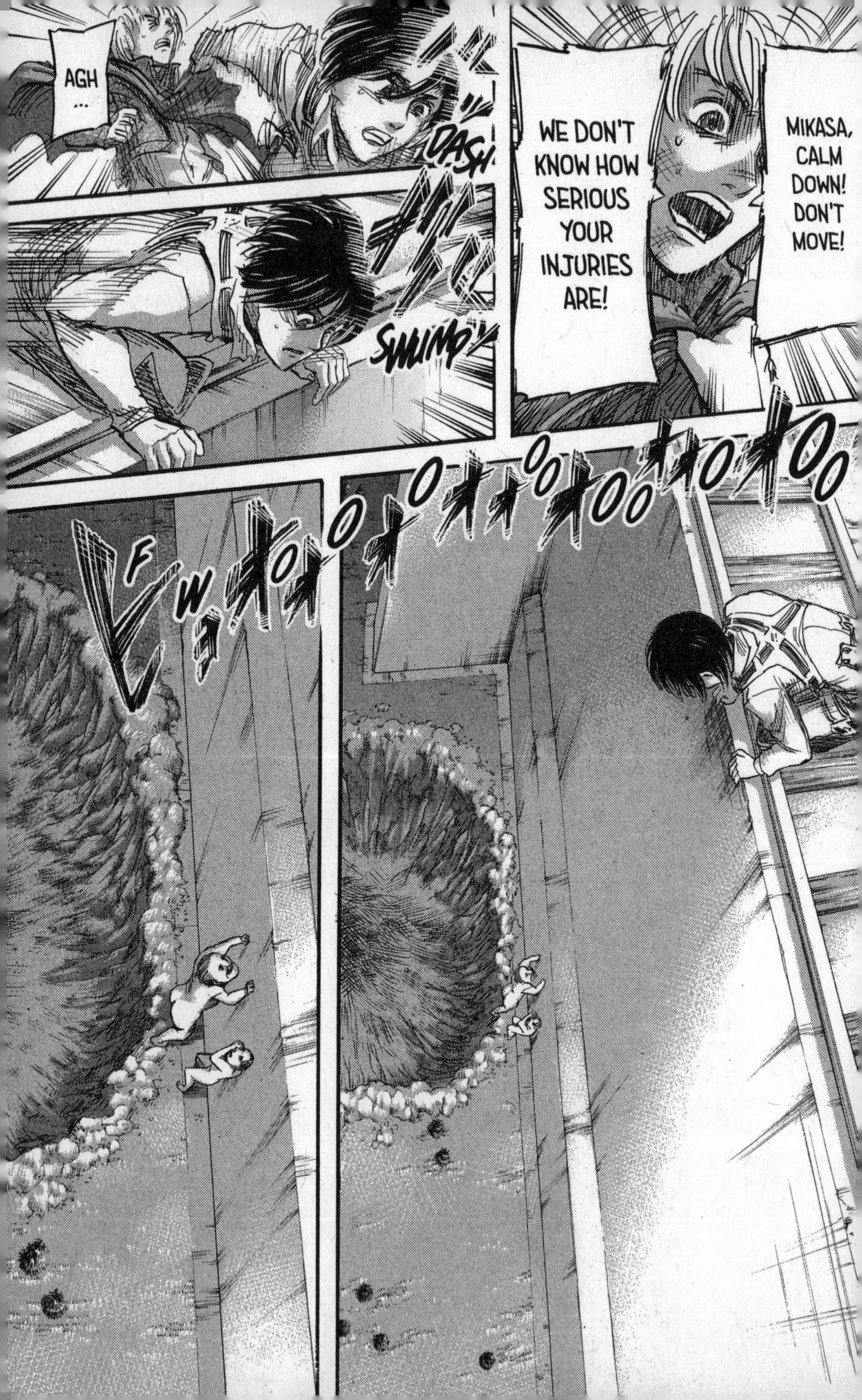
MIKASA, CALM DOWN! DON'T MOVE!
WE DON'T KNOW HOW SERIOUS YOUR INJURIES ARE!
AGH ...
DASH
SWUMP
FWOOOO

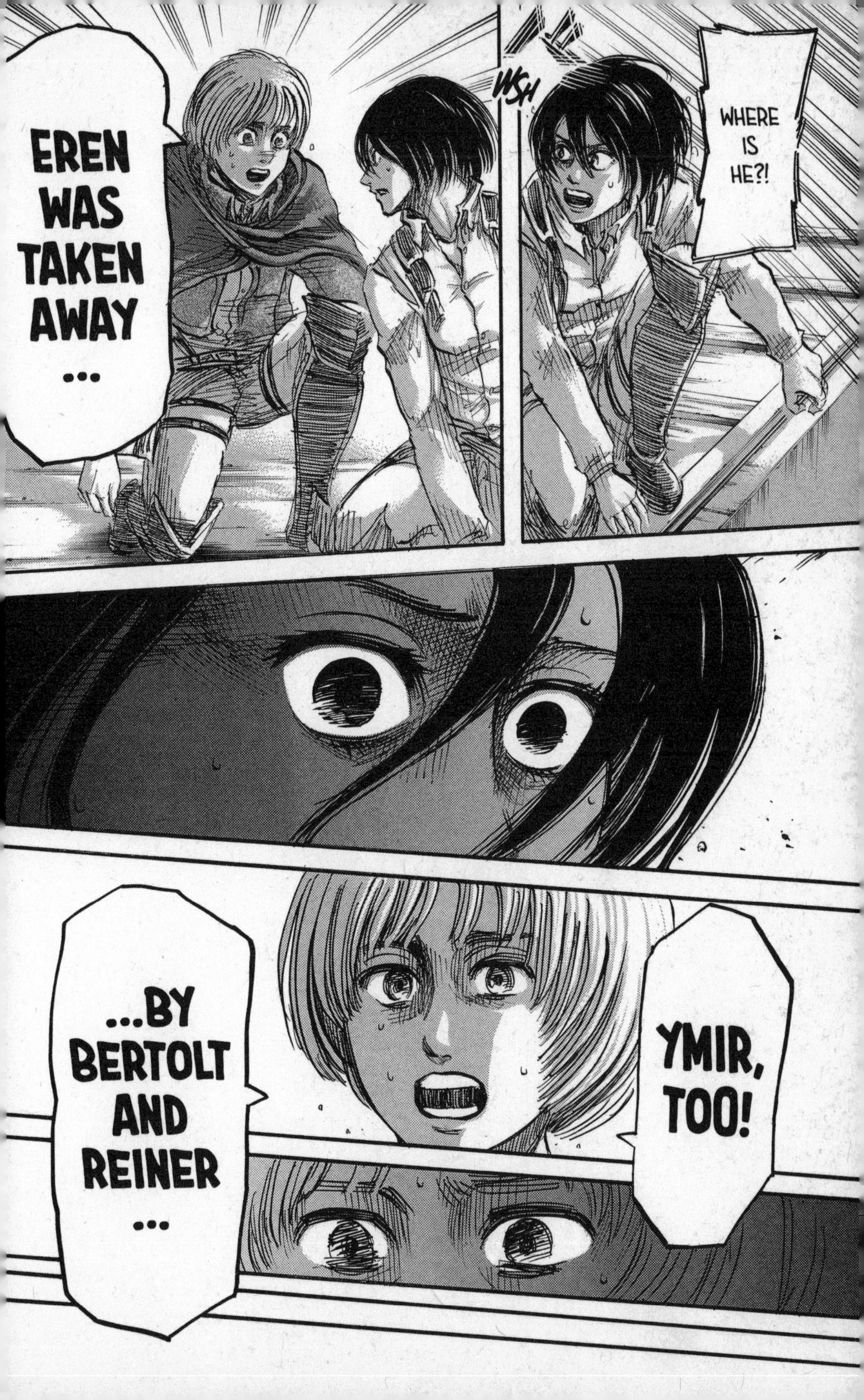
WSH
WHERE IS HE?!
EREN WAS TAKEN AWAY...
...BY BERTOLT AND REINER...
YMIR, TOO!

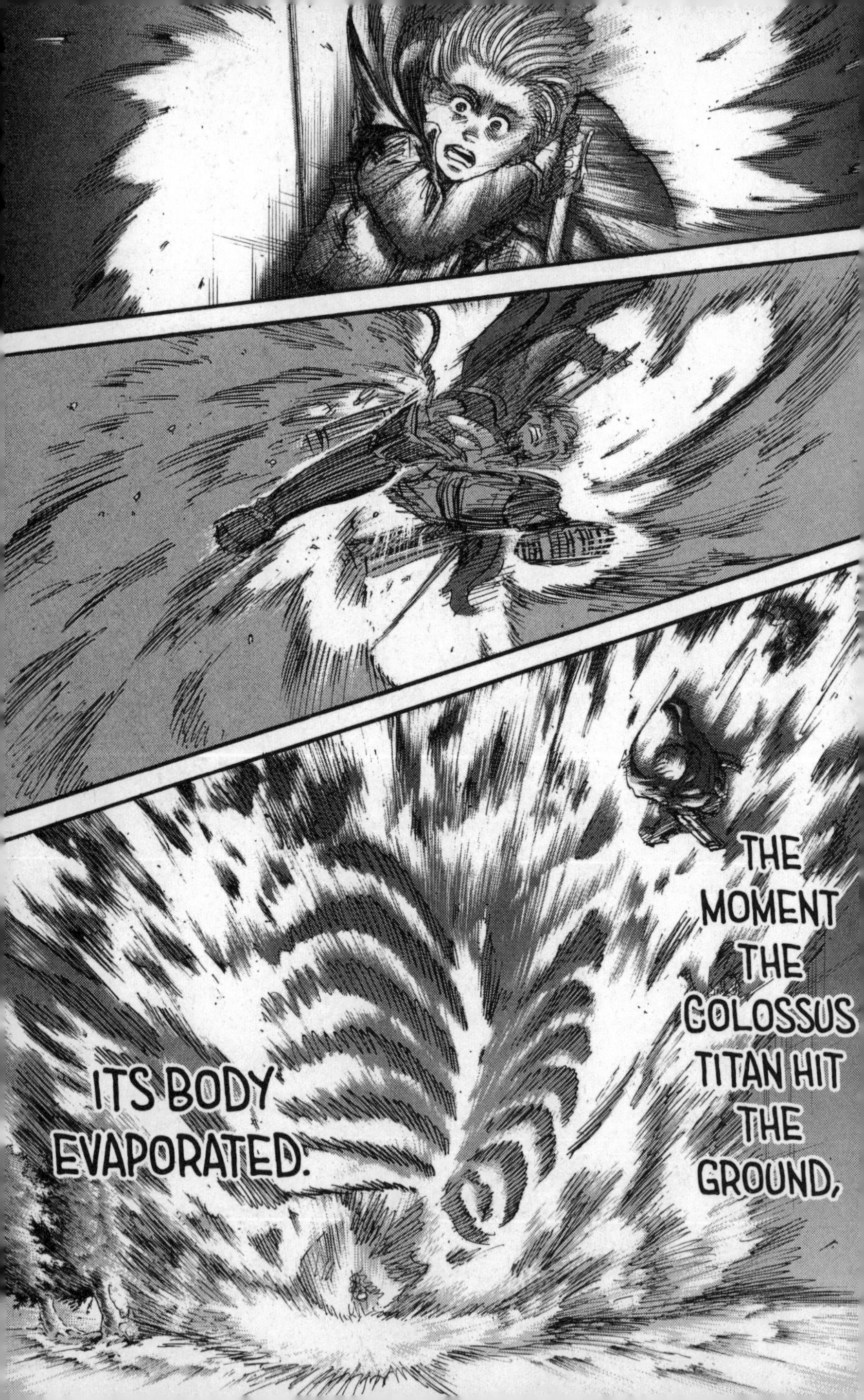
THE MOMENT THE COLOSSUS TITAN HIT THE GROUND,
ITS BODY EVAPORATED.

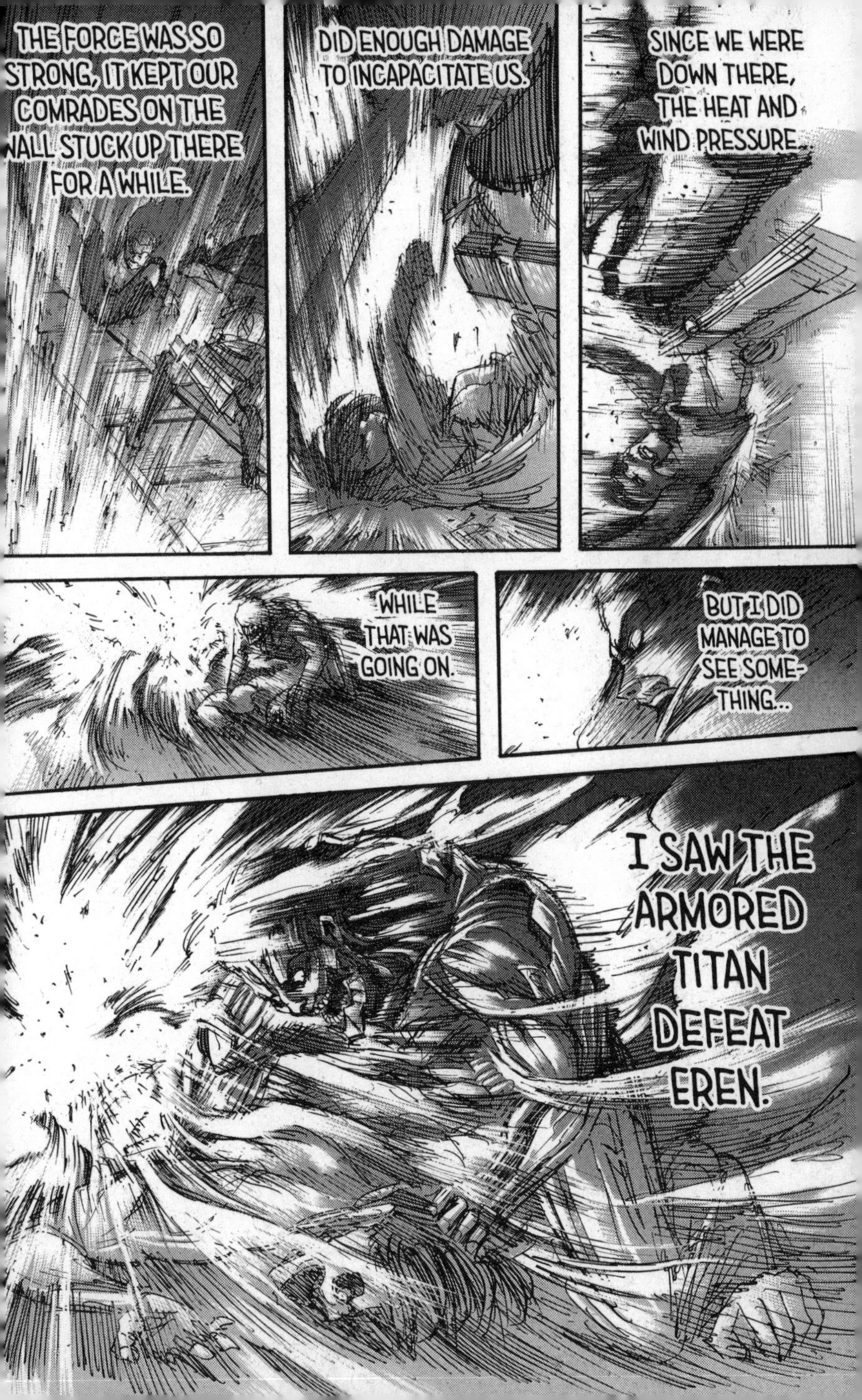
SINCE WE WERE DOWN THERE, THE HEAT AND WIND PRESSURE...
DID ENOUGH DAMAGE TO INCAPACITATE US.
THE FORCE WAS SO STRONG, IT KEPT OUR COMRADES ON THE WALL STUCK UP THERE FOR A WHILE.
BUT I DID MANAGE TO SEE SOME-THING...
WHILE THAT WAS GOING ON.
I SAW THE ARMORED TITAN DEFEAT EREN.

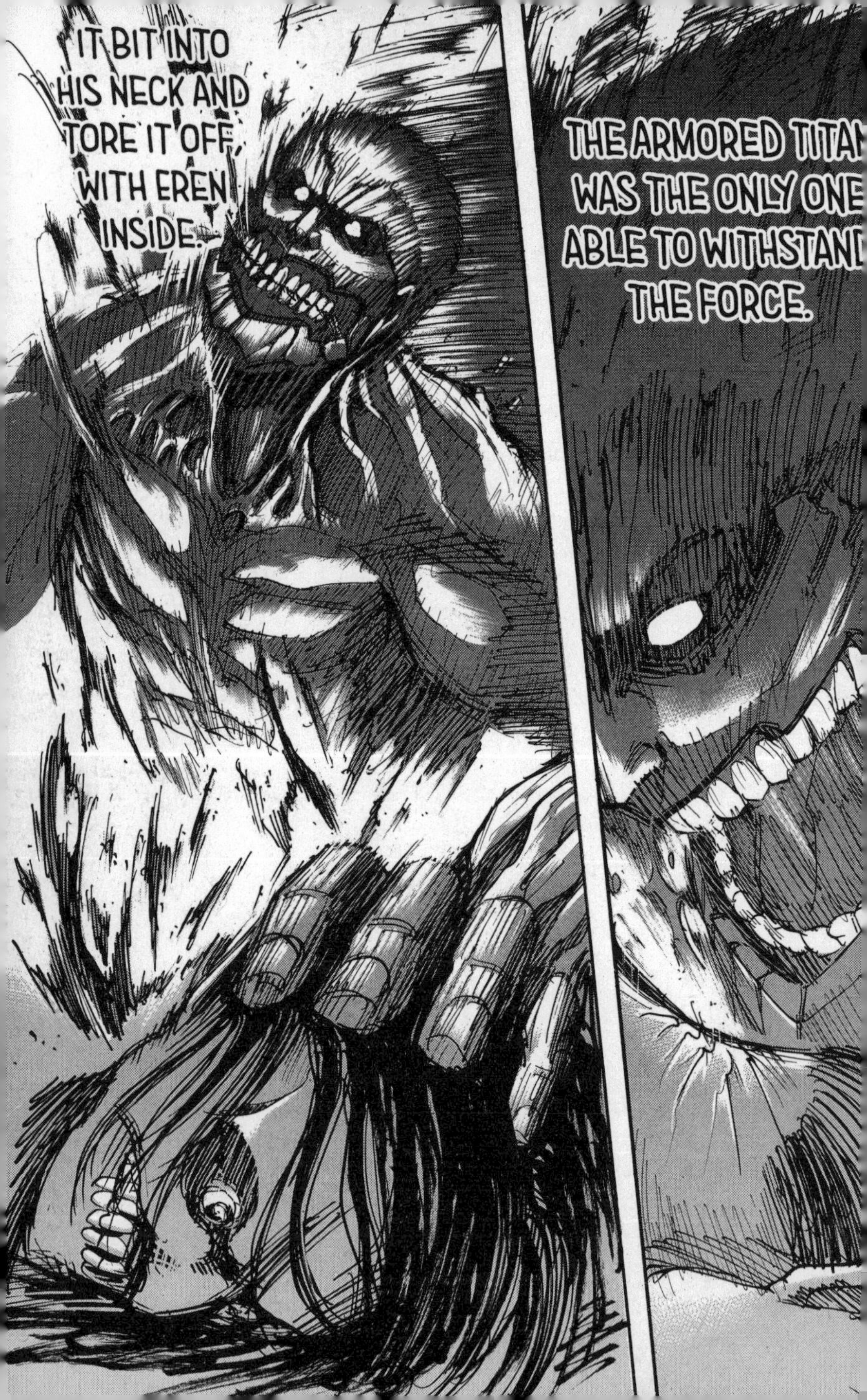
THE ARMORED TITAN WAS THE ONLY ONE ABLE TO WITHSTAND THE FORCE.
IT BIT INTO HIS NECK AND TORE IT OFF, WITH EREN INSIDE.

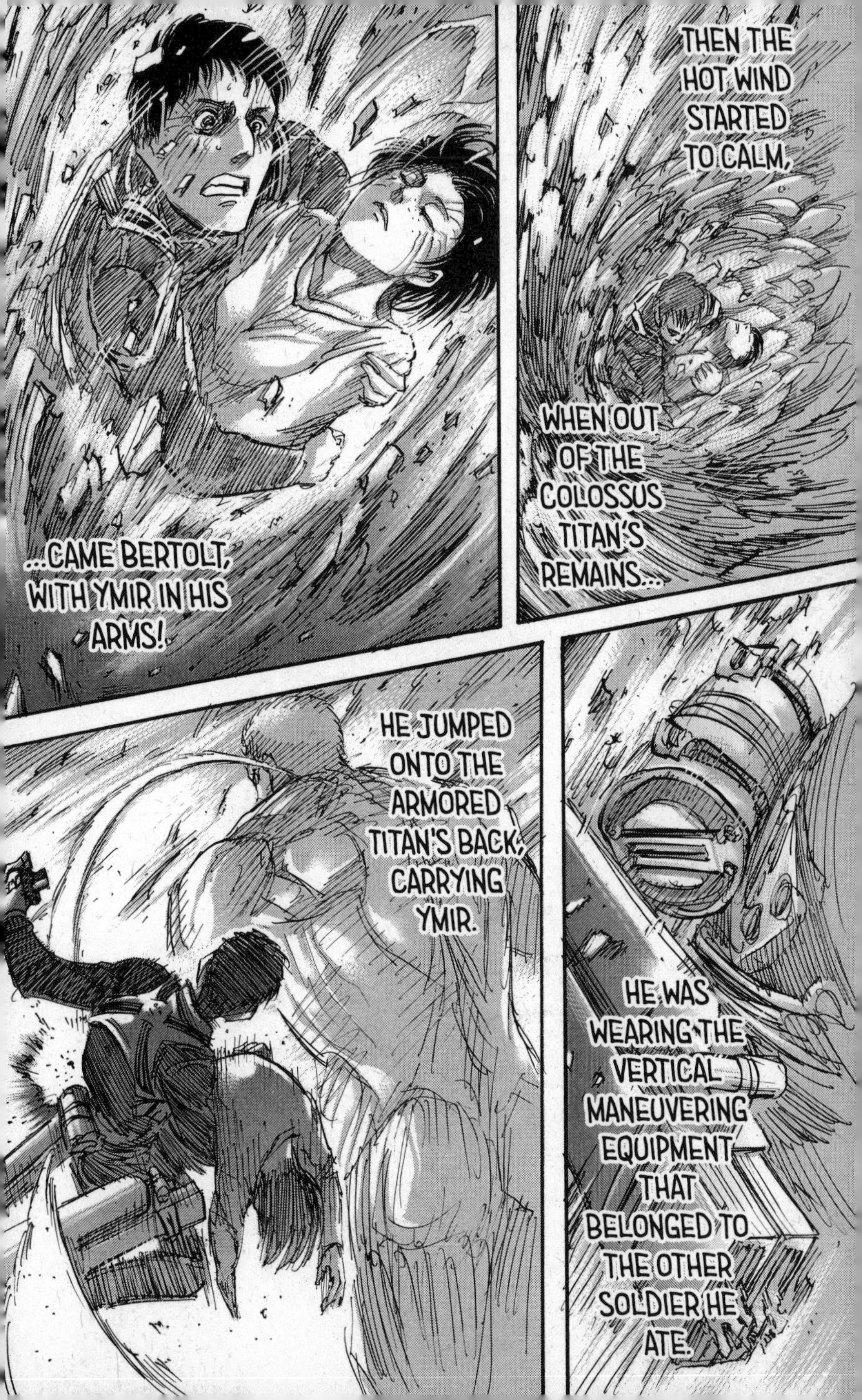
THEN THE HOT WIND STARTED TO CALM,
WHEN OUT OF THE COLOSSUS TITAN'S REMAINS...
...CAME BERTOLT, WITH YMIR IN HIS ARMS!
HE WAS WEARING THE VERTICAL MANEUVERING EQUIPMENT THAT BELONGED TO THE OTHER SOLDIER HE ATE.
HE JUMPED ONTO THE ARMORED TITAN'S BACK, CARRYING YMIR.

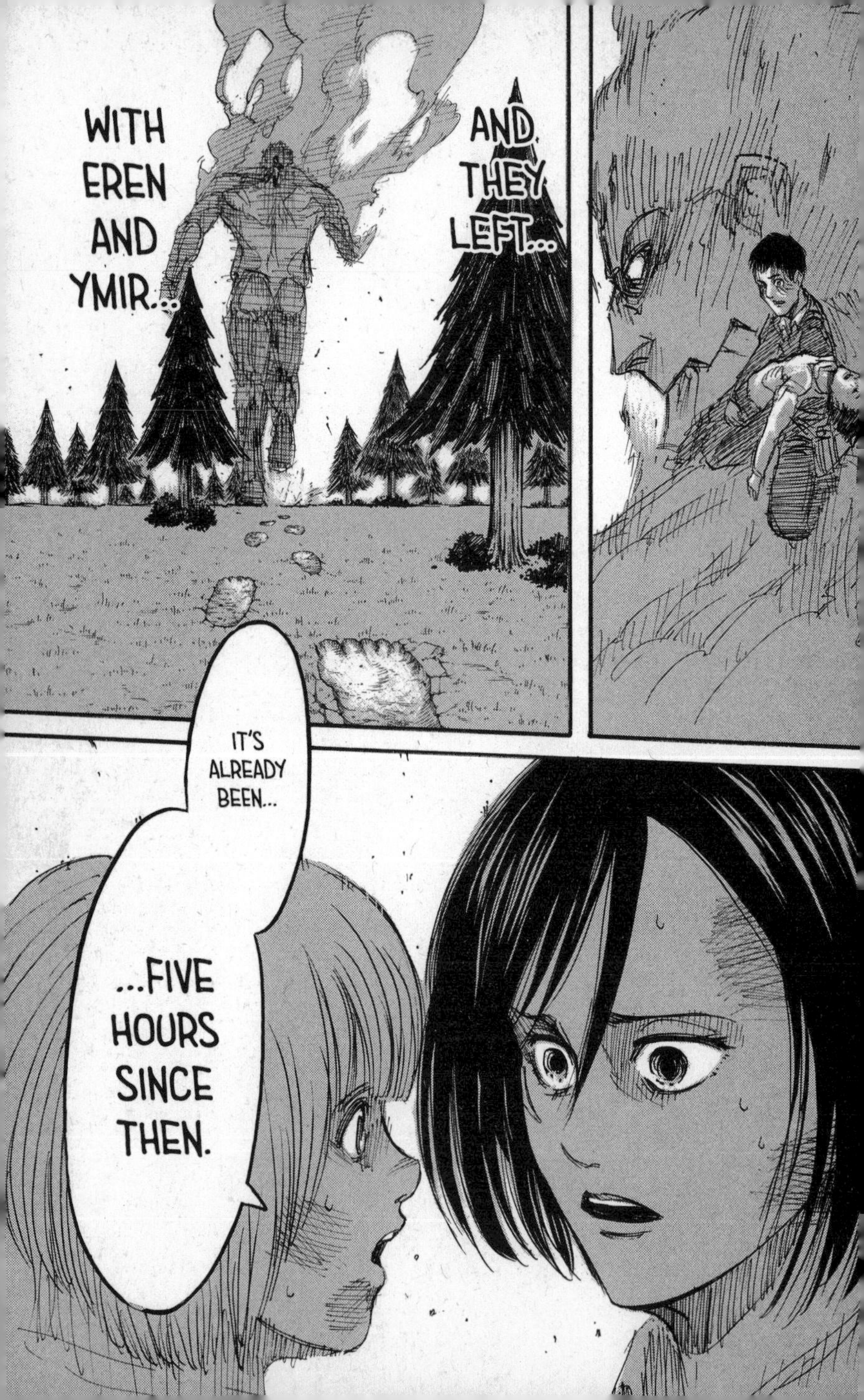
WITH EREN AND YMIR...
AND THEY LEFT...
IT'S ALREADY BEEN...
...FIVE HOURS SINCE THEN.

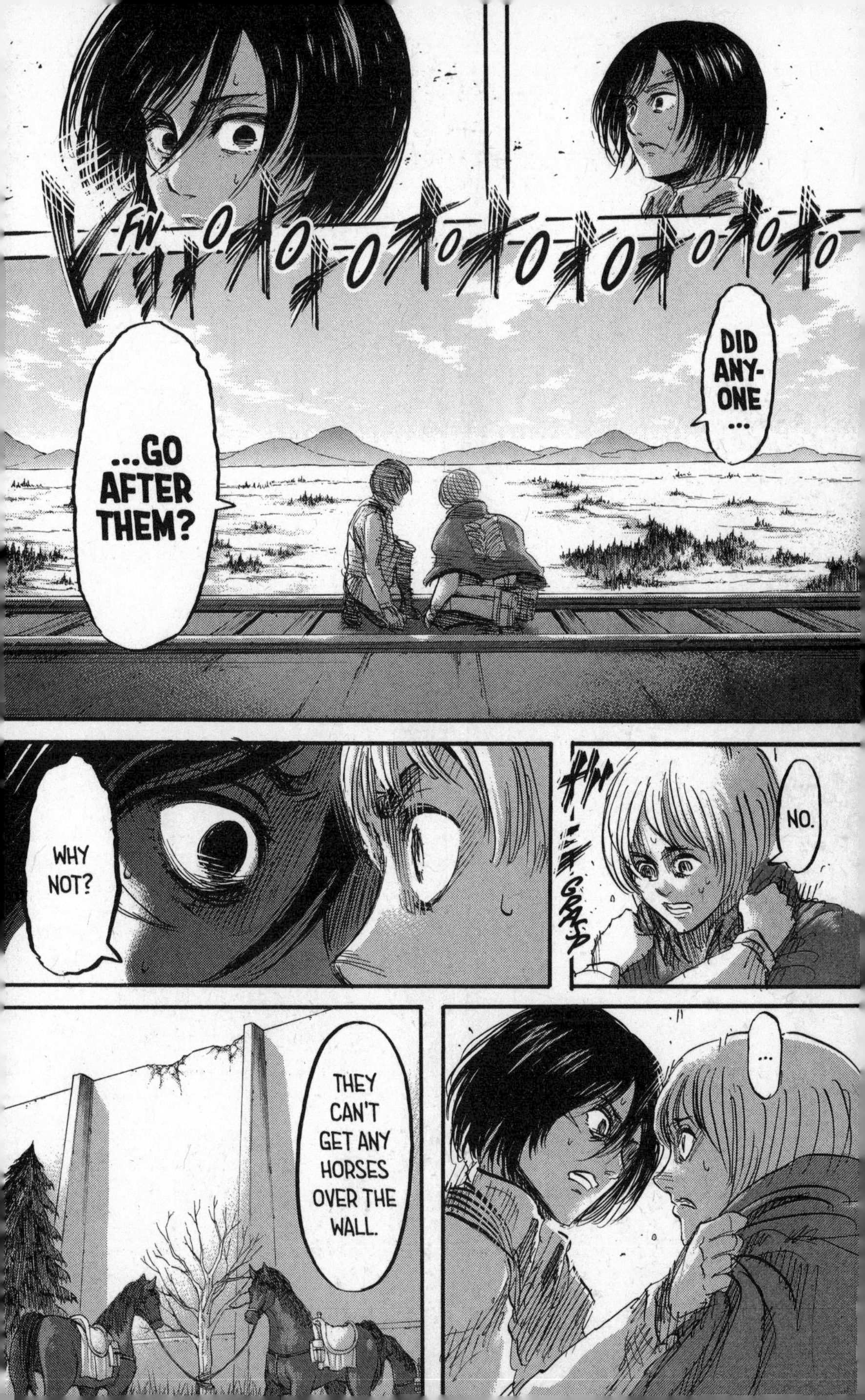
DID ANY-ONE...
...GO AFTER THEM?
NO.
WHY NOT?
...
THEY CAN'T GET ANY HORSES OVER THE WALL.

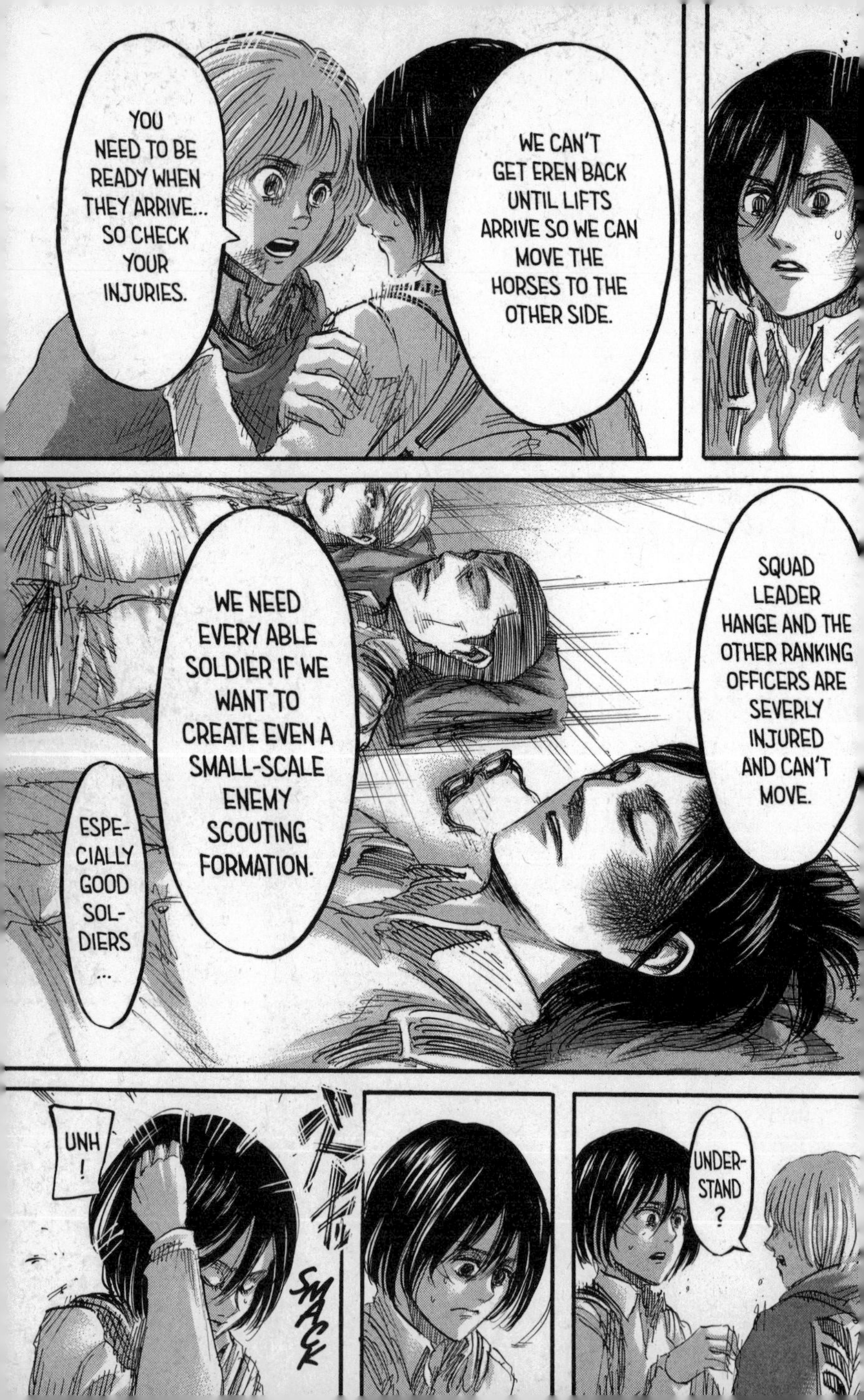
WE CAN'T GET EREN BACK UNTIL LIFTS ARRIVE SO WE CAN MOVE THE HORSES TO THE OTHER SIDE.
YOU NEED TO BE READY WHEN THEY ARRIVE... SO CHECK YOUR INJURIES.
SQUAD LEADER HANGE AND THE OTHER RANKING OFFICERS ARE SEVERLY INJURED AND CAN'T MOVE.
WE NEED EVERY ABLE SOLDIER IF WE WANT TO CREATE EVEN A SMALL-SCALE ENEMY SCOUTING FORMATION.
ESPE-CIALLY GOOD SOL-DIERS...
UNDER-STAND?
UNH!
SMACK

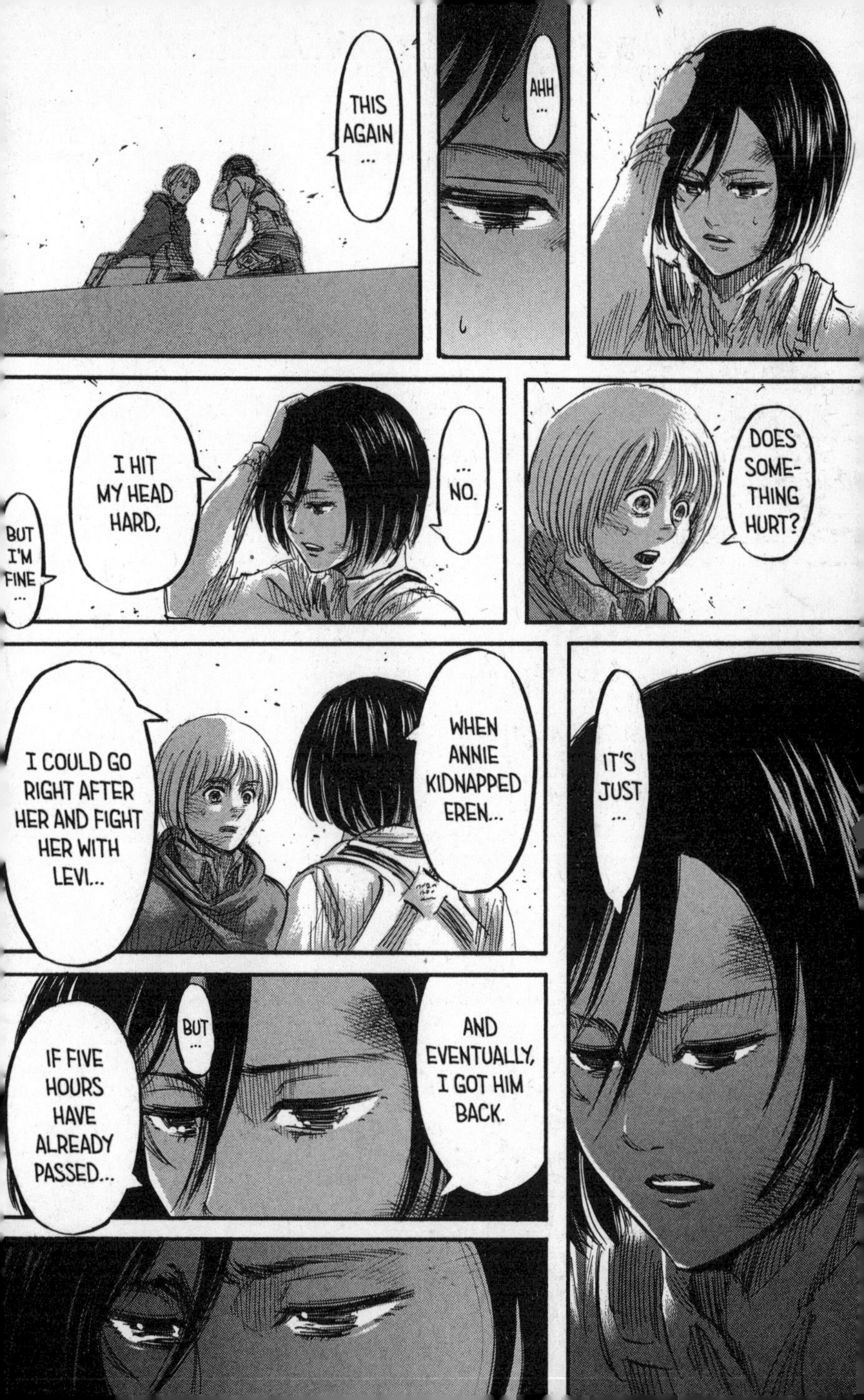
AHH ...
THIS AGAIN ...
DOES SOMETHING HURT?
... NO.
I HIT MY HEAD HARD,
BUT I'M FINE ...
IT'S JUST ...
WHEN ANNIE KIDNAPPED EREN...
I COULD GO RIGHT AFTER HER AND FIGHT HER WITH LEVI...
AND EVENTUALLY, I GOT HIM BACK.
BUT ...
IF FIVE HOURS HAVE ALREADY PASSED...

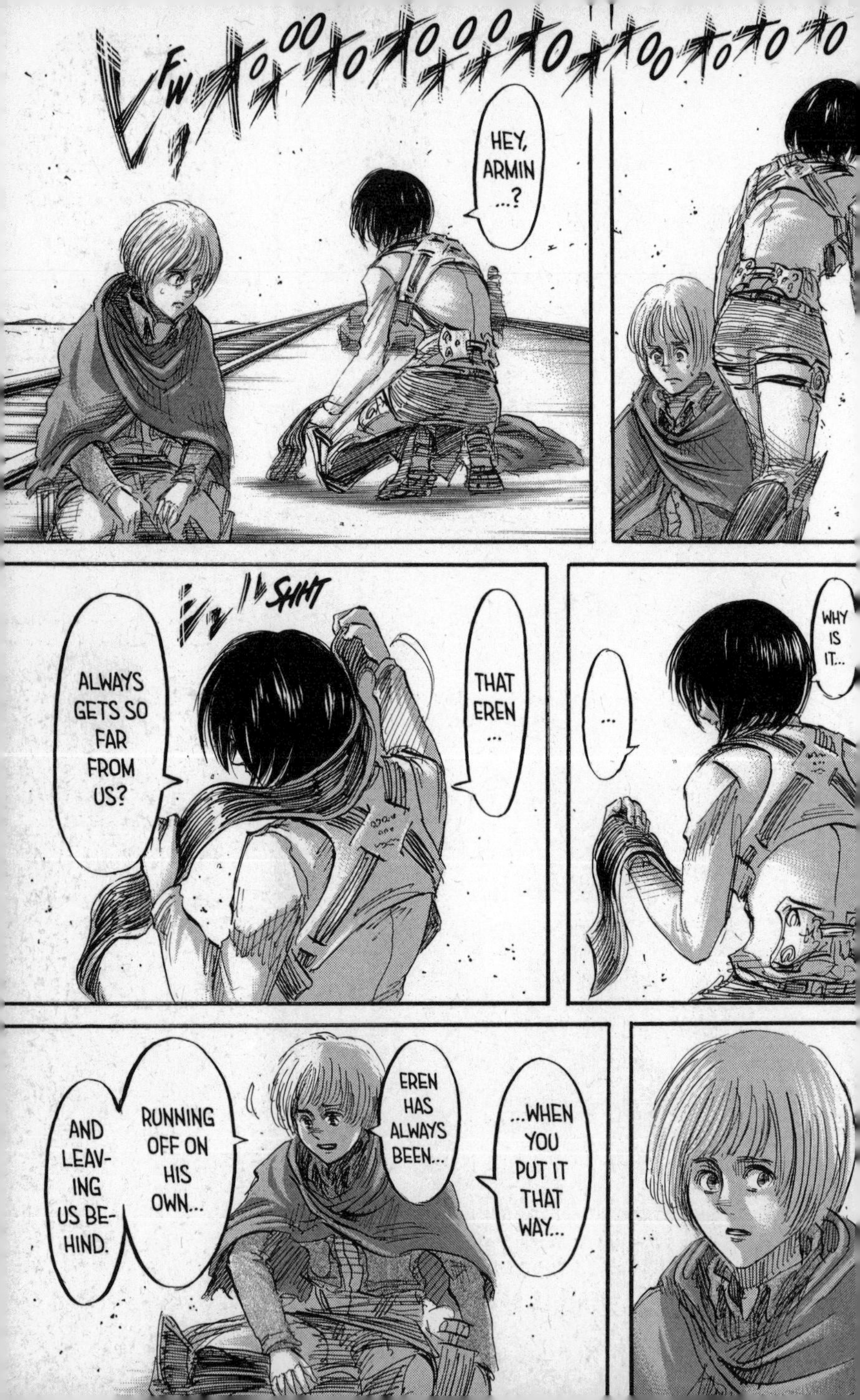
HEY, ARMIN ...?
WHY IS IT...
...
SHHT
THAT EREN ...
ALWAYS GETS SO FAR FROM US?
...WHEN YOU PUT IT THAT WAY...
EREN HAS ALWAYS BEEN...
RUNNING OFF ON HIS OWN...
AND LEAV-ING US BE-HIND.

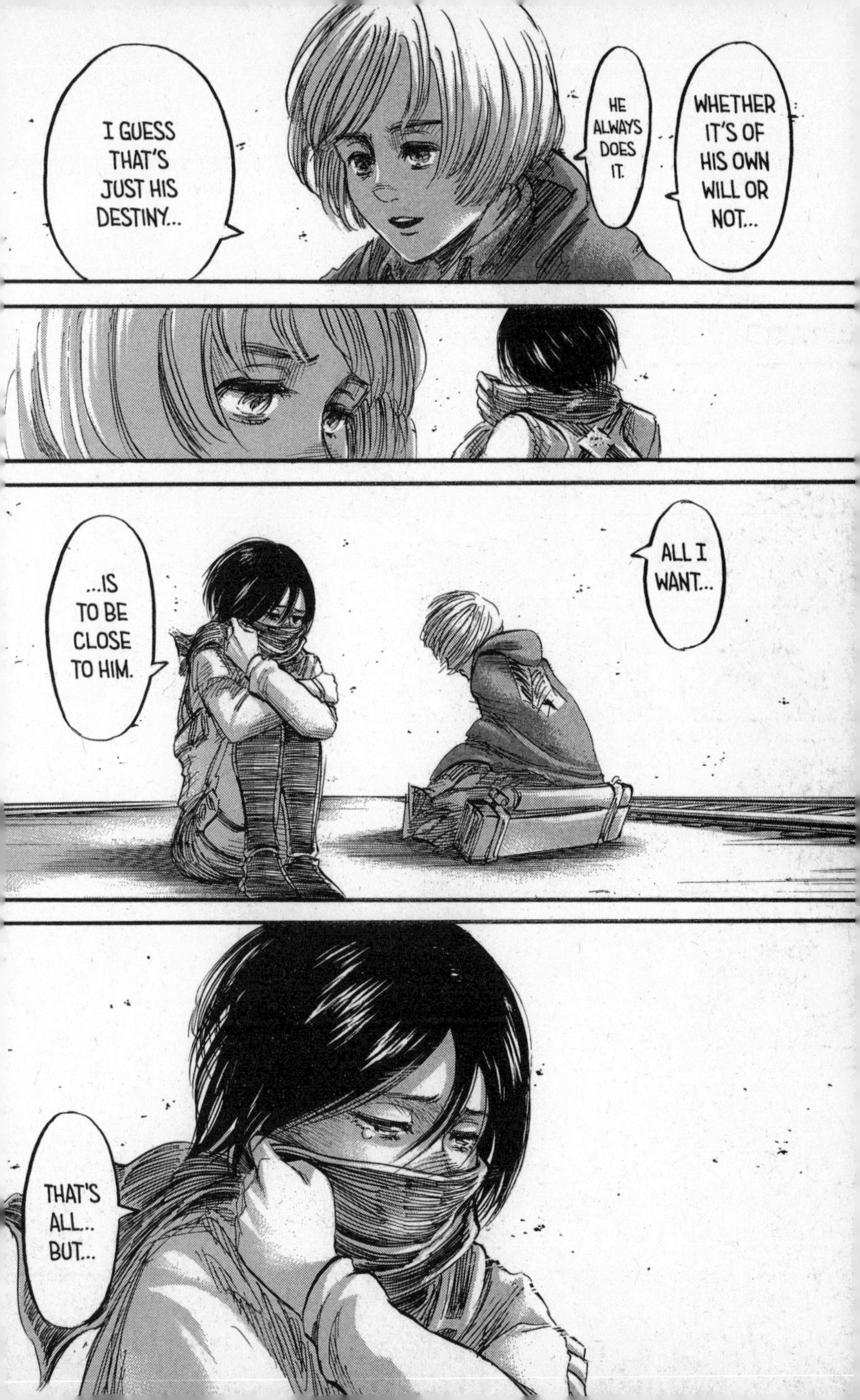
WHETHER IT'S OF HIS OWN WILL OR NOT...
HE ALWAYS DOES IT.
I GUESS THAT'S JUST HIS DESTINY...
ALL I WANT...
...IS TO BE CLOSE TO HIM.
THAT'S ALL... BUT...

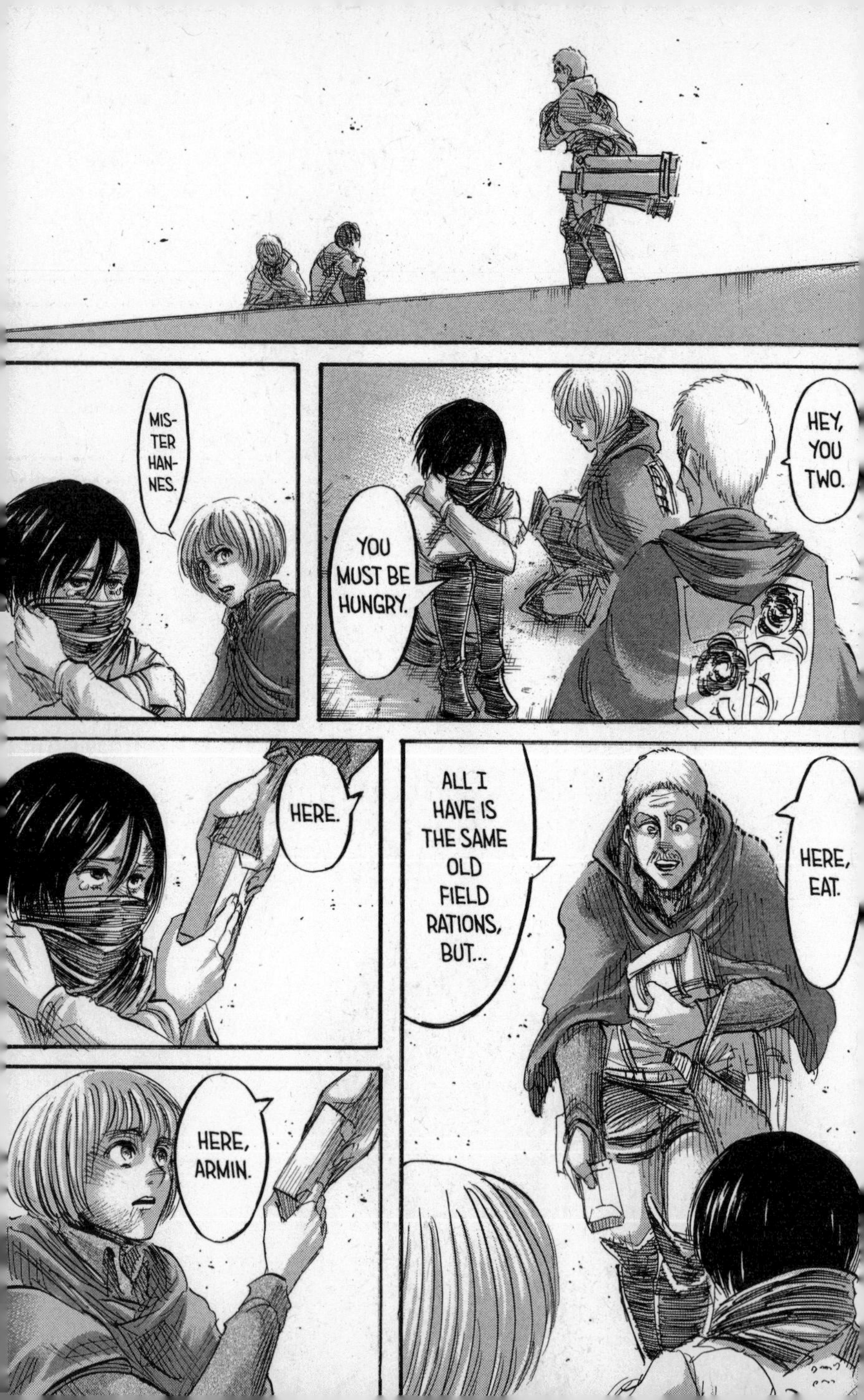
HEY, YOU TWO.
YOU MUST BE HUNGRY.
MISTER HANNES.
HERE, EAT.
ALL I HAVE IS THE SAME OLD FIELD RATIONS, BUT...
HERE.
HERE, ARMIN.

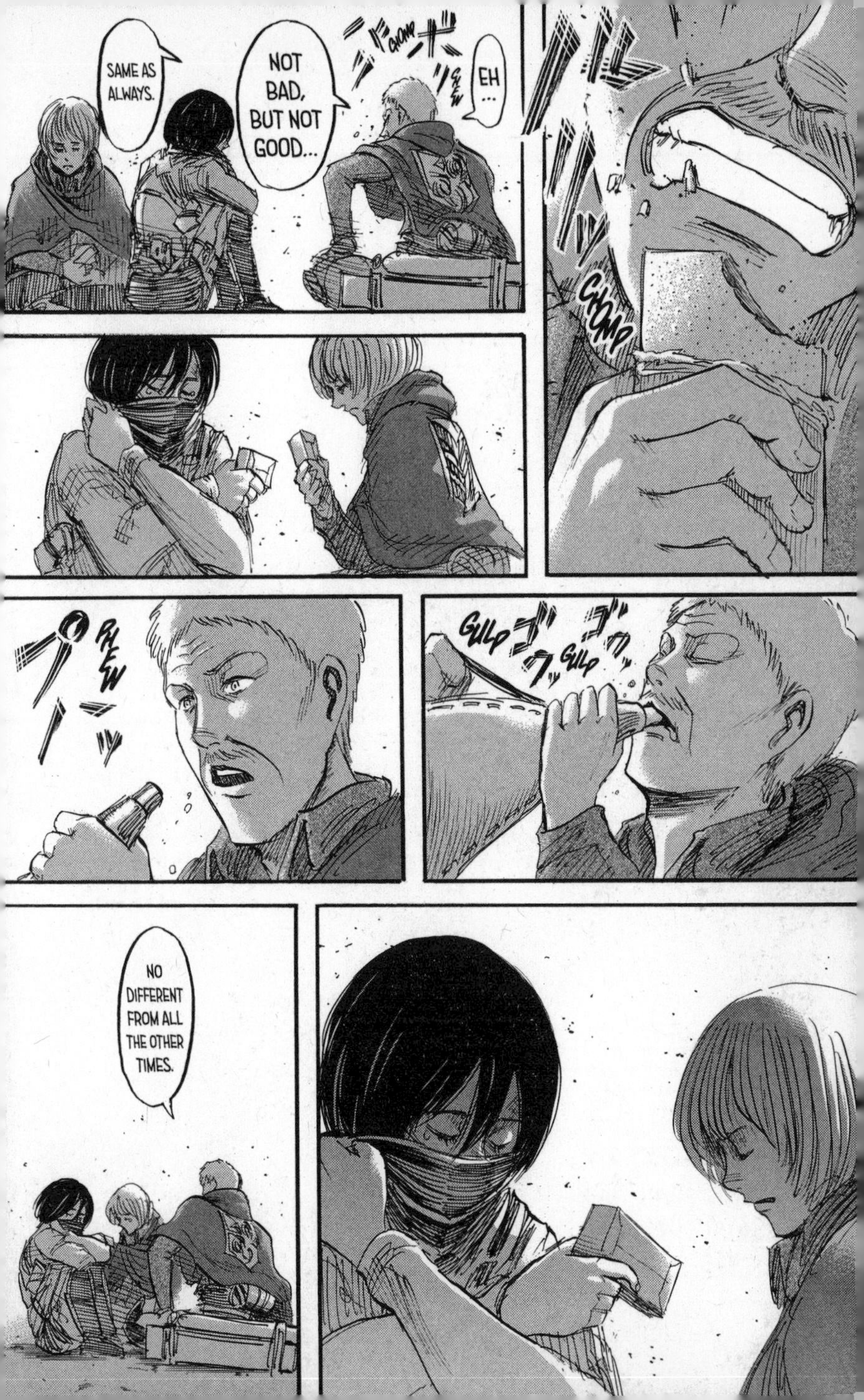
CHOMP
CHOMP
EH...
NOT BAD, BUT NOT GOOD...
SAME AS ALWAYS.
GULP
GULP
PHEW
NO DIFFERENT FROM ALL THE OTHER TIMES.

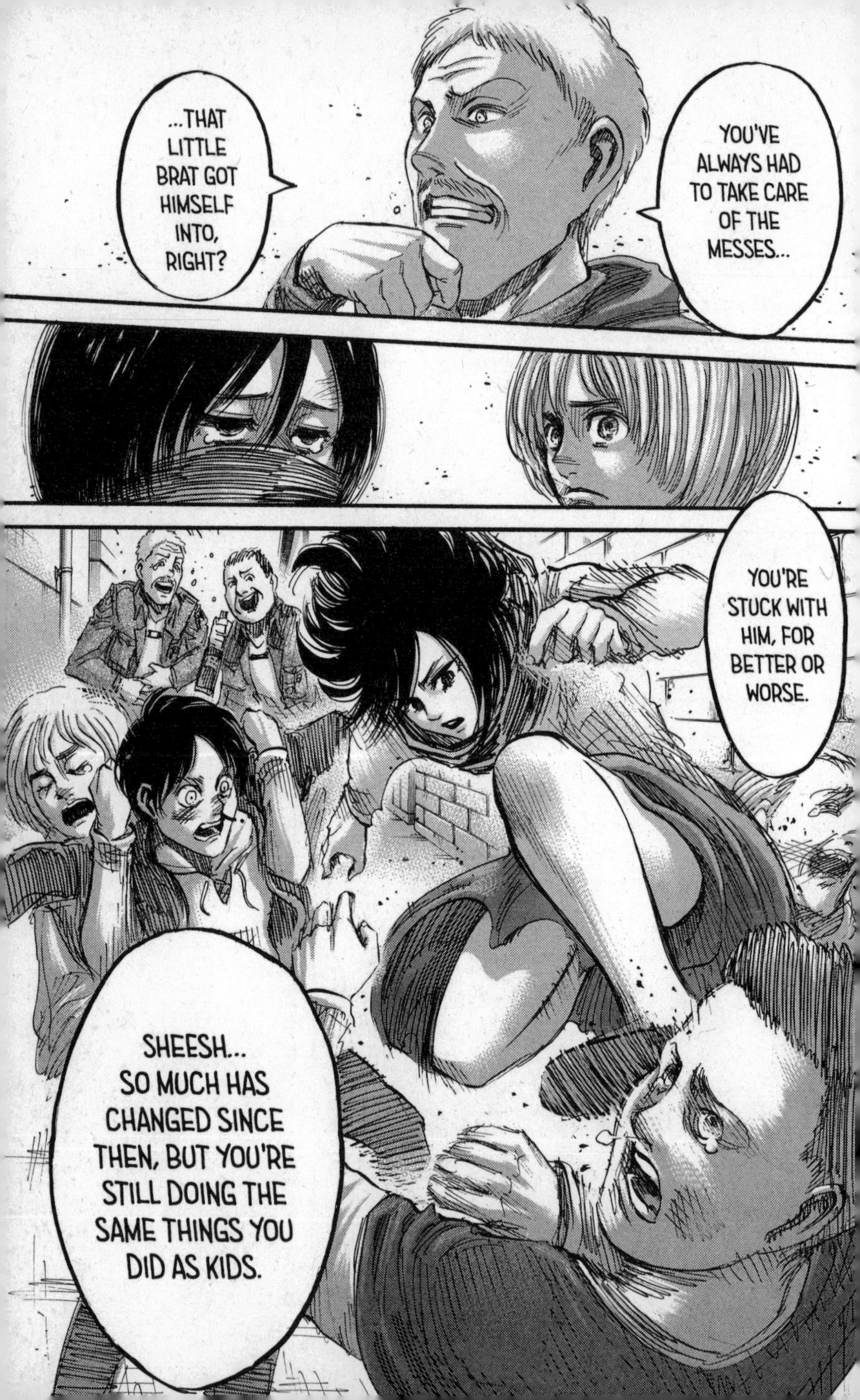
YOU'VE ALWAYS HAD TO TAKE CARE OF THE MESSES...
...THAT LITTLE BRAT GOT HIMSELF INTO, RIGHT?
YOU'RE STUCK WITH HIM, FOR BETTER OR WORSE.
SHEESH... SO MUCH HAS CHANGED SINCE THEN, BUT YOU'RE STILL DOING THE SAME THINGS YOU DID AS KIDS.

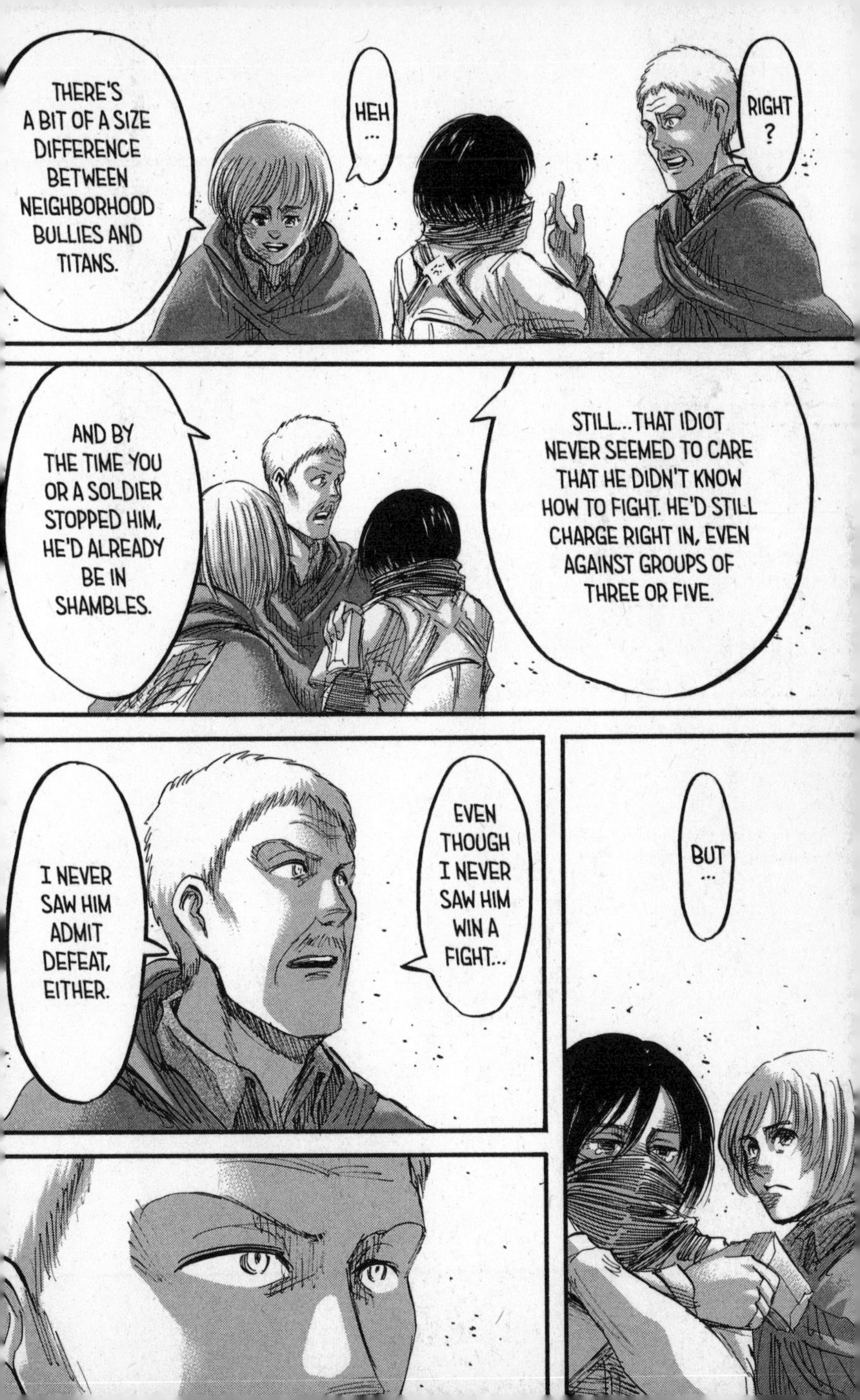
RIGHT?
HEH...
THERE'S A BIT OF A SIZE DIFFERENCE BETWEEN NEIGHBORHOOD BULLIES AND TITANS.
STILL... THAT IDIOT NEVER SEEMED TO CARE THAT HE DIDN'T KNOW HOW TO FIGHT. HE'D STILL CHARGE RIGHT IN, EVEN AGAINST GROUPS OF THREE OR FIVE.
AND BY THE TIME YOU OR A SOLDIER STOPPED HIM, HE'D ALREADY BE IN SHAMBLES.
BUT...
EVEN THOUGH I NEVER SAW HIM WIN A FIGHT...
I NEVER SAW HIM ADMIT DEFEAT, EITHER.

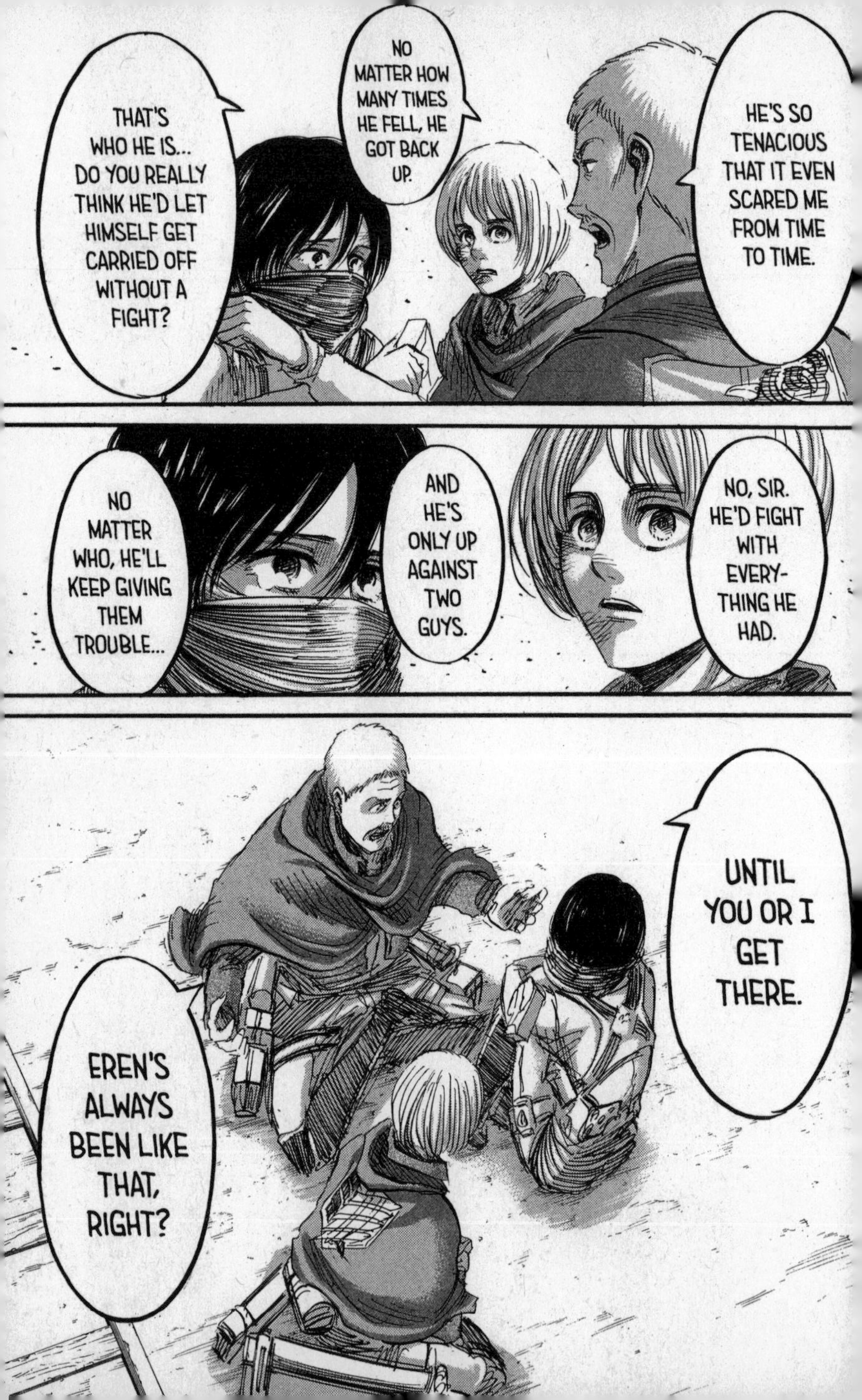
HE'S SO TENACIOUS THAT IT EVEN SCARED ME FROM TIME TO TIME.
NO MATTER HOW MANY TIMES HE FELL, HE GOT BACK UP.
THAT'S WHO HE IS... DO YOU REALLY THINK HE'D LET HIMSELF GET CARRIED OFF WITHOUT A FIGHT?
NO, SIR. HE'D FIGHT WITH EVERY-THING HE HAD.
AND HE'S ONLY UP AGAINST TWO GUYS.
NO MATTER WHO, HE'LL KEEP GIVING THEM TROUBLE...
UNTIL YOU OR I GET THERE.
EREN'S ALWAYS BEEN LIKE THAT, RIGHT?

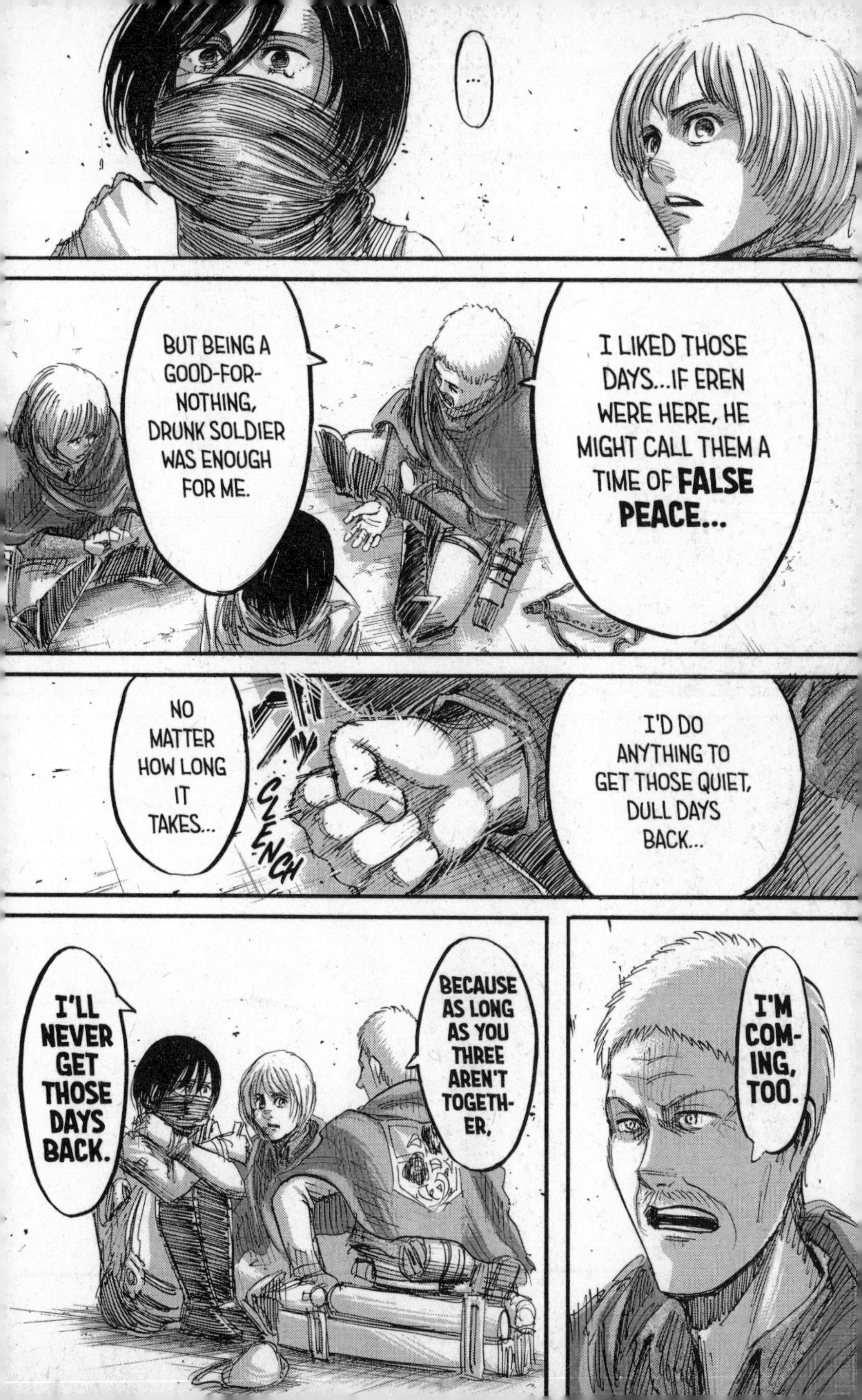
...
I LIKED THOSE DAYS...IF EREN WERE HERE, HE MIGHT CALL THEM A TIME OF FALSE PEACE...
BUT BEING A GOOD-FOR-NOTHING, DRUNK SOLDIER WAS ENOUGH FOR ME.
I'D DO ANYTHING TO GET THOSE QUIET, DULL DAYS BACK...
CLENCH
NO MATTER HOW LONG IT TAKES...
I'M COMING, TOO.
BECAUSE AS LONG AS YOU THREE AREN'T TOGETHER,
I'LL NEVER GET THOSE DAYS BACK.

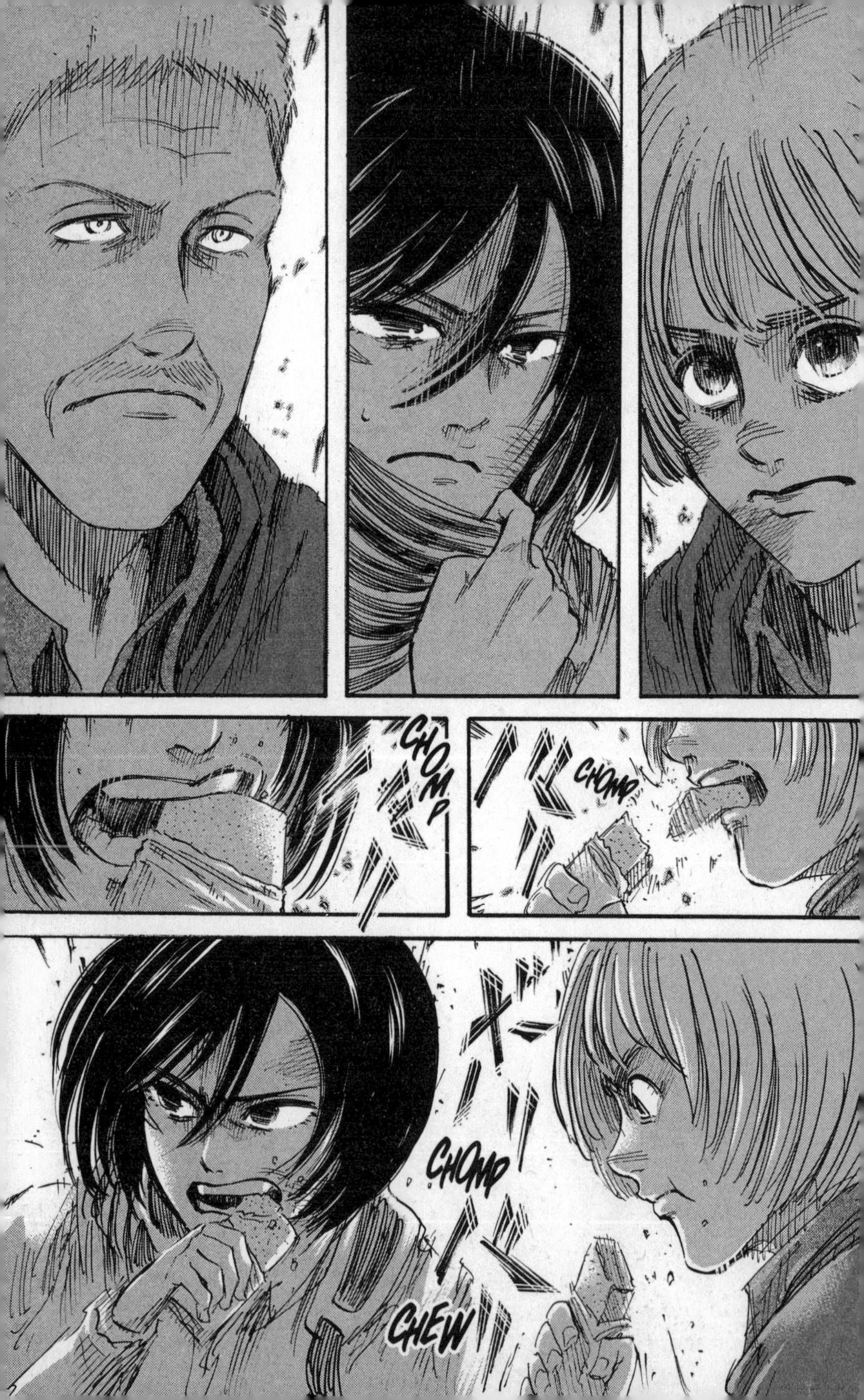
CHOMP
CHOMP
CHOMP
CHEW

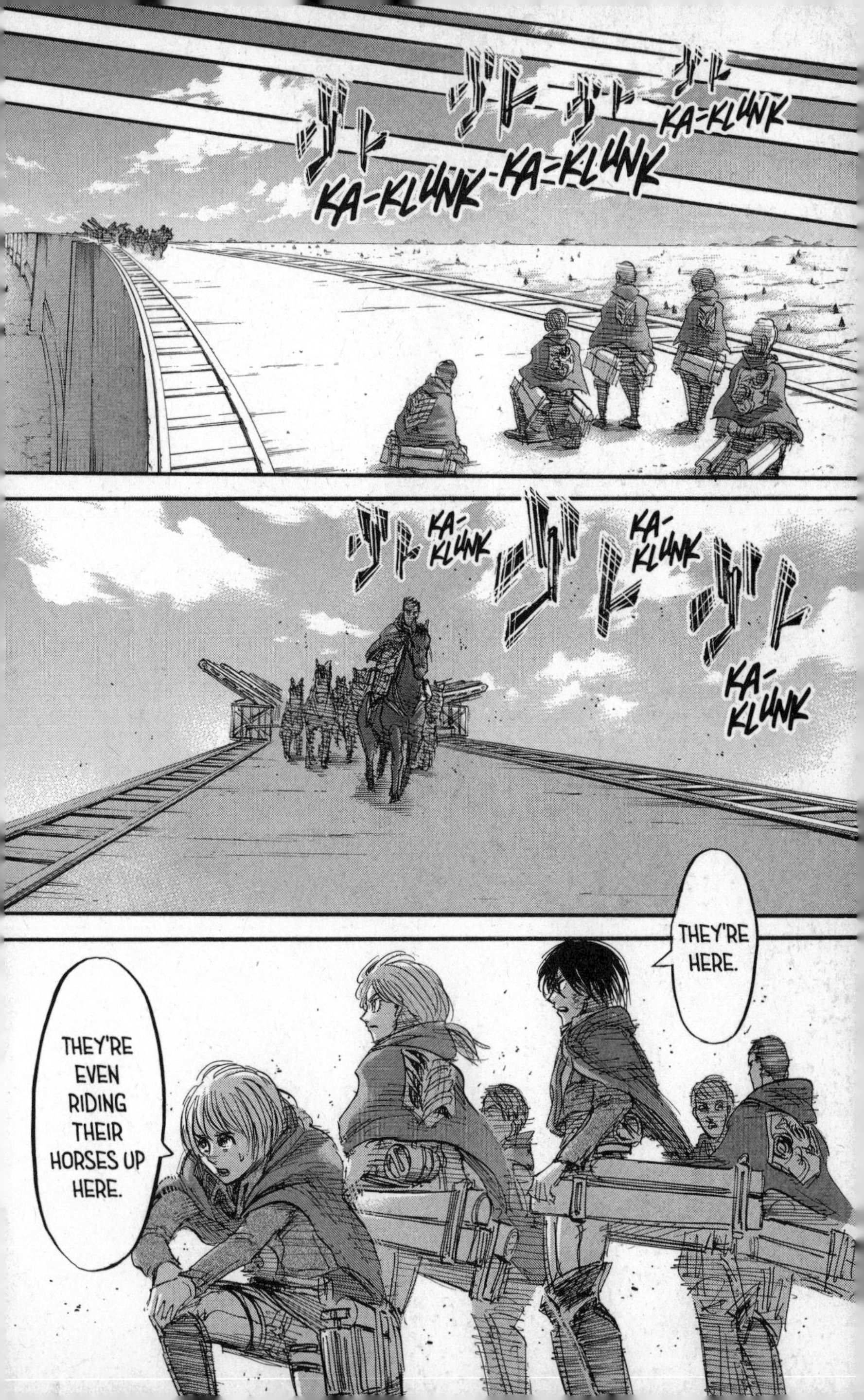
KA-KLUNK
KA-KLUNK
KA-KLUNK
KA-KLUNK
KA-KLUNK
KA-KLUNK
THEY'RE HERE.
THEY'RE EVEN RIDING THEIR HORSES UP HERE.

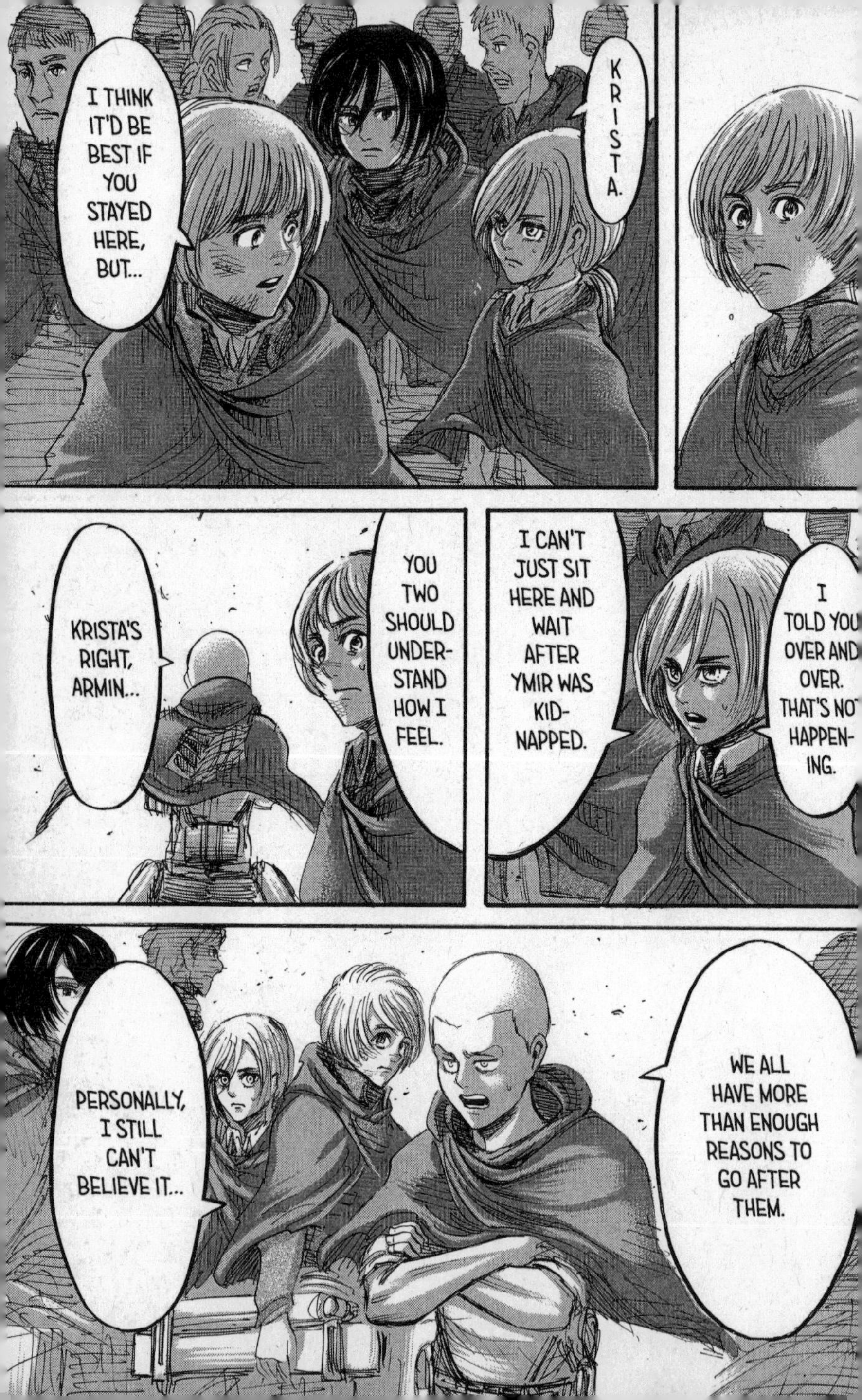
KRISTA.
I THINK IT'D BE BEST IF YOU STAYED HERE, BUT...
I TOLD YOU OVER AND OVER. THAT'S NOT HAPPENING.
I CAN'T JUST SIT HERE AND WAIT AFTER YMIR WAS KIDNAPPED.
YOU TWO SHOULD UNDERSTAND HOW I FEEL.
KRISTA'S RIGHT, ARMIN...
WE ALL HAVE MORE THAN ENOUGH REASONS TO GO AFTER THEM.
PERSONALLY, I STILL CAN'T BELIEVE IT...

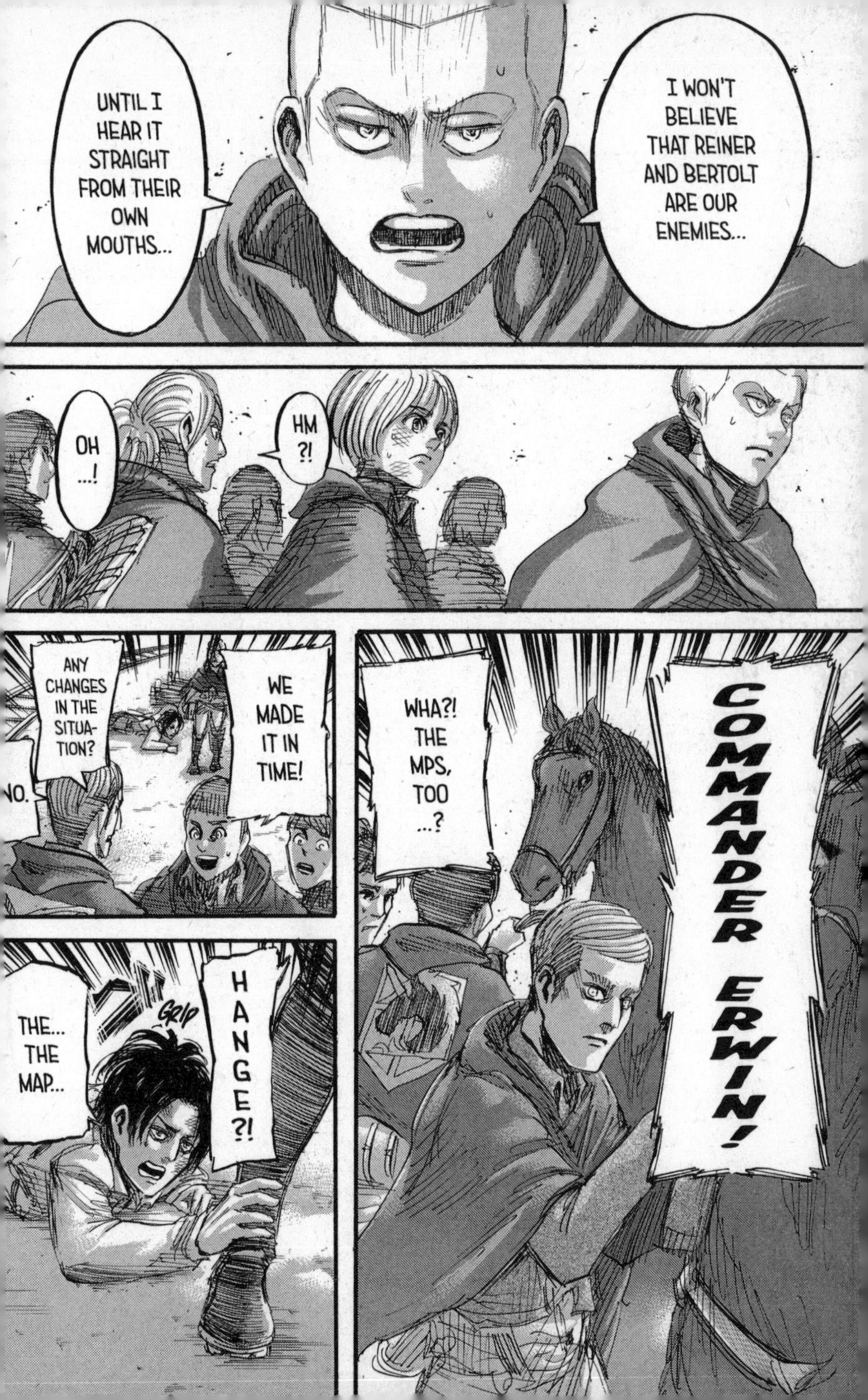
I WON'T BELIEVE THAT REINER AND BERTOLT ARE OUR ENEMIES...
UNTIL I HEAR IT STRAIGHT FROM THEIR OWN MOUTHS...
HM?!
OH ...!
COMMANDER ERWIN!
WHA?! THE MPS, TOO ...?
WE MADE IT IN TIME!
ANY CHANGES IN THE SITUATION?
NO.
HANGE?!
GRIP
THE... THE MAP...

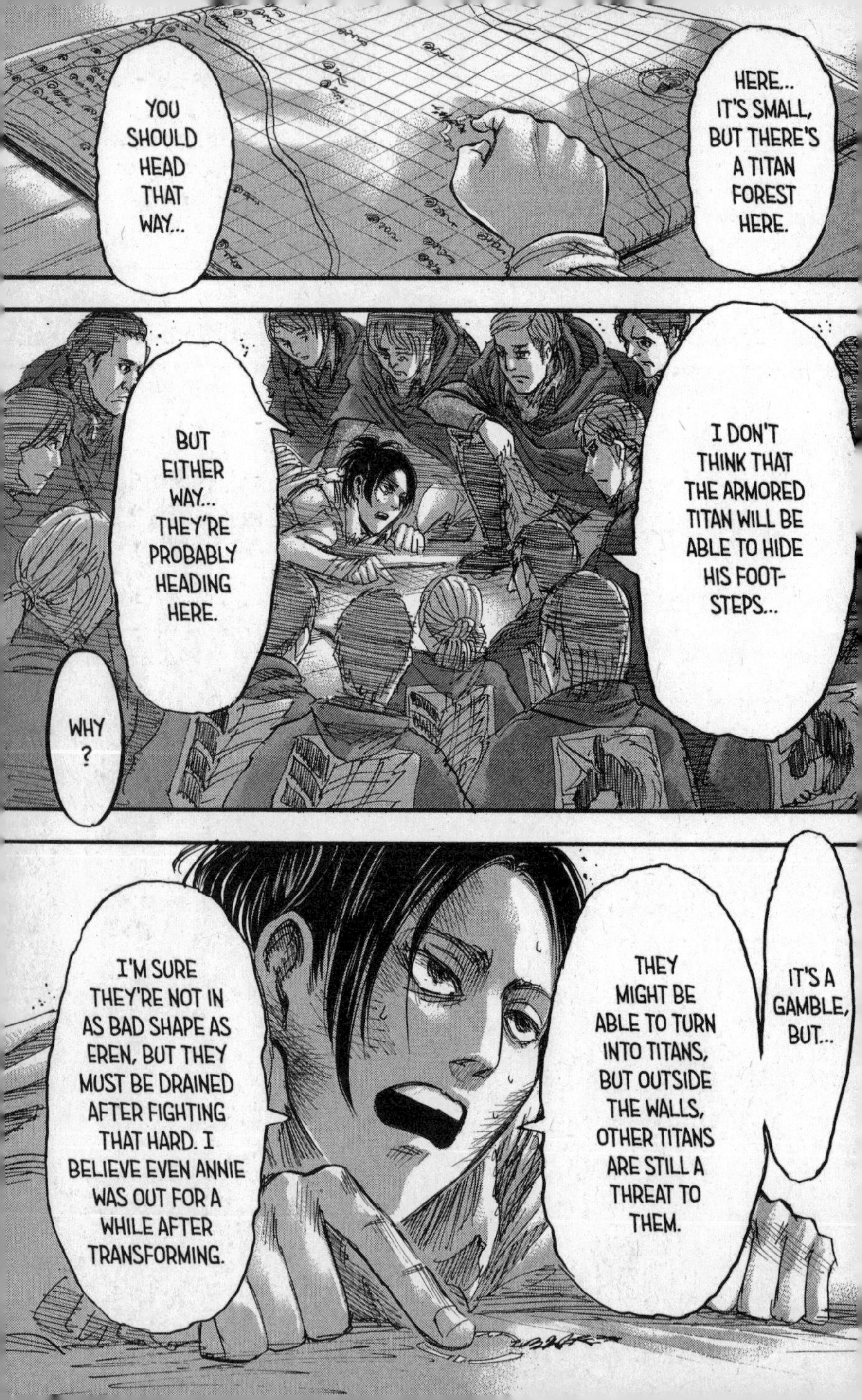
HERE... IT'S SMALL, BUT THERE'S A TITAN FOREST HERE.
YOU SHOULD HEAD THAT WAY...
I DON'T THINK THAT THE ARMORED TITAN WILL BE ABLE TO HIDE HIS FOOT-STEPS...
BUT EITHER WAY... THEY'RE PROBABLY HEADING HERE.
WHY?
IT'S A GAMBLE, BUT...
THEY MIGHT BE ABLE TO TURN INTO TITANS, BUT OUTSIDE THE WALLS, OTHER TITANS ARE STILL A THREAT TO THEM.
I'M SURE THEY'RE NOT IN AS BAD SHAPE AS EREN, BUT THEY MUST BE DRAINED AFTER FIGHTING THAT HARD. I BELIEVE EVEN ANNIE WAS OUT FOR A WHILE AFTER TRANSFORMING.

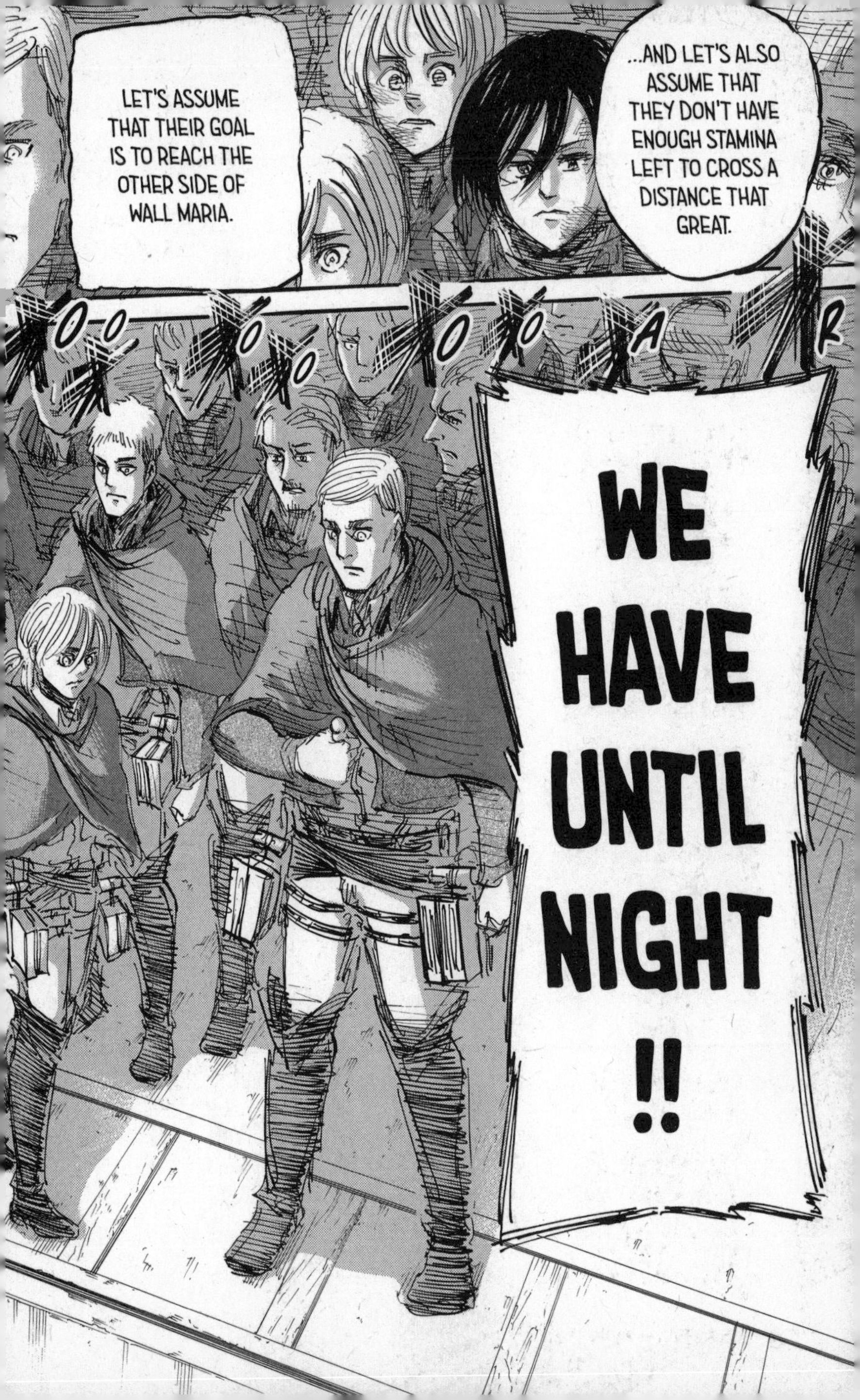

LET'S ASSUME THAT THEIR GOAL IS TO REACH THE OTHER SIDE OF WALL MARIA.
...AND LET'S ALSO ASSUME THAT THEY DON'T HAVE ENOUGH STAMINA LEFT TO CROSS A DISTANCE THAT GREAT.
OOOOOOAR
WE HAVE UNTIL NIGHT !!

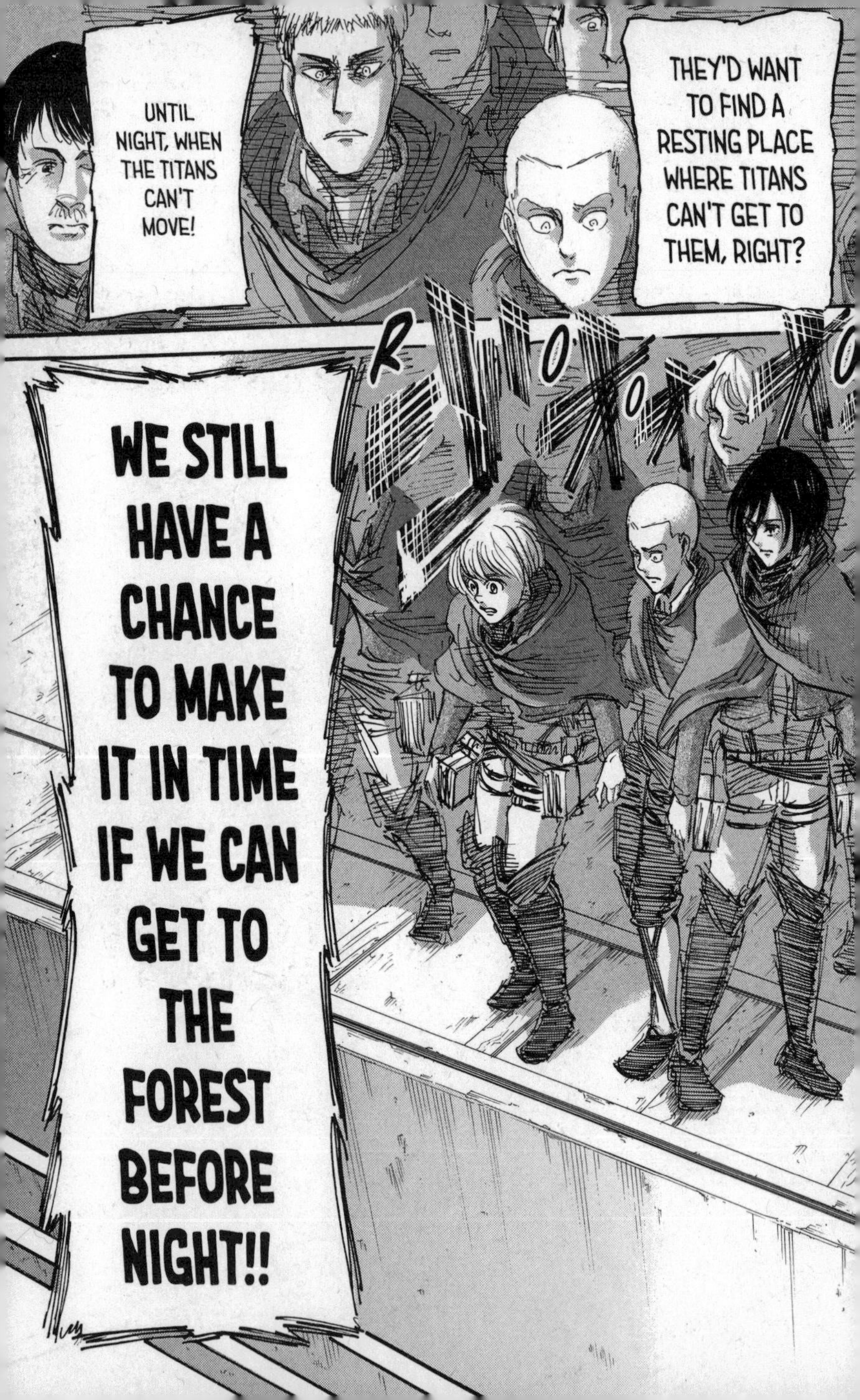
THEY'D WANT TO FIND A RESTING PLACE WHERE TITANS CAN'T GET TO THEM, RIGHT?
UNTIL NIGHT, WHEN THE TITANS CAN'T MOVE!
WE STILL HAVE A CHANCE TO MAKE IT IN TIME IF WE CAN GET TO THE FOREST BEFORE NIGHT!!

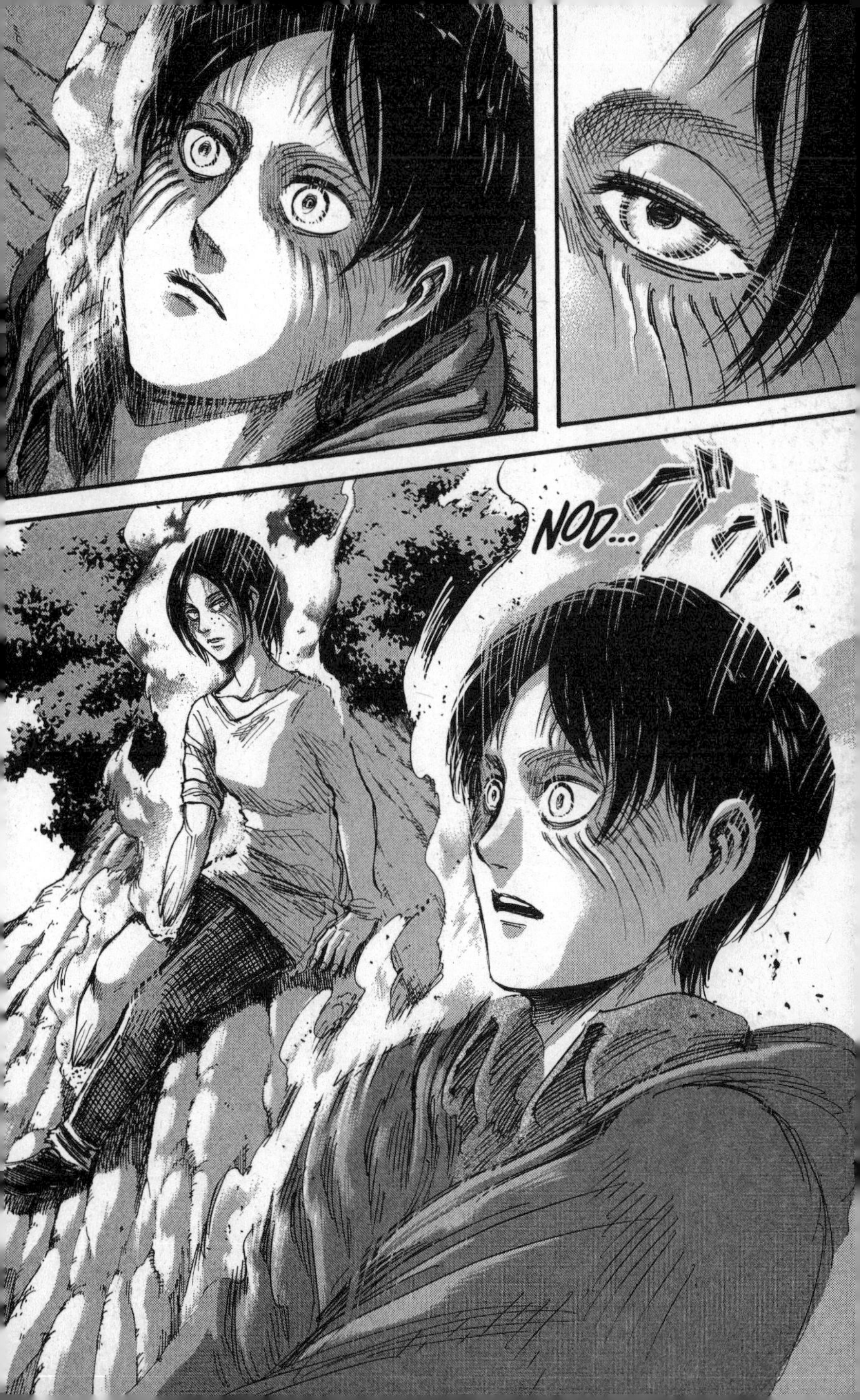
NOD...

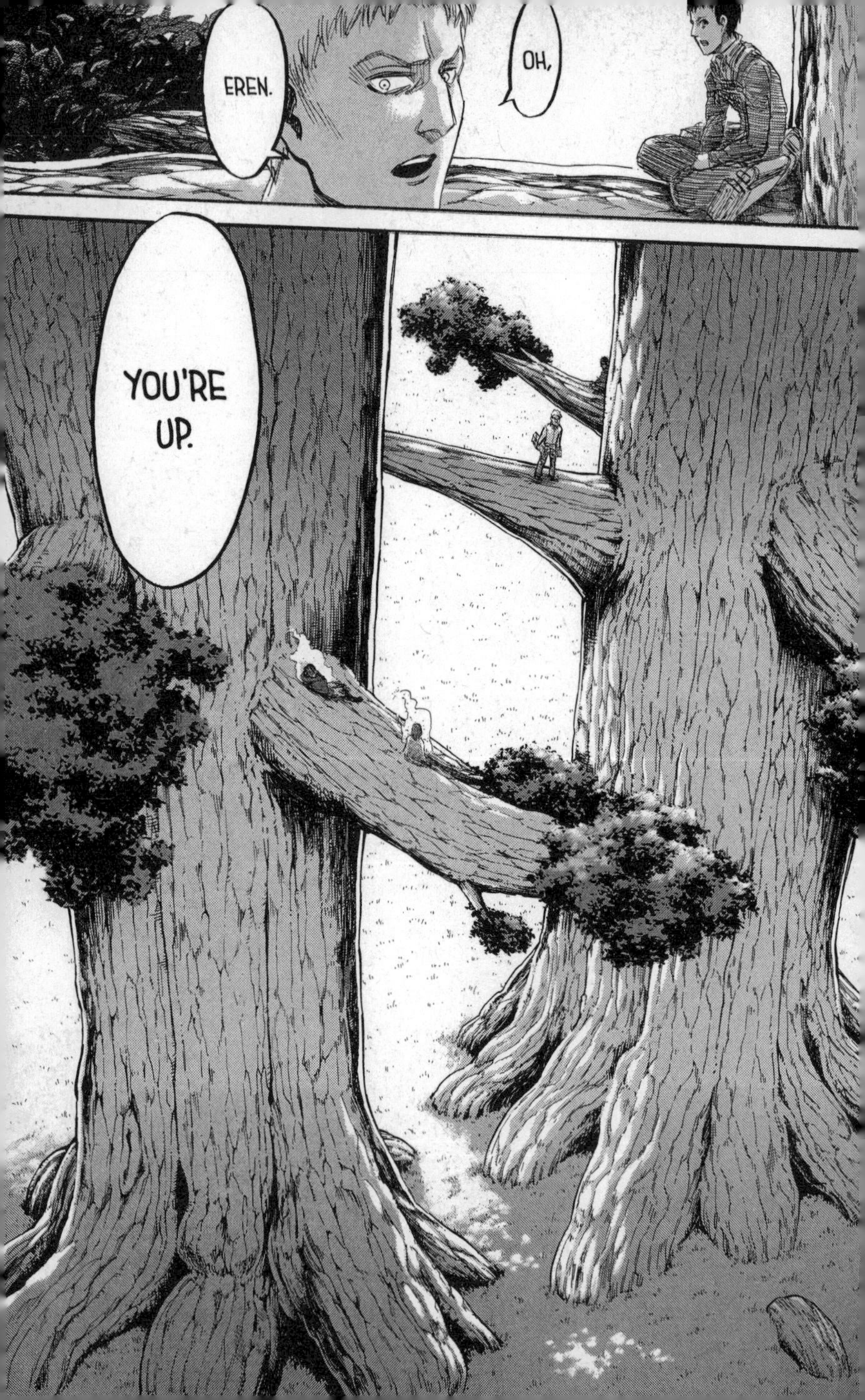
OH,
EREN.
YOU'RE UP.

ATTACK on TITAN

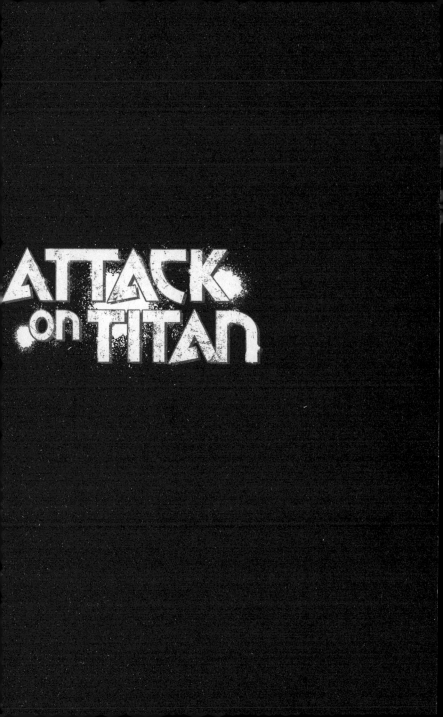

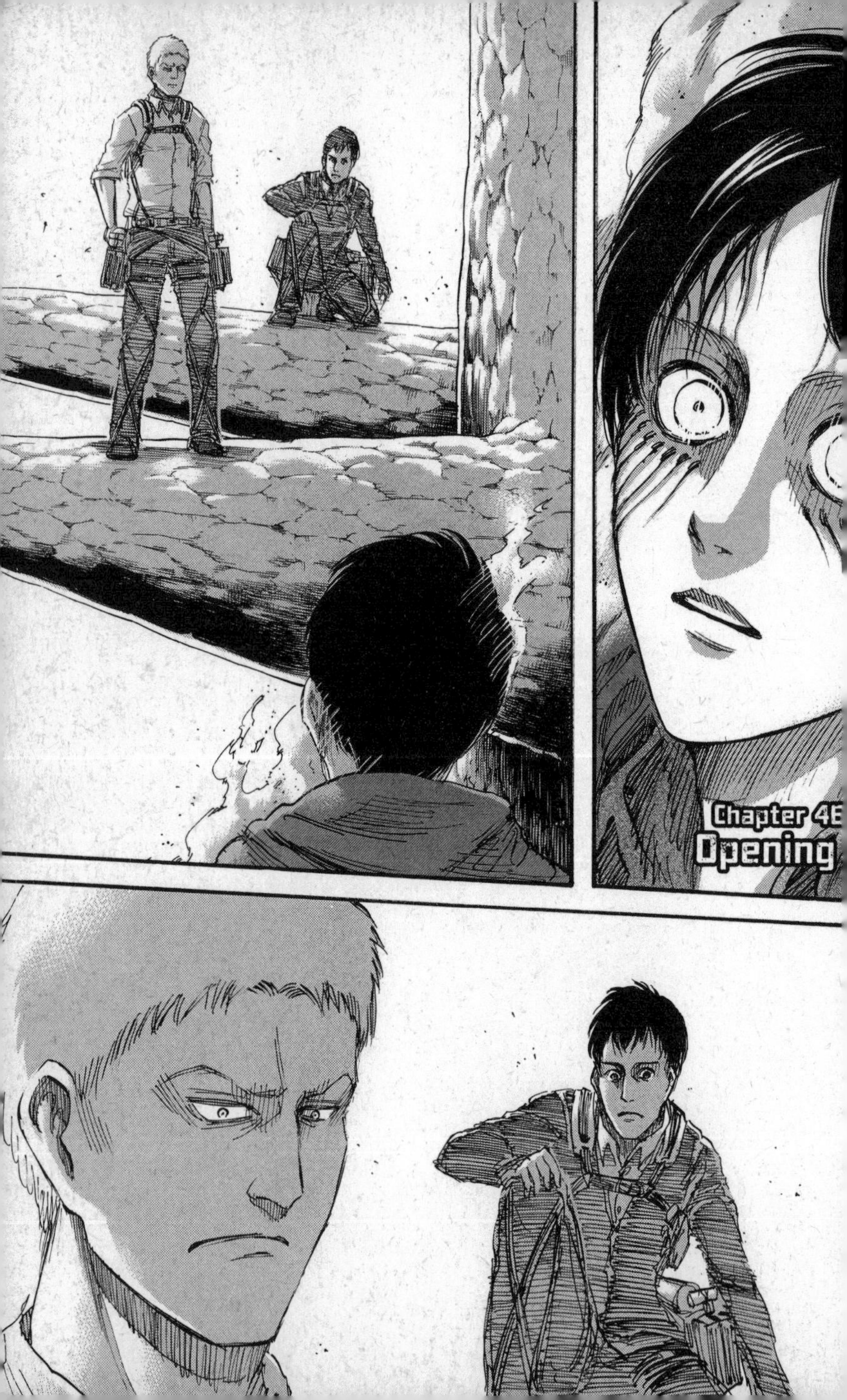
Chapter 4
Opening

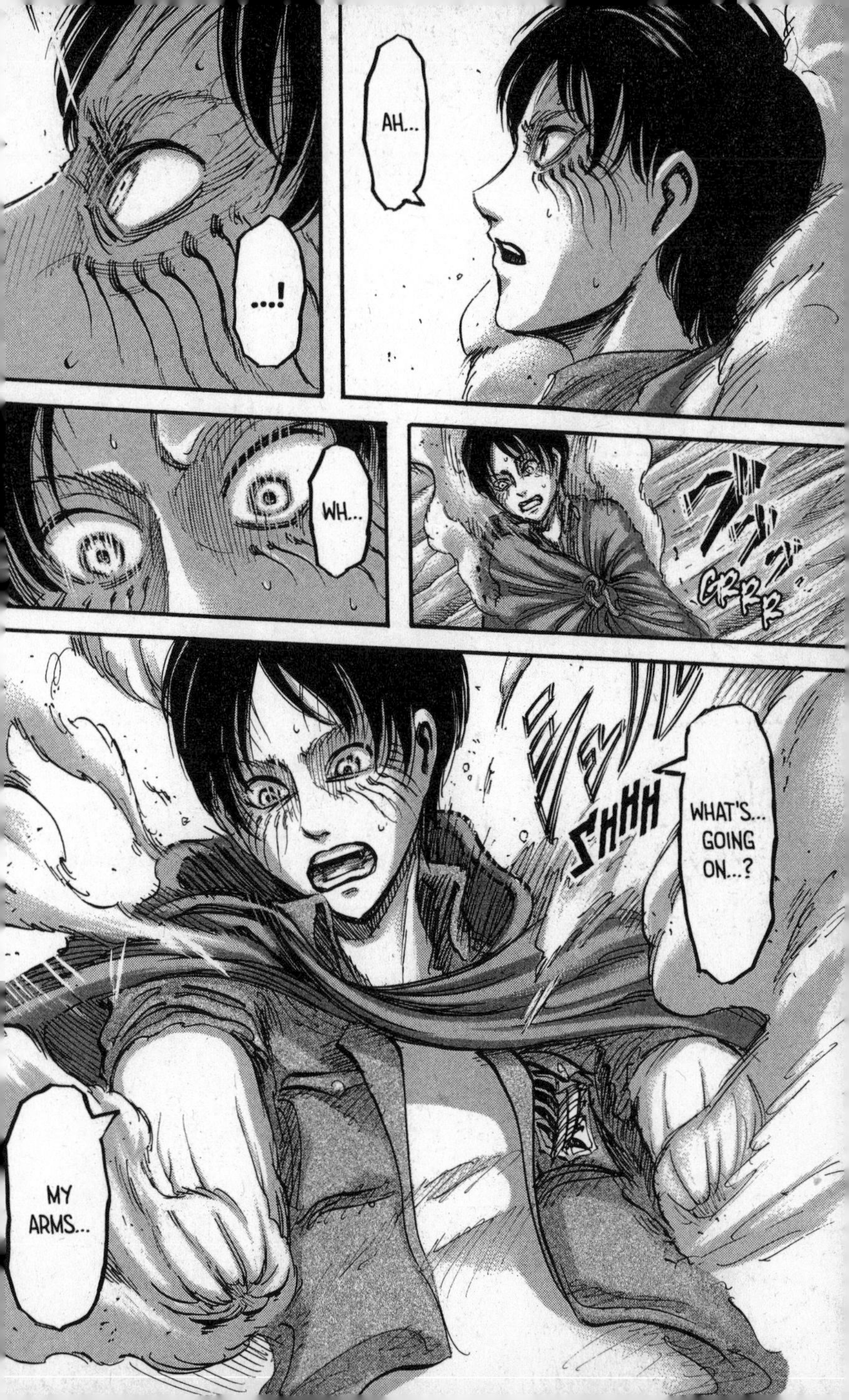
AH...
...!
GRRR
WH...
SHHH
WHAT'S... GOING ON...?
MY ARMS...

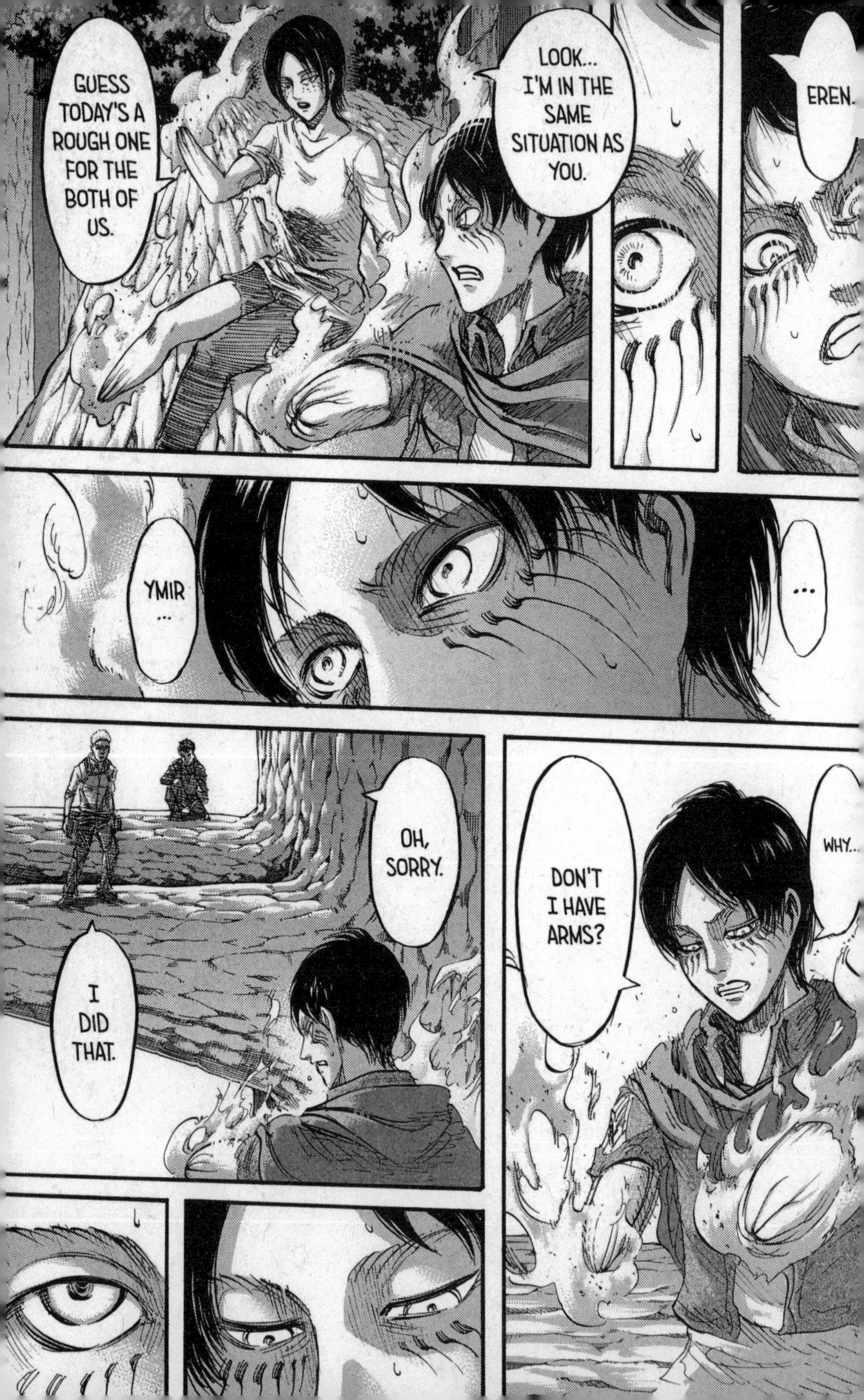
EREN.
LOOK... I'M IN THE SAME SITUATION AS YOU.
GUESS TODAY'S A ROUGH ONE FOR THE BOTH OF US.
...
YMIR ...
WHY...
DON'T I HAVE ARMS?
OH, SORRY.
I DID THAT.

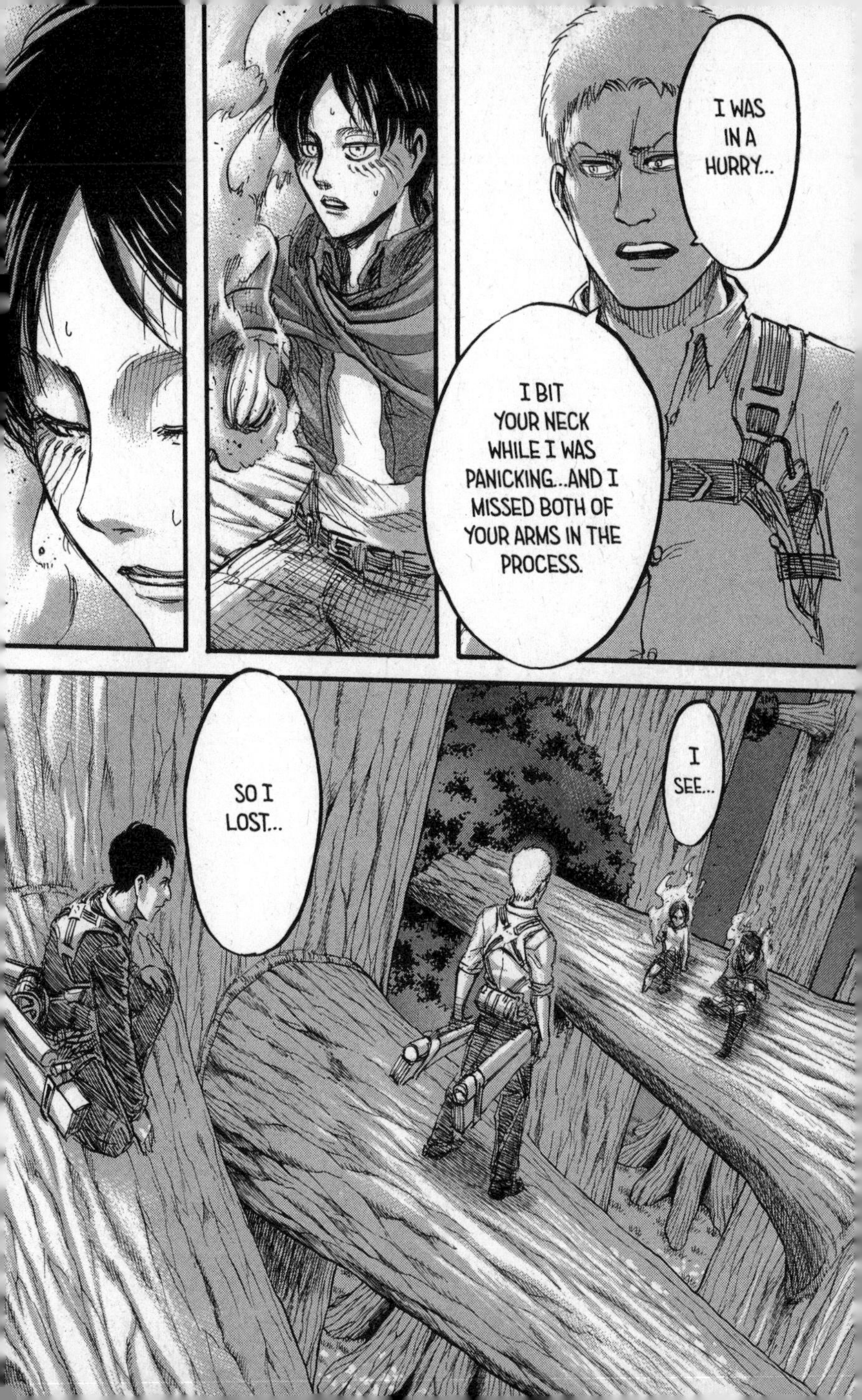
I WAS IN A HURRY...
I BIT YOUR NECK WHILE I WAS PANICKING...AND I MISSED BOTH OF YOUR ARMS IN THE PROCESS.
I SEE...
SO I LOST...

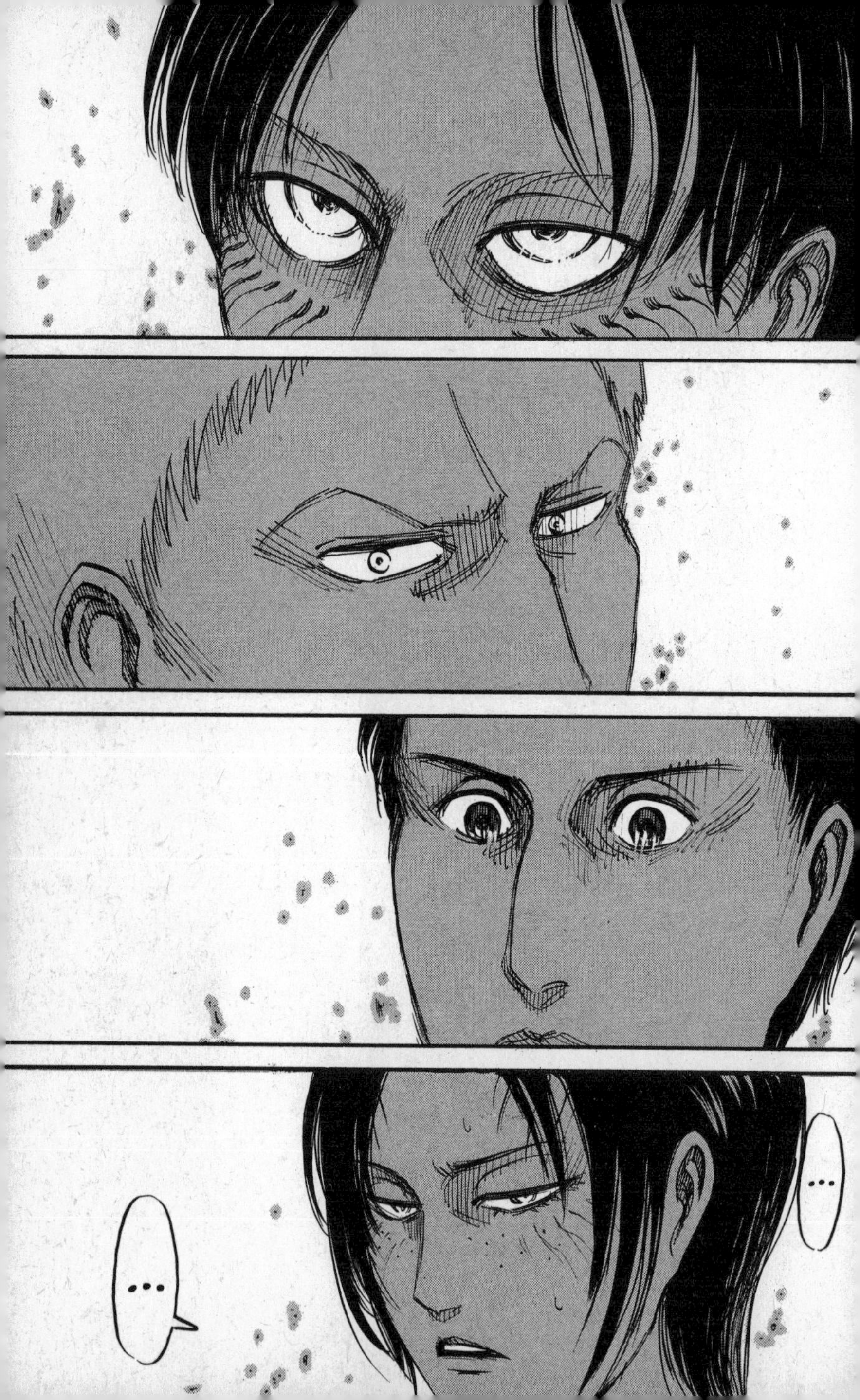
...
...

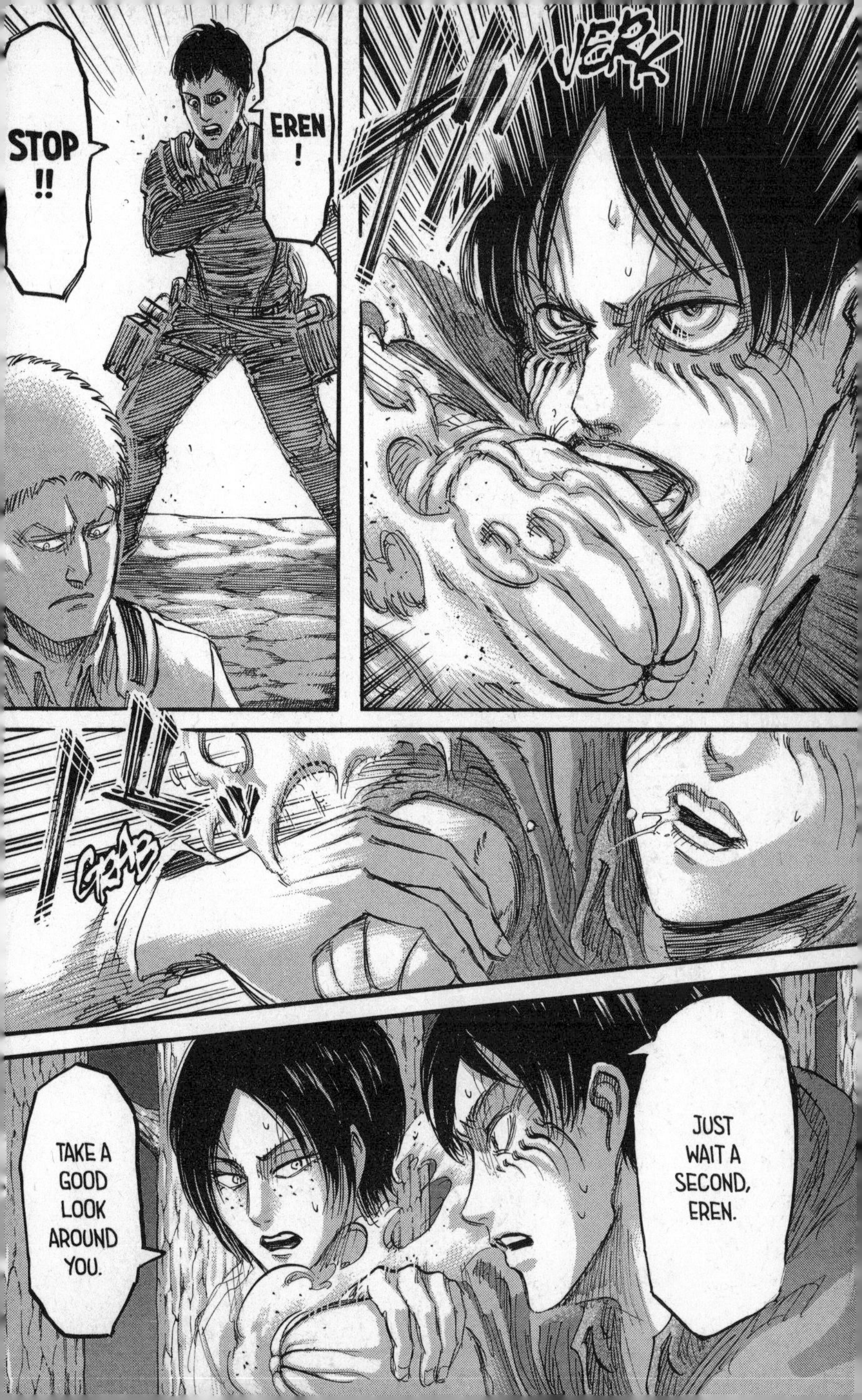

JERK
EREN!
STOP!!
GRAB
JUST WAIT A SECOND, EREN.
TAKE A GOOD LOOK AROUND YOU.

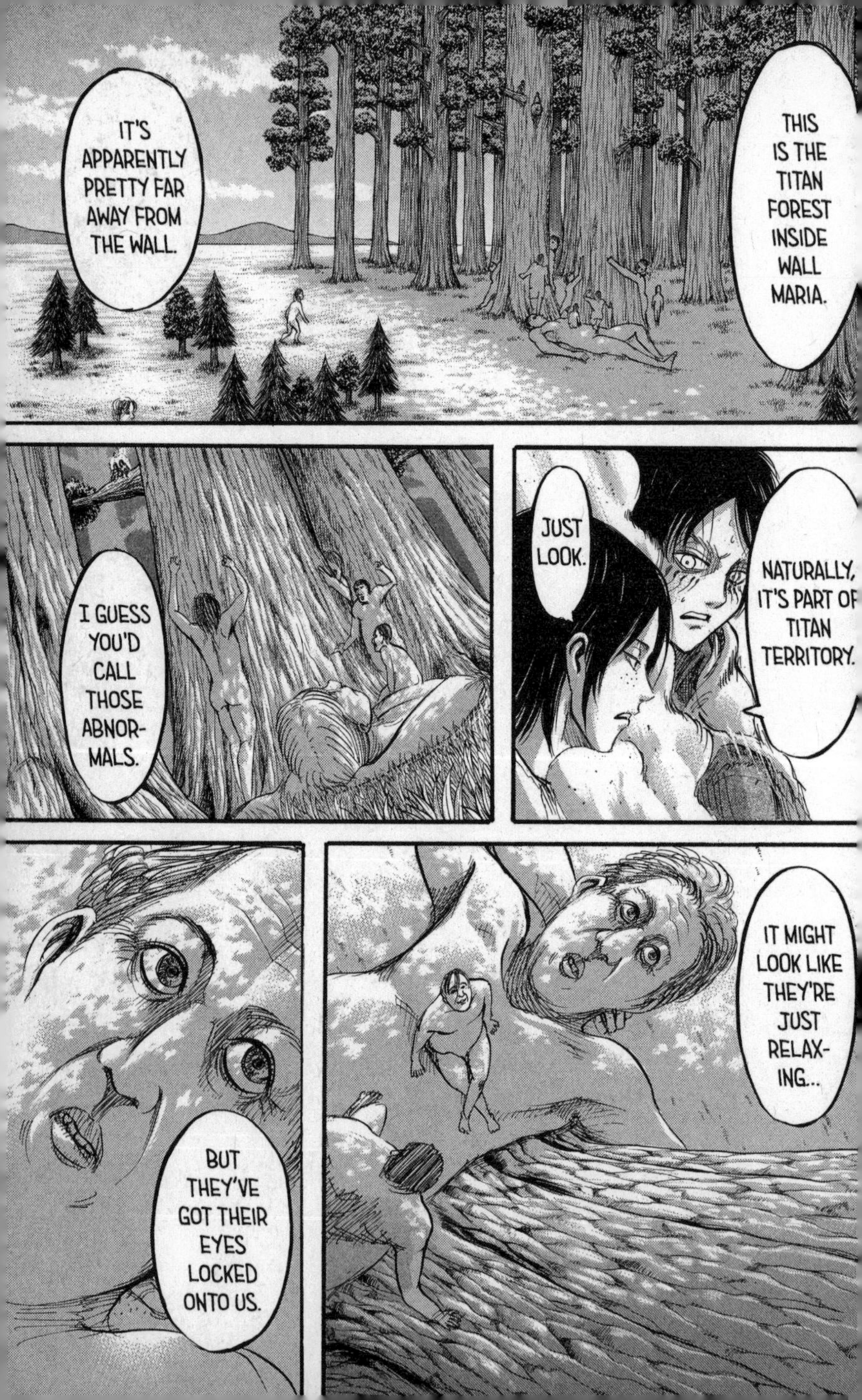
THIS IS THE TITAN FOREST INSIDE WALL MARIA.
IT'S APPARENTLY PRETTY FAR AWAY FROM THE WALL.
NATURALLY, IT'S PART OF TITAN TERRITORY.
JUST LOOK.
I GUESS YOU'D CALL THOSE ABNOR-MALS.
IT MIGHT LOOK LIKE THEY'RE JUST RELAX-ING...
BUT THEY'VE GOT THEIR EYES LOCKED ONTO US.

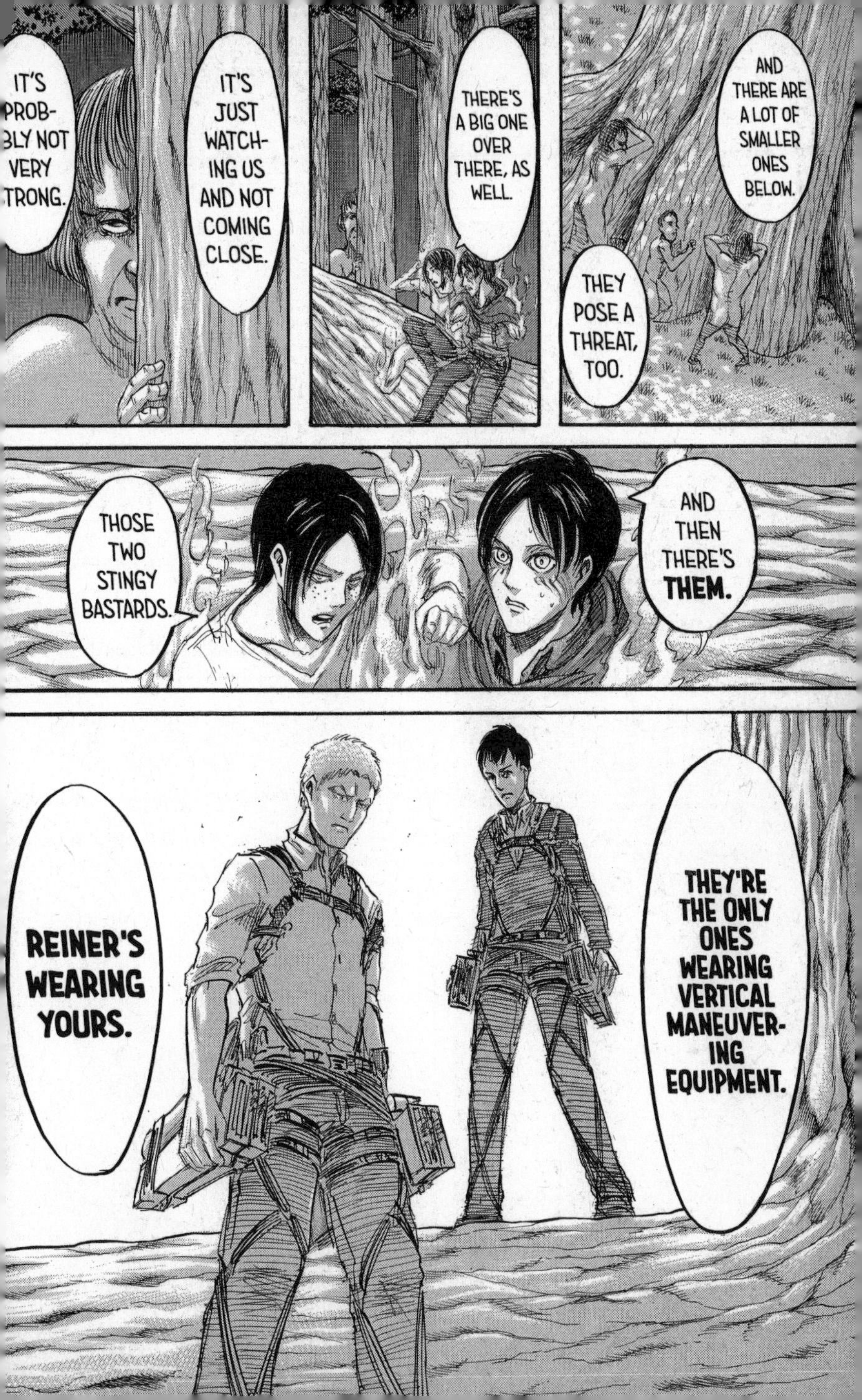
AND THERE ARE A LOT OF SMALLER ONES BELOW.
THEY POSE A THREAT, TOO.
THERE'S A BIG ONE OVER THERE, AS WELL.
IT'S JUST WATCHING US AND NOT COMING CLOSE.
IT'S PROB-BLY NOT VERY TRONG.
AND THEN THERE'S **THEM.**
THOSE TWO STINGY BASTARDS.
THEY'RE THE ONLY ONES WEARING VERTICAL MANEUVERING EQUIPMENT.
REINER'S WEARING YOURS.

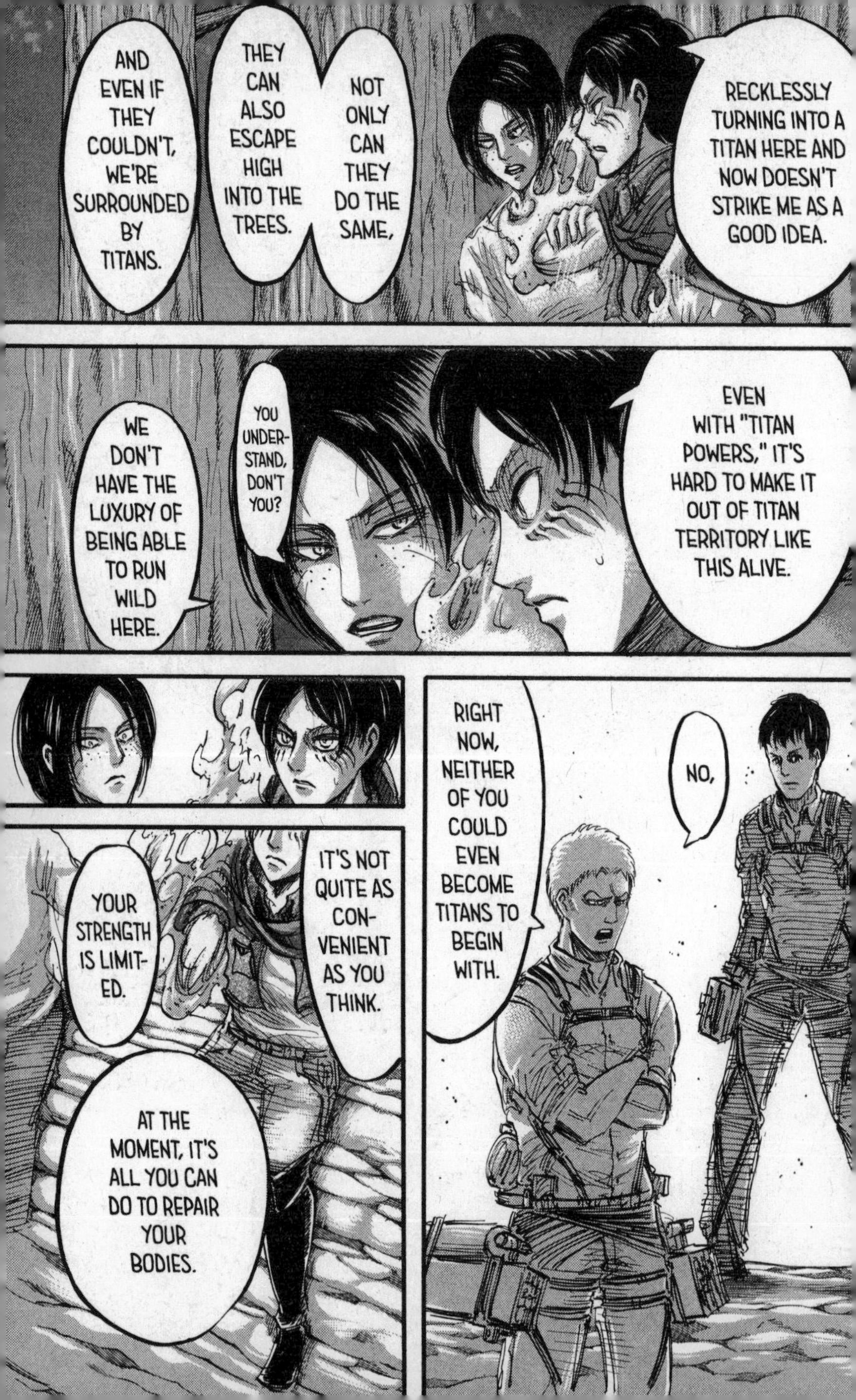
RECKLESSLY TURNING INTO A TITAN HERE AND NOW DOESN'T STRIKE ME AS A GOOD IDEA.
NOT ONLY CAN THEY DO THE SAME,
THEY CAN ALSO ESCAPE HIGH INTO THE TREES.
AND EVEN IF THEY COULDN'T, WE'RE SURROUNDED BY TITANS.
EVEN WITH "TITAN POWERS," IT'S HARD TO MAKE IT OUT OF TITAN TERRITORY LIKE THIS ALIVE.
YOU UNDER-STAND, DON'T YOU?
WE DON'T HAVE THE LUXURY OF BEING ABLE TO RUN WILD HERE.
NO,
RIGHT NOW, NEITHER OF YOU COULD EVEN BECOME TITANS TO BEGIN WITH.
IT'S NOT QUITE AS CON-VENIENT AS YOU THINK.
YOUR STRENGTH IS LIMIT-ED.
AT THE MOMENT, IT'S ALL YOU CAN DO TO REPAIR YOUR BODIES.

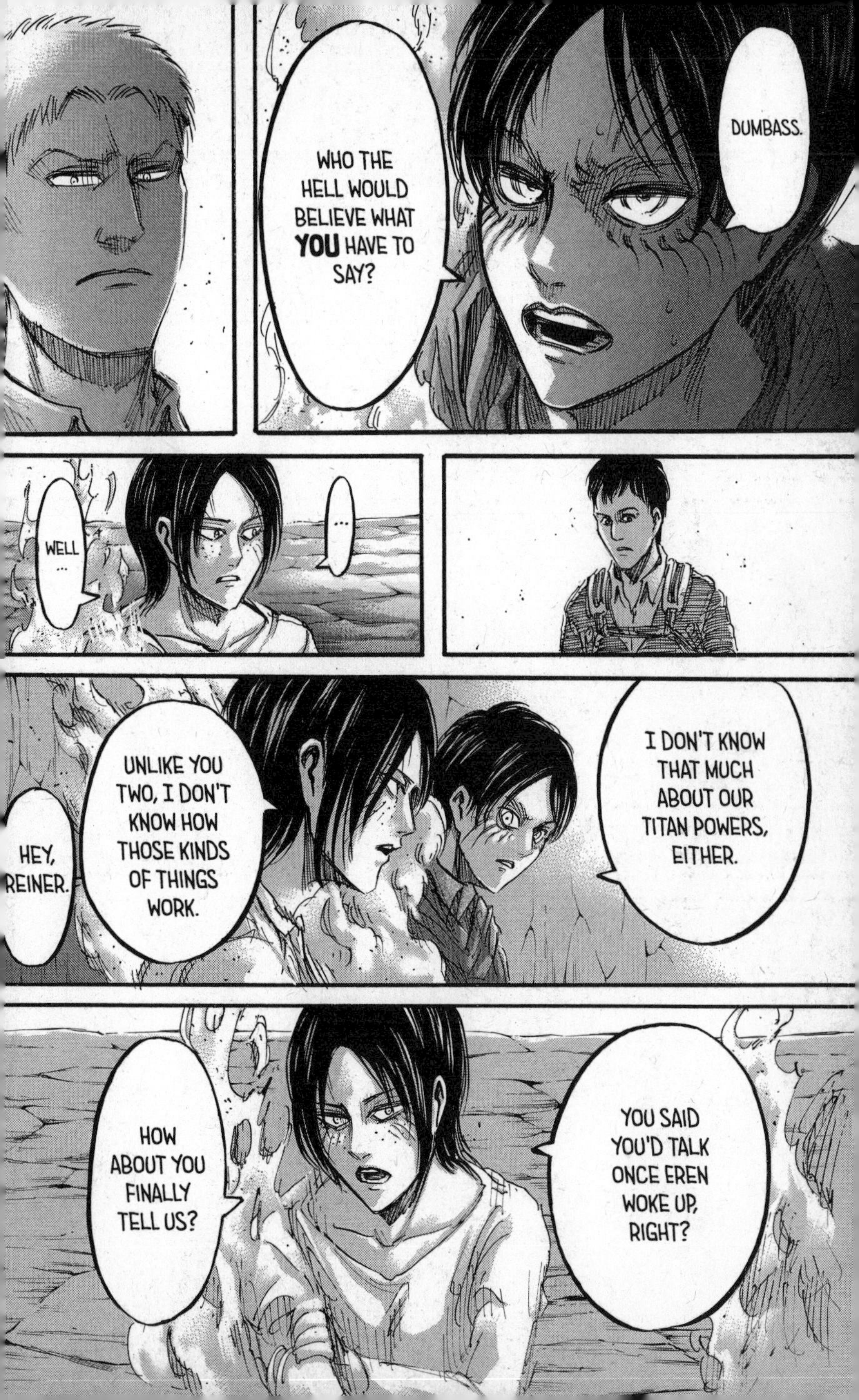
DUMBASS.
WHO THE HELL WOULD BELIEVE WHAT YOU HAVE TO SAY?
...
WELL ...
I DON'T KNOW THAT MUCH ABOUT OUR TITAN POWERS, EITHER.
UNLIKE YOU TWO, I DON'T KNOW HOW THOSE KINDS OF THINGS WORK.
HEY, REINER.
YOU SAID YOU'D TALK ONCE EREN WOKE UP, RIGHT?
HOW ABOUT YOU FINALLY TELL US?

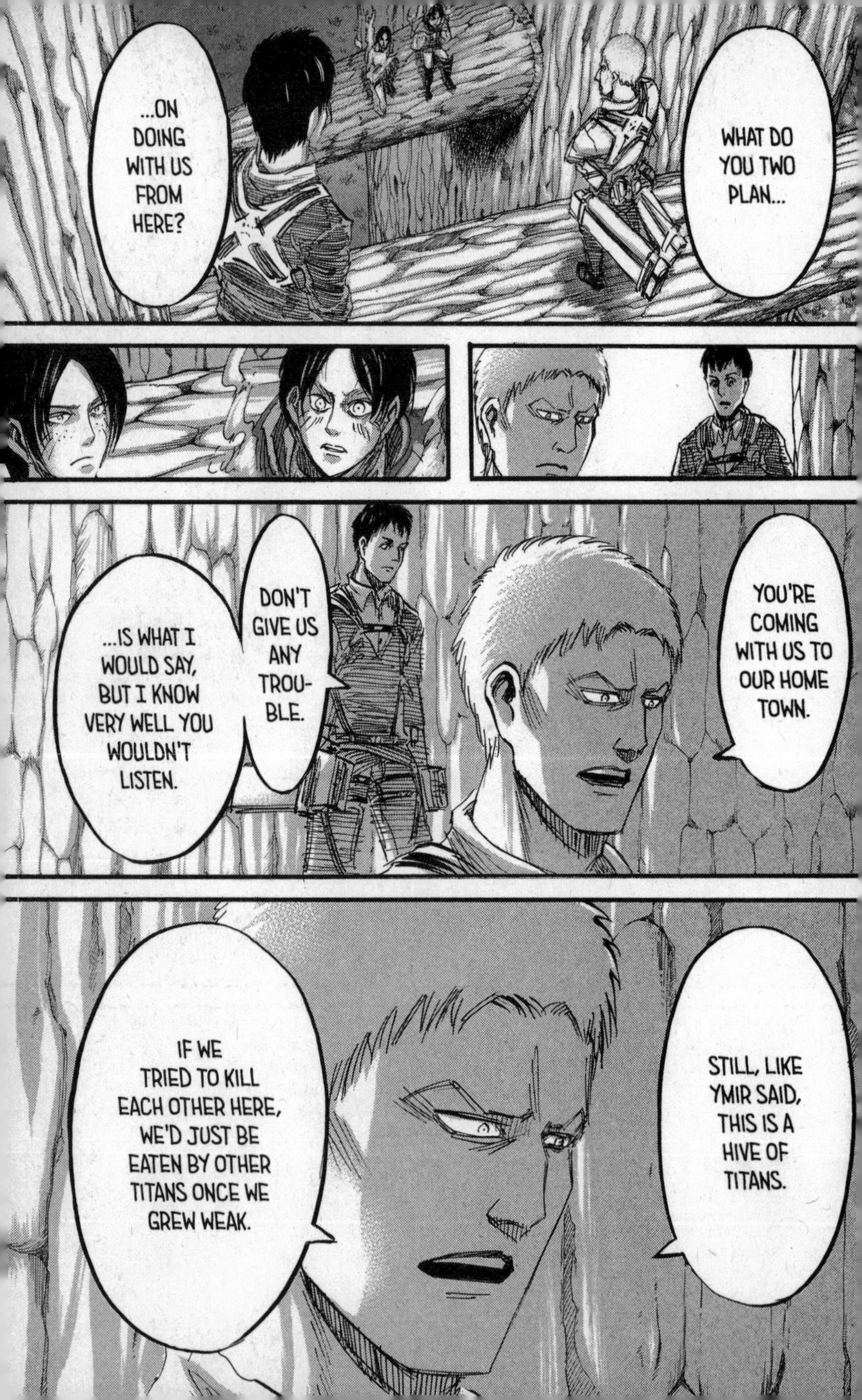
WHAT DO YOU TWO PLAN...
...ON DOING WITH US FROM HERE?
YOU'RE COMING WITH US TO OUR HOME TOWN.
DON'T GIVE US ANY TROU-BLE.
...IS WHAT I WOULD SAY, BUT I KNOW VERY WELL YOU WOULDN'T LISTEN.
STILL, LIKE YMIR SAID, THIS IS A HIVE OF TITANS.
IF WE TRIED TO KILL EACH OTHER HERE, WE'D JUST BE EATEN BY OTHER TITANS ONCE WE GREW WEAK.

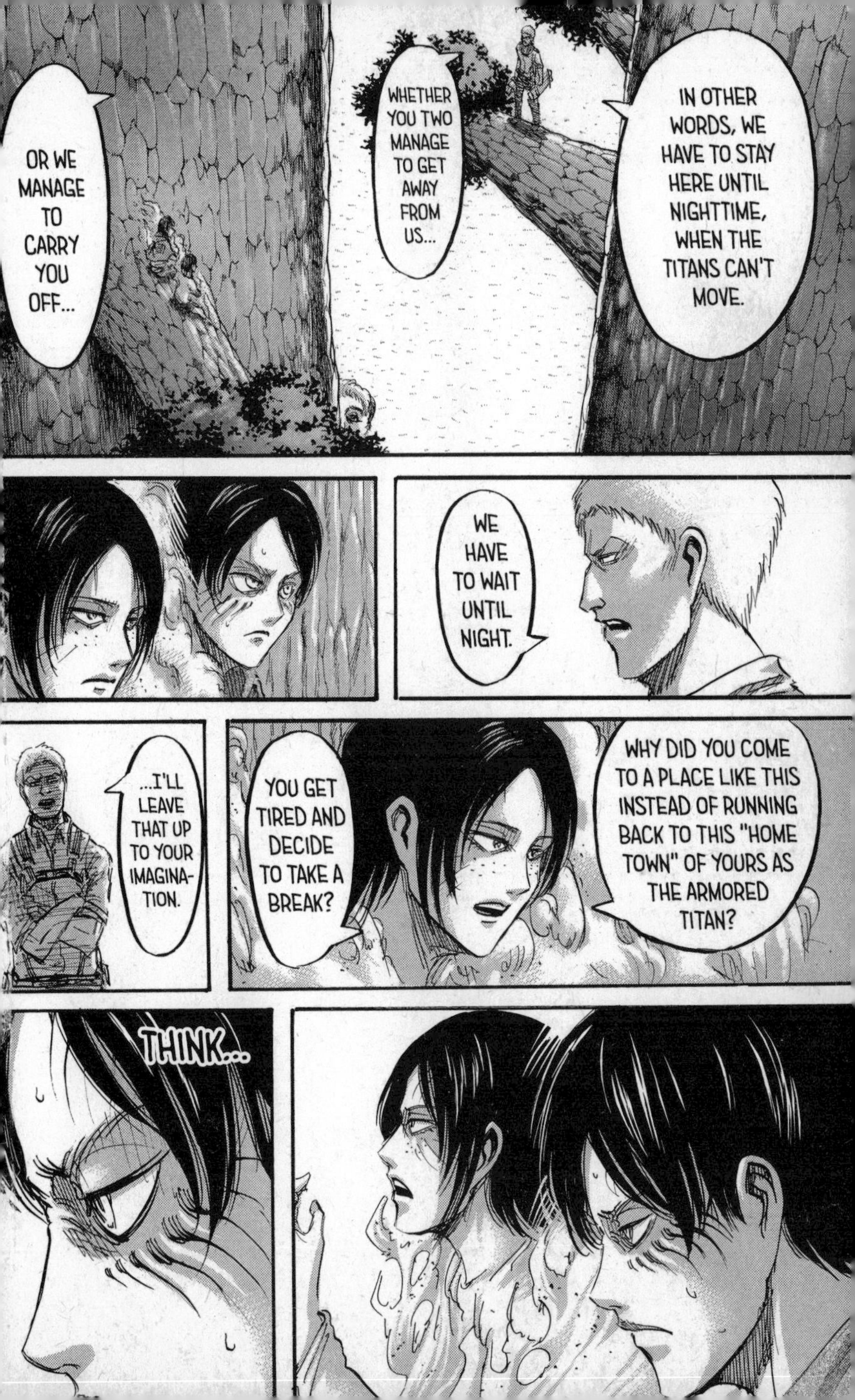
IN OTHER WORDS, WE HAVE TO STAY HERE UNTIL NIGHTTIME, WHEN THE TITANS CAN'T MOVE.
WHETHER YOU TWO MANAGE TO GET AWAY FROM US...
OR WE MANAGE TO CARRY YOU OFF...
WE HAVE TO WAIT UNTIL NIGHT.
WHY DID YOU COME TO A PLACE LIKE THIS INSTEAD OF RUNNING BACK TO THIS "HOME TOWN" OF YOURS AS THE ARMORED TITAN?
YOU GET TIRED AND DECIDE TO TAKE A BREAK?
...I'LL LEAVE THAT UP TO YOUR IMAGINATION.
THINK...

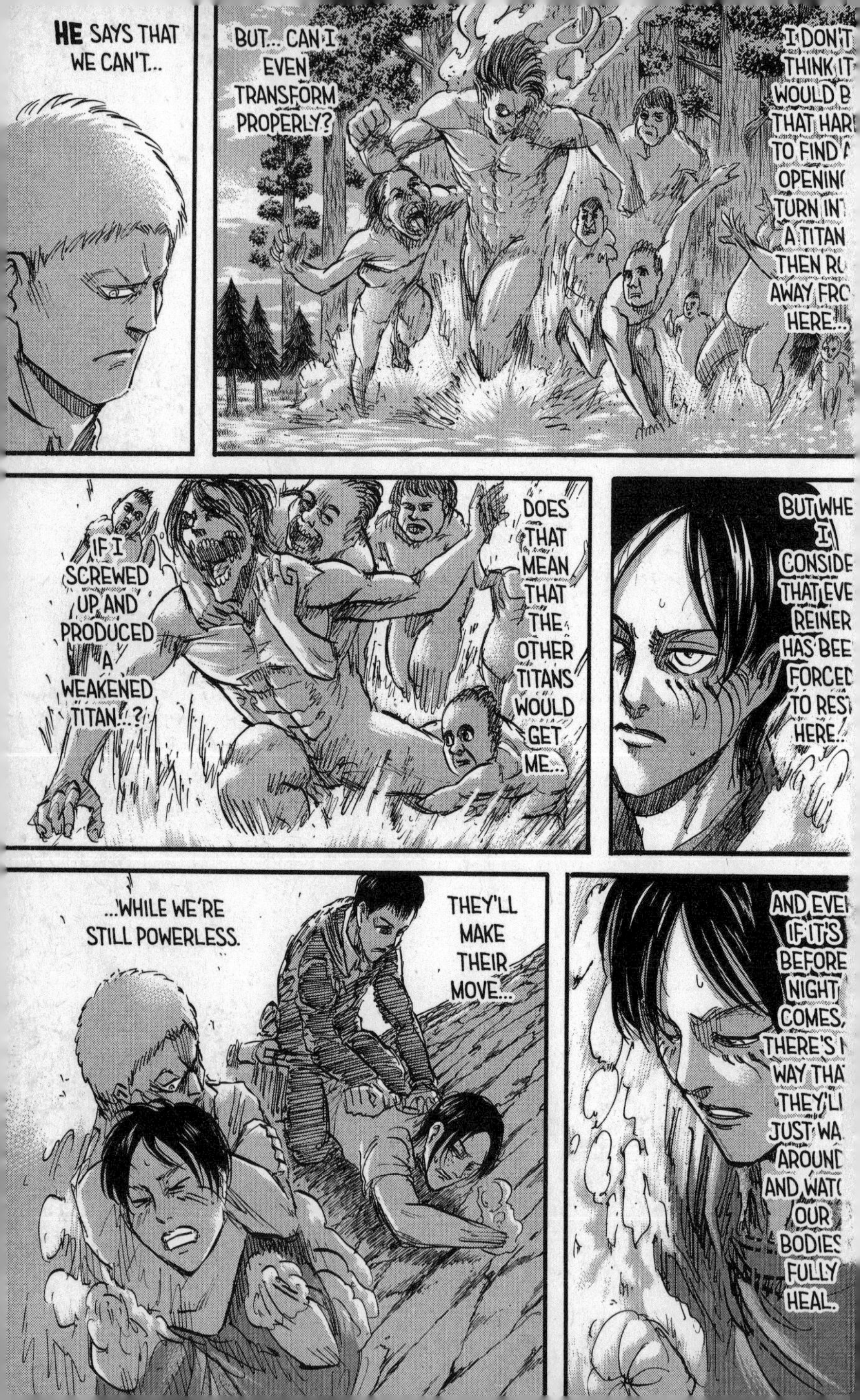

I DON'T THINK IT WOULD B THAT HAR TO FIND A OPENIN TURN INT A TITAN THEN R AWAY FRO HERE...
BUT... CAN I EVEN TRANSFORM PROPERLY?
HE SAYS THAT WE CAN'T...
BUT WHE I CONSIDE THAT EVE REINER HAS BEE FORCED TO REST HERE...
DOES THAT MEAN THAT THE OTHER TITANS WOULD GET ME...
IF I SCREWED UP AND PRODUCED A WEAKENED TITAN...?
AND EVE IF IT'S BEFORE NIGHT COMES, THERE'S WAY THA THEY'L JUST WA AROUN AND WAT OUR BODIES FULLY HEAL.
THEY'LL MAKE THEIR MOVE...
...WHILE WE'RE STILL POWERLESS.

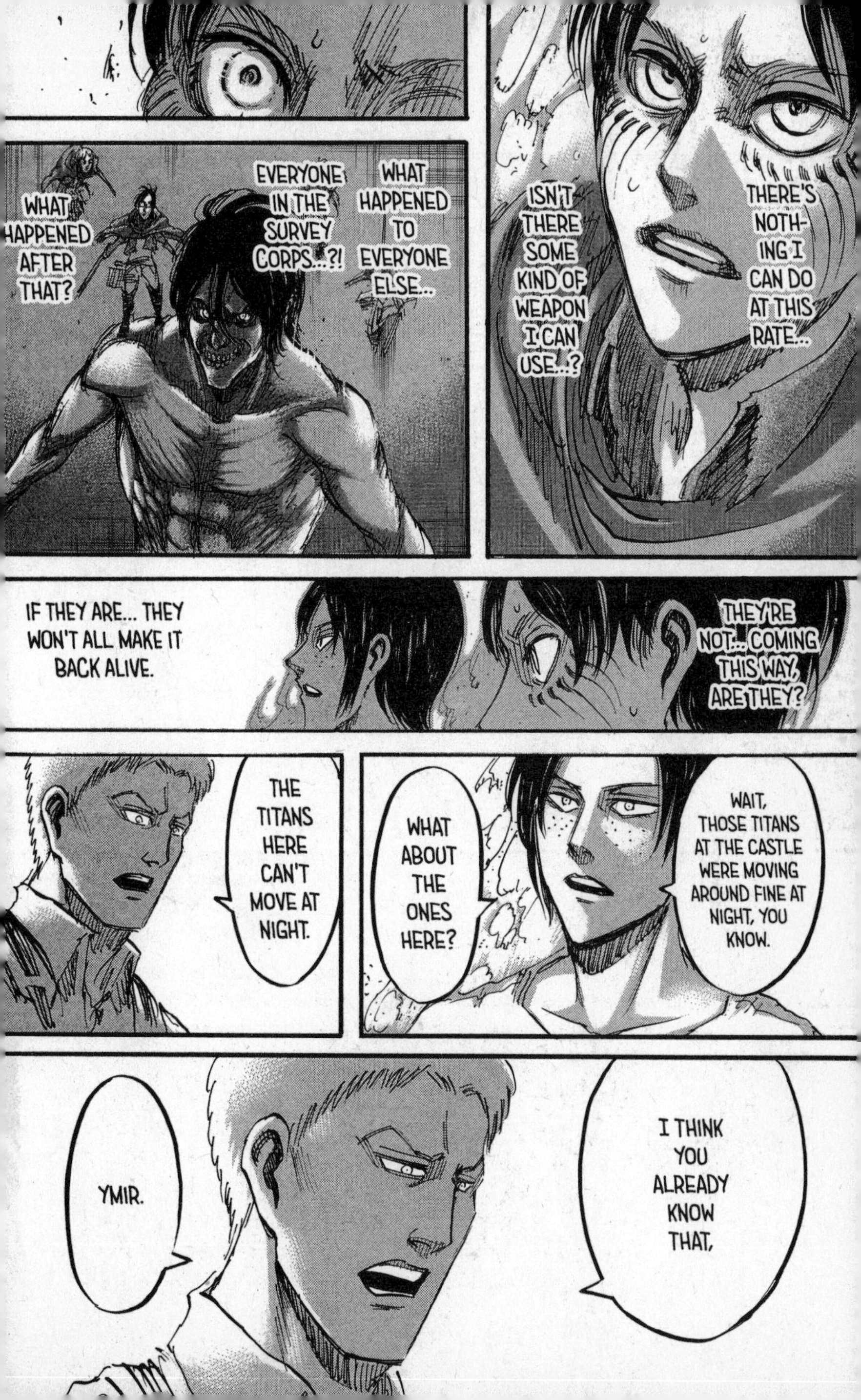

THERE'S NOTHING I CAN DO AT THIS RATE...
ISN'T THERE SOME KIND OF WEAPON I CAN USE...?
WHAT HAPPENED TO EVERYONE ELSE...
EVERYONE IN THE SURVEY CORPS...?!
WHAT HAPPENED AFTER THAT?
THEY'RE NOT... COMING THIS WAY, ARE THEY?
IF THEY ARE... THEY WON'T ALL MAKE IT BACK ALIVE.
WAIT, THOSE TITANS AT THE CASTLE WERE MOVING AROUND FINE AT NIGHT, YOU KNOW.
WHAT ABOUT THE ONES HERE?
THE TITANS HERE CAN'T MOVE AT NIGHT.
I THINK YOU ALREADY KNOW THAT,
YMIR.

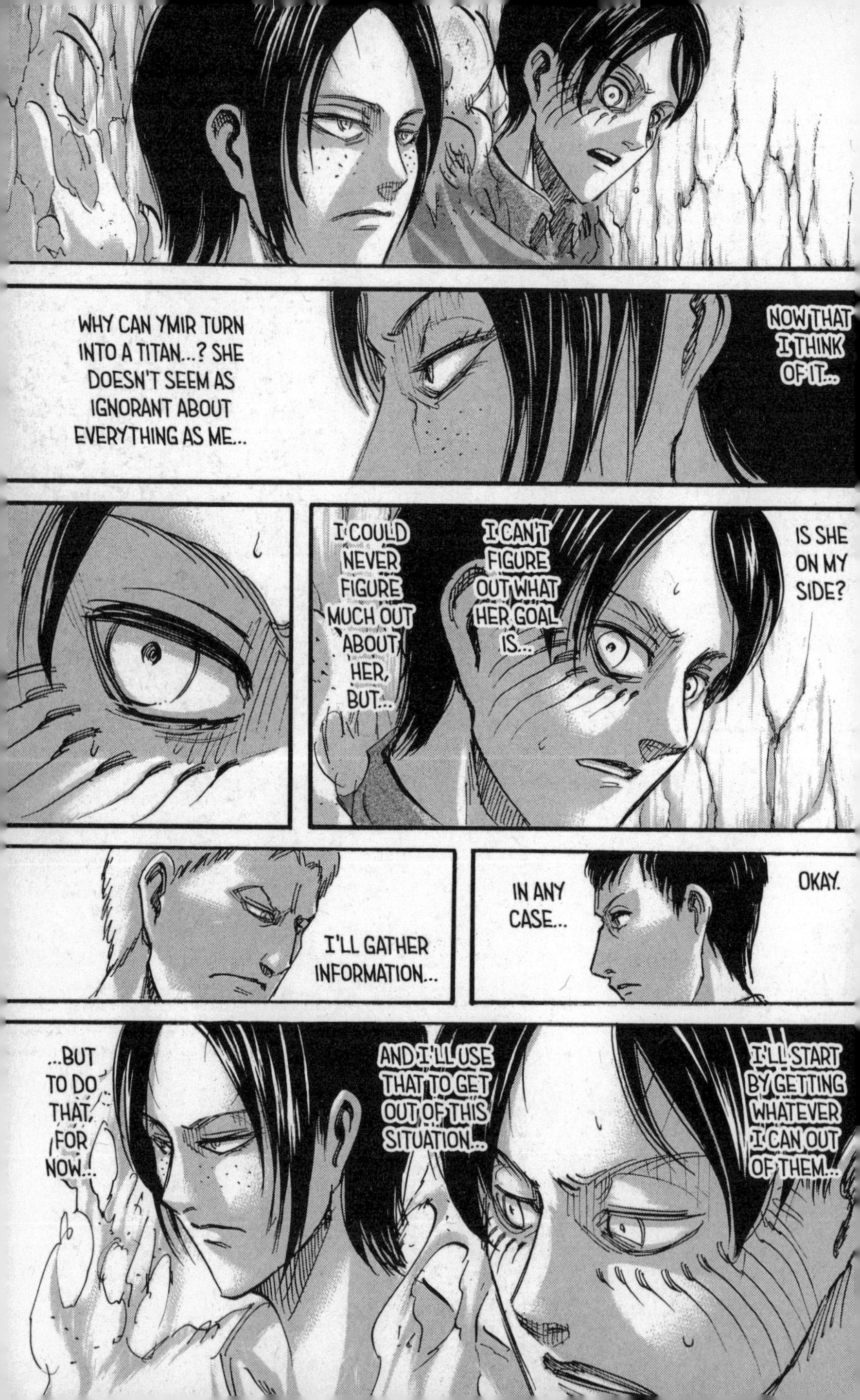
NOW THAT I THINK OF IT...
WHY CAN YMIR TURN INTO A TITAN...? SHE DOESN'T SEEM AS IGNORANT ABOUT EVERYTHING AS ME...
IS SHE ON MY SIDE?
I CAN'T FIGURE OUT WHAT HER GOAL IS...
I COULD NEVER FIGURE MUCH OUT ABOUT HER, BUT...
OKAY.
IN ANY CASE...
I'LL GATHER INFORMATION...
I'LL START BY GETTING WHATEVER I CAN OUT OF THEM...
AND I'LL USE THAT TO GET OUT OF THIS SITUATION...
...BUT TO DO THAT, FOR NOW...

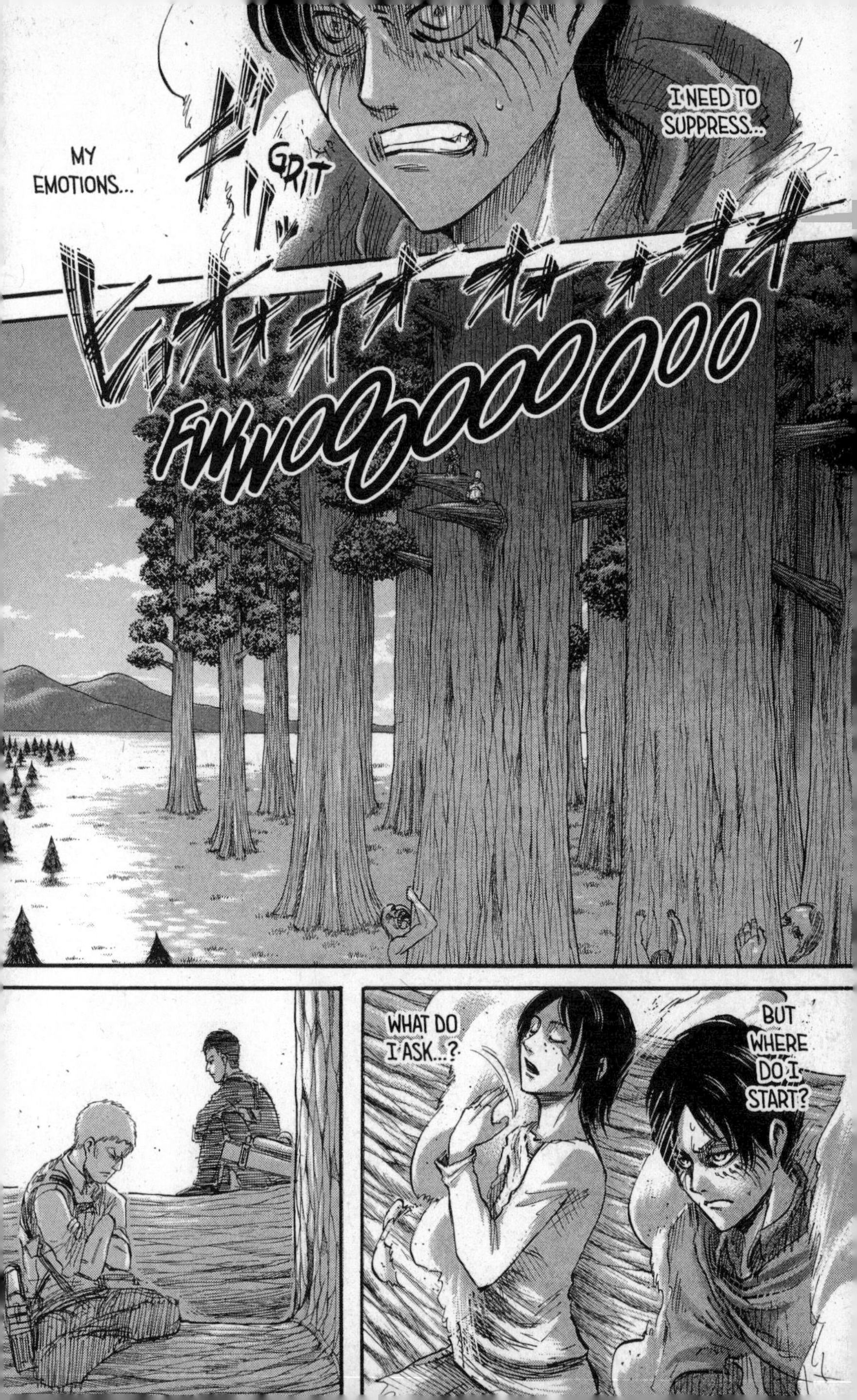
I NEED TO SUPPRESS...
MY EMOTIONS...
ギリッ
GRIT
FWWOOOOOOOOO
BUT WHERE DO I START?
WHAT DO I ASK...?

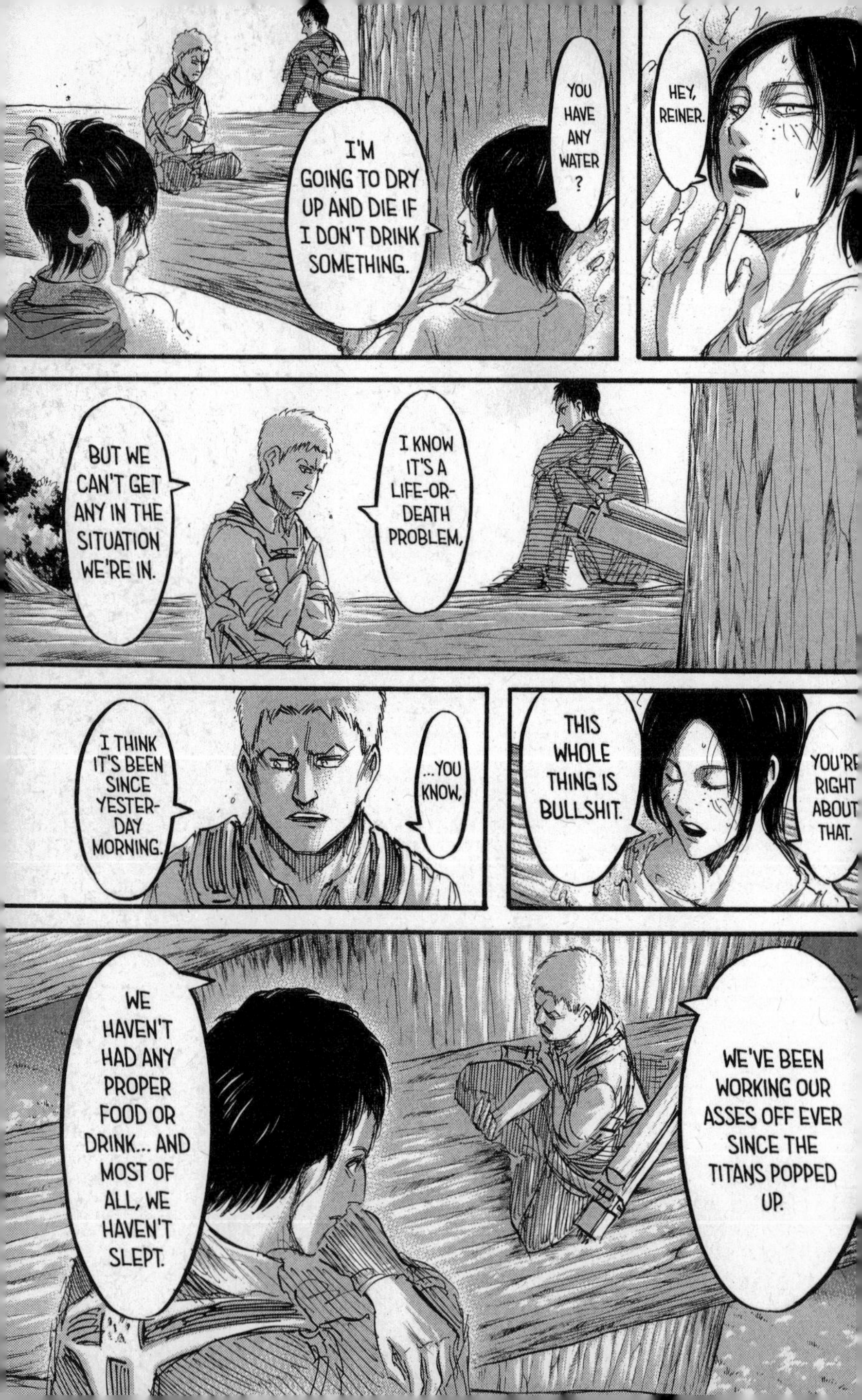
HEY, REINER.
YOU HAVE ANY WATER?
I'M GOING TO DRY UP AND DIE IF I DON'T DRINK SOMETHING.
I KNOW IT'S A LIFE-OR-DEATH PROBLEM,
BUT WE CAN'T GET ANY IN THE SITUATION WE'RE IN.
YOU'RE RIGHT ABOUT THAT.
THIS WHOLE THING IS BULLSHIT.
...YOU KNOW,
I THINK IT'S BEEN SINCE YESTER-DAY MORNING.
WE'VE BEEN WORKING OUR ASSES OFF EVER SINCE THE TITANS POPPED UP.
WE HAVEN'T HAD ANY PROPER FOOD OR DRINK... AND MOST OF ALL, WE HAVEN'T SLEPT.

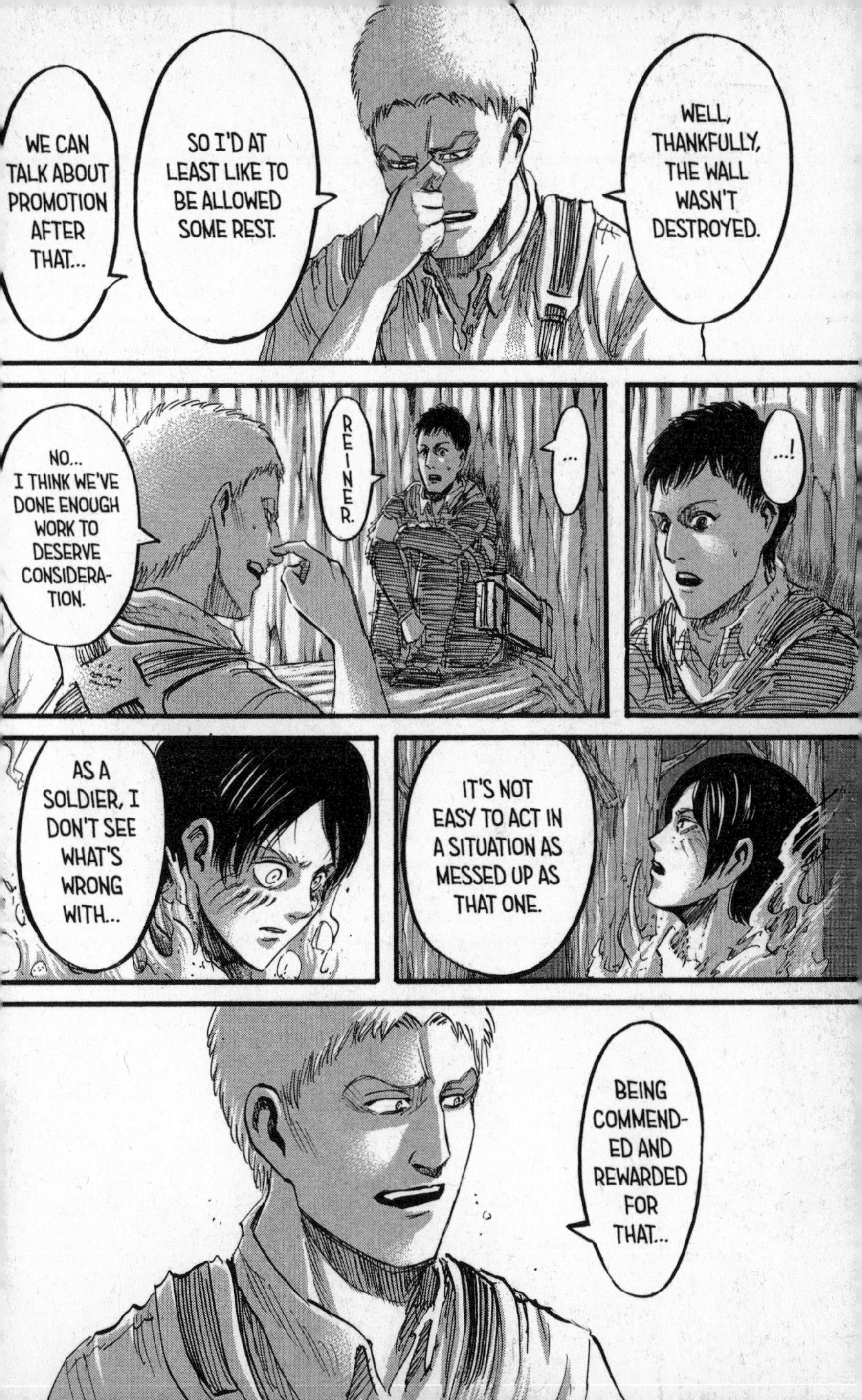
WELL, THANKFULLY, THE WALL WASN'T DESTROYED.
SO I'D AT LEAST LIKE TO BE ALLOWED SOME REST.
WE CAN TALK ABOUT PROMOTION AFTER THAT...
...!
...
REINER.
NO... I THINK WE'VE DONE ENOUGH WORK TO DESERVE CONSIDERA-TION.
IT'S NOT EASY TO ACT IN A SITUATION AS MESSED UP AS THAT ONE.
AS A SOLDIER, I DON'T SEE WHAT'S WRONG WITH...
BEING COMMEND-ED AND REWARDED FOR THAT...

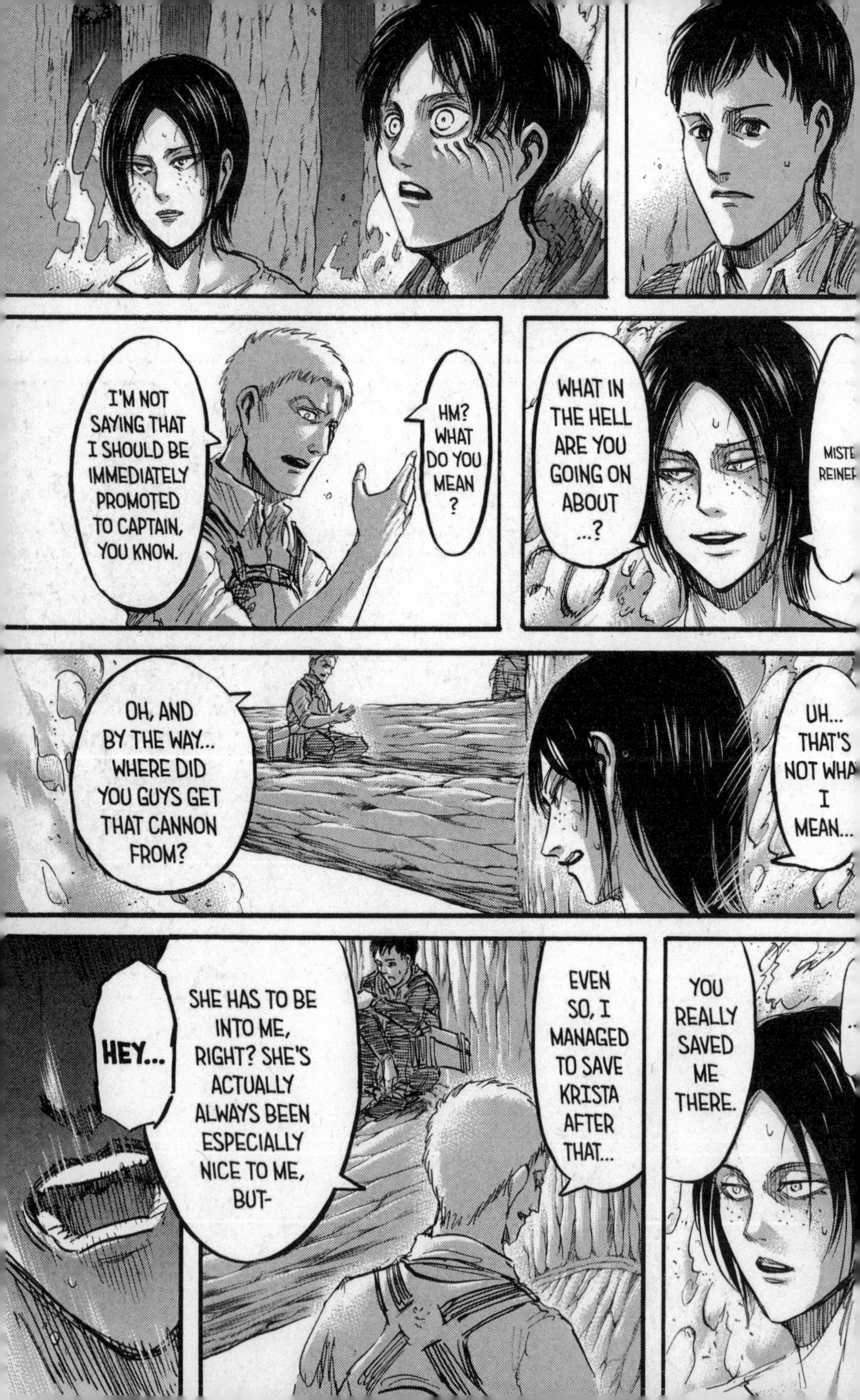

MISTE REINEF
WHAT IN THE HELL ARE YOU GOING ON ABOUT ...?
HM? WHAT DO YOU MEAN ?
I'M NOT SAYING THAT I SHOULD BE IMMEDIATELY PROMOTED TO CAPTAIN, YOU KNOW.
UH... THAT'S NOT WHA I MEAN...
OH, AND BY THE WAY... WHERE DID YOU GUYS GET THAT CANNON FROM?
YOU REALLY SAVED ME THERE.
EVEN SO, I MANAGED TO SAVE KRISTA AFTER THAT...
SHE HAS TO BE INTO ME, RIGHT? SHE'S ACTUALLY ALWAYS BEEN ESPECIALLY NICE TO ME, BUT-
HEY...

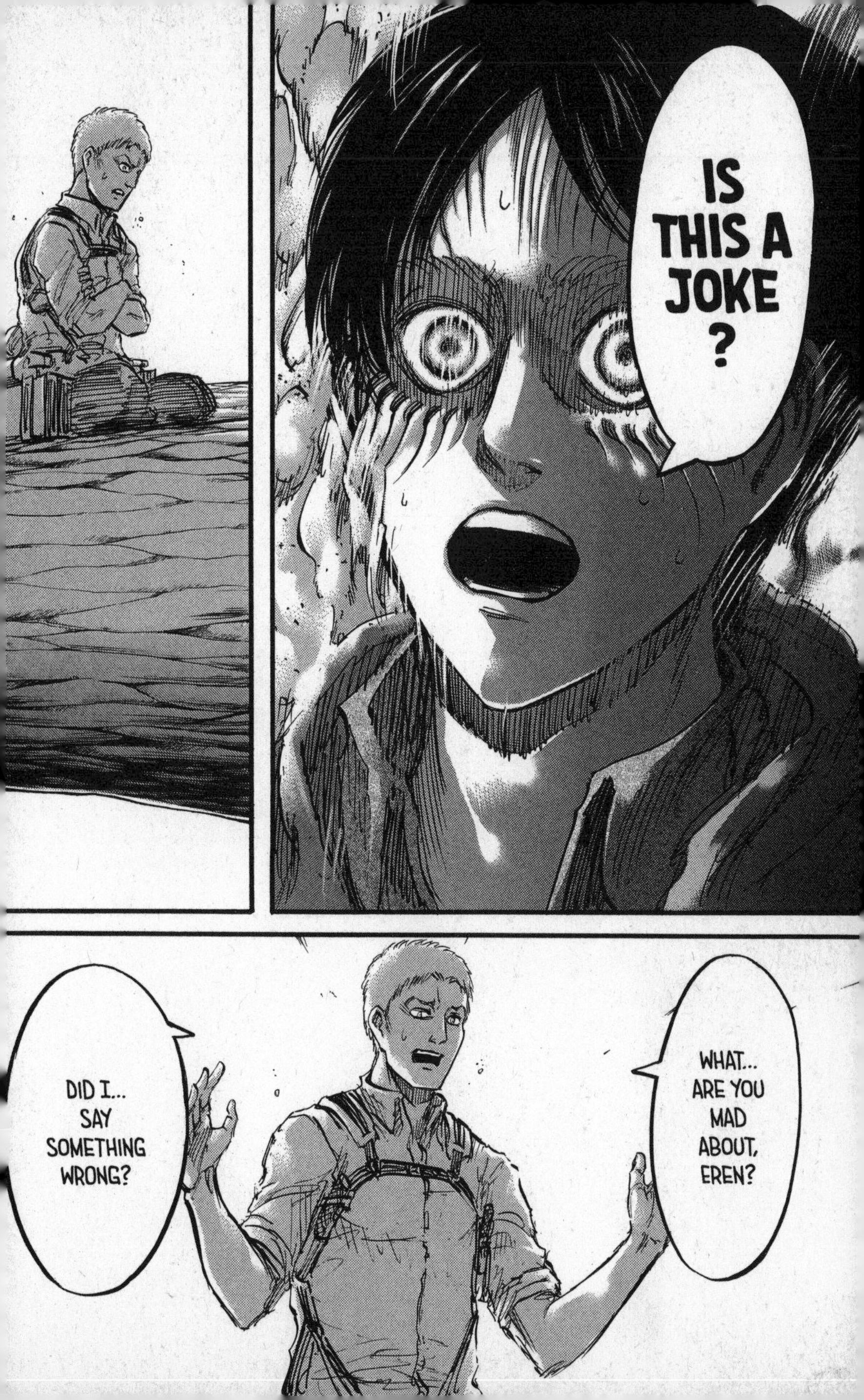
IS THIS A JOKE?
WHAT... ARE YOU MAD ABOUT, EREN?
DID I... SAY SOMETHING WRONG?

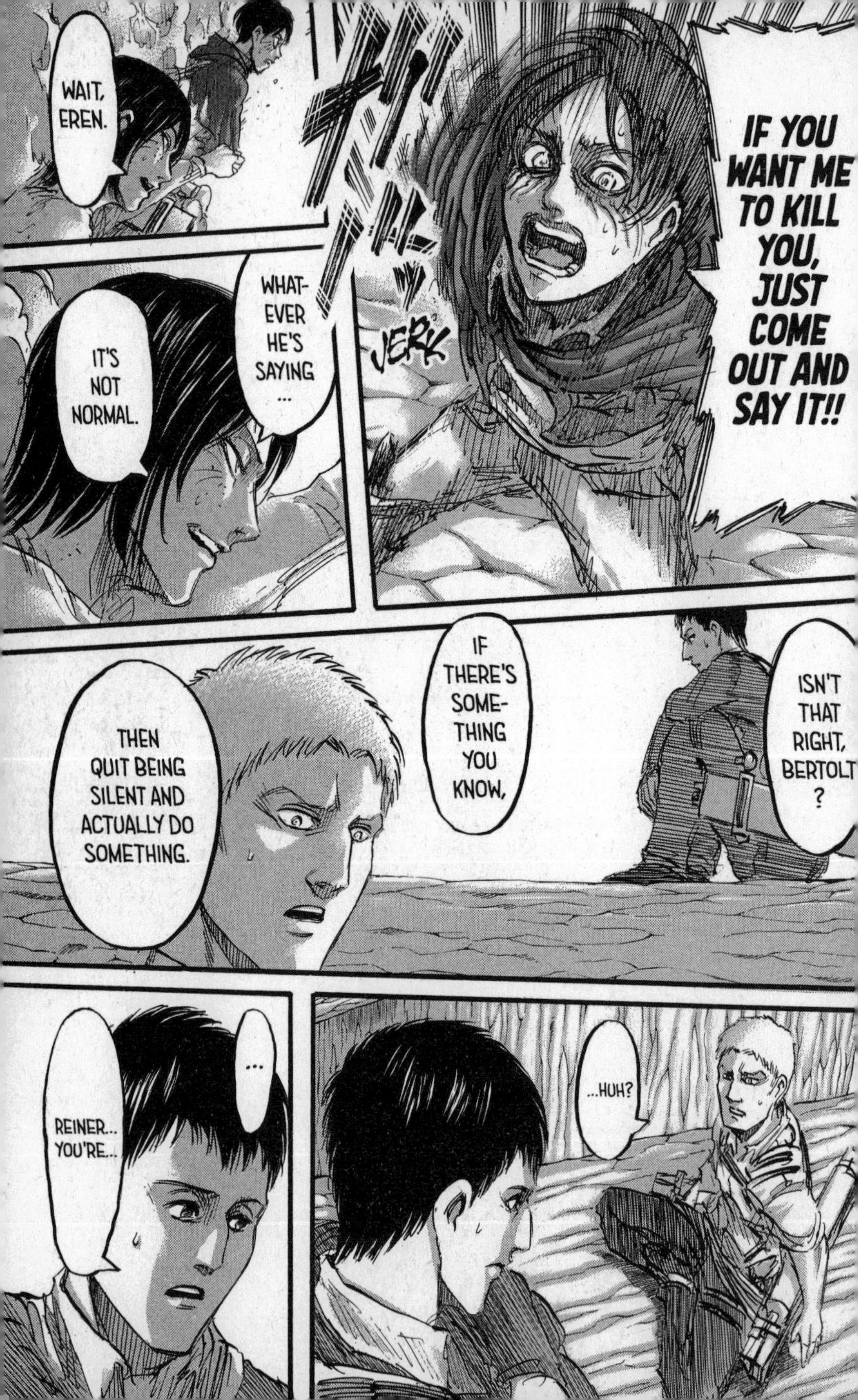

IF YOU WANT ME TO KILL YOU, JUST COME OUT AND SAY IT!!
JERK
WAIT, EREN.
WHATEVER HE'S SAYING ...
IT'S NOT NORMAL.
ISN'T THAT RIGHT, BERTOLT?
IF THERE'S SOMETHING YOU KNOW,
THEN QUIT BEING SILENT AND ACTUALLY DO SOMETHING.
...HUH?
...
REINER... YOU'RE...

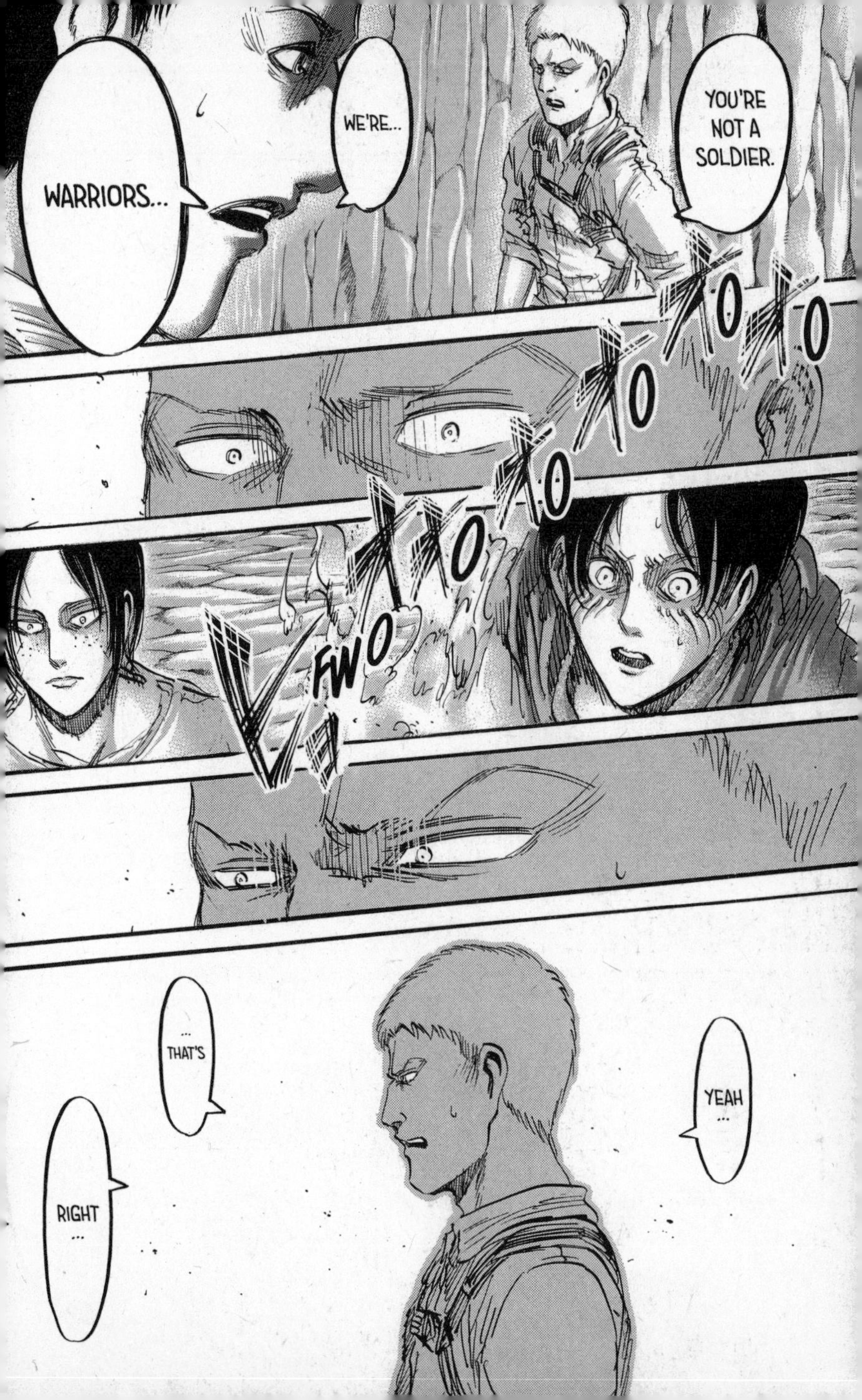

YOU'RE NOT A SOLDIER.
WE'RE...
WARRIORS...
FWO
YEAH...
...THAT'S
RIGHT...

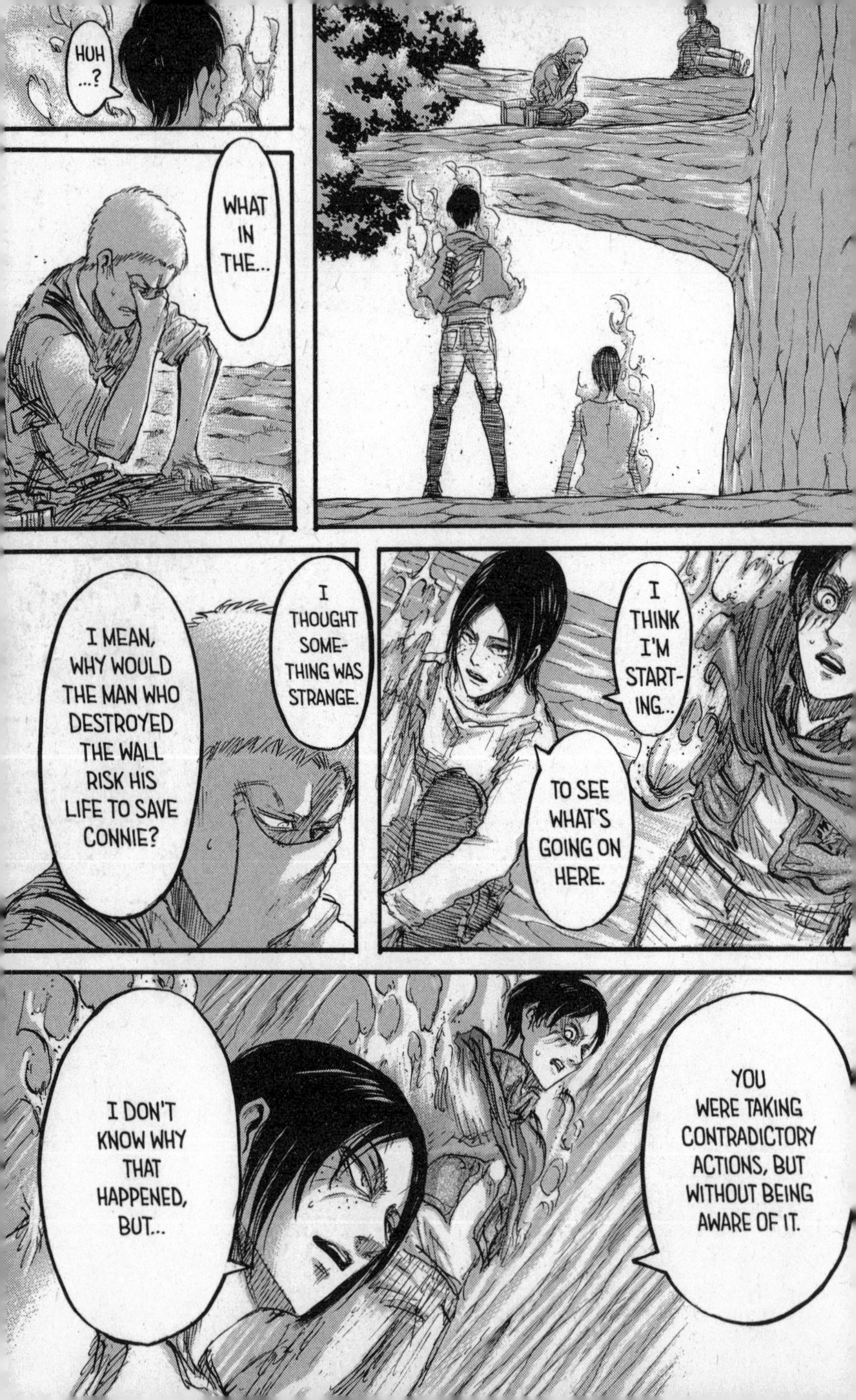
HUH ...?
WHAT IN THE...
I THINK I'M START-ING...
TO SEE WHAT'S GOING ON HERE.
I THOUGHT SOME-THING WAS STRANGE.
I MEAN, WHY WOULD THE MAN WHO DESTROYED THE WALL RISK HIS LIFE TO SAVE CONNIE?
I DON'T KNOW WHY THAT HAPPENED, BUT...
YOU WERE TAKING CONTRADICTORY ACTIONS, BUT WITHOUT BEING AWARE OF IT.

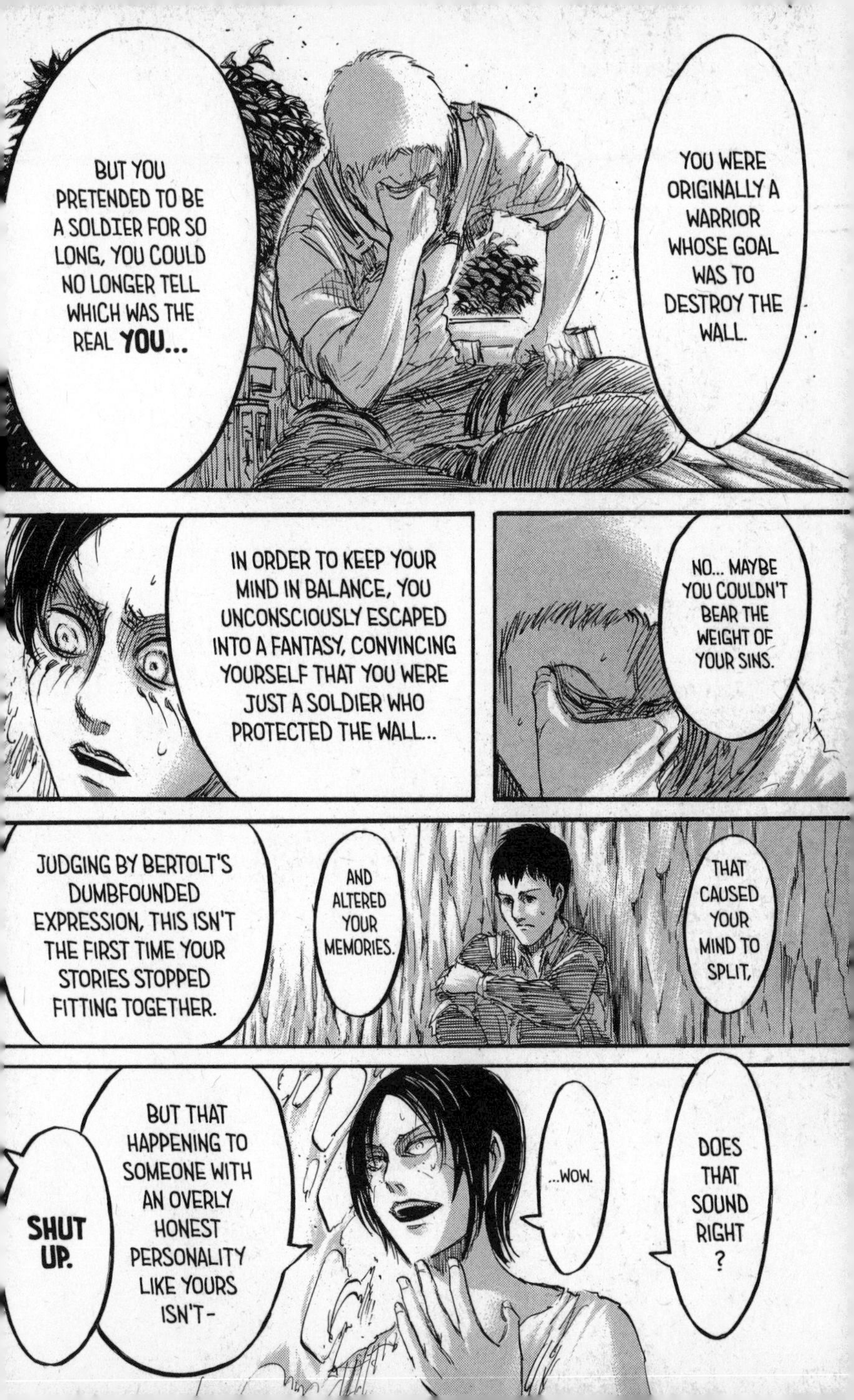
YOU WERE ORIGINALLY A WARRIOR WHOSE GOAL WAS TO DESTROY THE WALL.
BUT YOU PRETENDED TO BE A SOLDIER FOR SO LONG, YOU COULD NO LONGER TELL WHICH WAS THE REAL **YOU...**
NO... MAYBE YOU COULDN'T BEAR THE WEIGHT OF YOUR SINS.
IN ORDER TO KEEP YOUR MIND IN BALANCE, YOU UNCONSCIOUSLY ESCAPED INTO A FANTASY, CONVINCING YOURSELF THAT YOU WERE JUST A SOLDIER WHO PROTECTED THE WALL...
THAT CAUSED YOUR MIND TO SPLIT,
AND ALTERED YOUR MEMORIES.
JUDGING BY BERTOLT'S DUMBFOUNDED EXPRESSION, THIS ISN'T THE FIRST TIME YOUR STORIES STOPPED FITTING TOGETHER.
DOES THAT SOUND RIGHT?
...WOW.
BUT THAT HAPPENING TO SOMEONE WITH AN OVERLY HONEST PERSONALITY LIKE YOURS ISN'T-
SHUT UP.

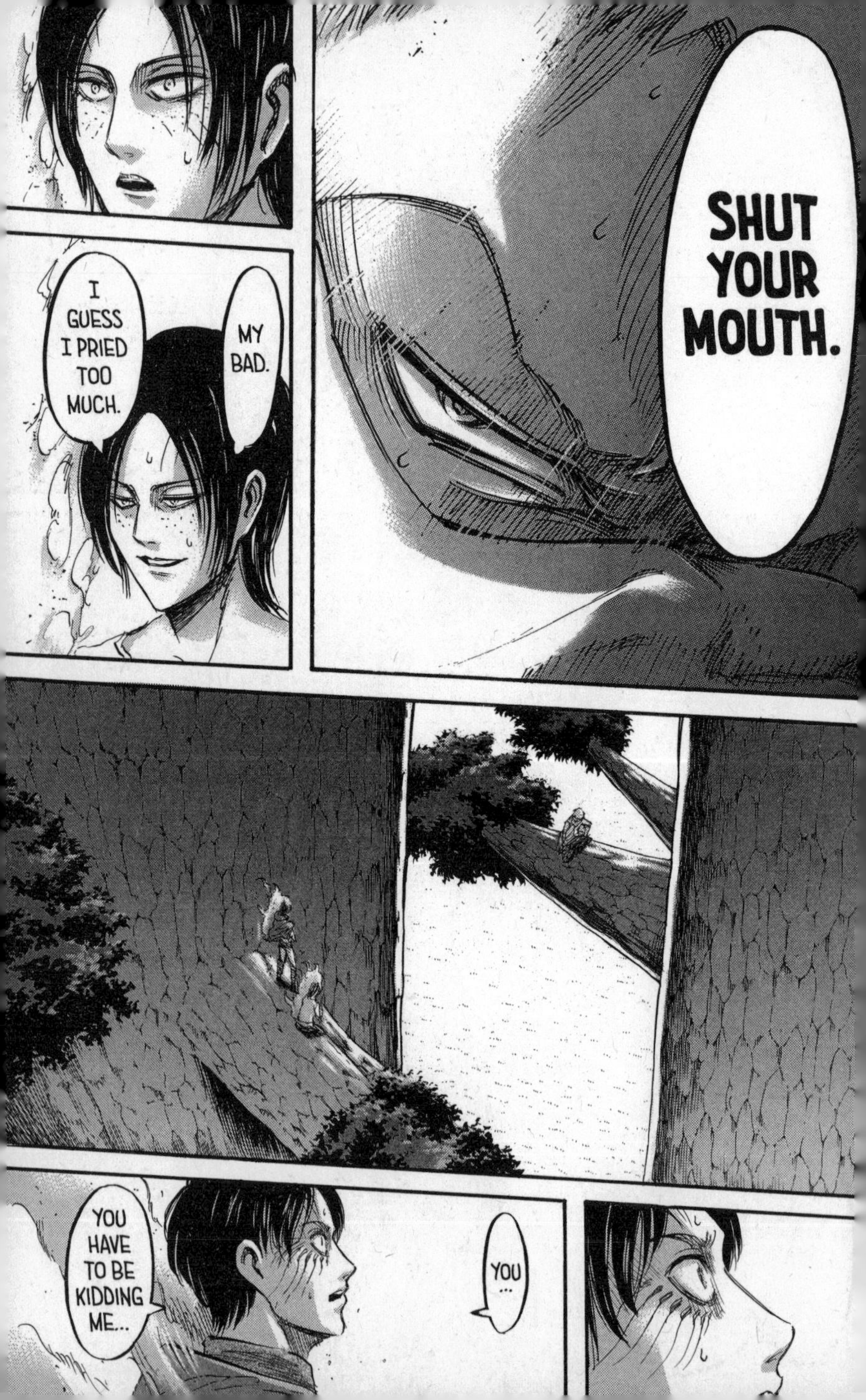
SHUT YOUR MOUTH.
MY BAD.
I GUESS I PRIED TOO MUCH.
YOU...
YOU HAVE TO BE KIDDING ME...

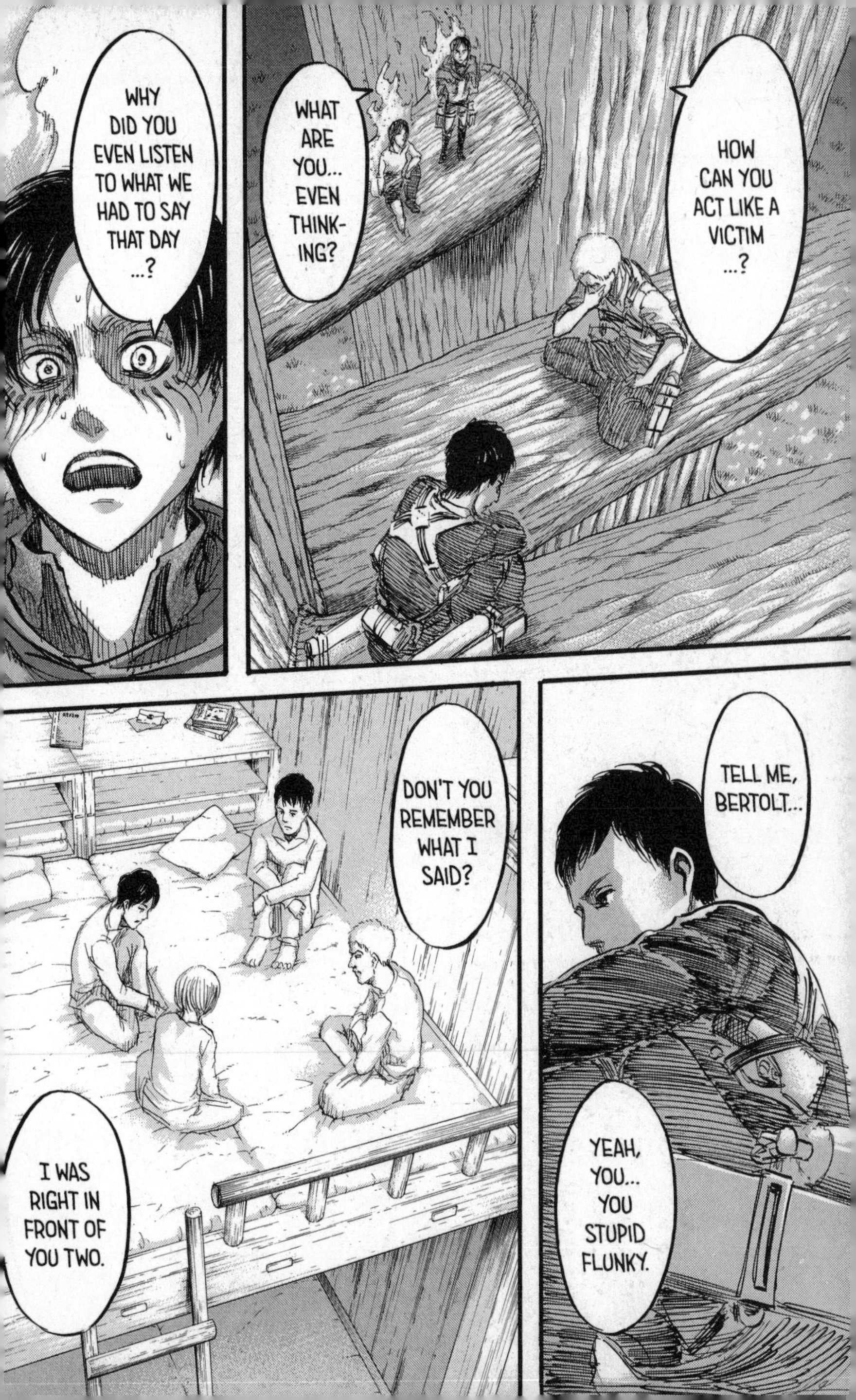
HOW CAN YOU ACT LIKE A VICTIM ...?
WHAT ARE YOU... EVEN THINK-ING?
WHY DID YOU EVEN LISTEN TO WHAT WE HAD TO SAY THAT DAY ...?
TELL ME, BERTOLT...
YEAH, YOU... YOU STUPID FLUNKY.
DON'T YOU REMEMBER WHAT I SAID?
I WAS RIGHT IN FRONT OF YOU TWO.

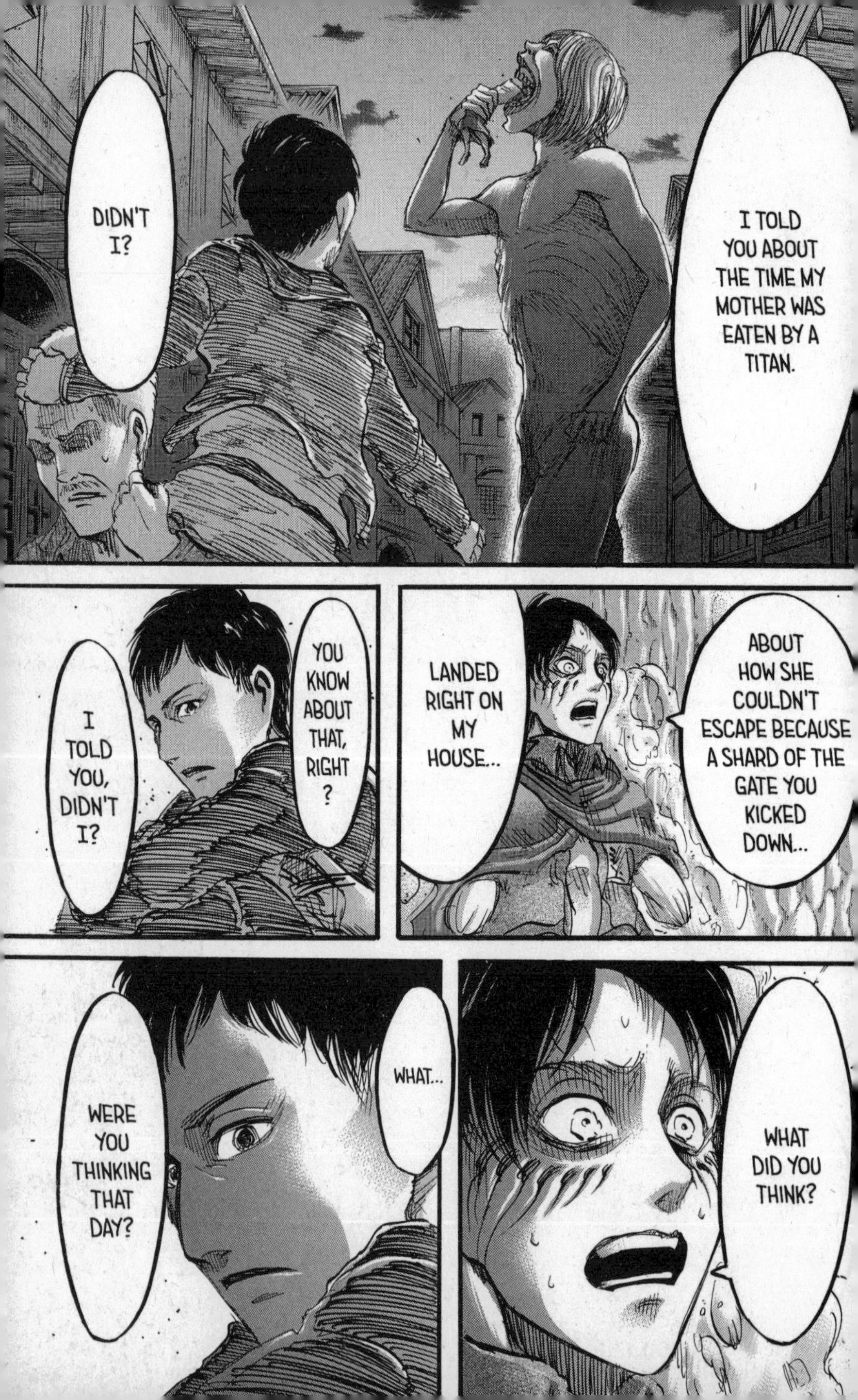
I TOLD YOU ABOUT THE TIME MY MOTHER WAS EATEN BY A TITAN.
DIDN'T I?
ABOUT HOW SHE COULDN'T ESCAPE BECAUSE A SHARD OF THE GATE YOU KICKED DOWN...
LANDED RIGHT ON MY HOUSE...
YOU KNOW ABOUT THAT, RIGHT?
I TOLD YOU, DIDN'T I?
WHAT DID YOU THINK?
WHAT...
WERE YOU THINKING THAT DAY?

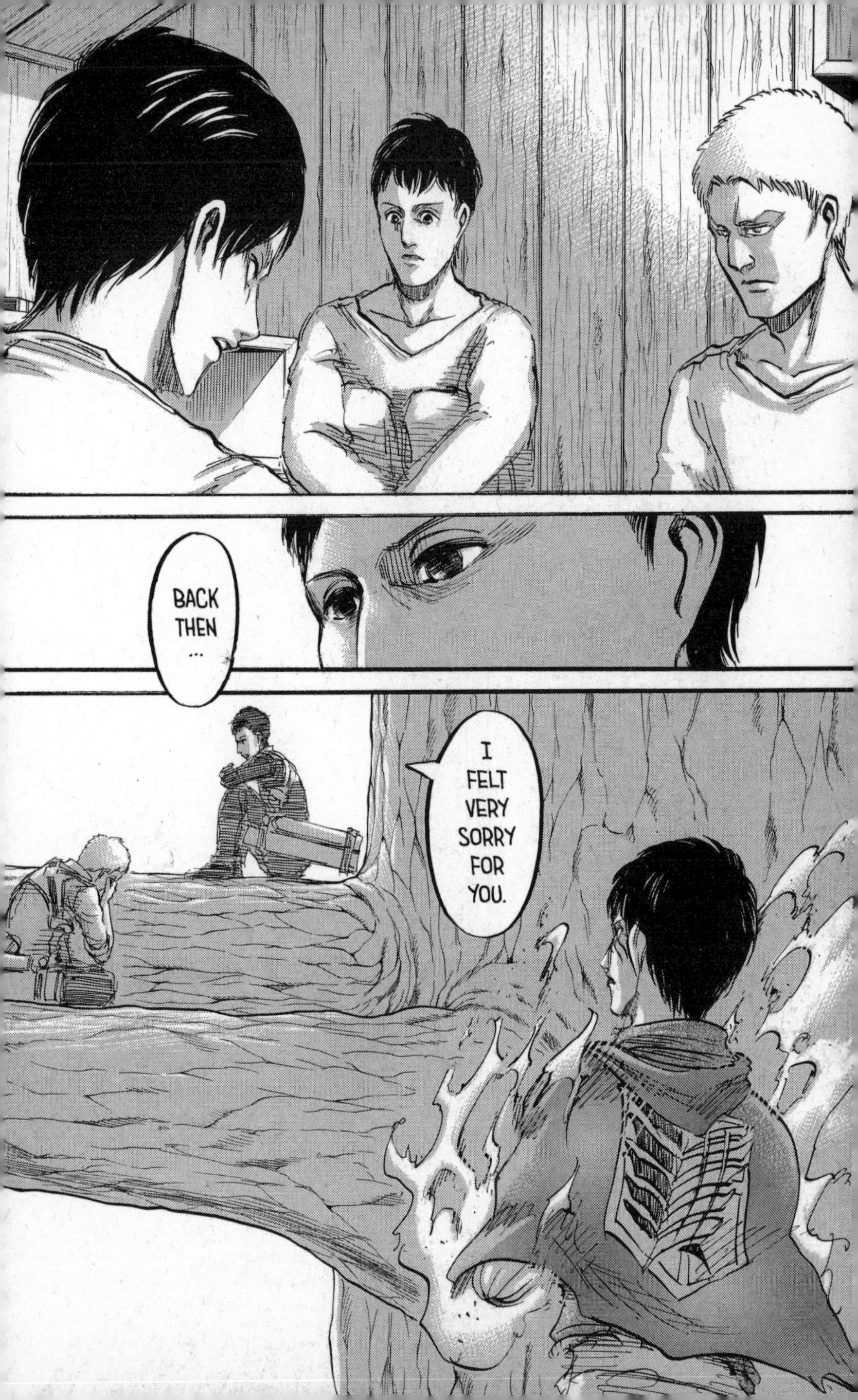
BACK THEN ...
I FELT VERY SORRY FOR YOU.

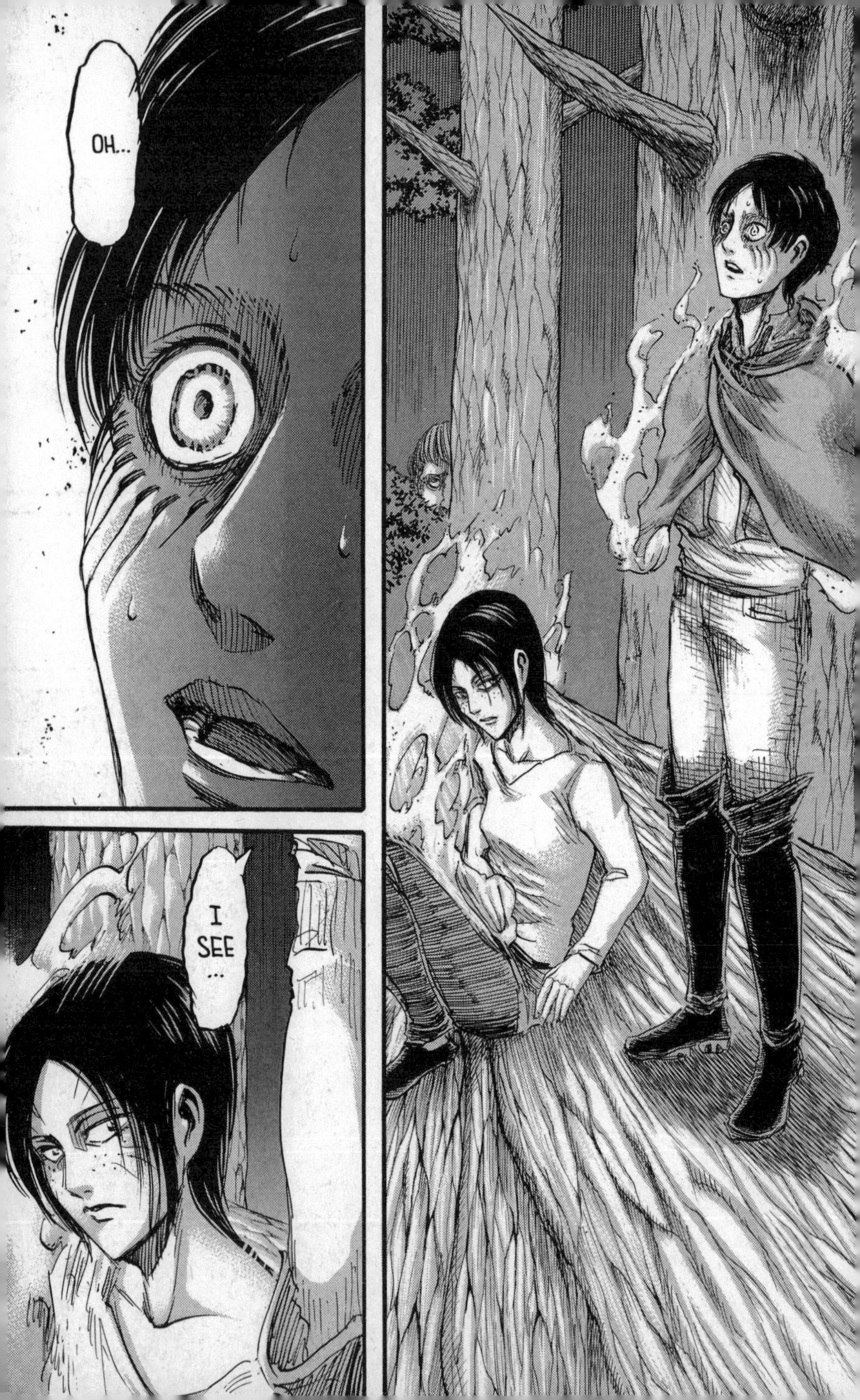
OH...
I SEE ...

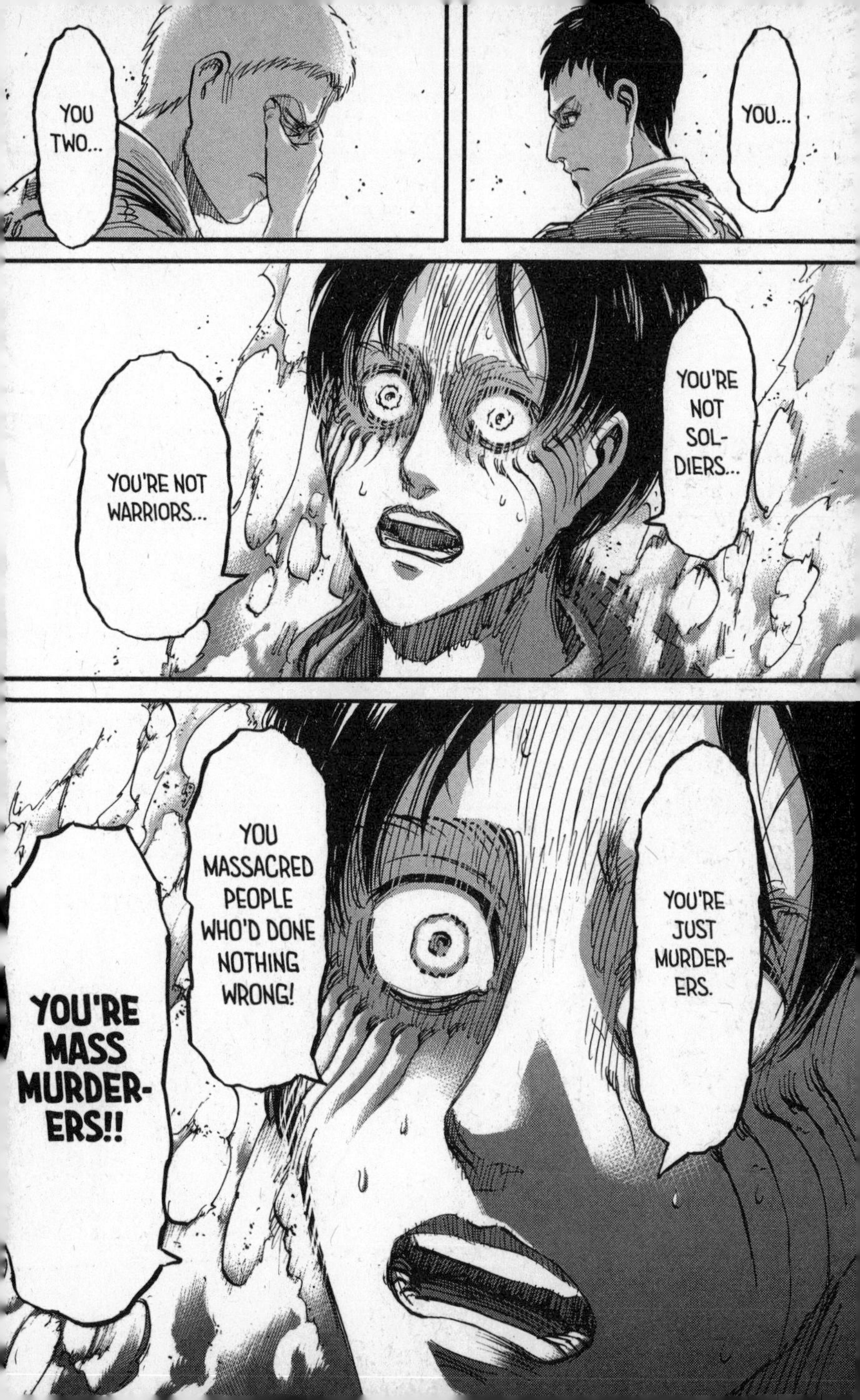
YOU...
YOU TWO...
YOU'RE NOT SOLDIERS...
YOU'RE NOT WARRIORS...
YOU'RE JUST MURDERERS.
YOU MASSACRED PEOPLE WHO'D DONE NOTHING WRONG!
YOU'RE MASS MURDERERS!!

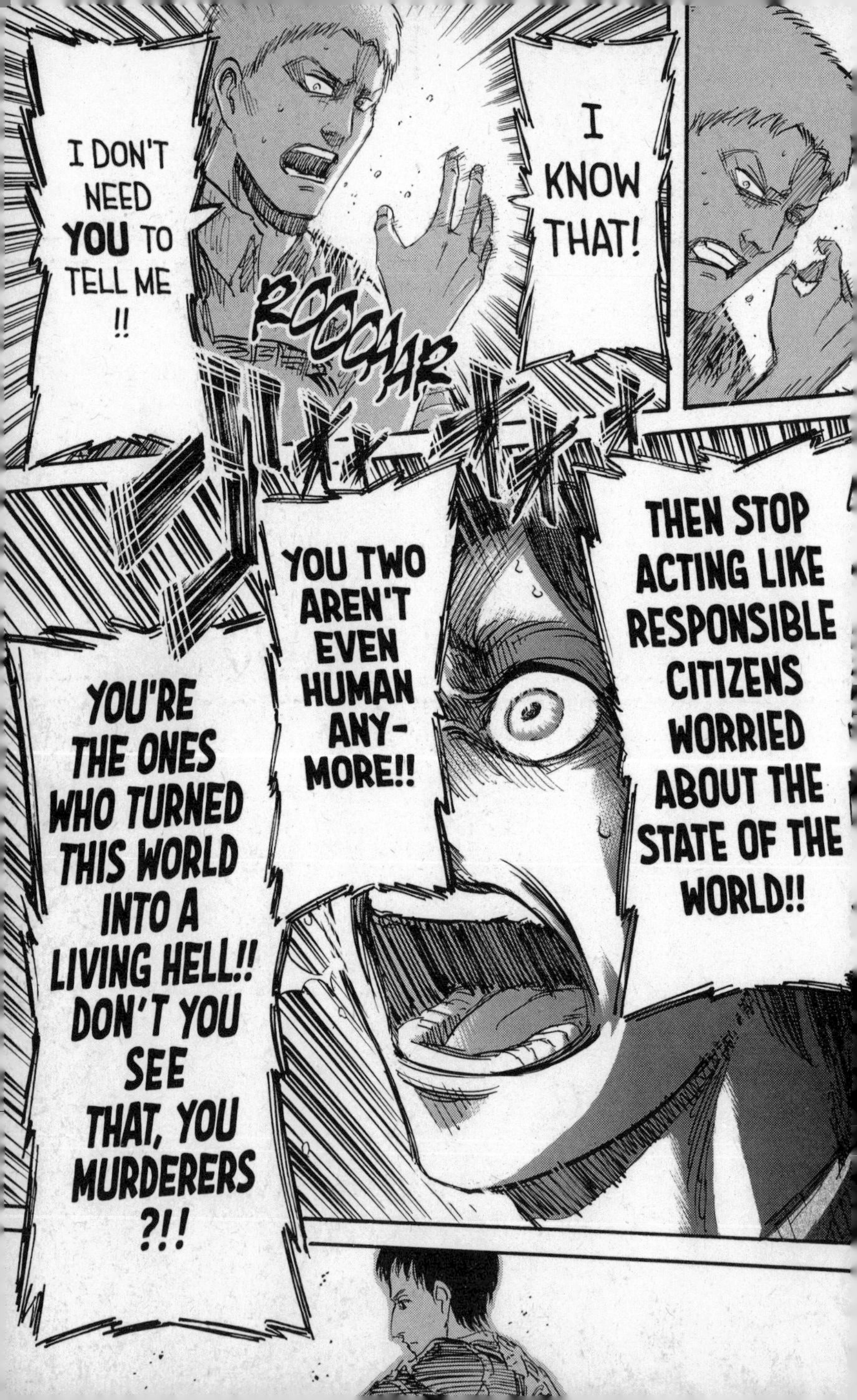
I KNOW THAT!
I DON'T NEED YOU TO TELL ME !!
ROOOAAR
THEN STOP ACTING LIKE RESPONSIBLE CITIZENS WORRIED ABOUT THE STATE OF THE WORLD!!
YOU TWO AREN'T EVEN HUMAN ANY-MORE!!
YOU'RE THE ONES WHO TURNED THIS WORLD INTO A LIVING HELL!! DON'T YOU SEE THAT, YOU MURDERERS ?!!

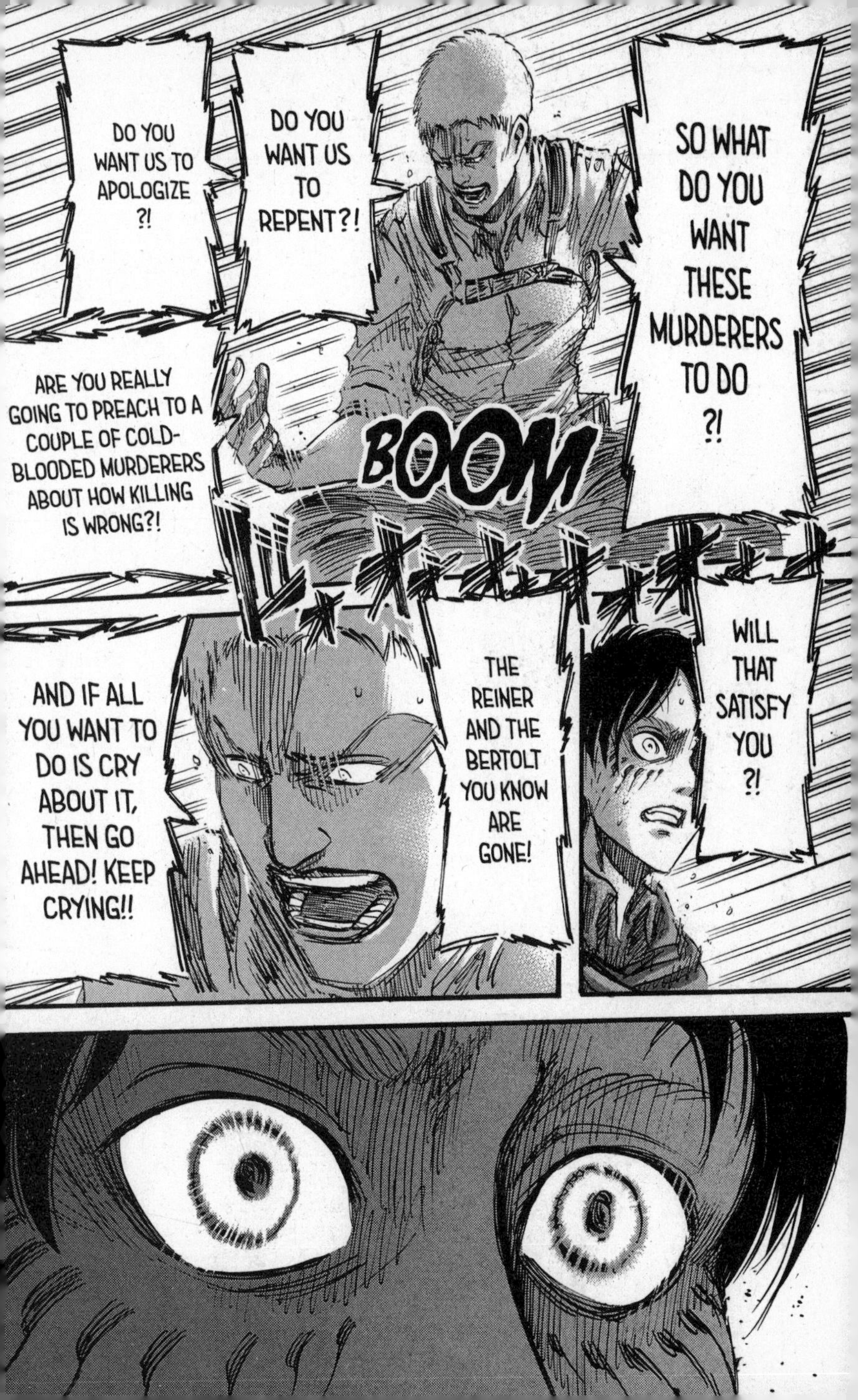
SO WHAT DO YOU WANT THESE MURDERERS TO DO ?!
DO YOU WANT US TO REPENT?!
DO YOU WANT US TO APOLOGIZE ?!
ARE YOU REALLY GOING TO PREACH TO A COUPLE OF COLD-BLOODED MURDERERS ABOUT HOW KILLING IS WRONG?!
BOOM
WILL THAT SATISFY YOU ?!
THE REINER AND THE BERTOLT YOU KNOW ARE GONE!
AND IF ALL YOU WANT TO DO IS CRY ABOUT IT, THEN GO AHEAD! KEEP CRYING!!

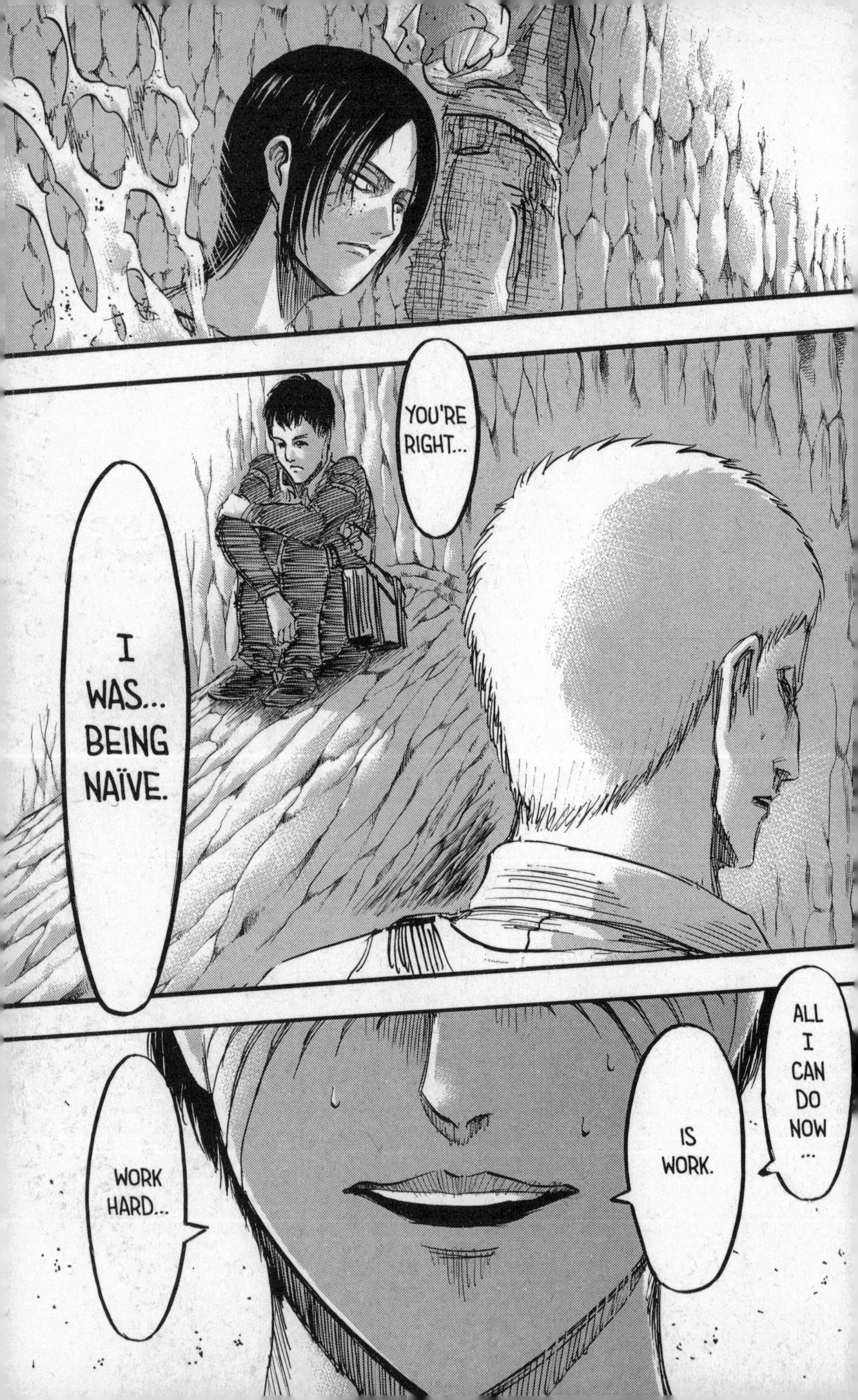
YOU'RE RIGHT...
I WAS... BEING NAÏVE.
ALL I CAN DO NOW...
IS WORK.
WORK HARD...

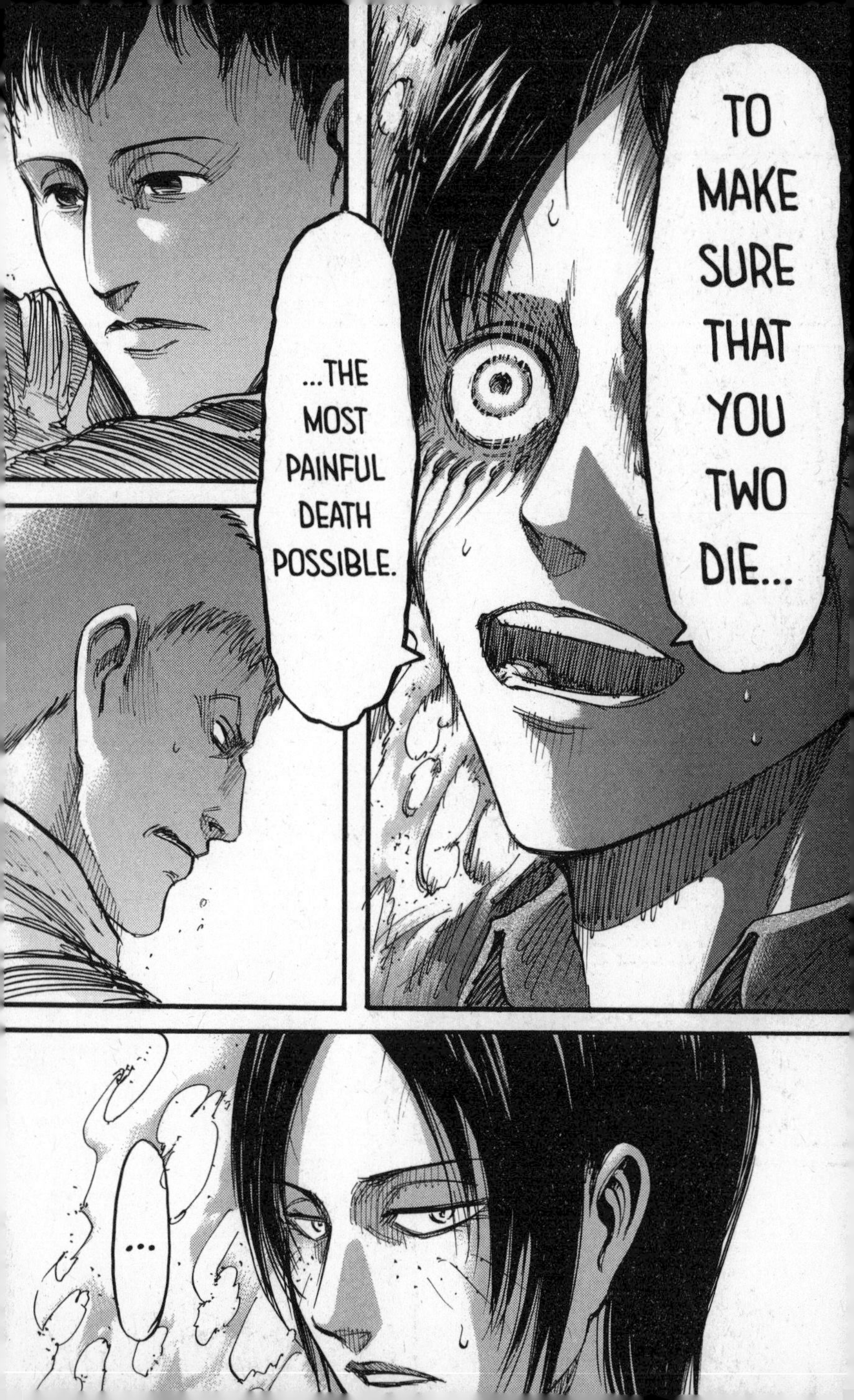
TO MAKE SURE THAT YOU TWO DIE...
...THE MOST PAINFUL DEATH POSSIBLE.
...

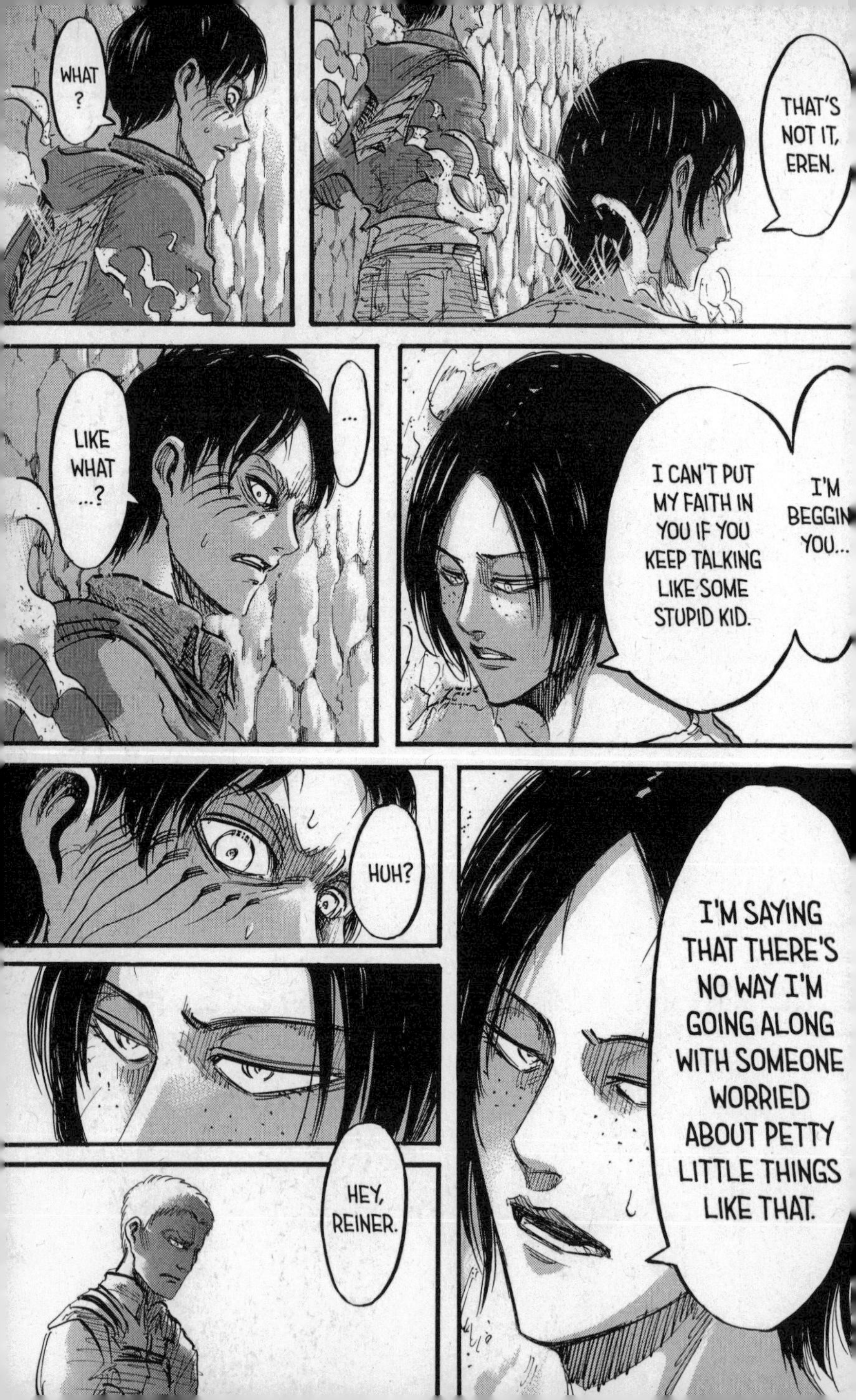
THAT'S NOT IT, EREN.
WHAT ?
I'M BEGGIN YOU...
I CAN'T PUT MY FAITH IN YOU IF YOU KEEP TALKING LIKE SOME STUPID KID.
...
LIKE WHAT ...?
I'M SAYING THAT THERE'S NO WAY I'M GOING ALONG WITH SOMEONE WORRIED ABOUT PETTY LITTLE THINGS LIKE THAT.
HUH?
HEY, REINER.

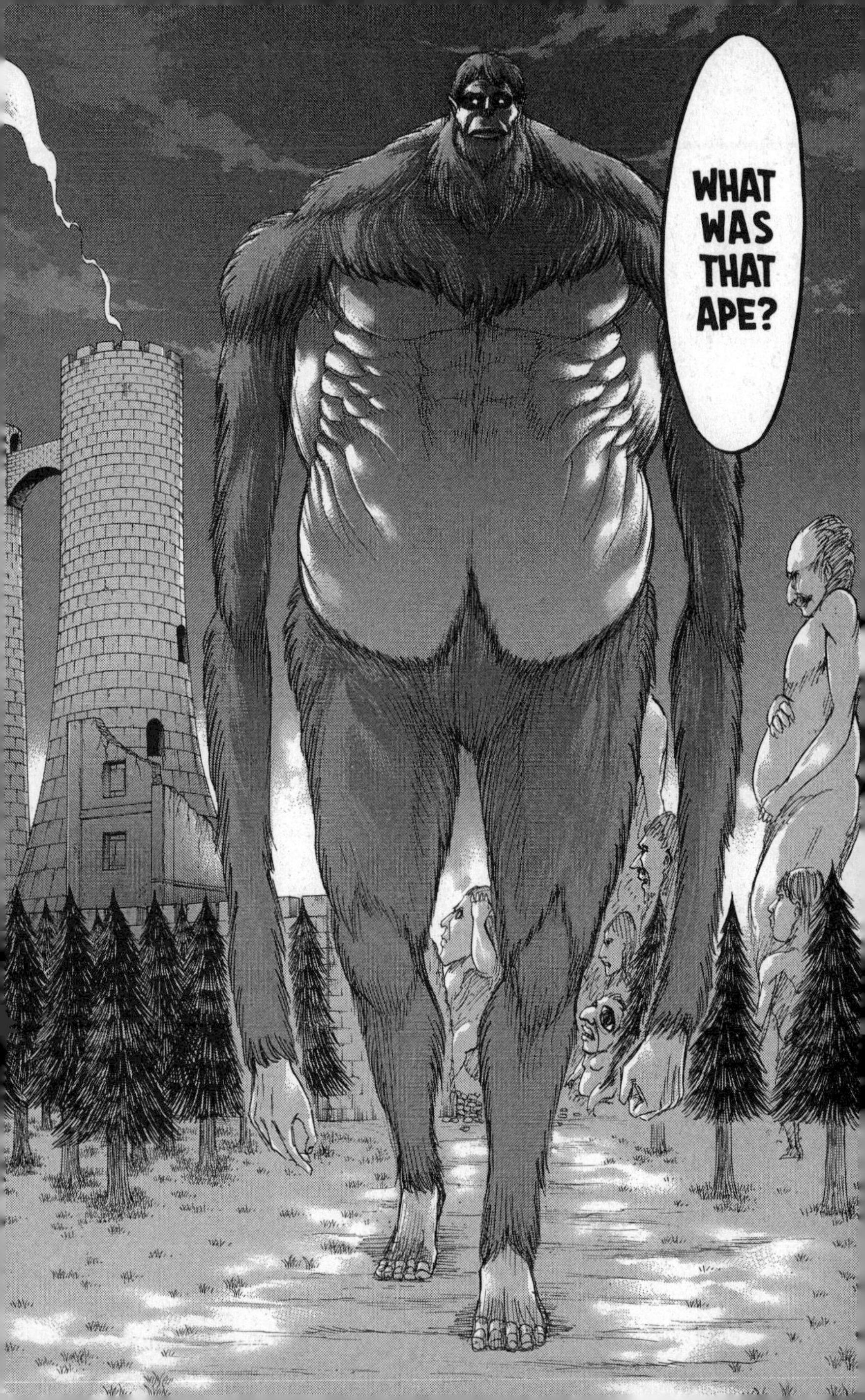
WHAT WAS THAT APE?

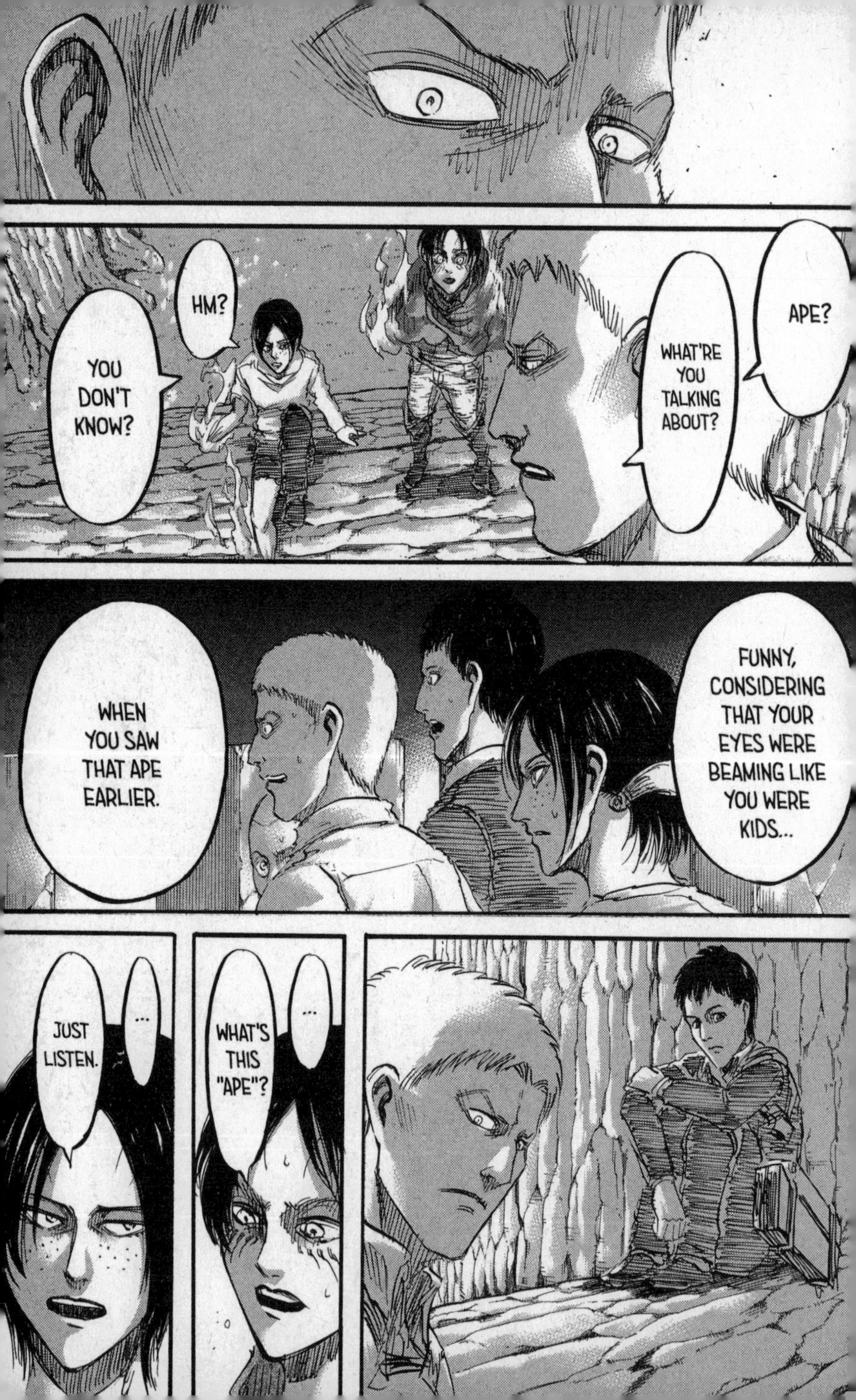
APE?
WHAT'RE YOU TALKING ABOUT?
HM?
YOU DON'T KNOW?
FUNNY, CONSIDERING THAT YOUR EYES WERE BEAMING LIKE YOU WERE KIDS...
WHEN YOU SAW THAT APE EARLIER.
...
WHAT'S THIS "APE"?
...
JUST LISTEN.

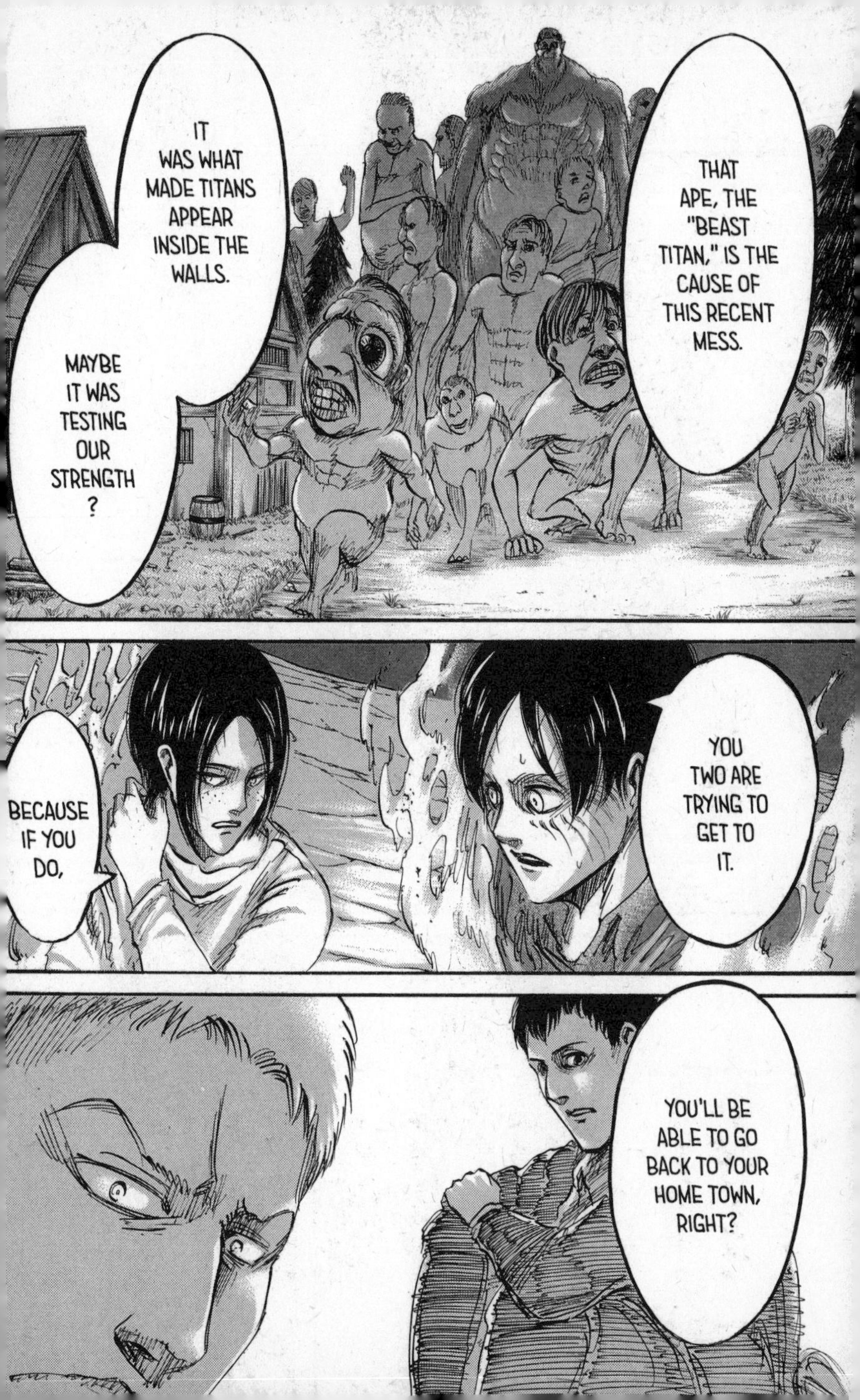
THAT APE, THE "BEAST TITAN," IS THE CAUSE OF THIS RECENT MESS.
IT WAS WHAT MADE TITANS APPEAR INSIDE THE WALLS.
MAYBE IT WAS TESTING OUR STRENGTH?
YOU TWO ARE TRYING TO GET TO IT.
BECAUSE IF YOU DO,
YOU'LL BE ABLE TO GO BACK TO YOUR HOME TOWN, RIGHT?

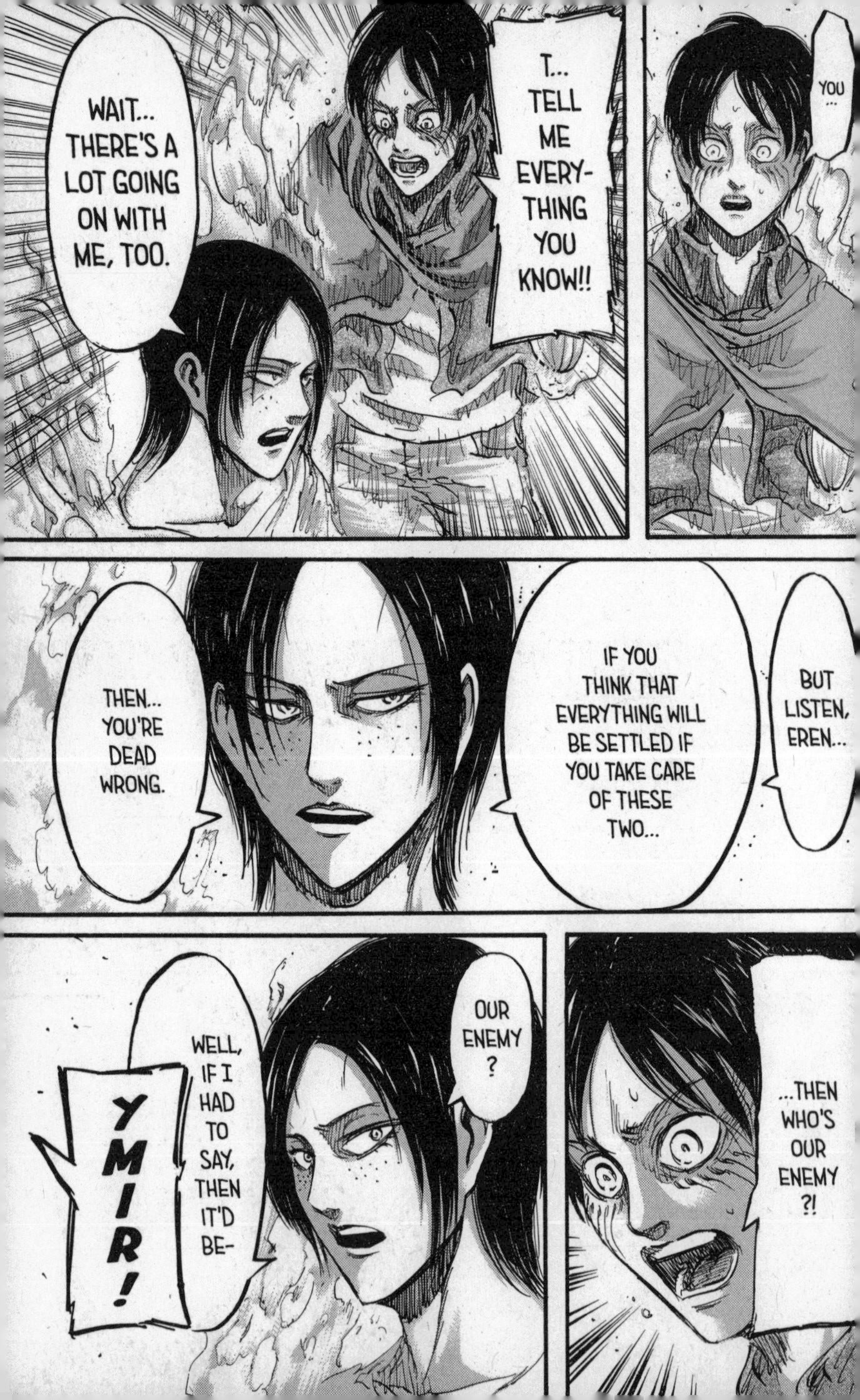
YOU...
T... TELL ME EVERYTHING YOU KNOW!!
WAIT... THERE'S A LOT GOING ON WITH ME, TOO.
BUT LISTEN, EREN...
IF YOU THINK THAT EVERYTHING WILL BE SETTLED IF YOU TAKE CARE OF THESE TWO...
THEN... YOU'RE DEAD WRONG.
...THEN WHO'S OUR ENEMY?!
OUR ENEMY?
WELL, IF I HAD TO SAY, THEN IT'D BE-
YMIR!

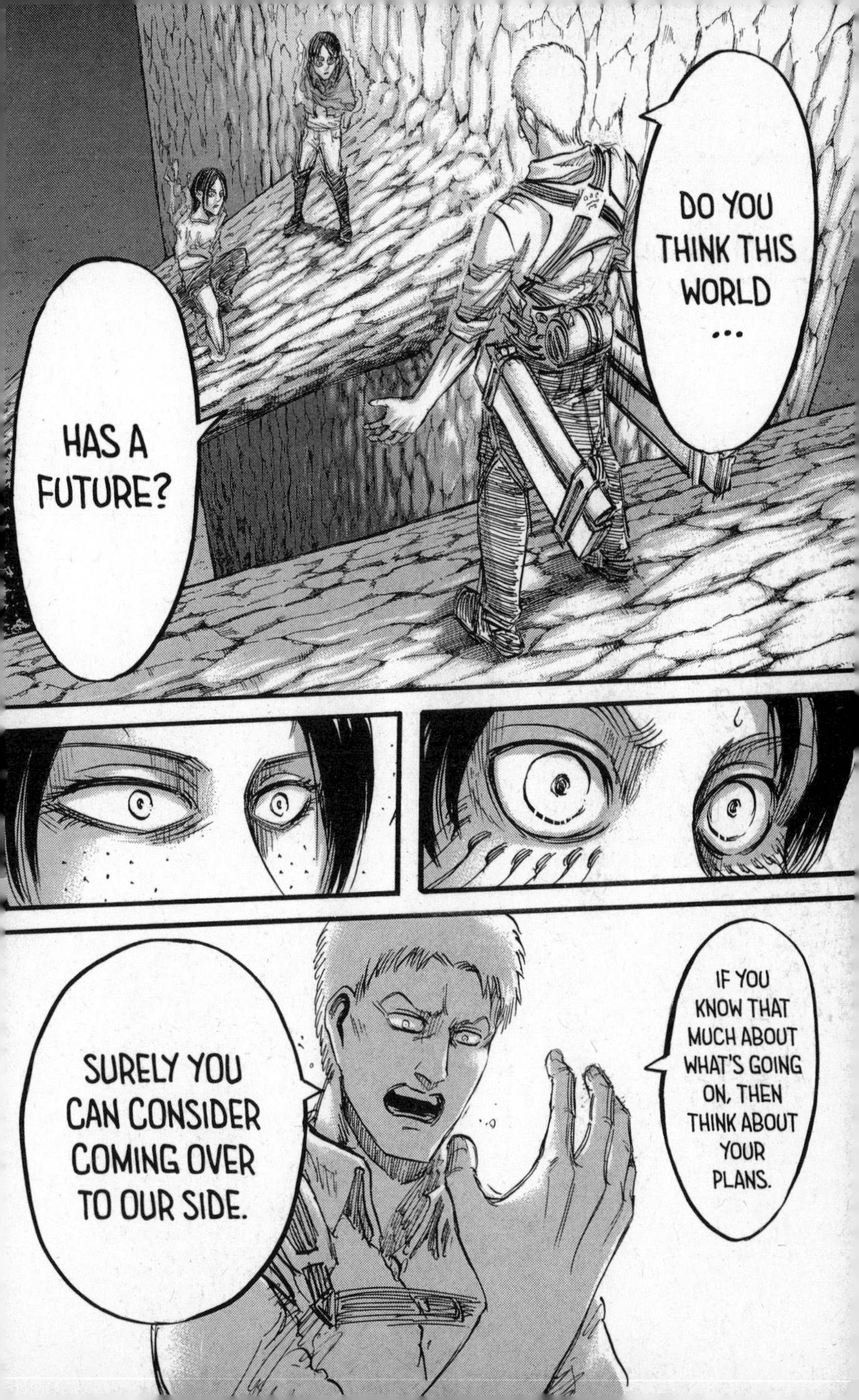
DO YOU THINK THIS WORLD ...
HAS A FUTURE?
IF YOU KNOW THAT MUCH ABOUT WHAT'S GOING ON, THEN THINK ABOUT YOUR PLANS.
SURELY YOU CAN CONSIDER COMING OVER TO OUR SIDE.

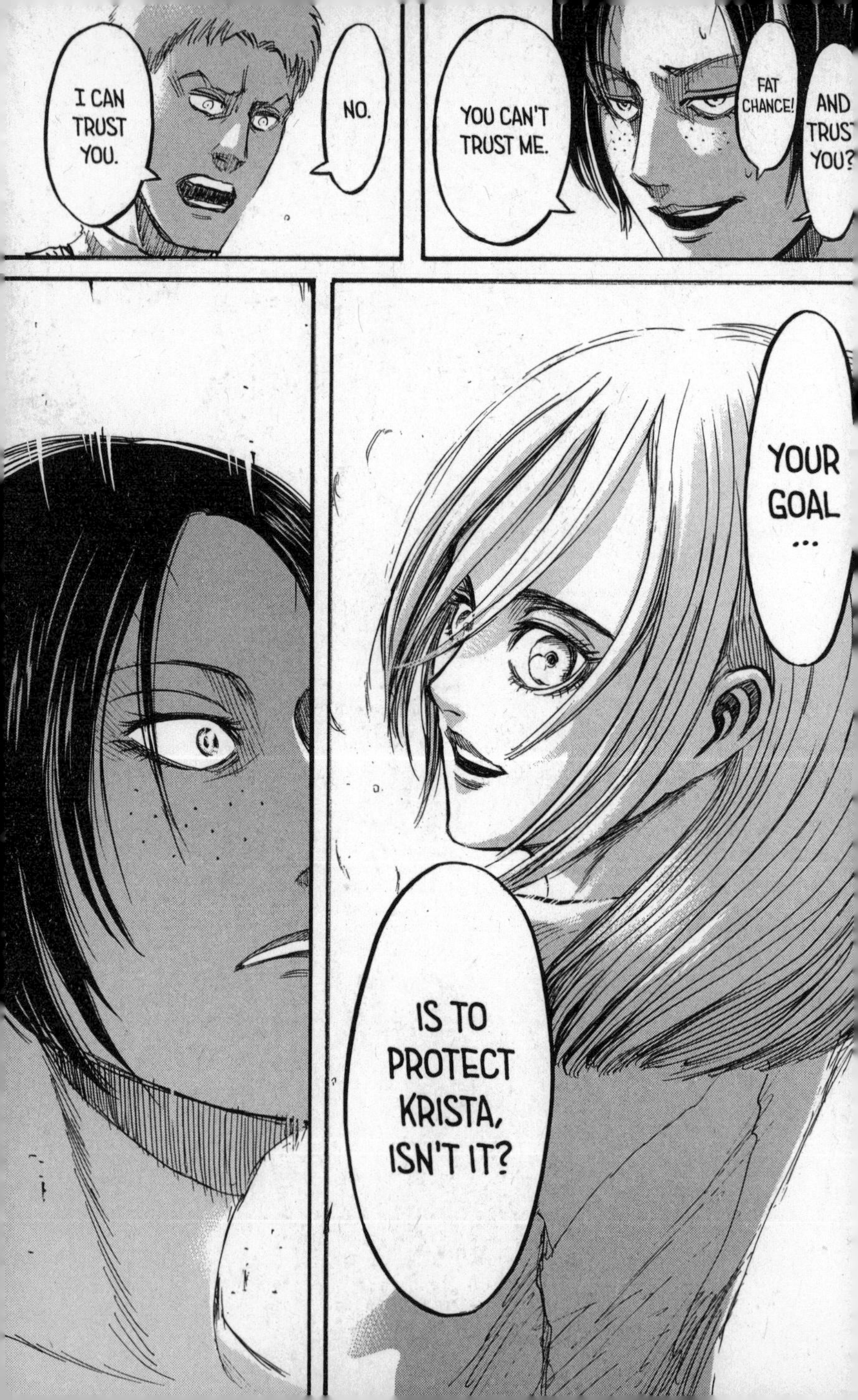
AND TRUST YOU?
FAT CHANCE!
YOU CAN'T TRUST ME.
NO.
I CAN TRUST YOU.
YOUR GOAL ...
IS TO PROTECT KRISTA, ISN'T IT?

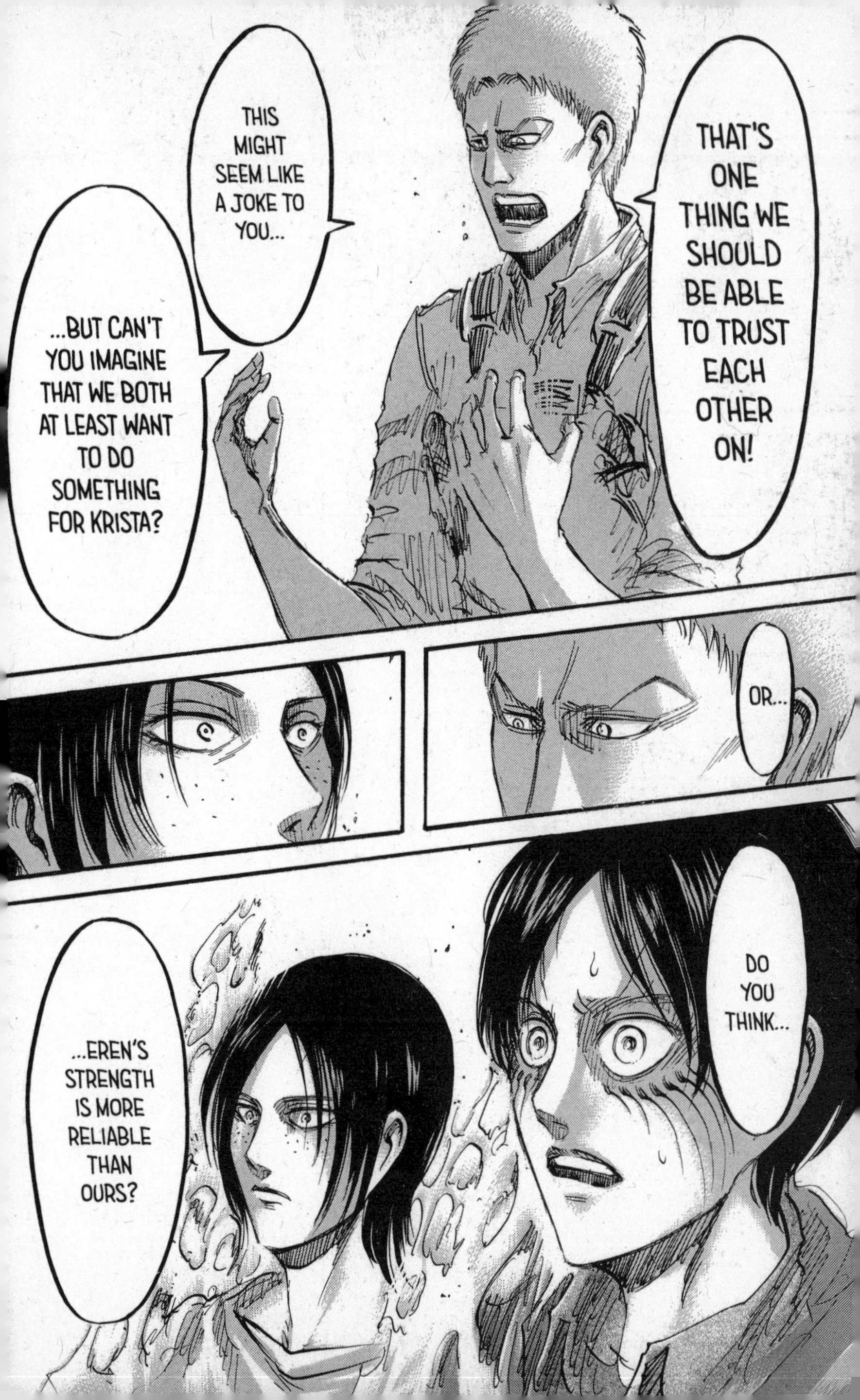
THAT'S ONE THING WE SHOULD BE ABLE TO TRUST EACH OTHER ON!
THIS MIGHT SEEM LIKE A JOKE TO YOU...
...BUT CAN'T YOU IMAGINE THAT WE BOTH AT LEAST WANT TO DO SOMETHING FOR KRISTA?
OR...
DO YOU THINK...
...EREN'S STRENGTH IS MORE RELIABLE THAN OURS?

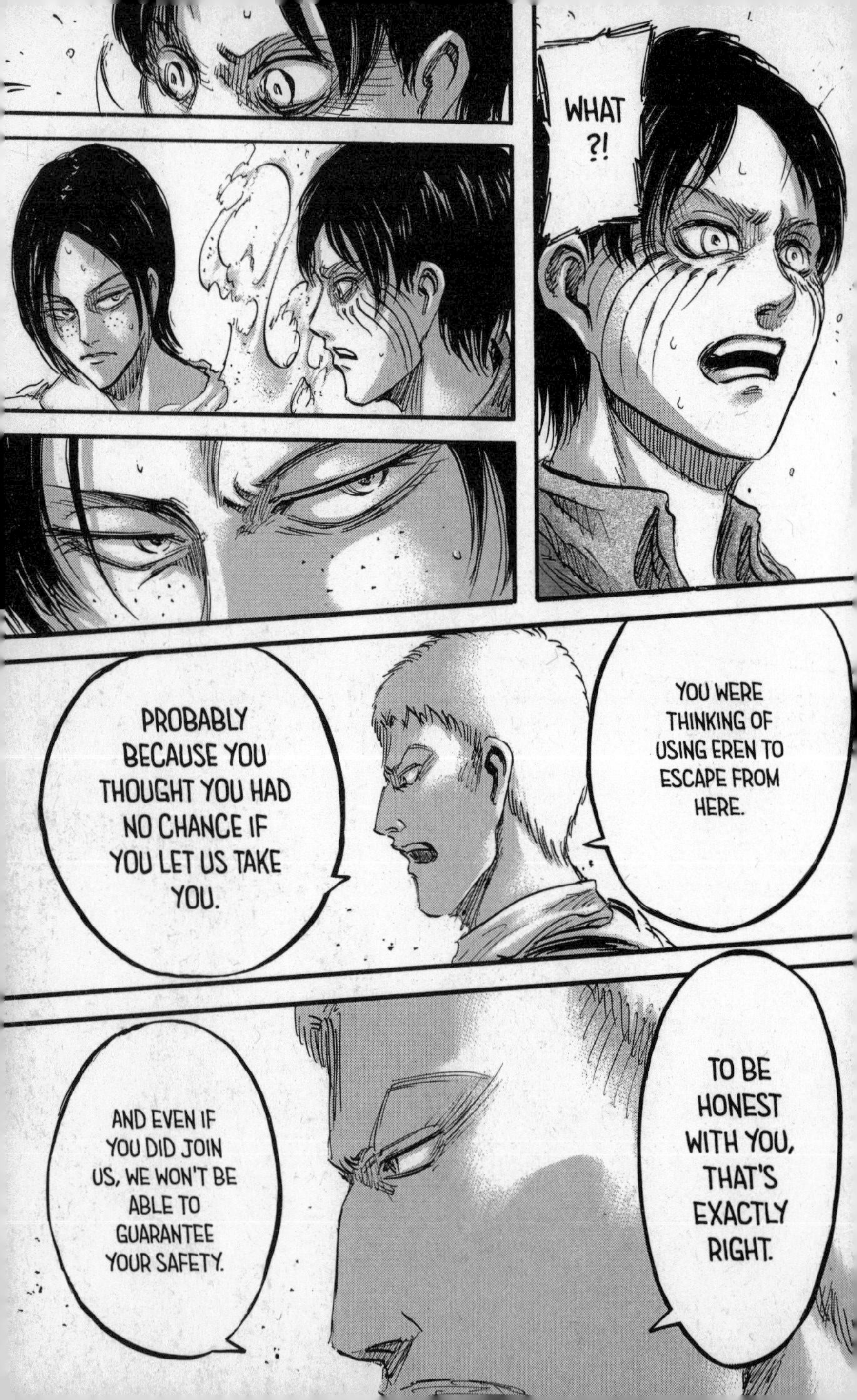
WHAT ?!
YOU WERE THINKING OF USING EREN TO ESCAPE FROM HERE.
PROBABLY BECAUSE YOU THOUGHT YOU HAD NO CHANCE IF YOU LET US TAKE YOU.
TO BE HONEST WITH YOU, THAT'S EXACTLY RIGHT.
AND EVEN IF YOU DID JOIN US, WE WON'T BE ABLE TO GUARANTEE YOUR SAFETY.

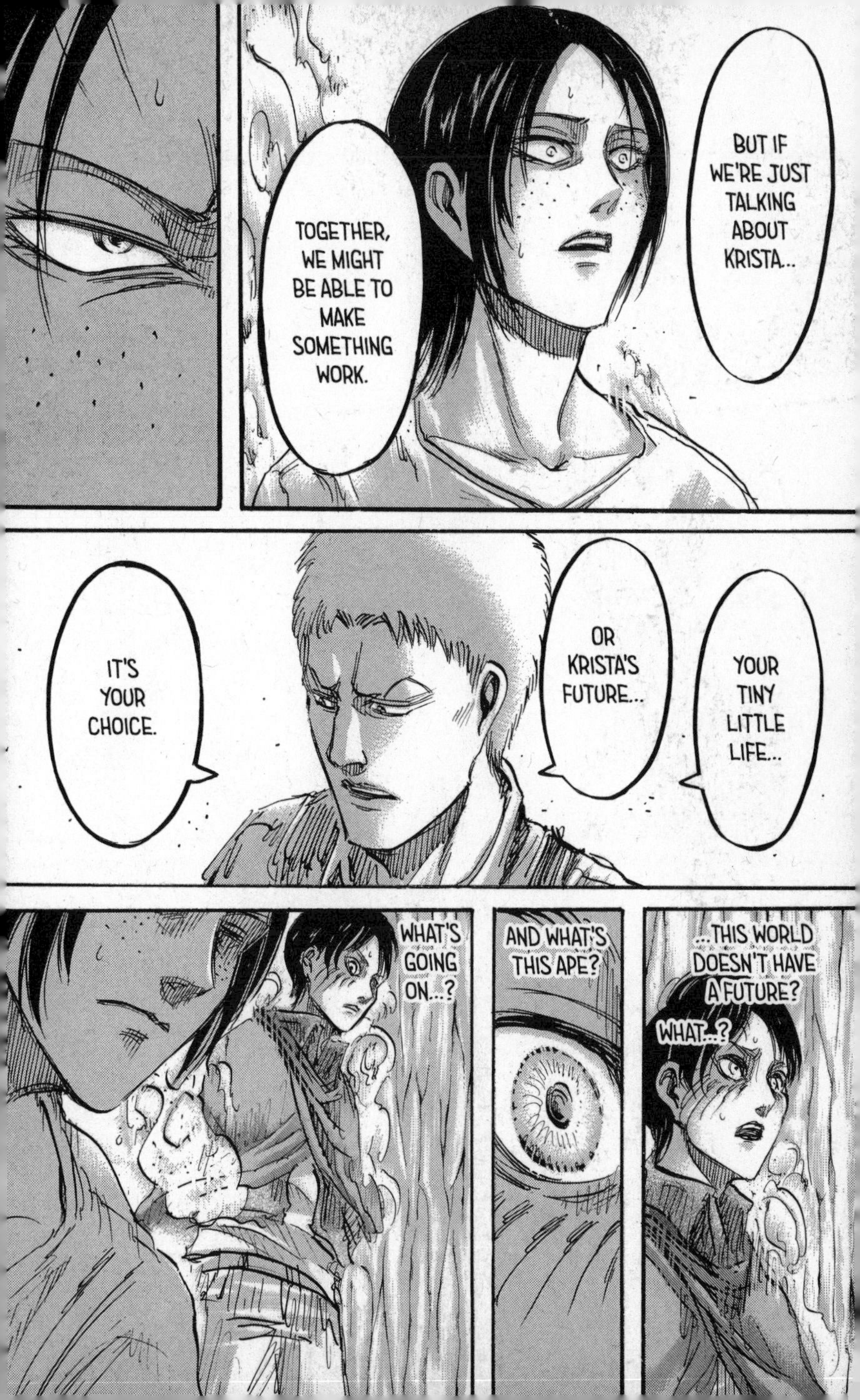
BUT IF WE'RE JUST TALKING ABOUT KRISTA...
TOGETHER, WE MIGHT BE ABLE TO MAKE SOMETHING WORK.
YOUR TINY LITTLE LIFE...
OR KRISTA'S FUTURE...
IT'S YOUR CHOICE.
...THIS WORLD DOESN'T HAVE A FUTURE?
WHAT...?
AND WHAT'S THIS APE?
WHAT'S GOING ON...?

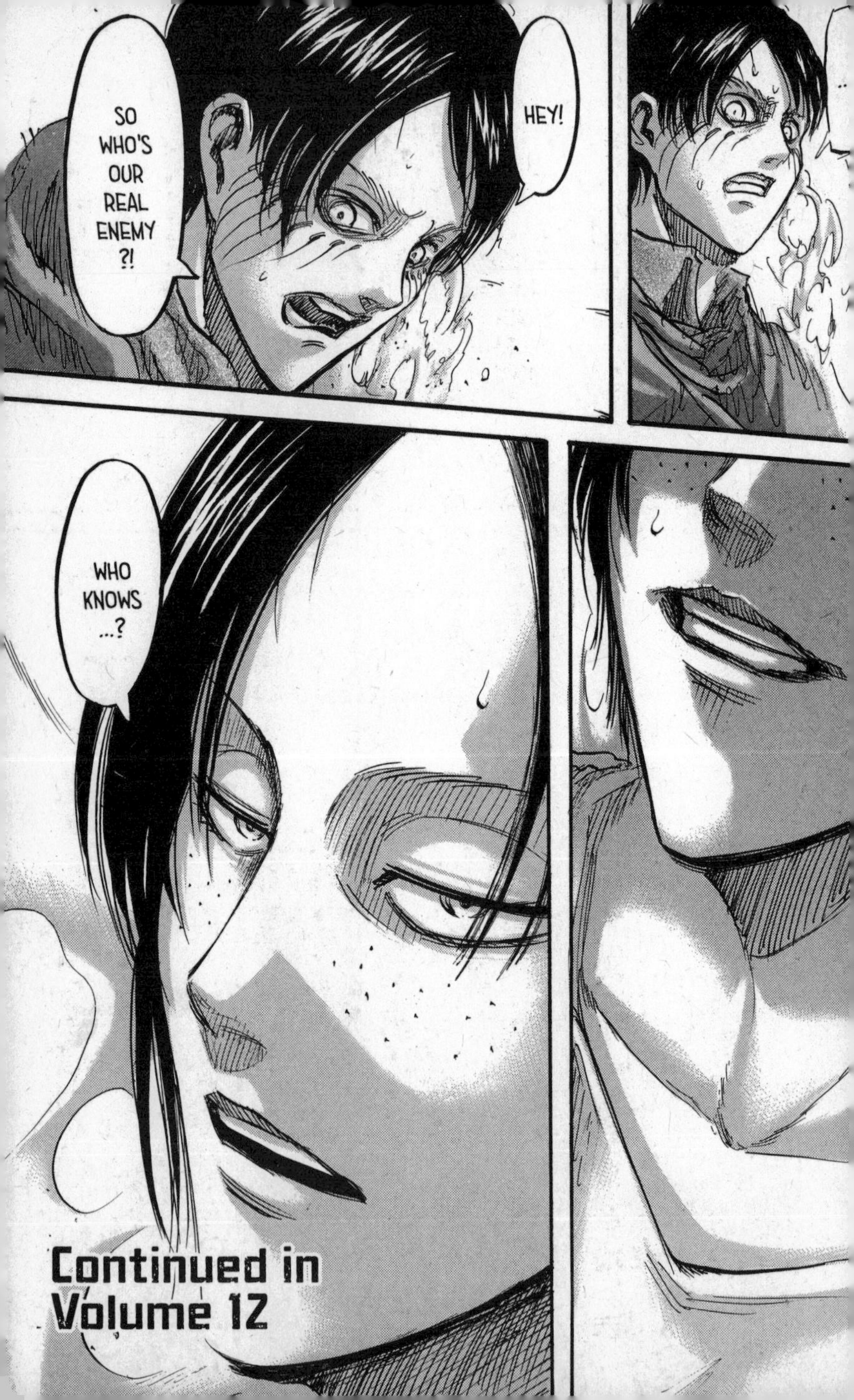
HEY!
SO WHO'S OUR REAL ENEMY?!
WHO KNOWS...?

Continued in Volume 12

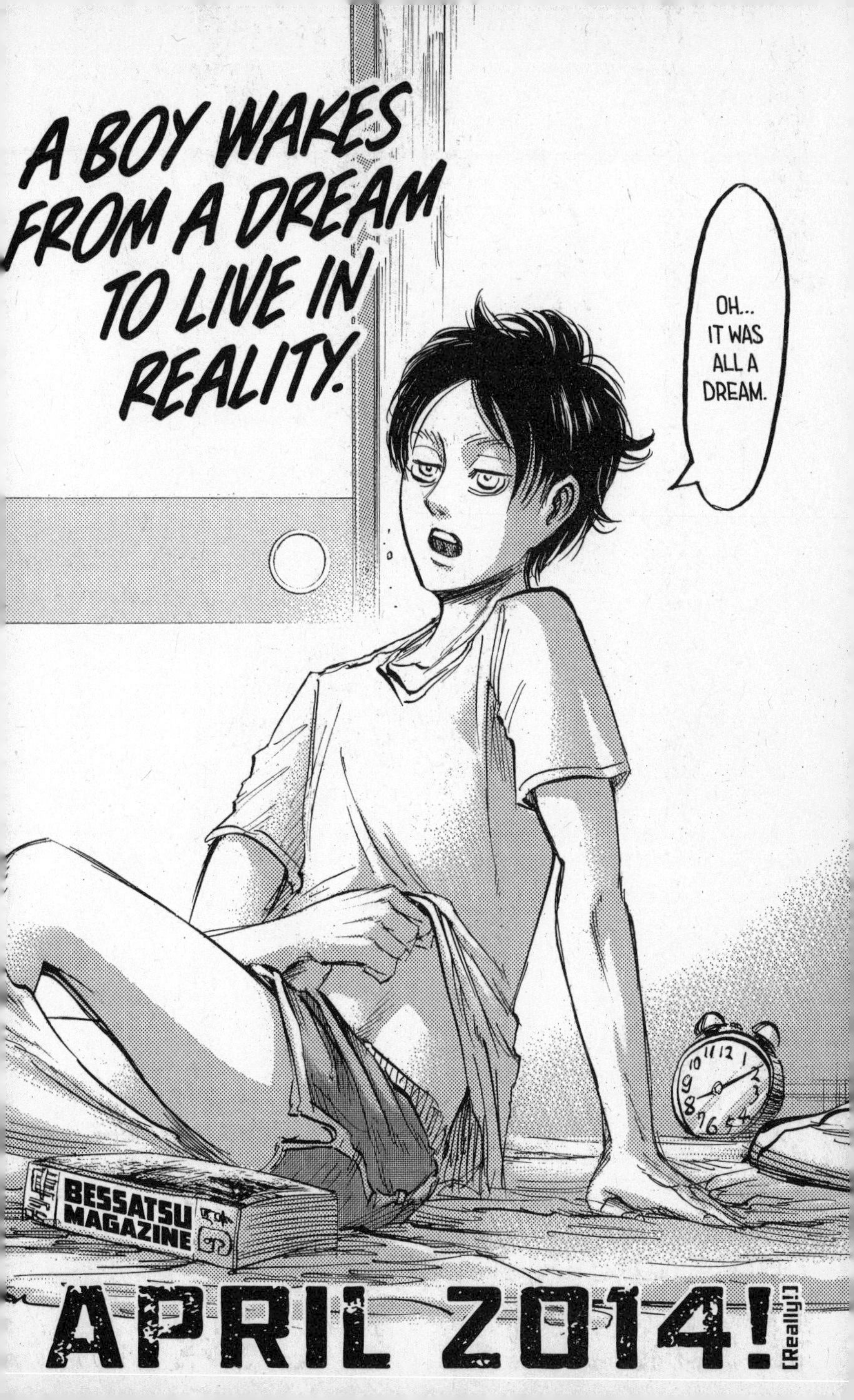
A BOY WAKES FROM A DREAM TO LIVE IN REALITY.
OH... IT WAS ALL A DREAM.
BESSATSU MAGAZINE
APRIL 2014!
[Really!]

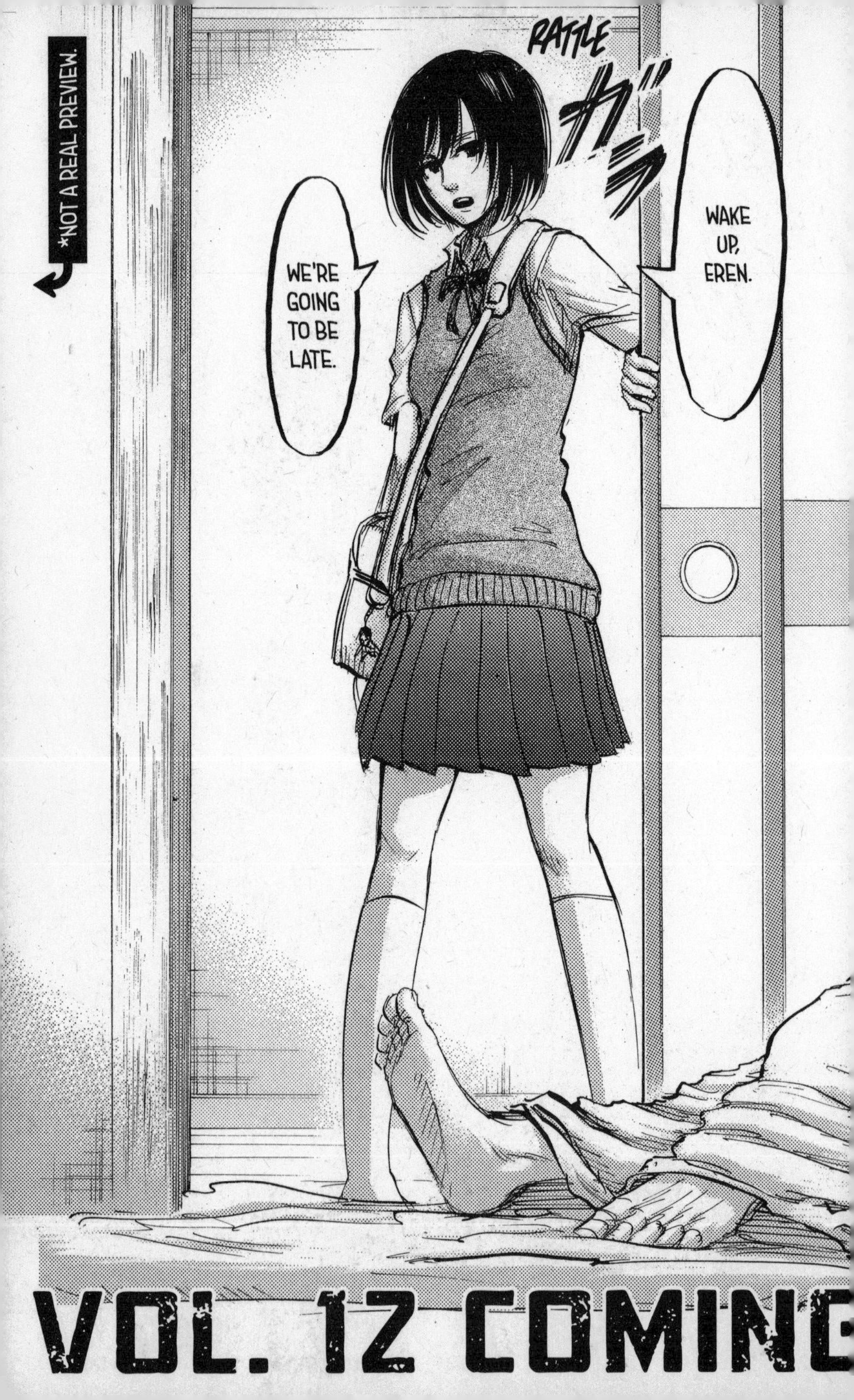
RATTLE
ガラ
WAKE UP, EREN.
WE'RE GOING TO BE LATE.
*NOT A REAL PREVIEW.
VOL. 12 COMING

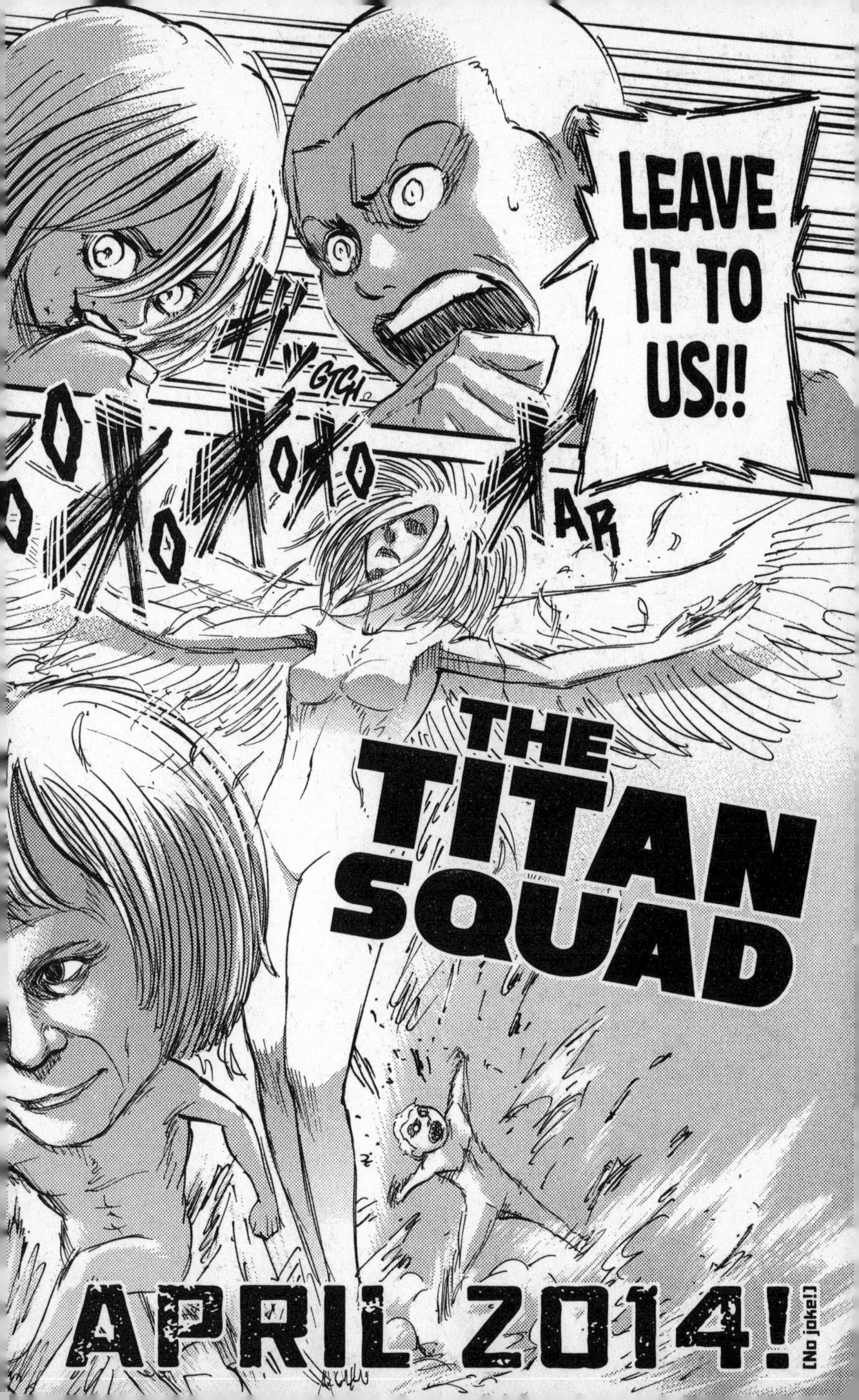
LEAVE IT TO US!!
Y-GTCH
OOOOOOOOAR
THE TITAN SQUAD
APRIL 2014!
[No joke!]

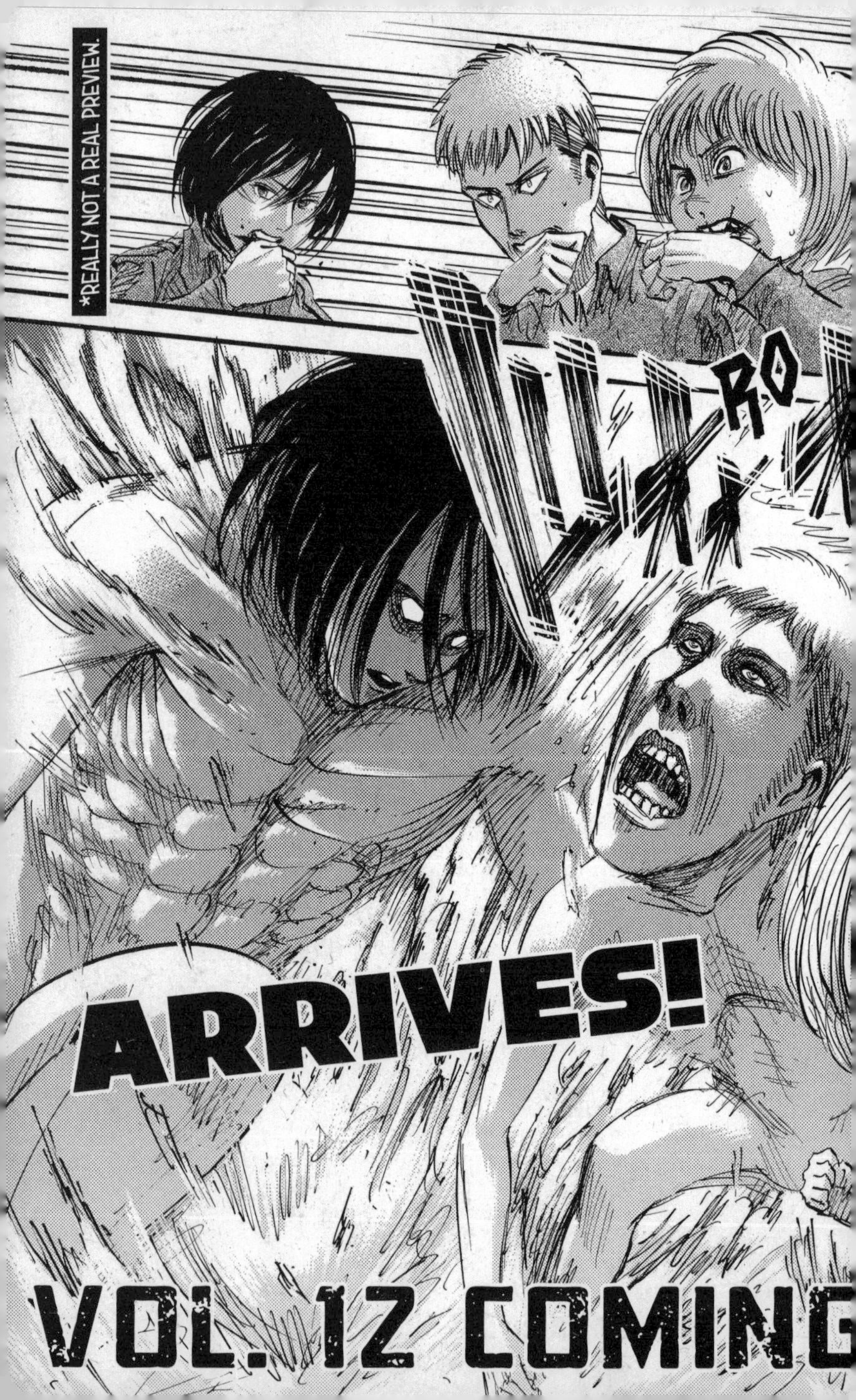
*REALLY NOT A REAL PREVIEW.
RO
ARRIVES!
VOL. 12 COMING

Translation Notes

STRIKE, THROW, SUBMIT, PAGE 49

THIS SLOGAN, DA-TŌ-KYOKU IN JAPANESE,
IS USED IN THE JAPANESE SHOOTO MIXED
MARTIAL ARTS LEAGUE.

Attack on Titan volume 11 is a work of fiction. Names, characters, places, and incidents are the products of the author's imagination or are used fictitiously. Any resemblance to actual events, locales, or persons, living or dead, is entirely coincidental.

A Kodansha Comics Trade Paperback Original

Published in the United States by Kodansha Comics, an imprint of Kodansha USA Publishing, LLC, New York.

Publication rights for this English edition arranged through Kodansha Ltd, Tokyo.

First published in Japan in 2013 by Kodansha Ltd., Tokyo as *Shingeki no Kyojin*, volume 11.

ISBN 978-1-61262-677-2

Original cover design by Takashi Shimoyama (Red Rooster)

Printed in the United States of America.

www.kodanshacomics.com

Lettering: Steve Wands
Editing: Ben Applegate